AGILE PROJECT MANAGEMENT

Making it Work in the Enterprise

J ROSS PUBLISHING

FIRST INDIAN EDITION 2017

ISBN : 978-93-8655-150-4

REPRINTED UNDER A LICENCE FROM AGREEMENT PUBLISHER: J ROSS PUBLISHING, 300 ROAD, #305, S PINE ISLAND PLANTATION, FL 33324 (USA)

FOR SALE IN INDIA, NEPAL, BANGLADESH, SRI LANKA, PAKISTAN, BHUTAN & MALDIVES ONLY.

Distributors:

BPB PUBLICATIONS
20, Ansari Road, Darya Ganj
New Delhi-110002
Ph: 23254990/23254991

BPB BOOK CENTRE
376 Old Lajpat Rai Market,
Delhi-110006
Ph: 23861747

COMPUTER BOOK CENTRE
12, Shrungar Shopping Centre,
M.G.Road, BENGALURU–560001
Ph: 25587923/25584641

DECCAN AGENCIES
4-3-329, Bank Street,
Hyderabad-500195
Ph: 24756967/24756400

MICRO MEDIA
Shop No. 5, Mahendra Chambers, 150
DN Rd. Next to Capital Cinema, V.T.
(C.S.T.) Station, MUMBAI-400 001 Ph:
22078296/22078297

Published by Manish Jain for BPB Publications, 20, Ansari Road, Darya Ganj, New Delhi-110002 and Printed him at Repro India Pvt. Ltd, Mumbai

Dedication

To Emma, Zoey, and Luke who helped press the keys!

Contents

Acknowledgments

There are many people to acknowledge who helped put this manuscript in a readable form and who lent their time and energies to making it a better book. Reading a draft manuscript is a challenge, and finding a way to tell the author what has to be fixed is an art, but to the beta-book crew who worked along with me, there is really no way to say thank you enough.

First, a tip of the hat to Andrew Willard, an experienced executive in information technology (IT)—recently retired as Vice President for IT at Alternative Asset Management—who writes game software as a hobby. Andrew read many of the most difficult chapters and gave generously of his time to critique and cajole and encourage a better product. Andrew first heard about the book during our mutual trip to Costa Rica in the spring of 2009. He got right into the project soon as we returned to the USA and provided inestimable help reviewing the draft text.

Second, my colleague from Harris Corporation in Melbourne, FL, Dr. Ken Ports, steeped in the science of project management and system engineering, provided valuable comments that I have incorporated throughout the text. Dr. Ports, now Director of Strategic Operations at Quantum Technology Sciences, particularly steered me straight on the chapters about quality and testing.

Karen Ellers, and Cathy Cortright, two terrific and experienced project managers, with whom I have worked on various web projects and ERP projects for Lanier Worldwide and Ricoh Americas Corporation, gave me many insightful comments, as always.

My many colleagues at Lanier Worldwide provided numerous opportunities to practice these ideas as Director of Development for E-Business and Lanier's web information portals. Bob Rhodes, as the Vice President and Chief Marketing Officer for E-business, ever demanding for customer value, patiently played the role of executive sponsor while my development team, led by Tim Pattison, worked out the kinks in agile methods.

At Ricoh Americas, Senior Vice President and CFO Dennis Dispenziere and Accenture partner Raymond Searles were instrumental in shaping my experience and attitudes about self-organizing teams and teamwork, value delivery, and benefit recovery on a very large scale.

And my grateful appreciation to the editing and production team at J. Ross Publishing particularly the copy editor, Ms Juli Geiger, who worked tirelessly to correct my many offending constructions.

Thanks to everyone for making this book possible!

John C. Goodpasture
Orlando, FL
August 2009

Introduction

This is a book about agile methodologies as seen through the looking glass of project management.

Dilbert: We need 3 more programmers.
Boss: Use agile programming methods.
Dilbert: Agile programming does not mean doing more work with less people.
Boss: Find me some words that do mean that and ask again.[1]

Dilbert™ is a creation of Scott Adams

There are new and challenging ideas in project management especially suited for managing innovation and technology projects—particularly software projects—that place ever-increasing complexity in the hands of users and consumers. The umbrella term for what we are talking about is *agile*:

> **The agile mission**
>
> *Agile* means small teams working collectively and collaboratively with this mission:
> *To deliver frequent, incremental releases of innovative functions and features, prioritized for need and affordability; evolved iteratively from a vision according to user reflection and feedback, and produced at the best possible value.*[2]

The methodologies included under the agile umbrella go by many names: SCRUM, Extreme Programming (XP), the Crystal Family, EVO, and RAD's agile variant: Dynamic Systems Development Method (DSDM).[3] And there are others: Feature-driven Design, Adaptive Software Development, Lean Development, Team Software Process (TSP), and Personal Software Process (PSP).[4] Before these, there were methodologies with longer legacies that set the stage: Spiral, RUP, JAD, and RAD to name a few.[5] And there are new methods that are intended to produce more reliable product, such as CleanRoom, but these methods are not agile.

All agile methods have one common denominator: Each in its own way addresses the ever-present dilemma encountered while building complex intangible deliverables with user interfaces, to wit, what the customer says they need and want is constantly uncertain. Indeed, the solution often defines the requirements—e.g., "I'll know it when I see it!"

Agile methods empower small teams to respond rapidly to changing landscapes and to deliver customer value quickly well within the longer cycles of business and markets. Agile teams work in small chunks of need that can be stabilized over relatively short periods, consulting customers and users as the solution emerges, frequently releasing product increments, and then inviting serious critique after every release.

Agile Methods Respond to the Root Cause

The industry did not arrive at agile methods overnight. Over many years the processes to address customer need have been refined—motivated by constant feedback that the projects and project management methodologies were unreliable for meeting business needs. Too many times the wrong thing was delivered or the right thing was delivered wrongly or nothing was delivered at all. *The right thing in the right way* seemed to be a minority of the project stories.

Many solutions have been offered and there has been improvement. Feedback and iteration were added to the waterfall,[6] maturity models were introduced to measure and motivate staff and organization, and there was an ever-increasing emphasis to be thorough regarding requirements. Interviews and storyboards, affinity analysis, tracking databases, UML models, and a myriad of other CASE tools and frameworks were introduced to ensure that nothing was dropped along the way.[7]

Now, as more and more projects have intangibles that interact in almost unimaginable combinations, it is all the harder to get things right. Much of the past emphasis on improving the art and science of project management has been placed on *doing things the right way*, building quality into project processes, and work streams. Certainly there is no doubt that project and program management has been raised to a high professional level in recent years in many industries. And there has also been a coalescing of doctrine among the various bodies of project management knowledge. A few examples include the Project Management Institute's Project Management Body of Knowledge (PMBOK®[8]) and its supporting standards and maturity model, the Software Engineering Institute's Capability Maturity Model: *Integration*, the United Kingdom's PRINCE2, as well as the U. S. Department of Defense program and acquisition management doctrine.

However, these doctrines decidedly are not agile. They are not identical in every detail. Nevertheless, they all embrace a strong command and control role for the project manager; they all value defined process capability to produce repeatable results, and they all feature a centrally planned sequential project methodology.

More recently, there is an ever-increasing emphasis on *doing the right thing* as a complement to *doing it the right way*. There is recognition that the right thing is often unknown or unknowable at the time the requirements are traditionally gathered and baselined. Experience has shown that developers may have to wait much later until there is user visualization of and experimentation with the real thing. Many have come to understand that the complexity, the interoperability with legacy systems, and the user experience have so many variables and combinations that it is hard to imagine and *imagineer* everything up front. Thus, agile methodologies depart from traditional thinking in important ways:

Agile departures from traditional

- Requirements are too important to be left to the beginning; they must be evolved with user interaction and interpretation as all the implications come into view.
- The process *emerges* to fit the circumstances; control metrics are empirically determined rather than defined by historical performance in the manner of Six Sigma.[9]
- Planning is important, but following the plan is not as important as satisfying the customer.

Traditional Approaches

The track record of traditional approaches is problematic.

Certainly, help is needed. The StandishGroup's *The Chaos Report (1994)* found the shocking results that among the software projects studied, nearly one-third did not finish and over one-half substantially exceeded the budgeted cost. Only 16 percent finished as planned.[10]

However, by 2007, *The Chaos Report* was reporting substantial improvement; the 16 percent figure for successful projects had doubled to about 32 percent according to a review by the online *SDTimes.*[11]

The review went on to report that Jim Johnson, founder and co-chairman of the StandishGroup, attributed this improvement to three reasons: better project management, iterative development, and the emerging web infrastructure.[12]

In the 2009 report, the StandishGroup reports a downtick in project success.[13]

Do Agile Methods Work?

A motivation for this book was to address these questions:

- When faced with unspoken or unknown requirements, is agile the answer? What confidence can a program manager have that agile methods produce acceptable project results?
- How applicable are agile methods to large scale projects, projects with legacy investment to protect, projects saddled with low trust, and projects needing commitment—that is, certainty for investors and enterprise managers?

Perhaps there is some reassurance to be drawn from the fact that even Microsoft and IBM are using agile methods on some projects.

The quick-read bottom line on agile methods is that they can work, they do work, they do shorten the schedule, and they do provide a high-quality product.[14] But agile is not a silver bullet. Its methods are not appropriate for every situation and only work if the proper environment and management mindset are committed to the project.

	Agile methodologies
A project management tip	• The agile methodologies described in this book depart from traditional project protocols for managing scope, cost, and schedule. • Agile is the method of choice when requirements are either changing, unknown, or unknowable until seen. • Agile methods work best in situations where there are fewer than a handful of small teams and typically fewer than 50 developers. • Agile methods work in-house better than they do through the constraint of a contract; they are inappropriate for firm fixed-price contracting. • Agile works with co-located teams better than they do through the cultural translation and limited communications channel of a virtual team. • Process-centric methods such as CleanRoom are required for programs where safety is critical, and for programs where high reliability is a requirement. These programs are unsuitable for agile methods.

Agile May Be the Answer

Project managers should look seriously at what is happening here. The troublesome shortfalls in performance and customer value—made all the more acute by the rapid business cycles in the web era—has motivated some industry innovators to look at the whole thing in an entirely different way. From the product development community, the software engineering community, and the system engineering community, truly imaginative and practical protocols have been devised and put into practice. Agile methods and practices not only apply project talent differently but also reorder the intuitive sequence of project events that has been the mainstay for generations. With the most recent drive to mainstream agile methods, a large number of project professionals are giving these ideas a careful look.

The practices you will read about in this book will provide new means to collaborate, assign work, and measure results. The customer takes on a different and more near-real-time role as product master; customer participation and accountability is more intertwined in project success. Satisfying the customer is of a greater value than is following a plan prescriptively. Certainly part of the appeal and recipe for success are attractive opportunities for early benefits and possibilities for self-pay projects. And, agile methods get a jump on customer satisfaction by rolling out value sooner than a traditional sequential method.

The ability to handle changing requirements and to handle them later in the project lifecycle is an advantage of these methodologies. Handling changes later at a lower cost flattens the *risk versus amount-at-stake* curve, thereby changing the dynamic for project governance.

For purposes of framing the discussion, four methodologies are featured in this book:

1. SCRUM. SCRUM is a management framework in the main; it is not prescriptive of actual technical practices, although there is a set of SCRUM rules. SCRUM is the simplest of the methods and it is perhaps the most popular today.
2. XP. This is a highly disciplined approach with specific definitive software practices. XP, more oriented toward engineering, is less directive about management practices than is SCRUM.
3. The Crystal family. This is the most empathetic methodology, calling itself *people powered*. *Family* recognizes that methods must adapt to scale. The Crystal Family is XP without a strong emphasis on personal discipline; documentation is a little heavier to compensate for less reliance on personal communications.
4. EVO. This is a true system engineer's approach to incremental and evolutionary software practices. EVO embraces the plan-do-check-act cycle; it makes no apologies for being a tandem string of incremental waterfalls.

The Spiral method is also described. Spiral came along a decade earlier than the four agile methods. Spiral addresses feasibility questions better than do any of the agile methods. The Spiral methodologists are expected to pivot to some other methodology for project construction.

Who Should Read this Book

This book is written by the professional for the professional. It is for experienced project managers, architects, and systems analysts who are comfortable in the classical and traditional methods of project management and now find they are about to embark on an uncertain journey. Managers, architects, and analysts who read this book will find not only succinct and practical explanations of new and different practices, but tips and advice as well to integrate and harmonize agile methodologies with those more familiar and mainstream.

You should read this book if you are involved with technology projects and programs and you are:

- Seeking awareness of new and alternative methods that are results oriented
- Looking to improve the value of project management
- Examining alternatives because there has been trouble with other project protocols
- Seeking knowledge because you are assigned to projects using agile methods

The Book by Chapter

Chapter 1 is a quick read of the four methodologies and practices that will be addressed in the body of the book. Subsequent chapters address specific project management topics in the context of agile methods.

Chapter 2 is about the business case. Projects are instruments of strategy for the betterment of the business and its beneficiaries. The agile business case respects and encourages the meld of business-cycle goals with the urgency and importance of customer need. In this chapter, there is discussion about how to efficiently align business-case practices with agile methods.

Chapter 3 addresses quality, perhaps one of the most important motivations for adopting agile methods. Quality is just not a matter of being error-free, but it is a more holistic concept: fitness to fit, function, and form; commitment to the customers' timeframe and fulfillment of their value proposition; fitness to economical use and maintenance; and commitment to stakeholder expectations for business performance.

Chapter 4 addresses testing. Testing is one of the primary quality tools in the agile and iterative space. Indeed, test-driven development is recommended as a design tool, a regression aid, and a quality tool. Because of testing's prominence in the agile methods, Chapter 4 explains how to plan a test, lay out a test scorecard, and how to incorporate other ideas such as sampling and hypothesis testing.

Chapter 5 is about scope and the means to gather and organize requirements. Chapter 5 addresses the work breakdown structure for agile projects, the means to assess complexity, and the techniques recommended for allocating requirements to releases.

Chapter 6 provides guidance for planning the cost and schedule. The place to start planning is the business case, but from that point, planning is about how teams will deliver all the features and functions demanded by the user. The main planning paradigm is the planning wave, divided into time-boxed development cycles.[15]

Chapter 7 is an explanation of estimating cost and schedule in numeric terms. Cost is a rollup of all the teams' efforts, but the total effort is dependent on schedule: how fast the requirements can be transformed to completed product. Cost and schedule depend on the throughput of agile teams. Velocity is the throughput metric commonly applied. Velocity measures the productivity of the project by measuring burn-down rate—the pace of completing product increments.[16]

Chapter 8 is about teams, the centerpiece of agile methods' organization model. Each methodology employs teams a bit differently, but the idea is the same: people working collaboratively in small teams to achieve synergy and collective results is a win-win for all concerned.

Chapter 9 takes up governance. Governance is a good thing if applied with common sense. It creates the opportunity for stakeholder buy in to evolving scope and delivery timelines. Governance brings resource commitment and provides a stable basis for the project to proceed.

Chapter 10 describes earning value and managing outcomes. Earning value means satisfying the customer, recovering investment, and setting up the benefit stream. Value tracking need not bring a large overhead to the project manager or to the teams. In this chapter we look at practices that are not only effective but also efficient in their application.

Chapter 11 provides ideas for scaling up and for allowing contracts and outsource agreements to become a wrapper for some of the project activities. The fact is that agile methods have been designed around small self-organizing teams. Scaling agile practices to the enterprise level is the challenge discussed in this chapter.

Chapter 12 is about benefits. No project worth doing is worth doing without a lasting benefit to the organization, stakeholder community, or customer base. Benefits mostly come after project closeout, but the agile methods introduce deliverables early and enable the possibility of collecting benefits as the project goes along, perhaps even making the project self-paying.

Appendix I contains details of the four agile methodologies featured in the book. Appendix II is a glossary for terms with unique meanings.

Endnotes

1. This Dilbert™ vignette was posted by *Eleclion* on Techcrunchit.com on December 21, 2008, http://www.techcrunchit.com/2008/12/21/will-this-economy-finally-push-the-toyota-way-into-software-development/, retrieved July 2009.

2. In this book, product base, product, system, deliverable, and outcome are used interchangeably to refer to whatever it is that the user or customer owns or uses at the conclusion of the project. The projects applicable to agile methods are software intensive, but may have many complex hardware components. Projects may produce only a software supported process, or they may produce a system or

application for internal use, or a system or product for business or the consumer. The project may be to make small or large changes to an installed base, called a legacy in this book.

3. XP is the acronym for extreme programming; EVO is the moniker for the evolutionary method championed by Tom Gilb; RAD is rapid application development, an older method that has evolved into DSDM.

4. TSP, Team Software Process, and PSP, Personal Software Process, are service marks of Carnegie Mellon University.

5. Acronyms in this list are RUP for Rational Unified Process, a product of IBM/Rational, RAD for rapid application development, JAD for joint application development.

6. Waterfall is the name given to a sequential project plan that roughly steps through gather requirements, design the solution, develop and test the solution, and then deliver the outcomes. It gets its name from the appearance on charts of a series of cascading steps. To improve the waterfall sequencing, iteration back to prior steps was added in the 1970s.

7. UML is the unified modeling language that is used to diagram and analyze requirements especially in systems with human interaction. CASE is the acronym for Computer Aided Software Engineering. It refers to a set of tools used to assist all facets of software design, development, and maintenance.

8. PMBOK is a service and trademark of the Project Management Institute, Inc. which is registered in the United States and other nations.

9. Six Sigma is a *defined control* methodology consisting of a multi-step problem identification practice and a defect control standard formally stated as requiring less than 3.4 million defects outside control limits per million opportunities out. The actual control limits are determined by analysis and historical measurements.

10. The StandishGroup has been reporting on Chaos regularly since the 1994 report. See the StandishGroup.com.

11. See a review of the 2007 report in the March 1, 2007, online edition of SDTimes: Rubinstein, D. "Standish Group Report: There's Less Development Chaos" *SDTimes*, March 2007, http://www.sdtimes.com/content/article.aspx?ArticleID;eq30247, retrieved July 2009.

12. Some industry experts take homage with the research done by the StandishGroup, saying that the results are not repeated in other surveys. Nevertheless, the 1994 results are widely cited and have entered the lexicon as fact. See his interview given to Infoq.com on August 26, 2006, http://www.infoq.com/articles/Interview-Johnson-Standish-CHAOS.

13. As reported in the April 2009 online version of the *SDTimes*. Retrieved June 2009 at http://www.standishgroup.com/newsroom/chaos_2009.php.

14. For some metric information on the track record of agile projects, see Appendix E, Empirical Information in: Boehm, B. and Turner, R. *Balancing Agility and Discipline*, Addison-Wesley, Boston, 2004, Appendix E.

15. Time-box concepts will be addressed in detail in many parts of the book. However, in a word, time-box is a preplanned duration for an activity within which time constraint everyone works. Work is either finished or not at the end of the time-box period—there is no partial credit. An *iteration* refers to a development step within a project. Iterations are time-boxed in agile methods. Each iteration is tasked to produce some number of features and functions within the time limit of the time-box.

16. Agile methods use some new terms for old concepts. *Velocity* is the agile word for throughput. It is a measure of how much product the team produces in the period of one iteration. *Burn-down* is a SCRUM term that is an earned-value concept (XP refers to burn-up, essentially the same idea). As each object is delivered to production, it is taken off the backlog list. Eventually, as the team works its way down the list, the backlog is vacated. *Burn* refers to effort. As effort is applied to each object, eventually the object is *burned* completely and is ready for production.

*Free value-added materials available from the Download Resource Center at **www.jrosspub.com***

At J. Ross Publishing we are committed to providing today's professional with practical, hands-on tools that enhance the learning experience and give readers an opportunity to apply what they have learned. That is why we offer free ancillary materials available for download on this book and all participating Web Added Value™ publications. These online resources may include interactive versions of material that appears in the book or supplemental templates, worksheets, models, plans, case studies, proposals, spreadsheets, and assessment tools, among other things. Whenever you see the WAV™ symbol in any of our publications, it means bonus materials accompany the book and are available from the Web Added Value™ Download Resource Center at www.jrosspub.com.

Downloads for *Project Management the Agile Way* include whitepapers that discuss the dynamic systems development method, agile quality drivers, the applicability of agile on DoD projects, and an agile slide presentation.

1

A Quick Read

The value of agile methods is the success that attends frequent, incrementally delivered features and functions, even in the swirl of complex and uncertain requirements.

> *Almost any methodology can be made to work on some project. Any methodology can manage to fail on some project. Heavy processes can be successful. Light processes are more often successful, and more importantly, the people on those projects credit the success to the lightness of the methodology.*
>
> *Alistair Cockburn*

This chapter is a quick read about management principles for agile projects—guidelines for actions and behaviors. Agile is about delivering business value quickly—quicker than needs change in business and market cycles—and about being adaptive and responsive to evolving customer needs and business circumstances.

Serious and compelling issues have motivated many thought leaders to invest their time, energy, and ingenuity toward developing agile values, principles, and practices. They have worked tirelessly to make them useful, and to promote them to project managers, architects, and developers. Perhaps stimulated by the increasing pace of business, especially since the advent of the Internet and all the allied electronic communication capabilities, and perhaps reacting to the frustration of unsatisfactory project results that seem a victim of misunderstood, unknown, or unknowable requirements, untraditional ideas about how to go about high-technology projects has taken root. All share one objective: to deliver *high-quality results that are beneficial to business and customer, even if there is volatility and uncertainty about what the customer needs and wants.*[1]

An agenda for improving the value proposition for the customer is something that no project manager can ignore, and it is an agenda that every project manager can embrace. Partly, improvement comes with better practices made specific to the project; other improvements come from better application of management regimes. And in all agile methodologies, the voice of the customer—in effect, the voice of the value proposition—is heard more often and heard in close proximity to the work results. Since those who read this book are project and program managers, business analysts, and other functional managers, the discussion that follows will look through the lens of management—specifically project management. This chapter presents these practices comparatively and provides the *CliffsNotes* for managers to size-up these ideas for potential application in their projects.

A project management tip	Agile methodologies are a management agenda
	• The story of agile methods is first a story about management approaches; it is an agenda for a different management framework on which to hang familiar implementation practices. • Agile is an agenda that places great trust in individuals. • It is an agenda that trades command and control processes and documentation for real-time face-to-face communication. • Agile enables managers to direct the maximum portion of project energy and activity towards value-added outcomes and allows users and end customers a near-real-time voice in the specification of value.

A Short History Provides Context

The genesis of agile methods was in the product development industry, first in Japan in the 1980s, and more recently in the U.S. software industry. Beset by the confluence of new-to-the-world concepts, software components that were hard to imagine until you saw them, and project cycles that were often longer than business cycles, products were often not meeting expectations. In the face of some unsettling performance, some in the industry set out to think of doing software projects a different way.

Early Thinkers

Some early research into untraditional methods began with two Japanese business research academics who examined product development projects at Honda, as well as at Fuji-Xerox, Cannon, NEC, and Epson in the consumer electronics industry. Hirotaka Takeuchi and Ikujiro Nonaka described their findings in a 1986 *Harvard Business Review* article, "The New Product Development Game."[2]

In that article, they coined the term *SCRUM* to describe the behaviors they observed in the businesses they studied. Scrum is a closely-knit team formation in rugby that involves the whole team working as a collective. The objective is to move the ball using tactics that are improvised and self-directed by team members in real time. Although software was not Takeuchi-Nonaka's focus, much of what they wrote about is similar to what is now embedded in the software methodology known as SCRUM. From his work done in the early 1990s, Jeff Sutherland is credited in the United States with being the early thought leader behind SCRUM. Ken Schwaber became a close associate of Sutherland, and together they drove SCRUM forward.

Another thought leader with early experience is Dr. Alistair Cockburn. Cockburn, the inspiration behind the agile method known as the *Crystal family*, and a prolific writer and thinker in the human and process aspects of software development, had occasion to work with IBM in the early 1990s and to observe the performance of many of IBM's software teams. He was struck by the fact that many of the most successful projects were rogues in the process sense. The team participants deliberately avoided the approved IBM processes in favor of their own invention. Although not formalized with a named methodology at the time, one characteristic that was common was developers sitting close together and talking to each other about what they were developing. Moreover, he observed that many of the teams that were following the IBM process were continually unsuccessful.

Another early agile experimenter was Kent Beck. In the late 1990s, Chrysler engaged Beck and his associates to help with a new software development for its payroll system. By the time Beck, Ward Cunningham, Ron Jefferies, and Martin Fowler arrived on the scene, the project was in trouble in spite of trying to follow a formal development plan. Not liking what they found, Beck et al. redid the project successfully—perhaps the first Extreme Programming (XP) project. As one of the earliest industrial projects to use XP, and, as reported in October 1998 in the publication *Distributed Computing*, the C3 Team was very complimentary about the favorable results.

In Sweden, American-born Tom Gilb, a renowned system engineer, was working around the same time as Beck, Schawber, and Cockburn on a better way to build complex user-centric systems. He recognized the need to develop incrementally, check with the customer with each release, and make adjustments for customer needs after each release. He thought *evolutionary development* was the best summary of his ideas and tagged his methodology *EVO*.

Group of 17

Cockburn, Schawber, and Beck were among 17 who, in 2001, gathered in a resort setting in Snowbird, Utah, with a mission to find common ground among competing and untraditional methods.[3] Although not a close-knit group at the outset, they were able to put together something they were all seeking: a framework they named the *Agile Manifesto*, purposed to guide practitioners of various lightweight methods. At that meeting they also agreed on the name *agile* as a better representation for what they were promoting. The drafting of the Agile Principles and the founding of the Agile Alliance followed.

Agile Manifesto and Agile Principles Set Up Agile Methods

The Agile Manifesto is a statement of values—of strongly held beliefs—expressed as preferences, not absolutes. Generally, all agile methodologies incorporate the manifesto into their value system, some more than others.

The Agile Manifesto

We are uncovering better ways of developing software by doing it and helping others do it. Through this work we have come to value:

- Individuals and interactions over processes and tools
- Working software over comprehensive documentation
- Customer collaboration over contract negotiation
- Responding to change over following a plan

That is, while there is value in the items on the right,

we value the items on the left more.

Source: www.agilemanifesto.org

Individuals and interactions over processes and tools: This first preference is for personal communications—face-to-face where possible—and recognition of the uniqueness of each individual and the contributions they make, as different from just staffing and then following a process. While defined processes certainly present a framework for activity, defined processes put situational awareness and responsiveness at risk. On the other hand, depending on interpersonal communication is an obvious limitation on scope and complexity. There is only so much people can keep in their head or on white boards, even if subdivided into multiple teams. It is self-evident that as the project scales up, documentation must be added to facilitate communications, record decisions and results, document performance, and provide audit trails.

Working software over comprehensive documentation: This value is perhaps better stated as working product rather than working software since the total product context needs to be considered. The main point is to apply effort where it really helps deliver value. A disproportionate effort applied to writing and updating documentation rather than developing and updating the product does not serve the sponsor well.

Customer collaboration over contract negotiation: Collaboration draws the customer into the development in an intimate way. But many customers will not be ready for their required responsibilities, and for many enterprises, close customer proximity will be countercultural. Contracts provide a little more distance, but contract negotiations are arm's-length, often adversarial, and difficult to make adaptive. Either way—close collaboration or within the framework of a contract—mentoring and coaching the customer's performance may become a significant project task.

Responding to change over following a plan: A clear point of departure with plan-driven methods is putting a higher priority on satisfying customers—that is, dynamically responding to needs that change with experience—than on following a project plan. *Responding to change* is reactive in tone but aligns with the XP value to keep product design as simple as possible and not to develop hooks for future capabilities not asked for by customers.[4] However, the caution is this: over simplification can damage product cohesion; the forest will be lost in the zeal to focus on pruning trees. Some proactive heads-up architecture is required to anticipate likely change. The promise of inexpensive opportunities to make changes late may be nullified if holistic system impacts are not considered early.

Subsequent to the Agile Manifesto, a set of agile principles was drafted. These principles, given below, guide specific project implementations by organizations practicing agile methods.

The 12 Agile Principles

1. Our highest priority is to satisfy the customer through early and continuous delivery of valuable software.
2. Welcome changing requirements, even late in development. Agile processes harness change for the customer's competitive advantage.
3. Deliver working software frequently, from a couple of weeks to a couple of months, with a preference to the shorter timescale.
4. Business people and developers must work together daily throughout the project.
5. Build projects around motivated individuals. Give them the environment and support they need and trust them to get the job done.
6. The most efficient and effective method of conveying information to and within a development team is face-to-face conversation.
7. Working software is the primary measure of progress.

The 12 Agile Principles (cont'd)
8. Agile processes promote sustainable development. The sponsors, developers, and users should be able to maintain a constant pace indefinitely.
9. Continuous attention to technical excellence and good design enhances agility.
10. Simplicity—the art of maximizing the amount of work not done—is essential.
11. The best architectures, requirements, and designs emerge from self-organizing teams.
12. At regular intervals, the team reflects on how to become more effective, then tunes and adjusts its behavior accordingly.
Source: www.agilemanifesto.org/principles.html

Project Development Lifecycle Covers Business Case-to-Business Delivery

A project development lifecycle is all the process, steps, and activities needed to transform a product vision into working product. The delivery vehicle is called a project: a one-time endeavor with a definitive start and end. All projects and all project methods have a lifecycle.[5]

Plan-Driven Lifecycle

Most project development lifecycles (PDLCs) have a simple organizing principle: build and deliver the specified outcomes according to a master project plan, a plan that specifies and baselines the scope, quality, budget, and schedule. The lifecycle is usually summarized in a few sequential steps as illustrated in Figure 1-1. The shorthand for this methodology is *plan-driven* and our acronym is PD-PDLC. Achieving outcomes according to planned predictions and commitments are the motivations for driving the project by the plan.

Plan-driven lifecycles begin with a business opportunity. If a new opportunity is a fit to the business and its strategic plan, sponsors may decide that a project to develop the opportunity's business potential is the next best step. The top-level and visionary requirements are gathered and approved by the business before any serious resources are expended. From the top-level requirements, a risk-adjusted forecast is made for the required resources, technology, environment, and myriad other commitments. Benefits are estimated and discounted for uncertainties. Upon sponsor approval of the business case, the project begins its lifecycle. The integrated master plan for design, development, and test is written and approved up-front. Many in the industry dub the plan-driven PDLC as the Big Design Up Front (BDUF). We will call it the PD-PDLC.

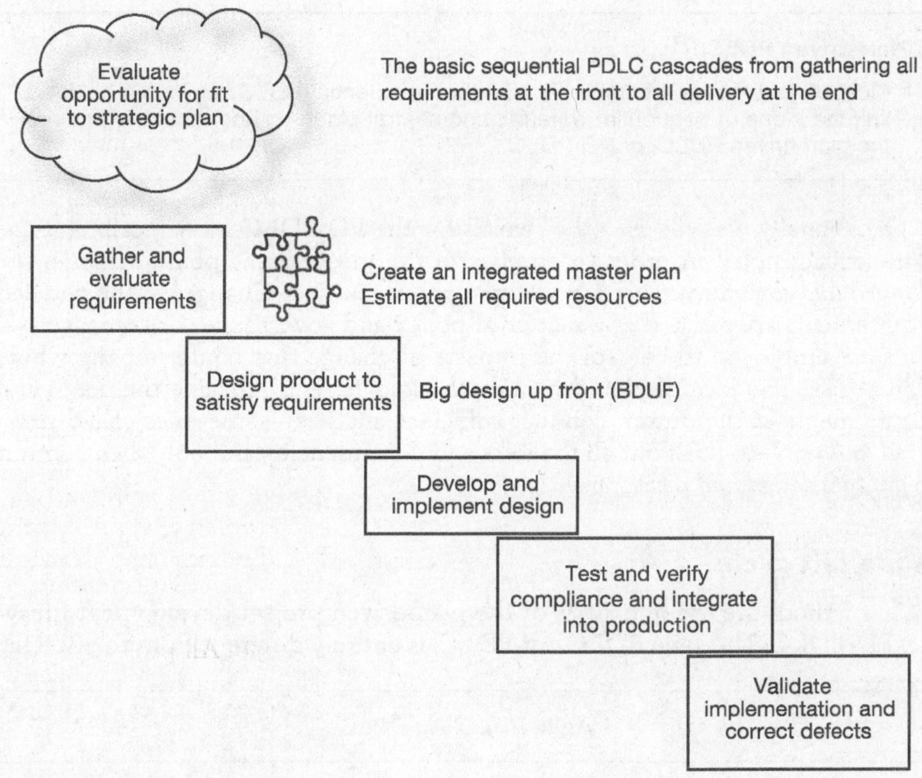

Figure 1-1 Basic sequential PDLC

The attractive thing about the sequential plan-driven PDLC is that it is a natural way of thinking about how to do something. And it fits any technology, industry, or engineering discipline. The plan-driven PDLC is deceptive in its simplicity: start with a vision of what is wanted; then, think of how that is to be done, step-by-step, in a chain of activities set down in a plan. Each step is allotted resources; each step depends on the results of the prior step in the chain. Each step is done only once. Progress through the lifecycle happens sequentially in a straight line, linearly in system-speak. Timelines are well behaved: they don't spiral about in expanding circles, or double back with iteration.

Because the usual graphic presentation of a sequential, plan-driven PDLC portrays each activity only once, and that unique appearance in the project lifecycle is shown top-to-bottom on a different line, displaced right-to-left according to time, the diagram takes on the cartoon appearance of a waterfall for which it is nicknamed. Recall Figure 1-1 and the cascade appearance of the project steps.

Plan-driven PDLC

- Most project managers centrally plan their sequential PDLC, so in this book we link the ideas of sequential waterfall and central planning and label the process the plan-driven PDLC, or PD-PDLC.

Occasionally we will use other words for the PD-PDLC model, calling it the plan-centric model in order to emphasize the most salient point: *activities are planned and committed to well in advance, not just-in-time.* Changes to the detailed requirements are resisted as a matter of policy and governance. Governance systems are employed to control the impacts of change that could put the whole plan at risk. The idea of plan-driven methodologies is to imagine the needs and requirements at the outset, conduct sufficient analysis—sometimes called *structured analysis*—to flush out all the risks and dependencies, and only then commit to *product design and development.*

Agile Lifecycle

Agile methods are the antithesis of the plan-driven project development lifecycle, PD-PDLC. The agile PDLC, Ag-PDLC, is entirely different from the BDUF:

Agile PDLC, Ag-PDLC

- Outcomes are incrementally planned and specified, built iteratively, and delivered in frequent releases.
- Agile projects are governed by a top-level business plan that envisions a product goal, top-level requirements, business milestones, and investment funding pegged to affordability.
- Scope and quality, the budget, and the schedule are framed by architecture at the top-level in the business plan but the details emerge as the project progresses.
- Value accumulates incrementally as outcomes are committed to production.
- Customers are allowed to change their mind from one release to the next in order to keep the value proposition ever in alignment with business and market realities.

The Ag-PDLC has three distinguishing characteristics that set it apart from the PD-PDLC:

> *Emergent:* The processes and procedures used by the implementation teams emerge from the team's analysis of the requirements and tasks. In effect, teams adapt; process control is achieved empirically by observation and reaction, not by defined process control with error bounds, as in Six Sigma.[6]

Iterative and evolutionary: The Ag-PDLC is a string of development cycles called iterations or sprints. With each iteration, some part of the requirement backlog is put into production and then the backlog is revisited in subsequent iterations until exhausted. The design evolves from iteration to iteration driven by product experience and feedback from customers—the design is iteratively adapted and improved as the backlog is worked off. Within the framework of the top-level architecture, the customer is allowed to reset priorities, add, delete, and change the backlog according to market and business need.

Incremental: The outcomes of iterations are packaged for release to production as an update to the product base.

To maintain alignment of deliveries with the value proposition in the business case, iterations are relatively short, from about two to three weeks in the XP and EVO methodology, 30 days in SCRUM, to something longer according to circumstances in Crystal. Releases are made as frequently as the business can absorb change, but typically no less frequently than a calendar quarter. There are no hard and fast rules; each project sets the agenda with the customer.

An Agile Manager's Agenda

Every PDLC has within it planning, managing, measuring, and accounting for results. In the Ag-PDLC, the project manager's agenda has a few featured elements. When these elements are present and effectively implemented, agile methods work smoothly, but if they are missing or poorly executed, agile methods give poor results. Here by topic are the most important things agile project managers do:

Customers: Coach customers' and end-users' project participation that is near real time and nearly continuous. Many customers require help to be effective in this role, and many organizations will have to make cultural adjustments for such customer intimacy.

Communications: Encourage communications that are open, honest, and real-time within and among teams. Manage the tradeoff between documentation and face-to-face discussion and interaction as a means to accurately communicate in a timely fashion.

Results: Maintain a focus on results, not specifically on process and activity. In this respect, value is earned only when product that serves the customer's need is put in production.

People: Internalize the idea *things are managed; people are led,* a principle embraced by Rear Admiral Grace Hopper (1906-1992), renowned computer scientist. Motivating and inspiring individuals are central to the success of high-performance teams that depend on individuals collaborating effectively, setting aside competitive secrecy, and attacking only problems.

Innovation and technical excellence: Champion innovation and technical excellence as enablers for successful projects, discriminating products, and satisfied customers.[7] Be the champion for coherent architecture, unassailable quality, and system cohesion as marks of best practices.

Agile managers are guided by these principles:

Plans are adaptive: Agile projects are not driven from a single plan. There will be a broad stroke plan in the business case, and there will be other detailed plans that are incremental, iterative, and just-in-time.

Value is the prerogative of customers: The value of requirements is ultimately a judgment by the business and the customer, envisioned in the business case and refined at each iteration.

Schedule and cost are derived: The business case frames the investment and major milestones, but actual costs and schedule are derived from the performance of teams deployed during the course of the project.

Change is embraced and encouraged: Change is not resisted. As a matter of policy and governance, agile practices encourage the end user to maintain the value proposition relevant to the state of the business and current to the market.

Documentation comes after personal interaction: Discourse and debate among individuals is recognized as a valid substitute for many formal documents. Documentation is still important, and acquires more importance with escalating project scale; documentation is just not as important as it is in the PD-PDLC.

Individuals are trusted: The concept of the high-performance team depends on trusting individuals to do the right thing the right way. In this context, doing the right thing means serving the interests of the customer, the project, and themselves while being committed and accountable for the results.

A project management tip	Agile commitments
	• Agile project managers commit to best-value for sponsors, customers, and users. • Total cost and resource consumption are dependent on value delivered, but are limited by investment funds and milestones given in the business plan. • The focus is on product quality in terms of form, fit, feature, and function as directed by customers and end-users. • Stakeholders and managers may have to give up the comfort of outcomes planned and forecast by central planning, but they do not have to give up an expectation for project outcomes consistent with vision, architecture, and the prospect of benefits.

Some Terminology to Make the Reading Easier

In this book we will adopt specific definitions for some of the most important terms and concepts that will be used in the text. We've already used most of the terms already as given in the working glossary in Table 1-1.

Table 1-1 Glossary of working terminology

Term	Working definition
Agile methods and practices	• Methodologies that are more situational-driven, less centrally managed and more self-managed, with an emphasis on near-continuous responsiveness to customer need. The focus is on the quality of the result, even if the result is not predictable at the outset and not according to plan. • Example: XP (extreme programming).
Business	• The organization or enterprise that hosts the project. The business may be a governmental unit, non-profit, or a business unit within a larger enterprise. • Organization, enterprise, and business are used interchangeably.
Customer	• The people and organization that are the principal beneficiaries of the project. • End users, or users, are customers with detailed functional knowledge. • Customers may be external or internal to the organization.
Knowledge area	• A body of knowledge about how to do tasks, or activities, that has a common association. • Example: Risk management.
Method or practice	• A means of doing a specific activity within a knowledge area. Generally speaking, there are inputs which drive actionable steps, thereby producing outcomes. • Example: Monte Carlo simulation of schedule outcome.
Methodology	• Activities linked to produce an outcome, with the specific methods or practices of each activity identified. In effect, a methodology is a life cycle of the project, a PDLC as we have described elsewhere. • Example: Crystal Clear.
Untraditional methodologies	• See Agile methods.
Practice standard	• An agreed upon way of doing a task, where the agreement is managed by a standards body (organization) with credentials in the standards community. • Example: ISO/IEC 12207 practice standard for software engineering.
Process	• Like a methodology, activities linked to produce an outcome, although the methods may not be specified. • Example: Project initiating process.

Table 1-1 (*continued*)

Term	Working definition
Product	• The intended outcome or deliverables of a project that is useful to a customer and fits the customer's idea of quality in the large sense: feature, function, effective in application, efficient to use, environmentally compatible, and economically operable and supportable throughout a useful lifespan. • Product may be tangible or intangible, and it may be a process, system, application, or product for internal or external customers.
Stakeholder	• Primarily a business unit or individual that is in the supply chain, or provides some resources to the project, but has no specific commitment to project success. In other words, involved but not committed.
Traditional methodologies	• Methodologies that are planned-out at the outset and managed centrally according to the plan to produce outcomes. The emphasis is on predictable results according to the specifications of the plan, a PD-PDLC as we have described elsewhere. • Example: Waterfall.
User	• See customer.

Plan-driven Provides Lessons Learned

We begin a discussion of methodologies with the poster child of the plan-driven lifecycle—the waterfall. Why do this? Two reasons: First, in spite of everything else said, the waterfall or other plan-driven variants such as CleanRoom, CMM (*I*)[8] and ISO 12207 still account for the lion's share of software developed today, although on a smaller number of projects. That is to say, as of surveys taken in 2004, small projects of 25 developers or fewer accounted for only 15 percent of all the code written, although they accounted for 65 percent of all the projects.[9] Large-scale projects containing 25 or more developers on staff—and often reaching in the multiple hundreds—account for 85 percent of all code written. Almost without exception, this latter group of projects is plan-driven.

Second, it is a worthy objective to set a baseline from which other approaches can be compared. It is also helpful to examine some of the lessons that have been learned with an eye toward stepping around the obvious difficulties.

The waterfall is a variant of the PD-PDLC that has been around for many decades during which it has acquired a rich history. The waterfall has a track record of producing projects of amazing scope with spectacular success, and by stark contrast there is also a track record of many failures and partial successes that continues in present time. It owes its longevity to its fit to projects of every size and complexity in almost every industry, from the smallest to the largest, and for its natural harmony with most manager's intuition that complex endeavors must be carefully planned and sequenced. The waterfall forms the basis for the traditional methodology in which most project managers are trained, and it is therefore fitting to present the waterfall as the PD-PDLC baseline.

The waterfall acquires its name from the usual way it is presented in a picture as a cascade of steps in sequence, finish-to-start.[10] Look back at Figure 1-1 as a much-simplified view of the waterfall. The steps are explained in Table 1-2.

Note in Figure 1-1 that the steps overlap, thereby relaxing a strict finish-to-start precedence that gates one task into the next. Strict adherence to a gated process is problematic because low priority and inconsequential tasks tend to lag behind. In more sophisticated renderings, feedback from a successor step is applied to the predecessor, allowing for some iteration of the predecessor to correct defects as early as possible. In another refinement, some product is delivered early on a fast track. However, even though sometimes incremental and iterative, evolution and emergence are missing. Evolution of the product after requirements are approved is not allowed unless a governance entity steps in and opens the design for change. Emergence of process and technique is also discouraged because emergent procedures are antithetical to maturity models that call for repeatable and predictable procedures.

Table 1-2 The basic waterfall

Waterfall step	Action
Charter the project	• The sponsor expresses a business need in a business case based upon an evaluation of an opportunity that holds value • The need is to be satisfied by a project • The need could be for a new or upgraded product or a new or changed process, or some other change in the organization's end-state
Gather all requirements	• The project team gathers all the requirements for the project outcomes, including all of the sales, marketing, supply chain, service and support, training, and features and functions
Implement deliverables	• The project team plans, designs, and implements according to the requirements • These activities may include design, development, test, pilot manufacture, and other compliance and regulatory steps
Verify requirements	• A verification team checks each requirement for satisfaction in the deliverables and for satisfaction of all external constraints and mandates
Deliver outcomes	• The business or customer receives the project deliverables

High Process, High Ceremony

Many say about the PD-PDLC that it is a methodology of *high ceremony*, meaning a methodology steeped in process, metrics, and documentation, all formally defined and made doctrine. The documentation becomes part of the handoff from one step to the next, provides a means to record approvals and also serves as a record and a history of what happened at each step. Thereafter, there are—or should be—more processes to maintain documentation with changes and modifications so that content is always current with the state of the project. These ancillary processes, and others that affect the project, all defined and set down in standards, guides, and plans, are what we mean when we say high ceremony.

Methodologies with high ceremony depend on documentation as a key means to communicate. These projects often run for years, so there must be protection from staff turnover that might result in key information walking out the door. High ceremony discounts to a degree the contributions of people as individuals: jobs are defined with the expectation that any qualified person can step in and effectively do the job. Indeed, there need not be high trust when there is high ceremony. In fact, high ceremony is often accompanied by low trust.

High ceremony is intended to foster a predictable outcome, leading to more mature organizations in the sense that, under similar circumstances, nearly identical quality will be produced repeatedly with projects of nearly identical performance.

Mr. Winston Royce

Perhaps one of the earliest industry descriptions of the PD-PDLC methodology and the ceremony that surrounds it is found in a well-known paper authored by Winston Royce, originally published by the aerospace firm TRW and presented to the 1970 IEEE WESCON.[11] Entitled "Managing the Development of Large Software Systems," Royce was actually reporting on his frustrations of delivering working software on time and within the budget. While explaining the cascading sequence very clearly in a short ten-page paper, he actually made the case for doing the process differently.

Perhaps prescient of the agile methods to follow some two decades later, Royce starts from the premise that if the project is of small scale and likely to be locally deployed and maintained, then the project methodology can be just two value-added steps:

1. Analyze the problem
2. Implement the solution

Obviously, such a simple approach is *low ceremony*, but it is also one of high trust and high value. By high value we mean that each step adds materially to the end product. By high trust, we mean that the project team need not provide extensive written proof of what is being done. There is little command and control exercised by project management, and there is little documentation preparation and approval.

If the project is to be of nontrivial scale—that is, not a two-stepper—then Royce perceives certain risks that must be mitigated. Years of experience by the project management community since Royce made his observations have not changed the risk picture very much. The principal uncertainties of centrally planned methods, pretty much universally recognized by managers, are given in *a project management tip*:

<table>
<tr><td rowspan="2">A project management tip</td><td>The principal risks in the PD-PDLC waterfall</td></tr>
<tr><td>• The requirements are never complete enough to forestall discovery late in the project lifecycle of latent, unknown, and unknowable requirements.
• Documents written early in the lifecycle are always at the risk of being overcome by events and rendered obsolete.
• Requirements discovered after baselines are set almost always impact unfavorably.
• The testing comes at the end. Testing invariably turns up issues and exposes unsatisfied requirements that should have been addressed much earlier when the cost and impact to project success was more manageable.
• Benefits come late and may not materialize because the business and the market have moved on, regardless of the project outcomes.</td></tr>
</table>

To combat these risks, Royce argued for more steps early in the process so that there are more opportunities to reveal hidden issues and requirements sooner. These steps came to be known as structured analysis. Royce also strongly advocated feedback and iteration; he also called for a parallel prototyping effort so that the customer would not receive version 1.0 in production. He advocated very elaborate controls and procedures to manage implementation, processes that came to be called governance. And he called for team discipline to abide by the control mechanisms as enforced by project management. Royce was quick to recognize that much of what he advocated would not be perceived as value-added, not by the end customer and perhaps not by the business stakeholders. Few would argue with him.

A project management tip	Mitigating risks in the waterfall methodology
	• Iterate between sequential steps and between non-contiguous steps in different phases to feedback errors and omissions for correction. • Be thorough and complete with the gathering of requirements and analysis of system design before any detailed implementation begins. • Incorporate sufficient prototyping and preproduction models so that the customer does not receive the first model of the deliverable. • Develop and maintain robust documentation of everything designed and developed and tested on the project. • Emphasize testing to the point that testing consumes more project resources than any other single activity. • Involve the customer early and often.

Role of the Customer in PD-PDLC

The customer is more at arm's length in the plan-driven methodologies, often separated by a contract from the development team. The customer is often quite distributed organizationally and spatially. The many disparate constituents are focused through an administrative channel that does the contracting. Nevertheless, the customer will often do a lot of homework to prepare for the contract, eliciting requirements from many widespread users; many customers even develop their own prototypes and run their own simulations as precontract preparation. After award, it is reasonable to expect that the customer will provide functional guidance and will participate in product validation. Unfortunately, the arm's-length relationship is often adversarial and detractive to the project's purpose.

PD-PDLC Advantages and Disadvantages

Table 1-3 provides a summary of the advantages of the plan-centric method.

The downside of PD-PDLC is summarized in Table 1-4. Although the list is shorter than the advantages given in Table 1-3, the disadvantages are profound; in some cases, such as dynamic requirements, the issues are outright showstoppers.

Table 1-3 Plan-driven methodology advantages

- Fits large and very large projects, distributed and outsourced workflow, contracted projects done at a fixed price
- Has the potential for developing exceptional process capability maturity for repeatable and predictable outcomes
- Does not strongly depend on exceptionally talented workforce
- Upfront structured analysis effectively supports high reliability and mission-critical safety-critical projects; e.g., space shuttle, medical instrumentation, and precision robotics
- Easily supports prototyping and other risk reduction preliminary efforts to ascertain feasibility
- Supports bridging to legacy projects, maintenance of a large installed base, and products or systems where incremental capability is an oxymoron; e.g., space shuttle ascent control system
- Lots of tool support
- Large trained base of practitioners, including contractors and consulting companies
- Supported by universities, certification organizations (e.g., PMI®), standards, and standards committees
- Enables historical databases to support parametric estimating; job-book estimating
- Intuitively simple to understand finish-to-start precedence of easily imagined deliverables
- Handles dependencies among large workforce and many deliverables
- Rich with reporting, as usually implemented
- Supports specification verification and functional validation
- Supports certification and regulatory compliance with robust documentation and repeatable process

Four Agile Methodologies Are Representative

As stated in the introduction to the book, among all the agile methods, four methodologies are representative of the points of the compass:

1. SCRUM because SCRUM is a management framework in the main; it is not prescriptive of actual technical practices.
2. XP because it is a disciplined software engineering approach to agile practices and is less prescriptive than SCRUM about management practices.
3. The Crystal family because it is the most empathetic methodology, calling itself *people powered*. Crystal directly addresses the scalability issue, proposing a ladder of methods with colors as the moniker. Crystal Clear is the single-team program; Crystal Orange is a multi-team scaled-up version.
4. EVO because it is a true system engineer's approach to incremental software practices. EVO embraces the Deming plan-do-check-act cycle (PDCA) discussed in subsequent chapters. EVO makes no apologies for building on incremental waterfalls.

Table 1-4 Plan-driven methodology disadvantages

- Inappropriate where requirements cannot be fixed, or where customer changes are frequent (inside the development or plan-driven cycle)[1]
- Inappropriate to small teams, fewer than 25 developers, since the cost of process often exceeds the cost of the business deliverables
- Inappropriate where uncertain application overwhelms process discipline, causing continuous re-baselining and re-analysis of earned value forecasts
- Delivery of business value is late in the life cycle; inappropriate where near-term value is paramount
- Values the plan, although the plan requires constant maintenance to maintain relevancy over long periods
- Encourages discipline but discourages process inventiveness
- Changes coming late are very expensive to insert, much more costly than the value of the upgrade in many instances
- Heavy, expensive, process and documentation, prone to errors discovered at the end
- Requires high discipline and commitment to maintenance of artifacts of process to keep them relevant and current over a long project life cycle
- Relies on and requires governance formality
- *Early stage* artifacts have to have a long life or the end result is incorrect

The Spiral method came along a decade earlier than these did. It is not an agile method in the sense of self-organized teams working on production software, but it is reasonably agile in that it is iterative, fast, exploratory, and innovative. However, the reason to include it in a discussion about agile methods is that Spiral addresses feasibility questions better than any other method. Once answered, the Spiral method is designed to pivot to some other methodology for project construction.

All four agile methods share a common idea, which is the main point to grasp:

A common idea

- Agile projects are a sequence of fixed-duration, variable-scope deliveries, each delivery guaranteed by its development team to add value and work as planned, but the planning starts anew after each delivery.

The image that comes to mind, as shown in Figure 1-2 is like a string of freight cars, each the same length, but the cars have varying capacity and functionality, each carload being important and useful to the customer.

Figure 1-2 Agile simplified

Addressing the Major Risks

Agile methods address the major risks of the waterfall methodology that are blamed for poor product quality and poor project performance. By topic, the agile risk mitigations are discussed below:

BDUF: Agile makes no attempt to do a big design up front that cannot sustain its relevance for the life of the project, nor is it assumed that complex systems can be fully imagineered by structured analysis at the beginning of the project lifecycle.

Unknown or unknowable requirements: Customers are allowed to add, delete, revise, and reprioritize requirements at the beginning of each iteration, but not during an iteration. This approach creates a piece-wise freeze to stabilize requirements for development.

Customers at arm's length: Customers are included on the development teams and coached for effective participation.

Testing and delivery is all at the end of the project cycle: In XP, test scripts are written as the first step in the development process. Test scripts are the means to document design requirements. Working product is delivered at multiple points in the project lifecycle. Only working product earns value, and only working product is integrated into the product base.

Documentation is not cost effective: Documentation is minimized insofar as instructions to guide development; documentation is replaced by daily collaboration and informal means to communicate: e-mail, instant messages, comments embedded in the product design, story cards, scorecards, and dashboards.

A Process of Cycles

All agile methodologies are about responsiveness, exercised iteratively. All methods embrace the concept of repeating nested cycles, although the terminology varies from one method to the next.

The building block is the standard day, ideally an eight hour stint of value-added activity. Each day begins with a team review that is time-boxed—that is, limited to a prescribed time duration—followed by development activity, automated testing, and ideally ending with the day's outcome integrated into the preproduction product base.

Iterations are built up of days, lasting a few weeks at most. In SCRUM, the iteration is called a sprint; in EVO it is called a delivery cycle or step. An iteration is planned as a time box during which the team develops a selected backlog of requirements. Once the selection is made, further changes to requirements are not allowed; for development purposes, the requirements are stable during the iteration. The finished deliverables, integrated into the product base at the end of the iteration, comprise a product increment.

Iterations, one or more, build up a release event. A release is one or more product increments going into production operations for internal or external use.

Releases are planned in waves. A wave is a planning horizon consisting of one or more releases. The planning horizon, typically not more than a few months, is the distance we can see ahead with reasonable vision of the evolving product.

Waves are synchronized with business cycles. The normal business cycles are quarterly, annually, and multi-annually to correspond to tactical results, yearly

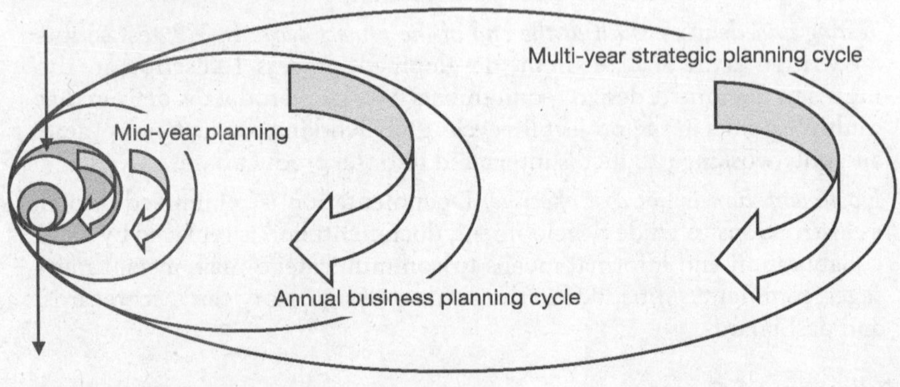

Figure 1-3 Agile in the business cycle

results, and strategic planning, respectively. Figure 1-3 illustrates the agile cycles embedded in the longer business cycles of annual plans and strategic planning.

Methodologies Compared

A good way to compare the methodologies is by looking at each from the point of view of people, process, and technology. People include stakeholders, sponsors, project managers, and team members that include the customer and end user. Process addresses management, communication, and measurement. Technology is really the technical practices that are main features of the methodology: estimating, developing, and closing.

Table 1-5, Table 1-6, and Table 1-7 provide a comparison of the four agile methodologies from the perspectives of people, process, and technology. More information about methodology-specific terms, including their definitions, is found in Appendix I (Methodologies) and Appendix II (Glossary).

Table 1-6 follows. Unique terms are explained in subsequent chapters and in Appendix I.

Table 1-7 addresses practices that are specific to agile methods; unique terms are explained in Appendix I.

Table 1-5 Comparison of agile methods—people

	EVO	SCRUM	XP	Crystal
Project management	Traditional project manager	SCRUM master[2]	Coach, coordinator, and facilitator	Project coordinator
Customer	Product experts	Product master	Embedded product manager	Business expert
Users	Product experts close at hand and instantly available	Other embedded functional users		Expert user close at hand and instantly available
Team leaders	From team members according to conventions of the project			
Team members	Routine system development qualifications by role	Highly talented and disposed to collaborative team work	Whole team of all required technical skills[3]	Highly talented and disposed to collaborative team work
Team roles	Architect, lead designer, programmer, tester, writer, users and domain experts, technical experts, system integrators, infrastructure experts			
Others	Executives, sponsors, stakeholders			

Table 1-6 Comparison of agile methods—process

	EVO	SCRUM	XP	Crystal
Rules and doctrine	EVO principles — Project rules	Agile Manifesto & principles — SCRUM rules[4]	XP values and principles[5] — XP practices[6]	Crystal principles[7] — Teams rules
Communications	Face to face preferred, but allowances for scale — Reasonable documentation to fit scale	Face to face preferred, but allowances for scale — Minimum documentation except for user	Face to face preferred, but allowances for scale — Minimum documentation except for user	Osmotic communications[8] — Documents as required to fit scale
Planning	Product vision & architecture Planning session for delivery cycle just-in-time	Product vision Product backlog Planning session for each sprint	Product vision Product backlog Planning session for delivery cycle just-in-time	Product vision & architecture Planning session for delivery cycle just-in-time
Estimating[9]	EVO day[10] — 26 hour weekly plan — Fatal date and 10-week planning horizon[11]	User stories and relative sizing; correct with experience and feedback	Velocity estimates Planning poker or equivalent	Use cases Delphi method Blitz planning
Delivery cycle	Multiple task cycles per delivery cycle (step) — 2-week delivery cycle — Progress by various charts	30-day sprint — Releases potentially after every sprint — Progress by burn-down charts	2-3 week iterations — Releases potentially after every iteration but more likely 2-3 iterations per release — Progress by burn-up charts	Short iterations planned by teams — Releases potentially after every iteration but more likely 2-3 iterations per release — Progress by various charts
Measurements[12]	Various charts	Burn-down charts	Burn-up charts	Burn charts Other various charts

Table 1-7 Comparison of agile methods—technology practices

	EVO	SCRUM	XP	Crystal
Developing	PDCA cycles as short waterfall cycles System architecture Time-boxing Frequent integration	Daily SCRUM meeting 24-hour inspection Time-boxing Sprint backlog Refactoring Frequent integration	Daily stand-up meeting Daily build Time-boxing Test-driven development Pair programming Frequent releases	Crystal techniques and strategies[13] Methodology shaping Short cycles Walking skeleton UML use cases Refactoring Frequent integration
Test and integration	Automated tests Frequent integration Daily builds, if possible		Test-driven development Automated tests Frequent integration Daily builds, if possible	Automated tests Frequent integration Daily builds, if possible
Closing	PDCA lessons-learned — Frequent deliveries	Reflection and lessons-learned — Frequent releases	Reflection and lessons-learned — Frequent releases[14]	Reflection Workshops — Frequent releases

Advantages and Disadvantages of Agile Methods

Table 1-8 and Table 1-9 summarize the material on agile methods. In many respects, these attributes are the mirror image of the PD-PDLC tables of advantages and disadvantages.

Table 1-8 Advantages of agile methods

- Rapid and frequent deliveries to production get the benefit stream going early; there is potential for the project to be self-supporting financially
- Relatively strong commitment to business milestones
- Efficient adaption to changing customer priorities and requirements keeps the project current and relevant
- Very cost effective for teams of 25 or less developers
- Customers get an influential *seat at the table* to shape the value proposition of the project as it unfolds
- The innovative potential of small teams working collectively only on the customer needs is unleashed
- A sense of accomplishment and a cause for celebration and reinforcement is offered at each successful iteration and release
- The project objective is customer-centric and not necessarily bound to a plan that is out of date
- Validation of customer value is built in and almost automatic by design
- Trust by stakeholder and customer is built with actual deeds

The Spiral Methodology Is a Risk Reducer

Headlines quoted by Barry Boehm as he begins his explanation of the spiral model.[12]

> *"Stop the lifecycle—I want to get off!" "Lifecycle Concept Considered Harmful." "The waterfall model is dead." "No, it isn't, but it should be."*

With sentiments like these, is it any wonder that anyone with a plausible alternative would get attention? Spiral is the invention of the well-known software methodologist Dr. Barry W. Boehm who worked many years in the aerospace and defense industry at the cutting edge of software development.

Table 1-9 Disadvantages of agile methods

- Weak commitment to overall cost and scope
- Vulnerable to turn-over in the team staffing
- Not architecture driven so there may be many dependencies discovered late
- Difficult to scale the small-team dynamics to an enterprise scope project
- Difficult to scale without commitment to documentation
- Difficult to contract the work team because requirements and scope are not known with adequate certainty
- Depends greatly on favorable logistics for team co-location, face-to-face communications, a pool of talented multi-disciplined staff, and instant access to knowledgeable and empowered customers or end users
- Testing is not independent
- Verification is by testing, not traceable to specifications
- High reliability and mission-critical requires strong verification that is missing

Motivations for Spiral

In the 1980s Boehm was working on the same dilemma that has motivated all the alternatives to the PD-PDLC: *How are risky, uncertain, and changing requirements to be approached?* Contemporary thinking at the time was to bear down on requirements analysis as the beginning step. Top-down design, structured analysis, and other analytical methods were introduced as additional effort into the front end of the project timeline. Recall that Royce proposed not only more analysis, but a parallel effort to work out the kinks before committing to production.

Dr. Boehm was well familiar with the work of Royce. Boehm was also familiar with evolutionary methods and McCracken and Jackson's criticism of the waterfall.[13] However, in spite of these insights, results on large systems remained stubbornly unacceptable.

Boehm accepted the notion advanced by Royce that many small-scale systems and applications could be successfully built and maintained with minimal documentation and formal process. He also bought into what has become a tenant of agile methods, to wit: users are notoriously poor at providing clear and complete requirements. However, in Boehm's opinion and experience, there were difficulties beyond requirements volatility. Technical feasibility was a frequent issue. Boehm felt that misunderstanding feasibility was a contributing factor to incorrect sequencing in the project schedule. Misunderstanding feasibility could start the project in the wrong direction, opening vulnerabilities to latent and unknowable risks.

Mind-Snap of Spiral

In getting to spiral, Boehm's insight was: *The nature and character of risks should be a leading factor in the order and sequence of development activities.*

No other methodology approaches sequencing this way. No other methodology sets the project starting point by first engaging in risk management, and doing so as a matter of doctrine. Absent a heads-up approach to identifying and addressing feasibility and practicality, the project may make many missteps of direction that could cause failures and unintended consequences. Identifying what to address first and what direction to take is the initial task to complete before any milestones are forecast.

A project management tip	Spiral is a risk-driven methodology
	• In order to determine the proper sequencing of activities within a process, the risks must first be determined. • The nature and character of risks may actually determine the order and sequence of activity within the project. • The spiral can be used as the launching mechanism for an agile project to complete the design, development, and delivery.

Spiral Cycles

Boehm described his methodology in a paper written in 1988.[14] The basic idea is represented visually by a spiral of activities that repeat with each cycle of the spiral. The spiral winds out from a hub or beginning point. The length of a path traced around the spiral is accumulating time. The radial dimension is cost. Cost increases as the spiral winds outward. Radiating from the hub are spokes that serve as boundaries between segments of activities or even phases of the project. Each segment is functionally unique and has a specified work product. As the spiral winds out from the hub, each work product influences the next. Each cycle of the spiral portrays an iteration of the lifecycle. Figure 1-4 illustrates the segmentation and phasing.

It's no surprise that in a risk-driven methodology such as Spiral, every cycle begins with a risk analysis. But analysis is not the main outcome. The main outcome is tangible evidence of feasibility or a means to mitigate identified risks. Getting to a working model rapidly is an objective similar to the motivation behind agile's refactoring: get something going quickly—the simplest possible solution—learn from it, and then come back to modify the solution later, all the while holding the black box parameters and functionality invariant.

In the first spiral cycle, the highest risk, or perhaps least feasible requirement, is prototyped and evaluated. Changes and adjustments are made until a move-on criterion is achieved. Each successive cycle builds on the success of the former. Low-impact artifacts are left to the latter cycles. At some point when uncer-

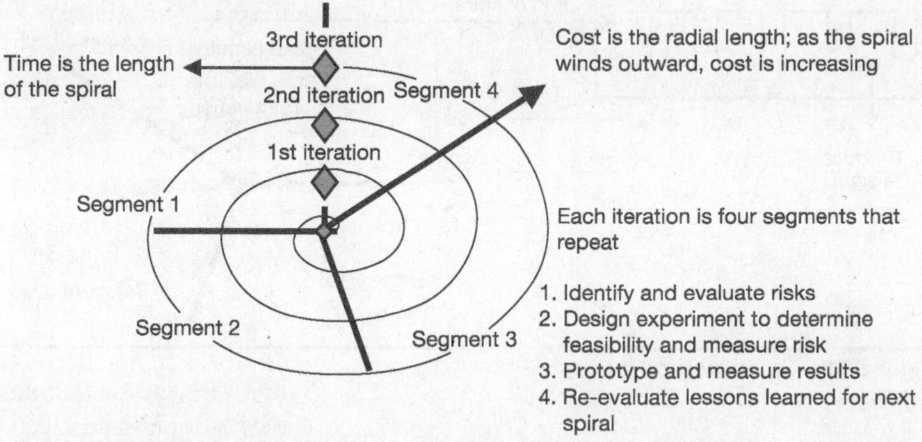

Figure 1-4 Spiral method

tainties are sufficiently understood, the management team transitions the project from a spiral into a more linear plan for development and deliveries.

Boehm envisioned the opening spiral cycles as the launch mechanism for the more linear PDLC that would follow. Picture a discus thrower winding up to launch the disc. The methodology explicitly allows for project management judgment and intervention to select the correct PDLC for the circumstances. The spiral could launch a Royce model, an agile model, or some other, as shown in Figure 1-5.

Spiral in a Linear World

The spiral pictorial reinforces the metaphor of systematically repeating risk analysis while accumulating more maturity at ever-increasing cost. The pictorial also reinforces the idea that in a risk-driven methodology repetitions cause the timeline to fold back upon itself. However, project managers must schedule the tasks and work packages according to the clock and calendar with tools like charts and graphs that show activity in linear segments of duration.

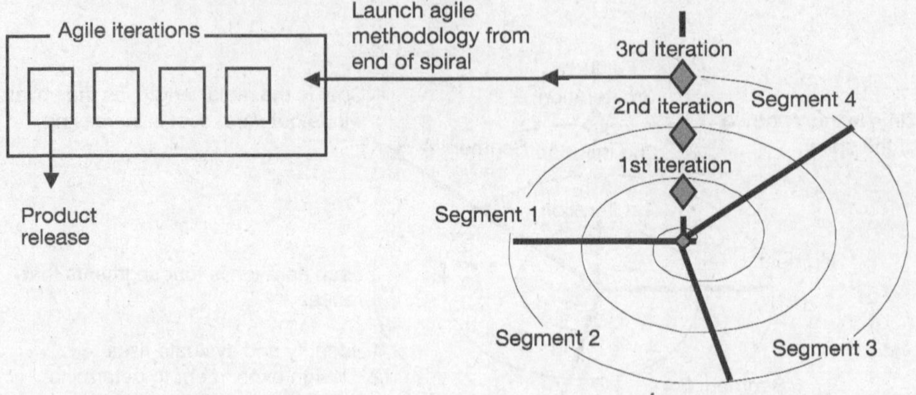

Figure 1-5 Spiral method launch

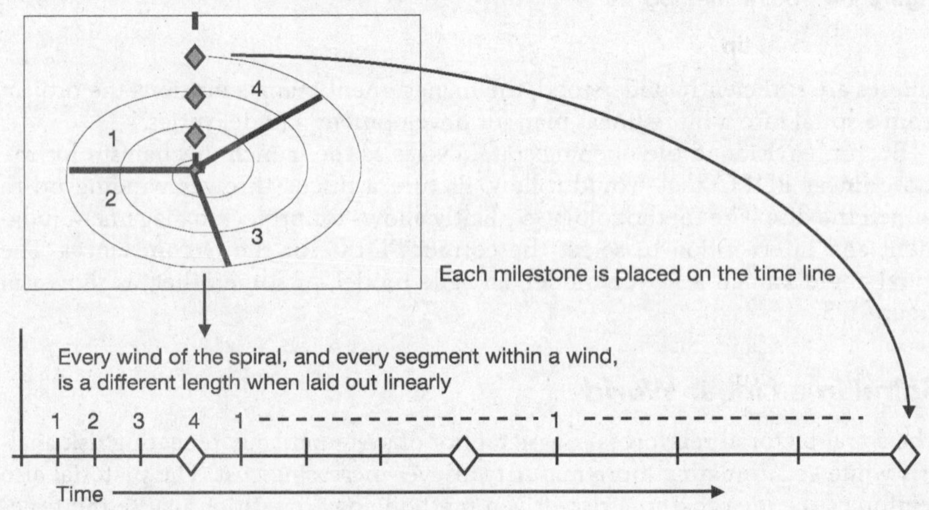

Figure 1-6 Spiral method launch (unwound)

To schedule the spiral, there are two things to do:

1. Unwind the spiral and lay it out straight as a string of linked tasks, as shown in Figure 1-6
2. Make an educated guess about a reasonable number of experiments and iterations, but also plan a generous time-buffer to absorb estimating errors

Putting the spiral on a calendar is unlike any other scheduling task. Different from agile methods that depend on fixed-duration iterations and time-boxes for control, spiral has no similar control mechanism. After all, Boehm's objective was to get the PDLC off in the right direction to maximize the likelihood of satisfying the majority of requirements, thereby improving the predictability of schedule or cost in the longer view.

A project management tip	Spiral methods can be laid out linearly
	• To actually manage a project with the spiral methodology, unwind the spiral into a linear progression, keeping the boundaries specified by the radial spokes. • Time buffers will be needed to allow for elasticity of effort and the possibility of repeating high-risk steps. • The overall forecast of the calendar date of the ending milestone must await risk analysis and prototyping. • After prototyping and experimentation results are known, the ensuing schedule is managed as a linear timeline.

Where does the spiral begin and end? Even Boehm said the answer to this question was a matter of judgment. To get started, begin with the highest risk. Evaluate it first and understand its impact to subsequent development and to the overall architecture. Follow up by evaluating lesser risks. The spiral ends when managers make a judgment that risks are sufficiently characterized.

Advantages and Disadvantages of the Spiral Method

Every methodology has its strengths and weaknesses. The spiral is not immune, as Table 1-10 illustrates:

Table 1-10 Spiral advantages and disadvantages

Advantages	Disadvantages
A strong advocacy for facing risks early and definitively	• There is no obvious starting point. The first risk cycle is a judgment what is known at the outset
Can be the front end for other methodologies	• There is no obvious exit from the experimentation and prototyping • Again, project managers and system engineers can only be guided by what is known and knowable at the time
Can be applied to any technology project	• Spirals do not naturally fit the linear world • Practical and conceptual adjustments are required to fit indefinite experimentation into a resource-constrained framework
Can be executed by reasonably skilled personnel	• There may be excessive throw-away from early experimentation
Can accommodate any book of best practices	
Appropriate in circumstances where the technology or concept is unproven, feasibility is questionable, and end-users interfaces are fuzzy	

Summary and Takeaway Points

In this chapter we have been developing this theme: *The value of agile methods is the success that attends frequent, incrementally delivered features and functions, even in the swirl of complex and uncertain requirements.*

Plan-driven methods have their place, particularly on projects of very high scale, safety-critical requirements, mission-critical objectives, and many contract situations. However, they are decidedly inappropriate in a dynamic requirements environment, inappropriate to fast and incremental delivery, and inefficient on smaller projects. The sweet spot for agile projects is teams of less than a few dozen developers where there is high value placed on rapid responsiveness to changing business imperatives, incremental product deliveries are practical and useful, and there is acceptance that responding to customers is more likely a winning strategy than following a plan that may have obsolesced.

There are many methodologies that subscribe to the agile manifesto and the agile principles. Each methodology's thought leaders had a particular point of view that set the tone of the method: SCRUM is a management method; XP is a set of disciplined practices; Crystal is about making methods habitable by mostly ordinary people; and EVO is a practical way to implement the PDCA cycle incrementally. Spiral as a launching point sets direction and answers basic feasibility questions.

All of these methodologies fit within a cycle of cycles: the daily cycle → the iteration → the release → the planning wave → the business cycle → the market.

At the end of the day, *agile* is small teams, working collectively and collaboratively, with this mission:

> **Agile mission**
>
> To deliver frequent, incremental releases of innovative functions and features prioritized for need and affordability.
>
> Evolved iteratively from a vision according to user reflection and feedback produced at the best possible value.

Chapter Endnotes

1. In this book, the words *business, organization,* and *enterprise* are used interchangeably. The words *customer* and *user* are also used interchangeably and refer to the target audience of the project results, whether internal or external.

2. Takeuchi and Nonaka, "The New Product Development Game."

3. The 17 drafters in Utah were Kent Beck, Alistair Cockburn, James Highsmith, Ward Cunningham, Martin Fowler, James Grenning, Andrew Hunt, Ron Jefferies, Jon Kern, Brian Marick, Robert Martin, Steve Mellor, Ken Schwaber, Jeff Sutherland, Dave Thomas, Arie van Bennekum, and Mike Beedle.

4. Simplicity is one of five specific values of the XP method. See: Beck, with Andres, *Extreme Programming Explained*, 18–19.

5. The consequence of a successful project is a product or a process which itself has a lifecycle. Beyond the project are the operational life and then some retirement phase, perhaps with reclamation of assets at the end.

6. Six Sigma is defined in Appendix II (Glossary). Defined process control is a concept from manufacturing, promoted strongly by the work of W. Edwards Deming and others in the post-World War II era. It presumes definable error limits that are acceptable in the finished product, means to measure, and means to correct. See Schawber, K., *Agile Project Management with SCRUM*, 2–4.

7. Highsmith, *Agile Project Management: Creating Innovative Products*, 27.

8. CMM (I) is the Capability Maturity Model—integration developed by Carnegie Mellon University. It integrates software and system engineering with

product integration in a set of recommended practices loosely framed in a methodology. CMM (I) is a service mark of Carnegie Mellon University.

9. Statistics taken from Boehm and Turner, *Balancing Agility and Discipline*, Appendix E.

10. Finish-to-start is a scheduling precedence taken from the Precedence Diagramming Method (PDM). It means that the finishing activity of a task must be completed before the beginning activity of the successor task can start.

11. IEEE WESCON is a western conference of the Institute of Electrical Electronic Engineers (IEEE). See WESCON Technical Papers, vol. 14, (1970), A/1-1 to A/1-9.

12. Boehm, "A Spiral Model of Software Development," 61.

13. McCracken and Jackson, "Lifecycle Concept Considered Harmful."

14. Boehm, "A Spiral Model of Software Development."

Table Endnotes

1. Boehm, B. and Turner, R. *Balancing Agility and Discipline*, Addison-Wesley, Boston, 2004 p. 31: Boehm recommends that requirement changes after requirements baselining should be less than 1 percent for a successful PD-PDLC project.

2. The three SCRUM roles—SCRUM master, product master, and the team—are explained in detail in: Schawber, K., *Agile Project Management with SCRUM*, Microsoft Press, Redmond, WA. 2004, Chapters 2, 5, and 8.

3. Beck, K. with Andres, C. *Extreme Programming Explained–2nd Edition*, Addison-Wesley, Boston, 2005, Chapters 4 and 10.

4. Schawber, K. *Agile Project Management with SCRUM*, Microsoft Press, Redmond, WA, 2004, Appendix A.

5. Beck, K. with Andres, C. 2005, op. cit., Chapters 4 and 5.

6. Beck, K. with Andres, C. 2005, op. cit., Chapters 7 and 9.

7. Cockburn, A. *Crystal Clear—A Human-powered Methodology for Small Teams*, Addison-Wesley, Boston, 2005, pp. 19–34.

8. Osmotic communications refers to communications by osmosis: absorbing information in your immediate vicinity, whether directly or indirectly intended for you. See: Cockburn, A. 2005, op. cit., p. 24.

9. Several unique terms are used to explain estimating in agile methods. See subsequent chapters and Appendix I for definitions, explanations, and examples.

10. Malotaux, N. *Evolutionary Project Management Methods*, Version 1.4b, 2007, accessed http://www.malotaux.nl/nrm/Evo/EvoEng.htm. June 2009, p. 9.

11. Malotaux, N. *Time Line: Getting and Keeping Control of Your Project*, Annual Pacific Northwest Software Quality Conference, Portland, OR, 2007, pp. 2 and 6.

12. Burn charts refers to earned value accounting wherein charts of planned and expended effort per deliverable object track progress toward accomplishing

all the work. Burn refers to effort. Burn-up or -down refers to working up or down a chart of required objects until the scope is complete.

13. Cockburn, A. *Crystal Clear—A Human-powered Methodology for Small Teams,* Addison-Wesley, Boston, 2005, pp. 46–105.

14. Beck, K. and Fowler, M. *Planning Extreme Programming,* Addison-Wesley, Boston, 2001, Chapter 17.

2

The Agile Business Case

The agile business case respects and encourages the meld of business cycle goals and strategy with the urgency and importance of customer need.

> *Every individual endeavors to employ his capital so that its produce may be of greatest value.*
>
> *Adam Smith, "The Wealth of Nations"*

The Business Case Adds Value to the Project

Agile methods do not make the business case unnecessary; indeed, the business case supports and justifies the project as a strategy step toward business goals. Even if the project is simply to burn-down a bug list, the project is made better by the effort invested to imagine and explore the opportunity and its alternatives, collecting everyone's thoughts in an organized way. Some put process labels on the effort, names like the *Envision* and *Speculate* phases or the *Explore 360* strategy.[1] Even simpler: *Scoping the project.*[2]

The business case is a capture document. It is an interface mechanism between the project and the business; and between the decision-maker sponsor, myriad stakeholders, and the project manager. The business case itself should be an example of lean and agile principles: simple; value adding; responsive; and evolutionary. To that end, we define three business-case levels corresponding to business impact:

- *Level 0:* A one-page form for small projects with one team working on the least intrusive projects. Level 0 is approved by a one-step workflow-managed approval process.
- *Level 1:* A simple template for more complex multiteam projects; it is approved in a two-step workflow.

- *Level 2:* For enterprise projects that have significant business implications; Level 2 requires executive approval.

Every project has an impact on the organization, so four sets of questions commonly arise in the business case:

1. Is a project the right approach to obtain what the business needs and wants? Is there an approach other than a project that should be considered?
2. Specifically, why is the proposed project the right project to undertake? Have alternative project choices been examined?
3. Can the project deliver the required business value for the resources available (e.g., time, money, people, and technology)?
4. What are the risks and how are they to be mitigated?

An Agile Business-Case Framework

The business case is a framework to hold content; the content is intended to be adaptable to many situations and amenable to iteration and evolution as the solution solidifies. The business case begins with a high-level idea from the business, a vision of the expected outcomes, discriminating features, and needed functional capabilities. At the top level, these intended outcomes are the project scope. The exact solution is value-driven by the end users or customers rather than plan-driven by sponsors and project management. In Chapter 1, agile projects were characterized as evolutionary, meaning that details evolve over time as customers evaluate each increment delivered to the product base.

There is an anticipated investment and expected payback, financial and otherwise. The investment goal is the limit on available funding; the payback is an anticipated benefit stream tied to the vision. Investment and payback are linked to milestones. Milestones establish a timeline and relate expected outcomes and benefits to the calendar as prioritized by value.

Take a look at Figure 2-1 for an example of the discussion so far. Each business element evolves during the project lifecycle.

Planning Element Relationships

To get a better handle on the business plan fundamentals, let's take a look at the relationships among planning elements as given in Table 2-1 on page 38.

Notice that there is a lot of entanglement among planning elements in the agile business case, many of which will change as the business case is developed and customers express their wishes. In a word, the agile business case is expected to adapt as the project particulars emerge. Adaptive planning requires a tradeoff between a *point solution* and a *best-value outcome.* The point solution is plan-centric;

Business case details hook to the framework that provides boundaries and limitations to govern project implementation

Example: Framework and its elements

Framework elements	Business case details
Opportunity	To improve new-order customer service in a manner that invites repeat business
Goals	Raise customer satisfaction metric by 50% in one annual business cycle Raise sales from existing customers by 25%
Strategy	Improve the environment and tools available to order entry processors; transfer some order entry to the customer
Project vision	An integrated, near-real-time order entry application useable by internal and external customers that reduces order entry time and improves the quality of the entry process by automated validation of data entry
Scope functionality	Web-based application that validates product, price, and customer account, useable by order processors and customers Integrates with product catalog and price books Supports sales credits for out-bound sales force
Milestones	M1: Internal order processor capability M2: External customer user capability M3: Automated sales credits
Investment	$1M total; M1: $500K, M2: $300K, M3: $200K
Beneficiaries	Order processors, sales team, billing and credit, and external customers
Benefit pay-back	Recover investment with increased sales and reduced operating expenses within two business cycles

Figure 2-1 Business case framework

it has seemingly precise estimates and predictable outcomes, but the track record is often otherwise: estimates and outcomes wind up with distressingly low accuracy and wide variances. On the other hand, the best-value outcome is empirically derived. Beginning with a product vision depicted in the business case, the best-value outcome progressively acquires definition and detail with each release, bound by a commitment to customer-driven value, and framed by architecture, the business case milestones, and available investment.

Table 2-1 Relationships in the agile business case

Customer-valued features and function	• All the product capabilities that depend on the value and importance assigned by the customer, as evolved with operational experience incrementally over the lifecycle of the project
Scope	• All the features and functions valued by the customer, and everything else needed by the project or the business even if there is no direct customer value
Resources	• All the people, technology, and environment needed to produce value for the customer in the prescribed schedule
Investment and funds	• Investment: the limit of affordability established by the business as the value of the opportunity • Funds: all the money needed to pay for resources as estimated by the project, but constrained by the available investment • There may be a gap between investment and funds as shown on the project balance sheet
Schedule	• Business milestones at which time features and functions are incrementally needed by end users
Value	• A best fit of features and functions to the available schedule and investment

Both the business—including by extension, the customer—and the project have rights and responsibilities as they mutually engage in business-project planning, as given in the project management tip that follows:

A project management tip	Rights and responsibilities in the agile business case
	• The business has a responsibility to provide a clear business vision. • The business has a right to a best-value response to the business need. • The agile project has a responsibility to be responsive to the value judgments of the business and provide a best-value solution. • The agile project has a responsibility to respect the limitations of funds and the business milestone identified by the business case.

Best-Value Is Derived

The value proposition of a project is always in the eye of the beholder—business leaders and customer alike—meaning that the beneficiaries bestow value. Ideas about values as beliefs generally come from the top of the enterprise; ideas about value as an opportunity come from all points of the customer base, internal and external. Best-value is a meld of beliefs and opportunity delivered at an affordable price.

Imagine a chain with links from the fuzzy front end of opportunity and visionary ideas, through goals, to strategy and operations. Think of opportunity as untapped value that is waiting to be captured and processed into business results. Tapping into opportunity provides the fuel to power projects. Figure 2-2 illustrates the relationships in the chain from opportunity to goal satisfaction. The chain is shown in the familiar *V* form so that lateral alignments are more apparent.

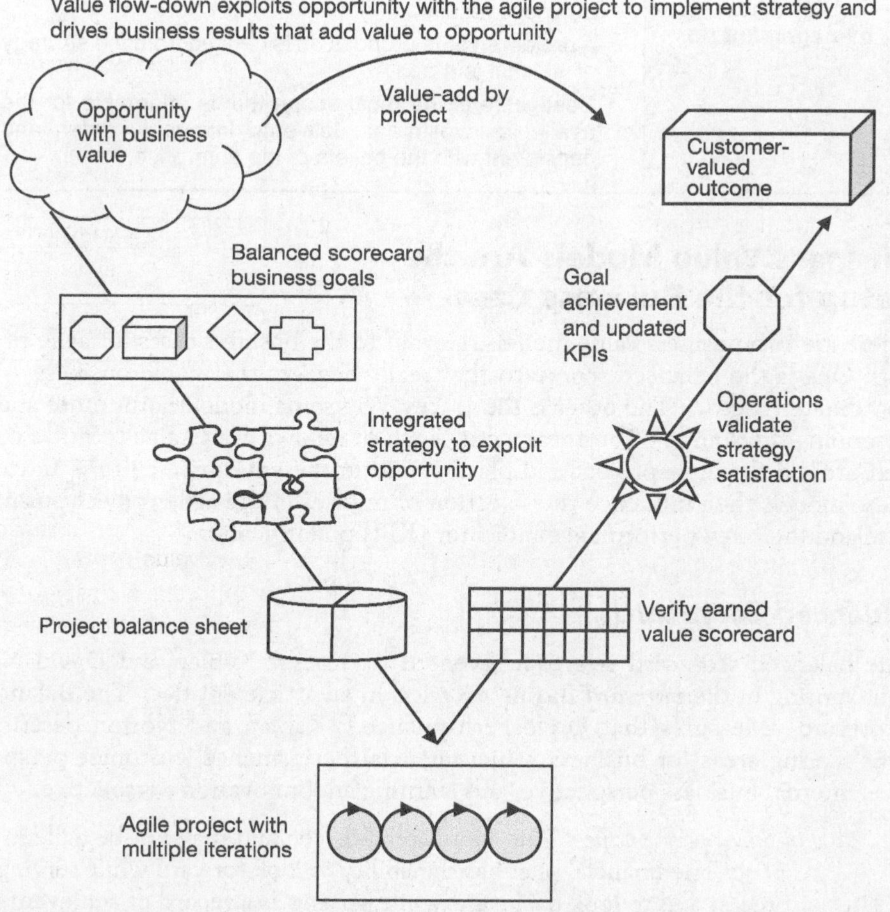

Figure 2-2 Value flow-down

Most organizations pull all this together in a strategic plan. As commonly practiced, strategic planning sets goals and identifies the means to achieve those goals. The means of achievement is called *strategy:* Strategy is a linked and ordered set of actionable steps that point unambiguously to a goal. Strategy is a plan for action set in the context of business culture, strengths and weaknesses, and threats and opportunities. The business makes projects part of the action, an element of strategy, and thereby an instrument to achieve goals.

A project management tip	Projects are valued for their impact on strategy
	• Opportunity is where the value is; a project becomes valuable if it can harvest and transform opportunity into business results. • A project's value proposition is derived from the strategy of which it is a part. • Best-value is the most scope that is affordable for the available investment, delivered in priority order, and consistent with the beliefs of the enterprise.

Business Value Models Are the Setup for the Business Case

There are two business value models relevant to the business cases for agile projects. One is the balanced scorecard that really engages the whole business with coordinated metrics. The other is the Tracey-Wiersema model that is more about describing the source of business value. Each in its own way helps to put a context around the agile project and place it within the enterprise culture. In turn, these models then influence the selection of metrics in the agile project business case and their key performance indicator (KPI) quantification.[4]

Balanced Scorecard

The balanced scorecard is a tool invented by Robert Kaplan and David Norton. Writing in the *Harvard Business Review* in an article entitled "The Balanced Scorecard—Measures that Drive Performance,"[3] Kaplan and Norton described four scoring areas for business value: financial performance, customer perspective, internal business perspective, and learning and innovation perspective.

1. *Financial performance:* This area is plan-driven and may not be agile in all respects. The financial plan has the ability to look forward while serving as a forecast and to look backward while serving as a record of achievement. Historical data is valued by agile managers as a basis to calculate trends

and evaluate risks for a look-forward forecast. The forecast is valued for its heads-up to all managers to take corrective action to reduce variances and stay within the investment limitation of the agile business case. All projects regardless of methodology must respond to financial performance.

2. *Customer perspective:* Performance indicators in this area measure how well customers are satisfied. Agile projects score well in this space because the customer must be an active project participant. The customer readily contributes to decisions regarding business matters and makes themselves readily available to interpret requirements.
3. *Internal business perspective:* In this area are measures of effectiveness and efficiency of internal programs, often referred to as the operational effectiveness (OE) perspective. Effectiveness is about impact—the degree to which a project makes a difference improving the lot of beneficiaries. OE is valued for bringing efficiencies and greater effectiveness to internal programs.
4. *The innovation and learning perspective:* The performance measures in this area not only gauge how the business is updating its products and services, but also how well the business is developing its human resources. This perspective is valued for the competitive edge it gives the enterprise. Innovation and learning fits naturally with the Crystal family. The Crystal methods are the human-powered methods that emphasize personal development and constant learning.

<table>
<tr><td rowspan="2">A project management tip</td><td>Balancing the scorecard for agile projects</td></tr>
<tr><td>• Every agile project has the potential to touch all four perspectives of the balanced scorecard.
• Customer satisfaction is the primary motivator of agile projects. The Agile Manifesto favors delivering customer value over following a plan.
• Financial measures and operational KPIs can be flowed directly onto the business case, but plan-driven KPIs will have to be adjusted for agile performance.</td></tr>
</table>

Agile and the Balanced Scorecard

In the agile project space, project measures have a different priority and emphasis compared to the traditional project plan. Agile priorities require some adjustment in thinking about what success is and how it is to be measured. From the financial perspective, it is already established that cost and benefits are dependent on the evolutionary value-driven outcomes. Obviously, there is a big change here: hitting a planned budget gives way to delivering as much scope as the available investment permits. The cost-recovery benefit stream becomes dependent on the choices made by the business and the customer during the course of the project—choices conditioned in part on how those chosen outcomes contribute to benefits.

Agile in the financial perspective: Every project requires investment. Evaluating an investment opportunity for its funding requirements touches on affordability, payback, and risk. Since there is no point solution to evaluate for cost, agile projects fall back to two parameters:

1. Affordability for the product envisioned in the business case
2. The likely payback if the imagined product is fully deployed and accepted

Affordability—the capacity and willingness to pay—limits the total project expenditures.

Risk colors business confidence about funding requirements. Confidence, capacity to pay, and tolerance for uncertainty drive a company's willingness to invest. Willingness is an election, a choice among affordable and beneficial alternatives. Ordinarily, the decision policy is to choose projects according to which provides the best performance against the balanced scorecard, including investment payback. Without a payback, no project goes forward. Payback drives the go-no-go decision. Payback first recovers the investment and then generates a return on the investment. Risk discounts the payback and thereby affects willingness. However, in the agile space, early incremental deliveries reduce risk and increase the value of benefits.

Figure 2-3 diagrams the relationships discussed thus far.

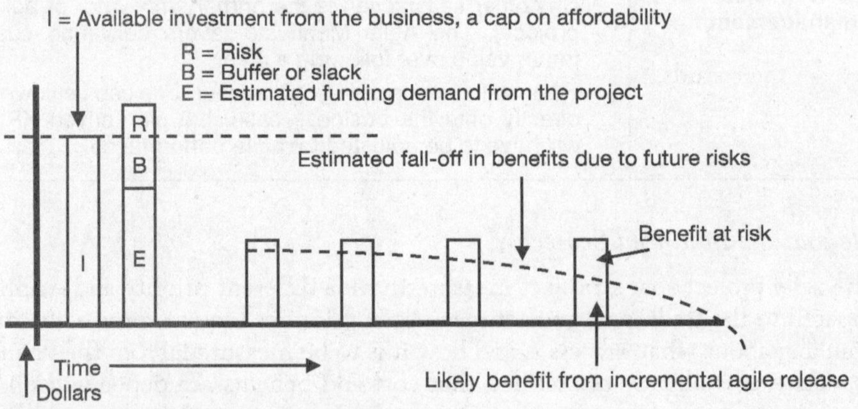

Figure 2-3 Investment and funding

Agile in the internal operations perspective: In the internal perspective, KPIs focus on reducing the friction of internal processes. Used in this context, friction means the impediments to a smooth and timely workflow that are not value-added or that detract from efficiency. Agile teams are self-organizing, require minimum supervision, and communicate in near real time to avoid surprises to managers and sponsors. Operational effectiveness—measured as the ratio cost of value-added work to the total work—is maximized by minimizing management overhead and other tasks not directly linked with producing product. Most noticeable is the absence of formal documentation of the kind recommended in IEEE 12207, as discussed in Chapter 1.

Agile in the customer perspective: The agile customer relationship is a strong suit. In SCRUM, the product master is embedded in the development team. In all agile methods, the customer is available and committed to team participation to set priorities, interpret requirements, test product, and provide feedback and evaluation. In the short run, this is all directed toward getting the most effective product development; in the longer run, this builds customer investment in the product, which should improve loyalty and satisfaction.

Agile in the learning and innovation perspective: The learning and innovation perspective is target-rich for agile projects. The small teams and multidisciplinary assignments foster learning. Small teams are typically more nimble and more innovative, less risk averse, and more likely to pursue unconventional ideas. KPIs to reinforce these behaviors include new feature and function inventions, time-to-market metrics, new product market-share capture rates, and responsiveness to new vision and direction.

Table 2-2 and Table 2-3 illustrate the measurement regime of the balanced scorecard as applied to agile projects.

Treacy-Wiersema Model

Michael Treacy and Fred Wiersema described an interesting model of business value in their study, "Customer Intimacy and Other Value Disciplines,"[5] which they expanded further in their book *The Discipline of Market Leaders*.[6] Closely aligned with the balanced scorecard, the Treacy-Wiersema model has three focus areas, each of which are relevant to the agile way of thinking:

1. Customer intimacy, meaning to have insight and understanding but also to have business–to–business relationships that create efficiencies on both sides
2. Product leadership, meaning product excellence, leading edge innovation, and discriminators that draw customers
3. Operational excellence, meaning exceptional efficiency and effective processes and procedures that produce business results at the least possible cost

Table 2-2 Balanced scorecard and agile projects—financial and customer

Perspective	Balanced scorecard values	Agile project measurements
Financial perspective	• Earnings after tax on ordinary operations	• Incremental deliveries may affect depreciation schedules for capital funds since capital depreciation usually begins when product is put into production
	• Risk-adjusted financial measures NPV and EVA for cash flows	• Cash flow benefits from early and frequent releases are more valued because they are less discounted than benefits that begin at the very end of the project
Customer perspective	• Loyalty and satisfaction measures	• Customer participation on agile teams should favorably affect adoption rate, trouble reports, and warranty actions post-project
	• Revenues by product line and product	• Customer participation on agile teams should favorably affect purchasing decisions about the product developed by the project teams

Treacy and Wiersema posit that an enterprise can truly excel in one of these three, developing the culture and mindset and operating incentives to be the best, but usually this happens at the expense of being ordinary in the others.

A project management tip	Customer intimacy and other value disciplines
	• Project managers can easily adopt agile practices to organizations that share any of the value models described by Michael Treacy and Fred Wiersema.

Organizations that put relationship management foremost as a business value also practice customer intimacy. Companies strong in relationship management understand each customer and user individually, but also in context with their larger community. Understanding is translated into nearly instant familiarity when a customer or user calls, logs in, or otherwise comes in contact.

Some organizations make their mark with product excellence and superiority. They have a vision that their products will always be the benchmark. They design with an expectation of an *ah-hah!* reaction from those that appreciate quality in all its dimensions. Obviously, such demand usually supports a price premium and returns a generous margin.

Table 2-3 Balanced scorecard and agile projects—internal and innovation-learning

Perspective	Balanced scorecard values	Agile project measurements
Internal perspective	• Operating efficiency measured as throughput per unit of resource applied	• Agile teams are benchmarked for throughput
	• Operating effectiveness measured as deployment and internalization of quality improvements	• Operating effectiveness measured as process improvements driven by feedback, iteration, and reflection on lessons learned after each agile iteration
Innovation-learning	• New features and functions added to the product line	• New features and functions added to the product line as valued by the customer
	• Quality of staff measured as skill diversity and skill achievement	• Quality of staff measured as skill diversity and skill achievement while serving on agile teams

The third area is operational excellence. Internal processes, methods, and procedures are made as frictionless as possible. Lean thinking prevails. Low expense is the mantra and usually this is passed along to customers as low prices. Every resource is directed toward only the value for which customers are willing to pay.

Tables 2-4, 2-5, and 2-6 provide comparisons of agile values with the value models proposed by Michael Treacy and Fred Wiersema.

Project Balance Sheet Helps Communicate with the Business Decision Makers

To move the dialogue from the business value models to a project model, we need common ground. Here is the operating premise: project sponsors and business executives who charter projects are really investors. As investors, they are betting a stake on success. The business case serves a purpose much like a prospectus, forecasting outcomes, estimating inputs, and warning of uncertainties. Like all investors, sponsors and executives understand that investment benefits come with some risk, and like all investors, they have an attitude about risk that is both institutional and personal. It is summarized in something called *risk tolerance*. Risk tolerance simply means that beyond a point, one more dollar at risk has a perceived impact to the business equal to many times its face value. If the perceived impact is too large, investment is truncated.

Decision makers with an agile mind-set know that the project proposition is multivalued. One value set comes from the business leadership who want

Table 2-4 Comparison of agile and Treacy-Wiersema—operational excellence

Value proposition	Agile Projects
Focus ruthlessly on operational efficiency	• Small, colocated teams that engage face-to-face with little overhead and minimum internal friction
Make it easy and convenient for customers to participate in the business	• Customers and end users embedded in small teams to state and interpret the business need
Remove barriers to flow—frictionless process	• Trust the team participants • Reduce the ceremony and formal procedures, including the supporting documentation
Make processes work across functional and organizational boundaries	• Include multidisciplined members on teams that can address cross-functional issues
Minimize overhead costs and pass savings to customers	• Trust the team participants • Reduce the ceremony and formal procedures, including the supporting documentation required to measure, control, and track progress
Internally disciplined	• Best represented by the XP methodology; assume high discipline as part of trust

Table 2-5 Comparison of agile and Treacy-Wiersema—customer intimacy

<table>
<tr><th>Value proposition</th><th>Agile projects</th></tr>
<tr><td>Products tailored to individual customers</td><td rowspan="2">• Customers and end users embedded in small teams to state and interpret the business need</td></tr>
<tr><td>High value placed on customer loyalty—customer for life—and loyalty programs to tailor service</td></tr>
</table>

to transform a perceived opportunity into real strategic value. Alignment with strategy imputes a longer cycle of change. Another value set, less definitive and fuzzier, comes from customers and end users, a phenomenon we call *customer-driven value*. Customer-driven value has these characteristics:

- All within the community may not fully share a common product vision
- Values are more diverse, reflecting the larger population of participants; the voice of the customer is vulnerable to being captured by the most vocal and urgent messenger
- Needs and wants are subject to a more rapid change than the business and are even self-conflicting among customer groups

Table 2-6 Comparison of agile and Treacy-Wiersema—product leadership

Value proposition	Agile projects
Product innovation with leading-edge feature and function	• Small, colocated teams that engage face-to-face discussing and experimenting new ideas
Place high value on new ideas regardless of source	
Move ideas through product development to the customer rapidly	• Rapid, frequent releases; typically spaced as rapidly as customers, users, and markets can absorb change
Self-cannibalize their own products for something new	• Constantly address backlog and reflection for new ideas for innovation and improvement

The project is successful only if both business and customer community constituents are satisfied. To that end, the project and the business seek alignment of business purpose and project performance. But in even in the best of cases there may be challenges. An alignment gap may remain between project capability and capacity on the one hand, and the value imperatives of the business and the customers on the other. What to do? The answer is: *Take a risk*. How much risk? Only as much risk as is necessary to balance business needs with project abilities. And who takes this risk? The project manager—the ultimate risk manager.[7]

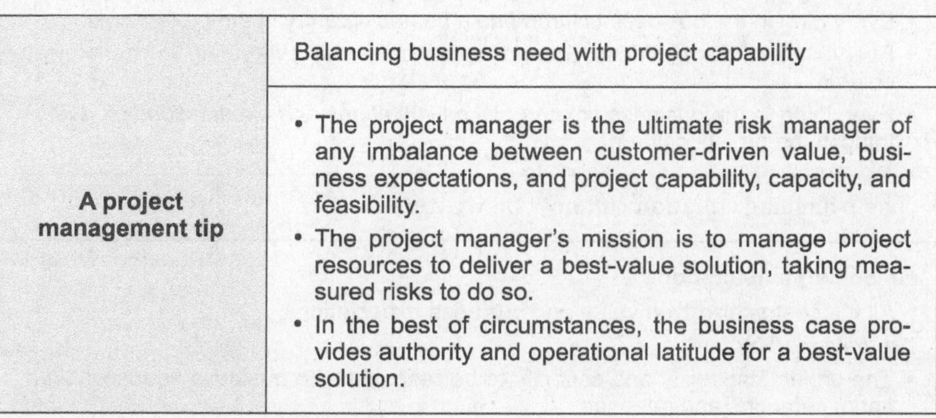

A project management tip	Balancing business need with project capability
	• The project manager is the ultimate risk manager of any imbalance between customer-driven value, business expectations, and project capability, capacity, and feasibility. • The project manager's mission is to manage project resources to deliver a best-value solution, taking measured risks to do so. • In the best of circumstances, the business case provides authority and operational latitude for a best-value solution.

A Framework for Value, Risk, and Capability: Project Balance Sheet

The value models just discussed provide a means for relating a business metric to a project metric. But they do not directly address how well expectations from the business side align with capacity, capability, and feasibility on the project side. For this task, we can use the *project balance sheet*.[8] The project balance sheet is a takeoff on its accounting counterpart. Similar to the accounting version, the project balance sheet is a double-entry, two-sided device with three elements that form a balance:

1. Business requirements and resources linked to milestones—the left side
2. Project capabilities and capacity to meet requirements in the prescribed timeframe with the allowable resources—the right side
3. The risk required to close the gap between numbers 1 and 2

A project management tip	Measurements reinforce performance
	• Measurements are stimulating, in effect a competition to exceed expectations. • The project balance sheet provides the opportunity and means to measure achievement in a framework of expectation and challenge.

Project Balance Sheet as an Agile Management Tool

The project balance sheet implements the balance equation, shown in three forms.

The balance sheet equation

- Everything in the business column *has a balancing* entry in the project column
- Everything in the business column *is the driver* for everything in the project column
- Everything in the business column *places limitations and expectations* on everything in the project column

The balancing equation can now be written:

Balancing expectations

- All the customer-driven value and business expectations

Are balanced by

- The project capability and capacity to be responsive to business needs within a set of iterations and releases

Another way to state the equation balances vision with facts and risk:

Balancing opportunity

- All the strategic business vision about the value of an opportunity

Is balanced by

- The project's ability to evolve a product that captures the value envisioned by the business

The project manager must risk values to balance *resource-scope-schedule-quality* estimates with business expectations.

The business

Resources	$250K investment Tools Facilities
Scope	Order entry application
Business case	$2000/mo savings after milestone 1
KPIs	Customer satisfaction Operational efficiency

The project

$240K - $275K cost range Tools Facilities	Resources
Order entry application	Scope
Basic order entry at milestone 1	Schedule
Satisfied customer	Quality
Cost: $25K	**Risk**

Figure 2-4 The project balance sheet

Figure 2-4 is a pictorial of the project balance sheet. The business is conventionally shown in the left column; the project and balancing risk are shown in the right column. The balance sheet is shown in a way that puts the business in a top-down position and the project in a bottom-up correspondence. Top-down is usually a more qualitative view driven by concept and imagination; bottom-up is more fact based, quantitative, and risk averse—meaning risk attitude reflects actual experience. Fred P. Brooks summed it up nicely when he wrote: "Good judgment comes from experience, and experience comes from bad judgment."

Planning with the Project Balance Sheet

The sponsor's view on the left side is conceptual and value oriented, sometimes oblivious to implementation practicalities as the project manager understands those. Often the sponsor has no specific understanding of project management, cost and schedule estimating, or risk management and statistical analysis. The project sponsor sees the project simply as a black box with every detail encapsulated within the project boundaries.

The Black Box
Black box is an architecture concept. It simply means that within certain boundaries, all internal details have been abstracted, made obscure, or encapsulated. Only the external parameters, features and functions are visible.

The project manager has the facts and estimates about the project, even if they are only rough estimates in the context of the business case. However, the project manager does not have the sponsor's expert knowledge about the business and markets. A bridge is needed to unambiguously couple the sponsor's imperatives, constraints, and understanding of the project with those of the project manager so that the business and the project are not talking past each other. That bridge is a common vision of scope and a mutual understanding of investment and benefits. Establishing the bridge is a key objective of the business case and the project balance sheet.

The Agile Business Case Is Built by Levels

Recall that the business case can be as simple as the information to fill a template web form. At Level 0, the form is routed to the decision maker by workflow. At Level 1, a similar but enhanced template is used; it is subject to two levels of approval, again by automated workflow if possible. Level 2 business considerations are more demanding. The business case may have to be presented to the organization's executives or C level.[9] Regardless of level, every business case for an agile project has requirements from two constituents:

1. Foundational and strategic requirements from the strategic plan and the balanced scorecard
2. Situational, customer-driven requirements that are only revealed in the course of the project, and are therefore fuzzy for planning purposes

Getting Started on the Business Case

There are a few elements of information that every business case requires. The agile idea about the business case is this: provide "just enough" information to obtain approval. The order of presentation is not critical. Many organizations have a standard template or checklist, as shown in Table 2-7, that states the actionable points.

Table 2-7 Checklist of business case content

The opportunity and the window of opportunity	• The value proposition in business terms, and the optimum timeline to take advantage of the opportunity.
The background	• What leads up to this point?
The solution and the product master	• What is proposed to address the opportunity? • Who speaks for the solution? • Who are the community of product users?
The sponsor	• Who is the project sponsor?
Project manager and team	• Who are the key participants needed for the project? • Consider roles for project manager, architect, lead designer, lead tester.
The benefits from the balanced scorecard	• What is the nature of the benefit proposition and how will it be measured? In effect, what is the payback to the project investors?
The beneficiaries	• The customers: Who is responsible for the value proposition? • The stakeholders: Who stands to benefit from the organization taking advantage of the opportunity? • Who is the community of beneficiaries?
Benefit realization	• To whom is the flag passed at project conclusion to follow-through on benefit realization?
Limits of affordability	• What is the maximum amount available for investment, either as capital funding or as expense funding? • To what extent is the project to be self-funding from an early benefit stream? Provide the estimated cash flow requirements and risk discounts. • What is the limit of the downside before the project might be canceled to limit losses?
The investment profile	• What is the investment over time needed to complete the project?
The known and knowable risks to success	• What may impede success? How feasible is the solution?
Business readiness	• Who will drive change for the organization? • What other organizations are involved: sales, marketing, supply, manufacturing, distribution, warranty support, etc.?

Summary of the opportunity: Answer these questions succinctly:

- What is it that brings us all to the table to discuss a new project?
- What is envisioned as the project's mission and scope?
- How will the enterprise and the customer constituencies be better off if the project is successful?
- How will the end state be changed or what goal will be reached?

A Seat at the Table

Regarding gathering at a *table*, we are using a metaphor. In point of fact, many organizations work exclusively by electronic workflow to review, comment, and approve business documents and never actually gather together face-to-face. Such behavior is somewhat at odds with agile methods that value face-to-face communications as a superior way to communicate.

See Chapter 1 for agile principles and specifically Principle 6.

Background and context: Describe what has led up to the opportunity at hand. A review of relevant historical performance is helpful background. Current operating results are always welcome. Examples: functional performance and process metrics, end-user evaluations and other voice-of-the-customer input, warranty or trouble reports, audit reports from across the balanced scorecard, supply chain metrics, and lessons learned from relevant history of other projects.

The project proposal: Lay out both sides of the project balance sheet. Present the business description of the whole value proposition: outcomes, expected benefits, quality fit, available investment, milestones with business importance, and customer needs. Describe the balance sheet project at a high level: scope, quality, cost, and schedule. The solution need not be too prescriptive but it has to be just enough to be credible. Identify any gaps necessary to balance the left side. Include mitigations, if known.

Operational results: Propose a *concept of operations* to describe who does what day-to-day in post-project operations with the deliverables. If there are KPIs, list and explain them.

Business preparation: Address business preparation needs that lead up to operations. Any reasonably sized project will require proactive change management and executive buy in; training for users, support staff, and maintainers; sales and marketing plans; rollout and market adoption strategy; beta trials; legacy retirement; and supply chain readiness, among other readiness needs.

Ask for approval: Last and perhaps most important, ask for an approval decision. An approved case is the project charter and authority to proceed.

Level 0, 1, and 2 Business Case

The business case hierarchy is a three-level pyramid as shown pictorially in Figure 2-5, stacked, not by accuracy of the estimates, but by their impact to the enterprise.

The Level 0 business case is driven by a backlog of requirements developed either by the end user, customers, or sÿstem operators and maintainers. The backlog requires prioritization by a Level 0 governance process and must fit within a Level 0 funding limitation. Level 0 is typically approved by simple workflow at a first or second level of management. Level 0 requirements fit within the context of existing systems, processes, and business models. Items from the backlog need not be just bug fixes, warranty repairs, or other trouble fixes. Requirements could represent new features and functions, but at Level 0 their scope is limited in this way: New functionality or features approved at Level 0 do not materially alter the relationship with the supply chain, customer or user constituents, or other commitments and certifications that may have the force of contracts, compliance, and regulation.

The Level 1 business case is a step-up in complexity; not only of the solution but also of the impact to the organization, its end users and customers, and perhaps to its regulators, suppliers, and other third-party associates. There may be, and usually is, more than one business unit involved, thereby complicating the

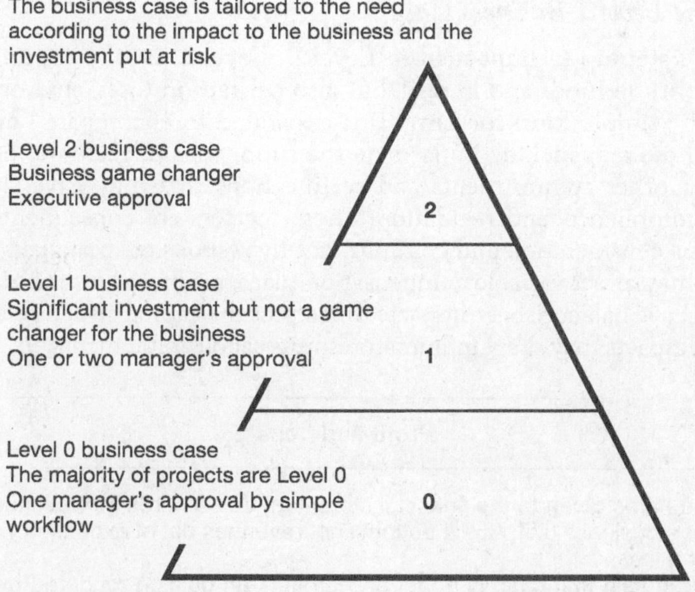

Figure 2-5 Business case pyramid

workflow for approval. There may have to be approvals from outside auditors, regulators, and certification authorities; supply chain units may need to consult. Technical feasibility may be in doubt. Business-to-business testing and certification of both process and technology may be required.

Opportunities at Level 1 fit these limitations. They are not bet-the-business in scope, do not materially alter the business model or the business values, and do not cannibalize other business units. In effect, at Level 1, projects are not a game-changer for the business.

The Level 2 business case addresses opportunities of such scope that a project might be threatening to business survival if not successful—Level 2 projects are business game changers. At Level 2, opportunities may go so far as to introduce a new business model, alter culture in some material way, and affect relationships across a broad landscape. Level 2 business cases are nearly always approved at the C level or by the governing board of the enterprise.

Building the Level 0 Business Case

Level 0 is a fill-in-the-form exercise. The information typically provided is given in Table 2-8 and is taken from the checklist in Table 2-7. In the best of cases, the form is web-based and operates with a database. Workflow provides a means for managers to review the business case, attach comments, and render an approval . Sometimes only one approval is required.

Building the Level 1 Business Case

Level 1 is a step-up in impact from Level 0. Level 1 usually commands more resources, both in funds and in staff, but also perhaps in tools, environment, and support. The simple form for Level 0 is expanded to encompass Level 1 complexities. These may include impacts on the supply chain, customer or user constituents, or other commitments and certifications that may have the force of contracts, compliance, and regulation. These matters are consequential and require serious consideration and commitment by responsible managers.

Level 1 may affect variable compensation plans, profit and loss (P&L) commitments, and have balance sheet impacts that affect the capital structure of the business. Such impacts may draw in human resourcesand capital managers.

Profit and Loss
P&L is the name given to the financial statement that records the revenue and expenses of a business unit. At the bottom line, revenues net of expenses yield either a profit or a loss. It is often said that cash is a fact and profit is an opinion rendered by accountants. Profit often results from non-cash adjustments to expenses and revenues. Companies can be profitable on the P&L but have no cash to pay bills!

Table 2-8 Level 0 business case

Date submitted	• Date usually assigned by the system when the form is submitted
Functional or system code	• An identifier to place the project in context with the business overall
Description of need	• The product vision • A narrative of the outcomes and deliverables as functions and features
Estimated benefit and benefit period	• Measures from the balanced scorecard or the KPIs of the affected functional users, and the timeline over which the benefits will occur
Reference to backlog or other requirements deck	• Typically, a requirements database holds all the bug reports, warranty claims, unsatisfied requirements from prior efforts, and other requirements according to some identifier
Source of need or primary beneficiary	• Who makes the case for the need? (This person may not be a member of the enterprise.) • Who is the primary beneficiary?
Requesting authority or sponsor	• Who is actually requesting the need? (In some organizations, users or external customers can not submit a business case, so an internal requesting authority is needed.)
Reason for a project solution	• Why does this need require a project; is there an alternative to address the need by means of routine operations?
Project manager Product master Architect Others	• Who are the primary project participants? (In effect, the project community or primary team members.)
Available funds	• Investment available for the project; to be considered a cap on affordability • Investment is a dollar-based value judgment by the business about the requested functions and features
Estimated complexity	• To be provided by the project as a value judgment
Milestones	• Business judgment on the timing of needed functions and features
Related or dependent projects, work orders, or other assumptions	• Dependencies that will affect outcomes and assumed conditions that are necessary and sufficient
Training need	• An assessment of business readiness requirements to receive and employ outcomes
Certifications, compliance to regulation, or other standards	• Identification of constraints on the solution not under the control of the business

Level 1 may still be a fill-in-the-form process managed by workflow. Almost without exception, Level 1 requires more than one approval.

A project management tip	Stakeholders focus on outcomes
	• The agile-thinking stakeholder has a bias towards outcomes; input and process are a means to achieve goals. • Agile managers forecast the outcomes based on the iteration backlog that is a small stabilized slice of the project backlog. • Each iteration or delivery cycle produces an increment of product as developed from the iteration backlog.

Table 2-9 Level 1 business case is an extension of the Table 2-8 Level 0 business case.

Table 2-9 Level 1 business case—additions to Level 0

Capital funds needed?	• Capital is used to fund items whose value depreciates with use. In some instances, labor to develop an asset of the organization can be capitalized as part of the cost of acquiring the asset. • Capital funding either for leases or purchases have multiyear impacts on cash flow and P&L expenses. • Beyond some limit, significant capital requirements materially affect the capital structure of the organization, which in turn could affect credit worthiness and borrowing costs.
NPV or EVA calculation required?	• NPV and EVA are a measure of cost and benefit. All the cost and benefit flows are put into a common time period by a calculation technique called discounting. • Discounting accounts for risk over a time period in the cash flows of both cost and benefit. • Discounting is usually managed by the organization's finance and accounting office. • Many companies impose a NPV or EVA calculation as a threshold for project approval. • Benefits should exceed costs, or the project should not be approved, at least on financial measures.
Cross-functional business units involved?	• The intradependencies among business units may become critical success factors and may affect the critical path of the project. • What are the assumptions about behavior and commitment of the involved units? • Does a customer or user team need to be formed?

Table 2-9 *(continued)*

Contractual changes required with the supply chain?	• Suppliers, dealers, distributors, and others with a relationship to the organization may be affected by a Level 1 project. • Modifying these relationships may be problematic and may be a risk to be identified on the right side of the project balance sheet.
KPI impact to P&Ls of affected business units?	• Many managers have P&L responsibility with a KPI attached. The KPI may affect compensation, promotion, or other success measures in the business. • In some cases, the project outcomes are designed to have beneficial impact to the P&L. KPIs for the affected P&Ls would then be changed.
Compensation changes recommended?	• Compensation is often used to motivate and incent performance on and about the project. • Team members who are drawn from the business to participate in the project and who are commissioned or variably compensated will require some compensation adjustments during their project service.
External threats to success	• Risks not under the control of the enterprise that could impact success. • Typically environmental, regulatory, financing, and certification authorities fit this category.
Upside opportunity not in scope	• Opportunity for upside that is not presently within the scope but is conceivably with within grasp given a project success. • Caution: opportunity not within the investment cap and not included in the product vision may violate the agile principle of simplicity.
Market and sales assumptions	• For products and services for sale, what are the market and sales assumptions that go into the benefit calculation?

Building the Level 2 Business Case

The Level 2 business case handles all the situations not within the scope and authority of Level 0 and Level 1. The protocol for approval invariably involves the executive staff.

Level 2 projects are projects of scale. One small team rarely executes them. Large scale does not rule out agile methods; however, scale complicates all management and technical parameters, disproportionately adding risk. Chapter 11 addresses how to scale agile methods.

Table 2-10 Level 2 business case is an extension of the Table 2-9 Level 1 business case.

Table 2-10 Level 2 business case—addition to Level 1

Proposed changes in business model	• Changes to the balanced scorecard or the Treacy-Wiersema model
Critical success factors requiring due diligence	• Analysis to support major conclusions of the opportunity assessment, benefit stream, and attendant risks
Outside regulators, certifying authorities, and creditors	• Identification of authorities who may have a say in the project success not under the control of the enterprise

Summary and Takeaway Points

In this chapter, the main point is: *The agile business case respects and encourages the meld of business cycle goals and strategy with the urgency and importance of customer need.* The business case is the top-level linkage between the decision-maker sponsor, stakeholders, executives, and the project manager. It provides just enough information to win approval and point the direction to the project manager.

The bridge between the business and the project is a common vision of scope and a mutual understanding of investment and benefits. Establishing this bridge is a key objective of the business case.

The project balance sheet compares the goals and strategy from the business with the project risks and capabilities that provide customers with important value in a timely fashion. The business case is simply the documentation of these facts and estimates, augmented with other information as the circumstances require.

The agile business case is designed to be consistent with agile principles: it is simple, timely, responsive to business and project need, and is open to adjustment as the value proposition evolves.

In its simplest form, the Level 0 business case is a one-page form that documents the envisioned product, the metrics from the balanced scorecard, and the project estimates. Level 0 is usually approved by a single decision maker.

Level 1 and 2 business cases are more robust, reflecting the greater impact on the business.

In the end, the business case is the setup for an agile response to customer need: a project responsive to an evolving need, early to production with beneficial product increments, and overall a best-value mix of cost and benefits.

Chapter Endnotes

1. Envision and Speculate are the first two of five phases proposed by Jim Highsmith. The remaining three are Explore (to develop), Adapt (to reflect on feedback) and Close. See: Highsmith, *Agile Project Management*, 81–82; Explore 360 is a strategy proposed by Alistair Cockburn in Crystal Clear. See Cockburn, *Crystal Clear*, 46.
2. Beck and Fowler, *Planning Extreme Programming*, Chapter 9.
3. Kaplan and Norton, *The Balanced Scorecard*, 71–80.
4. Key performance indicator (KPI) is a metric used by organizations to measure the performance of business units and individuals against certain benchmarks. Compensation is often based on achievement of the KPI results.
5. Treacy and Wiersema, "Customer Intimacy and Other Value Disciplines," 84–93.
6. Treacy and Wiersema, *The Discipline of Market Leaders*.
7. Goodpasture, *Managing Projects for Value*, 31, 46.
8. Ibid., 40–45.
9. C-level refers to the business executives with titles beginning with C, such as Chief Executive Officer and Chief Information [Systems] Officer.

3

Quality in the Agile Space

Quality is a nonnegotiable value. Quality is about making the customer ever more successful and about delivering more business benefits than the invested commitment.

> *Quality is never an accident; it is always the result of high intention, sincere effort, intelligent direction and skillful execution; it represents the wise choice of many alternatives.*
>
> *William A. Foster*

In this chapter, we address quality as an influence on the outcomes of agile projects. Many quality movements have come along over the years, but actually none have really disappeared entirely. The best ideas have adapted and conformed to modern practice. Scientific management, total quality management, zero defects, the Juran Trilogy, continuous improvement, quality function deployment, quality circles, defined process control, Six Sigma, plan-do-check-act, and others still have influence, each in their own way. Quality control—an early quality idea—morphed into quality assurance, and assurance has morphed into market-driven and customer-driven quality expectations. That is where we find ourselves today: *customers and markets are very much in command of the quality agenda.*

The Customer and the User
Recall that customers are those that set the value agenda and ultimately pay the investment; customers are the primary beneficiaries of the project. Customers are a community; they may be inside or outside the business. Inside the business, the community includes stakeholders of all means: executives, sponsors, and functional users; post-delivery support, supply chain members; and perhaps sales and marketing. Users are the functional experts within the customer community.

Quality Is Built Around Values, Principles, and Practices

Quality is a relentless goal of agile projects. Most agree that quality is hard to define: indeed, for many there is no satisfactory definition. Quality is one of those things that we know when we see it. To begin, quality is a value; values are ideas we believe in and care about. Things of value are things for which we are willing to work and pay. And so it is with quality.

Quality is inextricably linked with price through value. In this book, we think about the relationship this way: When quality as perceived by the customer or sponsor meets or exceeds the price to be paid, the product has true value. That is, the most fundamental definition of a *best value* is that quality exceeds investment. Chapter 10 addresses value in more detail; suffice it to say that when customers draw deep satisfaction with the quality of the product, they also believe they have received the best value for their investment. And, the term *customer* is meant in the broad sense: executives, sponsors, users, and those that pay, whether internal or external. Throughout the text, we will build on the quality values given in Table 3-1.

Table 3-1 Quality values

- Quality of communications: A respect for courtesy, timeliness, and accuracy of communications
- Product quality: A commitment to a product that is fit for use—reliable, maintainable, available, and conforms to standards and conventions; fit to form and function and fit to its environment, both societal and globally
- Quality practices: A commitment to standards of practice: it can be taken on faith by the customer that the product meets all required certifications and standards of practice
- Resource conservation: A respect for resources, especially timeliness, and a pledge of integrity in all financial matters
- Quality of performance: A commitment to personal and collective performance that is lawful, moral, and trustful
- Quality of relationships: A respect for each individual as an individual; in effect, a commitment to a safe and enriching environment that values each member's contribution

Every methodology includes principles labeled *quality principles*. Principles are the domain-specific guidelines that point the way and set boundaries for behavior and action. Principles support values, but principles bring the action. Every project dashboard should advertise the principles that guide their specific project and reflect upon their organization. The list in Table 3-2 can be a part of every agile project.

Within every project and every methodology there are quality practices. Quality practices are the things actually done to deliver and improve quality. Practices

Table 3-2 Universal quality principles for agile methods

- Everyone will be respectful of time
- Everyone will be respectful of other points of view; diversity is honored
- Problems are attacked, not people; a safe and trustful environment is everyone's concern
- Team members have a responsibility to add value to their team
- Everyone will consider learning and self-improvement part of their job, personally and for the mutual benefit of the team
- Every team member will work to benefit the team and the project, eschewing self-optimization
- Every object delivered to the customer will have met its quality measures
- Every object is the simplest possible object for the task, although the simplest may be quite complex at times
- Every object will have sufficient redundancy to ensure availability of feature and function to satisfy customer need
- No iteration is complete until its lessons are learned
- Everyone will have the common goal to economize effort and maximize throughput

are implementations of principles. There are many more than the most important few listed in Table 3-3. Each of the quality dimensions—fitness to use, fitness to standard, fitness to cost, fitness to societal and global environment, and others—are achieved most easily when fully internalized by all the project participants.

Table 3-3 Quality practices

- Communications will be answered promptly and courteously within a timeframe that is reasonable and customary
- Time boxes will be enforced and respected for their specific time limits
- Daily stand-up meetings will be planned so every team member has an opportunity speak in a safe environment
- Users have a right to influence the functional design, but users have a responsibility to work for the best value to the enterprise
- Work assignments will reflect a reasonable adjustment for risk and uncertainty
- Performance will be honored by incentives or other recognition and will be targeted and timely to the event
- Every object will be proven to a *fitness to use* standard with a unit test, followed by a user functional test and a system integration test
- Defects will be fixed when first discovered, provided there is economic justification
- All implementations will comport with the certified standards of the organization
- Object designs will honor system architecture
- Object designs will honor the user's evaluation of feature and function according to a best-value standard

Thought Leaders Set Up Agile Quality Values and Principles

Until the industrial revolution and the turn of the twentieth century, there had been no formal study of business quality or business methods to achieve quality. But all of that began to change with Fredrick W. Taylor.

F. W. Taylor's Lean Thinking

Fredrick Winslow Taylor, more popularly known as F. W. Taylor, was one of the first to study business systematically. He brought *Taylorism* into the business culture in the years leading up to World War I with a concept he called *scientific management*, a proposal to reduce waste through the careful study of work.

Unwittingly, he was the lean thinker of his day. According to Taylor, managers must acknowledge and accept this principle: *Managers have responsibilities to design efficient and effective process and procedures*. Waste must be eliminated! It is not enough that the trains run—they must run on time! Every action requires definition and a means to measure results.

Taylor came up with the original time and motion studies, perhaps one of the first attacks on nonvalue work. Peter Drucker, a management guru par excellence who coined the term *knowledge worker*, has ranked Taylor as one of the seminal thinkers of modern times.[1]

Taylor believed that workers must be divided by skill and by role; quality is achieved by careful job design, handing off from one skillful person to another. Any residual errors are caught at the end by independent inspection. Taylor's ideas made mass production of process results possible: people, properly trained, were to be as interchangeable as standard mechanical parts; defined processes staffed with qualified people should be capable of consistently repeatable results. And Taylor ushered in quality control as an independent and external practice to catch anything the functional process did not detect and correct.

Kent Beck in *Extreme Programming Explained*[2] confronts the legacy of Taylor: Beck believes that Taylorism lies latent in our business culture and unconsciously affects day-to-day activity. Worrisome to Beck is Taylor's idea that quality is a responsibility external to the mainstream work. The idea of quality outside the mainstream should be worrisome to all of us. As this chapter will present, quality is an equal partner with scope, resources, and schedule. Quality, as they say, is *built-in* and *job one*.

A project management tip	F. W. Taylor's impact on agile projects
	• Fredrick Taylor was the first lean thinker. • Taylor was first to study and quantify nonvalue work and put emphasis on eliminating wasteful and time consuming processes, procedures, and *environmental impediments.* • In a similar vein, Steve McConnell, respected author of *Code Complete,* states that the "general principle of software quality is that improving quality reduces development costs . . ." and that "The best way to improve productivity is to reduce the time reworking . . ."[3]

W. Edwards Deming and the PDCA Cycle

Deming introduced very practical ideas of process control as a means to limit variations in product quality. Today, it is called *defined process control.* Deming came at quality from the point of view of the product: make the product the same way each time and make it work within limits that are acceptable to the customer. The modern poster child for defined process control is Six Sigma.

Six Sigma
Six Sigma is a problem solving methodology and defect control strategy with the purpose of identifying and mitigating error sources in defined process control. The control limits are established such that production yields less than approximately 3.4 errors in one million opportunities either above or below the control limits. This figure is derived from the error possibilities within six standard deviations of a bell-shaped curve, after allowing 1.5 standard deviations drift of the long-term average defect rate. The process derives its name from the Greek lower case *s,* called *sigma* and denoted σ; σ is the symbol used by statisticians for the standard deviation of a probability density function such as the bell curve.

Ken Schwaber—a leading SCRUM methodologist—objecting to defined process control, puts it this way, "[defined process control] is based on processes that work only because their degree of imprecision is acceptable . . . When defined process control cannot be achieved because of the complexity of the intermediate activities; something called *empirical process control* has to be employed."[4] In Schwaber's view, software is too complex to expect defects to be contained within predefined error limits. Empirical control is the answer; empirical control is derived from observed facts, adapted to the situation, and not determined by preplanned limits from previous projects.

In spite of the fact that software projects offer little opportunity for statistical process control in the Six Sigma and Deming way, perhaps Deming's most noteworthy accomplishment from the perspective of project management and agile methodologies is his famous plan-do-check-act (PDCA) cycle that he originally adopted from Walter Shewhart. PDCA envisions planning for what is to be done, then doing it—that is the *plan-do*. Next, measure results—measuring is the *check* activity—and then *act* on the measurement results. To *act* in the PDCA sense means to reflect upon lessons learned and provide feedback for corrective actions to the next iteration of the plan.

Walter A. Shewhart
Deming was influenced by the work of the process statistician Walter A. Shewhart who is credited with identifying that processes have two variables: *assignable cause* and *chance cause*. The former is systemic and capable of being corrected and maintained to an economical minimum; the latter is randomly occurring in frequency and intensity, not always present in the process, and is mitigated by establishing performance limits for a given process.

Agile methods are not plan-driven from the top. PDCA is applied by the team at the iteration level. All iterations begin with a planning meeting; all end with a lessons-learned meeting that feeds the next planning session.

A project management tip	W. Edwards Deming's impact on agile projects
	• Deming introduced the PDCA cycle, which is wholly embraced by the EVO method. • The cycle really applies to all agile iterations. The plan-do is equivalent to the planning session followed by development, test, and integration. • Especially relevant is the *check-act* that provides measurement and feedback for continuous improvement. • Deming focused on eliminating unsatisfactory results before they reached the customer. In agile parlance, every object must pass its unit, functional, and system test.

Joseph Juran Favors the Customer

Joseph M. Juran was a contemporary of Deming but they worked separately in Japan in the 1950s. He is known for his advocacy of the Juran trilogy: *quality improvement, planning, and control.*

Juran began the quality shift away from Deming's product focus and toward a customer focus. Juran stressed the quality concept of *fitness for use*. He believed that meeting a specification is a necessary condition, but insufficient without fitness to use—that is, honoring the customer's idea of product value and utility. In a word, features are not valuable unless they are everyday useful. Juran's ideas are what agile practitioners think of as favoring customer value over following a plan.

Juran defined five parameters that make up *fitness to use*:

1. Quality of design, a judgmental parameter with grades of goodness
2. Conformance to standards and customary expectations of the market
3. Availability, a consequence of frequency of breakdown and rapidity of repair
4. Safety in use
5. Usability in a customer's setting

Among tools, Juran popularized the Pareto chart, which he named after Italian economist Vilfredo Pareto who recognized the phenomenon of the 80-20 rule in his study of business activity.

Pareto Chart
The Pareto chart is a histogram arranged in descending order that shows distinct problems according to how frequently each occurs. One distinct problem might be a paper jam, and it might occur 100 times a quarter. The paper jam might be the most frequently occurring problem observed. The 80-20 rule states that most histograms show that 80 percent of all problem occurrences are linked to only 20 percent of distinctly identified problems. So, if by example, 1000 occurrences are reported, and there are 80 distinct problems among the 1000, by the 80-20 rule, 800 of every 1000 occurrences are forecast to be attributable to 16 of 80 distinct problems.

A project management tip	Joseph Juran's impact on agile methods
	• Juran shifted quality toward a concern for the customer and away from the goodness of the product. • The agile interpretation of Juran is to value customer satisfaction over following a plan. • The concept of fitness for use, a synonym for customer satisfaction, was promoted by Juran as a quality management concept. • The Pareto chart helps to focus agile teams on the most important features and functions.

Philip Crosby: Zero Defects and Free Quality

Philip Crosby came along a generation after Deming and Juran. Working in the aerospace and defense industry, Crosby became fixed on pushing Deming's ideas of assignable cause to the point of zero defects. He also authored the principle of *doing it right the first time,* known as *DRIFT*.

Crosby is best remembered for inventing the idea that *quality is free!* In his formulation, the cost of conformance is just a cost of doing business the right way. Thereby, the cost of quality is free; only the cost of nonconformance is an add-on.

A project management tip	Crosby discovers that quality is free!
	• Agile teams understand and practice the DRIFT principle. • Although zero defects is laudable, agile methods look to the customer to put a priority on fixing defects. Some defects are not economically repairable and will not be fixed.

Six Sigma Revolution

Six Sigma was not designed for projects, software, or agile methods. Projects generally, and software specifically, do not remotely approach the error rates championed by Six Sigma. Six Sigma is not agile; its methods are supported by myriad documents, practices, and analysis. Six Sigma is the crown of the defined process control paradigm eschewed by Schwaber and others. So why is Six Sigma in the discussion about quality for agile methods? Six Sigma has interesting practices helpful to agile projects. Consider these two:

1. *Problem identification and solution design:* Six Sigma employs a problem identification and solving practice that builds off Deming's PDCA. Six Sigma is said to *follow the defect,* which means to reflect on the product results and work back through root-cause analysis to identify defect sources. *Follow the defect* fits the agile mandate to always deliver a working product.[5] In Six Sigma-speak, the practice is referred to as Design-Measure-Analyze-Improve-Control (DMAIC). DMAIC really implements the *check-act* component of PDCA in a more sophisticated manner.
2. *Opportunity space:* Six Sigma promotes the idea of an *opportunity space* where quality measurements are made. Opportunity results are par-

titioned between good and not good, acceptable and unacceptable, or nondefective and defective. The opportunity space for software systems is unique to the nature of software. In modern software, with few exceptions and certainly different from mechanical and electronic systems, program logic always works as designed, and works repeatedly the same way given the same initial conditions and operating data; there are no effects from wear and tear, age, environment, and material differences. But software does have defects:

- *Logic errors:* Defects from logic constructs that actually work, but not as wanted by the customer.
- *Technical errors:* Defects that arise from technical issues such as incorrect language syntax, incorrect or inconsistent variable and data definitions, spelling errors, data out-of-range, or other similar construction problems.[6]
- *Data errors:* Defects from data that does not conform to data definitions.
- *Conformance errors:* Actual practices that do not conform to the quality standards.

Software complexity complicates the opportunity space. The opportunity space is populated by defects that are known, unknown but knowable, and unknowable. Known defects are those that are already discovered and in a backlog; they may or may not be fixed according to priority and the cost of fixing. The unknown but knowable errors are a matter of discovery and testing, again subject to priority and economics. The unknowable defects are those that arise from unlikely conditions and conditions that only the user can recognize once the product is in an operational context; a developer, who is not an expert in the business, may not ever recognize certain defects for what they are.

The idea of continuous improvement is to make the best bet in partitioning the opportunity space, improving performance with every iteration. Figure 3-1 illustrates the discussion points. The opportunity space is sampled after iteration. All the counts are expected to change from one iteration to the next. Some defects will be deferred for a later fix; others will be ignored; most will be fixed in the iteration in which they are discovered.

Because agile methods are iterative and the design is refactored, containment per se—a concept that seeks to prevent defect *creep* from one code base to the next—is not strongly enforced.

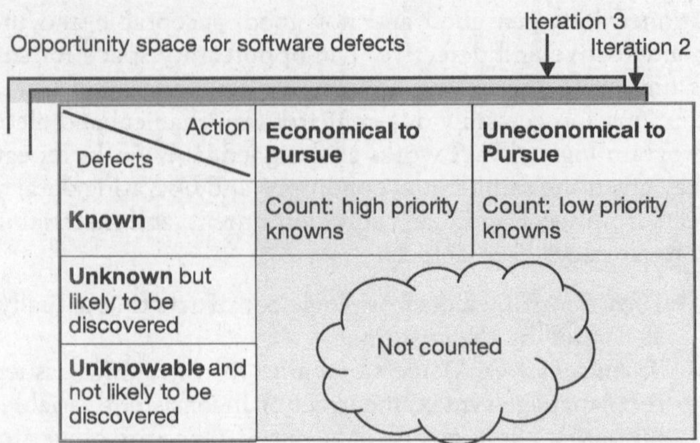

Any time the opportunity space is sampled for a measurement, a quality metric is computed.
Typically, the measurement is taken at the end of the iteration when the increment is integrated to the product base:

$$\text{Quality (Iteration N)} = \frac{\text{Count known defects fixed in Iteration N + Count all prior fixed defects}}{\text{Count all known defects, economical and uneconomical}}$$

Figure 3-1 The opportunity space

The Software Opportunity Space

In the agile world where the emphasis is on verifying quality with robust testing, both technically and functionally, the opportunity space is challenging.

Historically, the error rate in software code is a 1000 times worse than that of the popular Six-Sigma boundary.

In a 2005 *Business Week* interview, Watts Humphrey, a fellow of the SEI, declared that companies that comport with SEI's capability maturity model were averaging a one in one thousand error rate.[7]

Obviously, such performance is target-rich for improvement possibilities. In fact, in an NIST study released in 2002, the government reported that the impact of software errors had reached 0.6 percent of the U.S. GDP, almost $60 billion in that year![8]

Continuous improvement is a means to better performance; it is a quality concept and a project practice driven by root-cause analysis and feedback of lessons learned.

A project management tip	Six Sigma is supportive of agile
	• Six Sigma provides a very effective problem solving method, DMAIC, which enhances the PDCA cycle. • The principles of DMAIC are usable without invoking other aspects of Six Sigma. • Six Sigma brings understanding of the defect opportunity space, and promotes the idea of setting limits at the boundaries of customer satisfaction. • Many defects will never be known and others are not economical to fix. All have the potential to contribute to the customer experience.

Lean Practices for Quality

Lean practices began in manufacturing a century ago. Before World War I, Taylor was thinking lean. More recently, lean has come to mean a laser focus on making every practice value-added from the customer's perspective. Lean also means smoothing the flow from one step to another so that unproductive idle time is minimized, reducing or eliminating batch queues, substituting real-time processes, and minimizing overhead setup time. Lean also means deferring production decisions until just-in-time to avoid inventory buildup and premature commitments.[9] But perhaps most important for the customer-developer relationship, and also as a centerpiece of lean and agile methods, is the concept of *pull*. *Pull* means that features and functions are pulled into the product design as a consequence of customer request rather than being pushed out by a developer's whim.[10]

Pull and the concept of simplicity work in complementary ways. Simplicity is avoidance of complex interactions but it is also avoidance of complexity caused by incorporating design before its time—before the customer states a need or sets a priority.

Quality Values and Principles Are Planned into the Agile Methods

The discussion so far is the setup for actionable quality practices in agile projects. Values and principles such as respect for courtesy, timeliness, and accuracy of communications, are guidance for day-to-day activity. Tools and techniques such as customer-driven value and plan-do-check-act, come from the legacy of Taylor, Deming, Juran, and Crosby among others. It now remains to apply this quality inventory to agile projects.

Planning and Deployment

Planning for quality is much like planning for the project itself: Establish goals, conceive a strategy, adopt principles to guide action, and define practices. Ideally, the project's quality goals and principles will:

1. Align with the quality elements of the balanced scorecard
2. Reflect the values and principles of the organization as given in Table 3-1 and Table 3-2
3. Reflect the principles of quality practices in projects as given in Table 3-3
4. Respect the values and principles of the specific methodology followed

Suggested quality goals are given in Table 3-4.

Table 3-4 Quality goals

Goal	Measurement	Commentary
Customers will be satisfied with the value obtained in the product feature and functions	• Subjective measures: not satisfied, satisfied, and very satisfied	• Agile projects value customer satisfaction over following a plan
Project sponsors will judge the project a best-value fit to the business case	• Subjective & quantitative measures of how well the vision is realized for the intended investment	• The business case establishes milestones and funding affordability for the envisioned product
The business will feel that it is ready and able to accept and effectively deploy the project outcomes	• Operational metrics, such as training readiness, supply readiness, and manufacturing process and procedures	• Change management and business preparation adopt the product and drive benefits
Stakeholders on the balanced scorecard will judge that the impacts on key performance indicators (KPIs) are within the range of expectation	• Balanced scorecard metrics	• Sometimes stakeholders establish constraints rather than open doors, but still expect a favorable impact on KPIs
Team members will feel that they had a fair and reasonable opportunity to provide a best-value solution to the customer	• Subjective evaluation of the team and project experience	• Principles given in Table 3-2 are adhered to

Deployment of a quality regime is first and foremost a communications task to inform, train, educate, and to document principles, standards, benchmarks, and practices. Deployment drives internalization. By deployment and internalization, we mean that while it is necessary to inform and educate, it is imperative for each project member to take matters to heart to have an effective program, to make the project principles personal principles, and to make quality practices natural and routine.

Quality-program deployment steps for agile projects are listed in Table 3-5.

Table 3-5 Deployment elements for agile projects

Deployment task	Commentary
Publish values and principles of the project in a written form Make standards and benchmarks readily available	• Think lean: Make it efficient to access the necessary information on a project dashboard
Establish scorecards for recording performance in the defect opportunity space	• Use electronically accessible scorecard templates for data entry and updates where possible
Establish workflow for approving scorecards	• Think lean: Require only as much approval authority as necessary to maintain the integrity of the scoring
Hold team meetings or other forums to inform and educate on the quality program	• Time box the team meetings; be respectful of time and respectful of all ideas and discussion
Establish audit procedures for performance on key practices that drive quality	• Inspect what you expect • Caution: Overly intrusive audit procedures may affect results[1]
Establish improvement goals	• Use every iteration reflection and lessons-learned session as an opportunity to raise the performance bar for the next iteration
Use TQM tools to identify problems and measure progress	• Pareto charts and fishbone cause and effect diagrams are among the most used in agile projects

Scorecards for Quality

In physical systems, quantitative quality metrics are numerical measures compared to a benchmark or control limit. This we know is *defined process control.* Among many similar objects, the actual measurements—usually slightly different from one object to another—will largely cluster around the nominal value. Acceptance limits are established to separate the good objects from the bad.

Numerical measurements are recorded on a scorecard that is often called a control chart because the measurements are plotted between the control limits as shown in Figure 3-2.

With intangible outcomes, physical parameters such as size and weight are not usually measured; instead, functionality and performance are measured. Because many defects are unforeseen consequences of interactions among system elements, the system's latent chaos and entropy are unknown. Thus, the practical import is a near-real-time strategy to set quantitative defect limits empirically, meaning the quality standard is adapted to the observations of the actual situation. To gather empirical data, discriminating differences are observed and recorded.

At the unit test level, there are all manner of technical errors:[11] Syntax, spelling, definitions, and others. At the integration and functional level, users find errors of logic—such as retrieving only a last name instead of a first and last from a

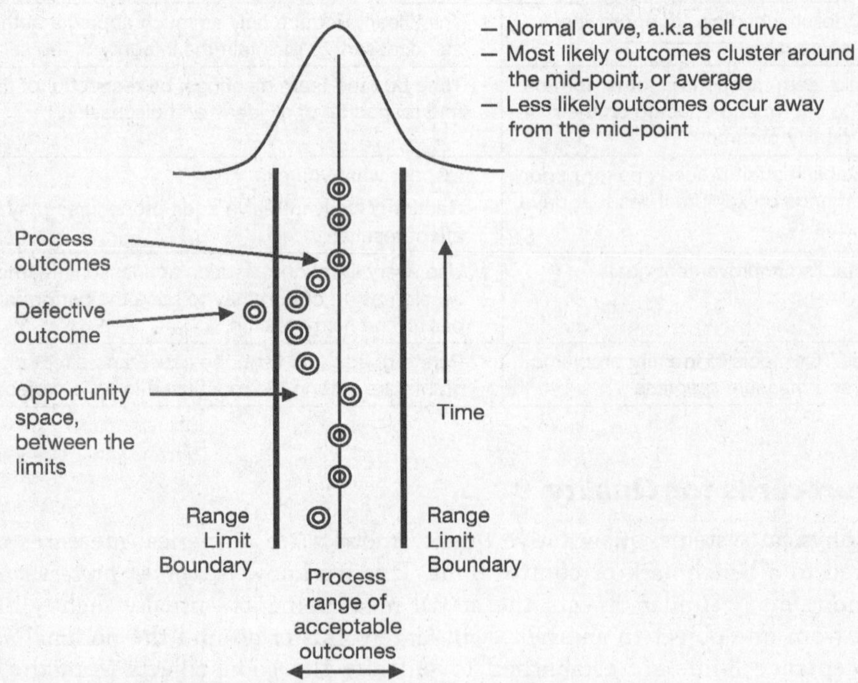

Figure 3-2 Example error control chart

database—and errors of performance, such as too much time taken to populate a data field. And there are other defect categories such as defects of conformance to standards, and missing or inappropriate features and functions.

To develop a quality performance scorecard, design entries for:

- *Error condition:* The error condition is the unique problem observed, like retrieving only the last name rather than first and last.
- *Error condition frequency:* Occurrences of unique errors are scored as a *1* or *0*—at each observation instance, the error either occurred or did not occur. The total frequency count is simply the sum of the error scores.
- *Error impact:* Impact is a judgmental factor about how much an error condition affects product effectiveness and customer satisfaction. Impact is often given as an ordinal (e.g., low, medium, or high). But numbers in a sequence such as one, two, and four are handy for computing a quality figure of merit by weighting error condition frequency with the condition's impact:

Quality metric

The (error condition frequency × error impact) calculation is a numerical figure of merit for quality—the higher the number, the lower the customer satisfaction will be.

Figure 3-3 shows an example scorecard for hypothetical Error Condition 1. The project situation portrayed in Figure 3-3 is described in the in the panel below:

Project example

- An object is under examination for error conditions as a validation of quality.
- Six instances are examined.
- Each instance is allowed zero, one, or two occurrences of Error Condition 1; this allowance is the baseline quality condition.
- Error Condition 1 is judged to be of low impact—3 on a scale of 10.

On the scorecard, there are four data elements:

1. A planned baseline or standard value
2. The operating plan value. The operating plan may be different from the baseline because of just-in-time circumstances that could be different from when the baseline was set
3. The actual performance
4. The computed quality

On the scorecard, note these points:

- The operating plan is more optimistic than the baseline, 10 errors in six instances are forecast, rather than 12 in six instances forecast in the baseline

Quality is a consequence of the number of error occurrences and their impact on the product

Example for quality measurement for "Error Condition 1"

Planned		Observed	Computed
Baseline quality standard	Operating plan	Actual error count for 6 instances	Actual average quality* Baseline average quality*
≤2 errors per instance	≤10 errors in 6 instances	1, 0, 2, 3, 0, 3 Total = 9	Average actual quality Total observed (9) × Impact (3) Total instances (6) = 4.5 Average baseline = 12 × 3/6 = 6
Impact of Error Condition 1 is 3 on scale of 10 *Average Quality = [Impact × Average Error Count], a smaller number is better			

Figure 3-3 Error Condition 1 scorecard

- The actual observed errors are even a bit better than in the operating plan, 9, rather than 10, in 6 instances
- The average baseline figure of merit is six; the actual computed quality is somewhat better at 4.5

Sampling for Quality Validation

Sampling is an advanced topic for readers interested in additional quantitative quality measures. Most experienced project managers and developers understand that it is impossible to validate every quality consideration; there are just too many conditions and combinations. There are economic limitations, schedule constraints, undiscovered or unknowable defects hidden behind obscure functionality, and operational flukes. Therefore, validation is led naturally to sampling.

Sampling

Sampling shifts the mind-set from *descriptive statistics,* in which piles of data measurements describe actual conditions, to *inference statistics.*

An inference is a conclusion that is *assumed to be true* based on observation and analysis of similar or closely related facts.

Usually, an inference is accompanied by a statement of confidence about how certain the assumed conclusion is.

In project terms, drawing an inference is a pretty big shift from measuring every outcome. Drawing an inference introduces the idea of *trust me* into the validation results, thereby adding complication when communicating with executives and sponsors. Opinion polls are an everyday example of inference statistics: the opinions of only a few thousand seem to represent those of many millions with a reasonable margin of error—in other words, with relatively high confidence.

In projects, the situation is much the same as in political polls. From a relatively small number of observations, validators infer those same results on a larger population that is too numerous to evaluate. For example, when testing database systems, there may only be opportunity to validate a few thousand records out of tens of millions. But if the validation is designed correctly, then there can be confidence that the remaining data population will have the same quality. In most practical situations, it is possible to actually quantify the confidence of the test results.

Sampling is a big subject, but there are a number of simplifying assumptions and heuristics that make sampling a practical tool for day-to-day use, as shown in Table 3-6.

In Chapter 4, sampling is addressed in more detail and there is information about how to pick the sample size and how to estimate the confidence that the validation can be reasonably inferred to the whole population. Suffice to say that if the population is more than ten times that of the sample drawn from the population, and the error conditions are random occurrences distributed among

Table 3-6 Simplifying ideas for sampling

The idea	Commentary
A population is a collection of objects having similar attributes	• The population need not be contiguous or uniformly populated • The population can have time-sensitive properties such as time-of-day, or location properties such as elevation • It is possible to sample object A in order to infer performance of object B, as in a prototype versus a production model
All members of the population do not need to be known before sampling begins	• A sampling *frame* defines the known elements of the population; the true size of the population may be unknown • Example: the exact size of the voting population cannot be ascertained prior to an election, but a *frame* of a likely set of voters can be known
The best plan for picking samples from a population is to have no plan at all	• Pick samples randomly for validation
The sample size need not be precisely sized in order to get good results	• The sample needs to be large enough but it can be quite small compared to the population size

all objects in the population, then many simplifications come into play to make sampling practical for projects.

Quality Measures from Users

Since most of the project outcomes we have been discussing end up in a user community, it is common to ask, *How do you like them?* The answers often come back as *good-better-best,* and sometimes ranked on a scale of 1–10. Some caution, however: in the absence of objective standards for numerical ranks, the ranking is often no better than good-better-best. Subjectivity, however, affords flexibility because all the interpretation is driven strictly by the information given to us by our customers—another example of empirical analysis rather than fit to a defined standard.

Empirical analysis of subjective information benefits from something as simple as a histogram or Pareto chart. A Pareto chart is a ranking tool, as shown in Figure 3-4.

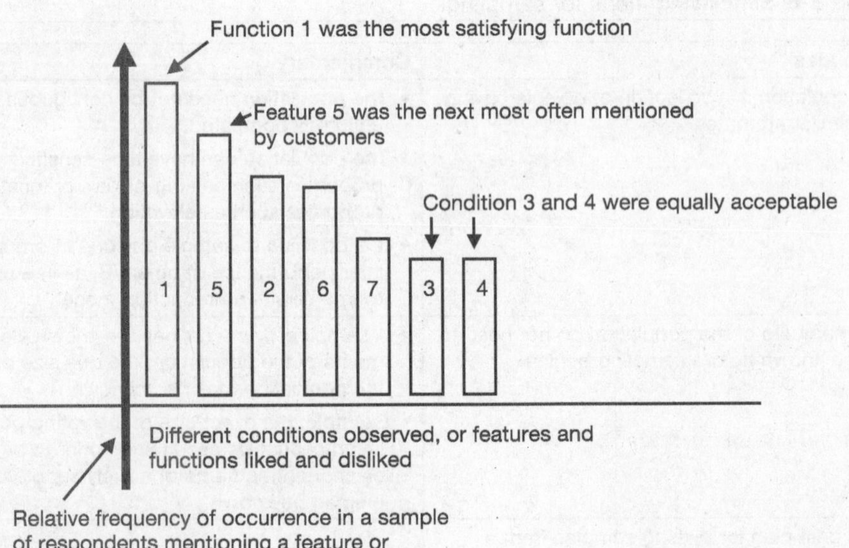

Figure 3-4 Histogram for quality measures

Summary and Takeaway Points

Our theme for this chapter is that *quality is a nonnegotiable value*. Quality is about making the customer ever more successful, and delivering more business benefits than the invested commitment.

There is no single definition of quality. Quality is expressed by its values, principles, and practices. Each of the agile methods has values, principles, and practices, but in this chapter, universal ideas are offered that are applicable in any methodology.

Early leaders in business quality set up many of the practices that are still useful today. Taylor introduced lean thinking and the concept that some activity adds no value to outcomes. Deming told us to reflect upon every outcome and offered the PDCA cycle; Juran said to focus on the customer. Crosby declared: *Quality is free!*

Six Sigma and the lean thinking paradigm are relatively recent quality movements. Although not designed for projects and software specifically, they are useful concepts and practices, such as the opportunity space and the idea of pull that are applicable to agile methods.

Even though the mantra of agile methods is to make quality performance happen every day, there is a place to plan for quality. Publish values, principles, and practices to a dashboard. Set up quality goals that are measurable; celebrate success. Proactively validate for customer satisfaction. In the end, quality is bestowed by beneficiaries. It is good only if they say it is good!

Chapter Endnotes

1. Wall Street Journal, "Frederick Taylor, Early Century Management Consultant," A1.
2. Beck with Andres, *Extreme Programming Explained*, 131–133.
3. McConnell, *Code Complete*, 567.
4. Schwaber, *Agile Project Management with SCRUM*, 2.
5. See Hallowell, "Software Development Convergence: Six Sigma-Lean-Agile."
6. Software as now designed is generally stationary in the statistical sense. That is, given the same initial conditions and the same data, the program will execute repeatedly in an identical fashion. Older practices that self-computed statements and variables, and thereby changed the program on the fly, creating nonstationary effects that are not necessarily repeatable, are for the most part no longer followed.
7. Business Week, "Watts Humphrey: He Wrote The Book On Debugging."
8. NIST, *Software Errors Cost U.S. Economy $59.5 Billion Annually.*
9. Poppendieck, *The Agile Customer's Tool Kit*, 4.
10. Womack and Jones, *Create Wealth in Your Corporation*, 67.
11. The terms *error* and *defect* are used interchangeably.

Table Endnote

1. The uncertainty principle: measuring actually changes that which is being measured.

4

Managing Test

Agile methods rigorously test to prove quality is designed-in.

> *All truths are easy to understand once they are discovered; the point is to discover them.*
>
> *Galileo*

To discover errors, demonstrate quality, and prove compliance—these are the reasons to test. It seems like an obvious statement, but the point of agile methods is to deliver working product at every iteration. There is no value earned if the product does not functionally perform. And certainly there is less value earned if performance, features, and esteem appeal do not attract and satisfy. Testing is essential to agile methods, first by the development team to verify proper design and development, and then by users to validate functionality, features, and operating performance.

Principles and Practices Guide Testing-in Quality

Customer satisfaction is the ultimate goal of agile product development. As described in Chapter 3, quality is the driver behind meeting or exceeding expectations. Unlike Taylor's theories of scientific management, for the agile practitioner quality is not a property to be controlled or assured by outsiders. Quality is a daily goal of every agile team member—an achievement to be demonstrated every day by automated tests that prove red failures can become green passes.

Quality has many dimensions, and many of those dimensions can be verified and validated by testing. Testing—to include user validation—is valued by agile methodologists as the one sure way to close any gap between what was asked for and what is to be delivered; testing is less to prove compliance to a specification and more to prove a satisfactory outcome for beneficiaries.

Principles and Practices

To that end, rules are needed that bind behavior but otherwise allow the self-direction of the development team to determine and modify day-to-day tactics.[1] Five principles to guide testing—in effect, the top-level rules—are summarized in Table 4-1:

Table 4-1 Test principles and practices

Principle	Practices
Don't kill the messenger	• Provide a safe and transparent environment; celebrate inquisitiveness • Scorecard each result • Provide opportunity for timely reporting; avoid accumulating a surprise • Look to the underlying cause with reasoned analysis
Every requirement must be testable; every test must relate to a requirement	• Decompose user stories until they are actionable; involve users in the interpretation of stories into the actionable descriptions • Link specific requirements to test, and the other way around • Apply test-driven development [TDD]* techniques that translate user stories directly into test scripts • Provide a means for users to understand and approve test scripts at the functional level
Anticipate some failure and make room for correction and retest	• Plan effort and duration anticipating failures and correction tasks • Update a working plan from actual test results • Plan regression tests that do not cause the entire iteration test series to be re-executed • Allow for regression testing after refactoring
Embrace learning	• Involve more than one person in the test scripting and execution. Build off pair programming if that practice is in place • Follow proven lessons-learned techniques: ask why at least five times to push down through a hierarchy of related reasons • Apply logical reasoning Deduction: *b* as a likely consequence of measuring *a* Abduction: Imagine that *a* is a possible explanation for *b*, although *b* may have many causes Induction: Imagine that *a* is a likely antecedent or condition that sources the *b*'s Inference: because *b* is true, so must *a* be true • Educate others on the team with the lessons learned • Apply what has been learned; modify best practices where necessary

Table 4-1 *(continued)*

Principle	Practices
Avoid isolation	• Use the buddy system; design and implement in pairs, test in pairs, or at least engage your buddy for critique and advice • Crosscheck with your buddy; think of independent means to verify results • Design the team and the project for socialization: sit together, communicate daily if not more often, communicate with a sense of urgency, share on the project test portal or on wiki, encourage boundaries according to natural breaks in the project • Integrate into the design base often and maintain awareness of the evolution of the project
*Test Driven Development (TDD) is defined in this chapter	

Test-driven Development Is the Starting Point

Test-driven development (TDD), is a practice that was proven first in XP.[2] The general TDD cycle is to "Write a test; . . . Make it run; . . . Make it right".[3] However, TDD is not restricted to the XP methodology, and as a concept, not even restricted to software.

Main Idea

Here are the main ideas of TDD, and they are a mind-bender for the traditionalist: Requirements are documented in the form of test scripts, and test scripts are the beginning point for product design. TDD works this way: detailed design and development, after consideration for architecture, is a matter of three significant steps:

- *Step 1: Document development requirements with test scripts.* Beginning with functional requirements in the iteration backlog, and in collaboration with users, the developer writes technical design requirements in the form of a test script, and writes the script in a form to be run with test-automating tools. Automated tools enable quick turnaround. Automated tests run fast, run on-demand, run repeatedly the same way, and run under various data and system conditions.
- *Step 2: Run the test, modifying the object design until it passes.* If the test fails, as it often will, the developer implements the quickest and simplest solution that will likely pass. Step 2 is repeated until the test passes.
- *Step 3: Refine the detail design of the object.* After the solution passes the test, the developer iterates the detail design to be compliant with quality

standards. In doing so, only the internal detail is changed and improved; no change is made to the object's external characteristics. To verify no external changes and continued functionality, the modified solution is retested internally.

A project management tip	TDD, unit tests, and acceptance tests
	• TDD was invented as a design practice; it is commonly applied to the lowest level design units. • "TDD's origins were a desire to get strong automatic regression testing that supported evolutionary design."[4] • Unit tests, distinct from TDD tests, are post-implementation design-verification tests. In most respects, unit tests and TDD tests are very similar, but the purposes are very different: one drives design and the other verifies implementation. • The concept of automated tests is also applicable to higher-level tests, such as product integration tests and user acceptance tests, but these are not for the purpose of driving design. • At higher levels, designs that pass unit tests are being tested in a larger context and by independent testers, including end users.

Beginning with a test script is to begin with the end in mind, an idea very much like Steven Covey's second habit for success.[5] Beginning with a test is, for all intents, beginning with the end-state features and functions written in the form of a script. The developer must think about how the object will work when it is finished, and write that working description into the script. To be as accurate as possible, the user must be present to converse with the developer during the course of the scripting. In fact, the dialogue begins before scripting with discussion of user stories in the iteration backlog. User stories, as will be described later, are vignettes of functional needs as told by expert users.[6] User stories themselves are not specific or technical enough to be actionable by developers. Thus, as seen in Step 1 there is interaction between developer and user to synthesize design requirements from user stories.

The Step 1-2-3 sequence is tagged as the *Red-Green-Refactor* sequence because the first test results are often *red* meaning failure, then *green* meaning a success, and finally *refactor* meaning the design is refined and brought compliant with quality standards. Refactoring only changes the internal detail of the object; the object's external appearance, functionality, and performance at its interfaces are unchanged.[7]

Of course, at Step 1, the test may pass; passing is a good thing when it happens. Depending on circumstances, if the first test passes before any design is done, then a reasonable conclusion is that the system already satisfies the requirement and additional design is not needed. A first-test success avoids redundancy and avoids adding unnecessary complexity to the product base.

<table>
<tr><td rowspan="2">A project management tip</td><td>TDD works best with new products</td></tr>
<tr><td>• Legacy complexities can greatly complicate a new project intended to integrate with the legacy, making the testing process both time consuming and complex in order to regressively prove that no harm is done with new functionality.
• Legacy testing scope often dilutes much of the advantages of practices such as TDD if automated tests are impractical.
• More conventional requirements documentation may be a better approach if it proves too complex to write the requirements as a test when modifying a legacy system.
• Legacy tools and product base may not support the tools and frameworks for efficient TDD practices that depend on automated tests.</td></tr>
</table>

Testing with Asserts

Among the things that make TDD work is the testing concept called *assert*.

The Meaning of *Assert*
Assert as a testing concept was invented and described by C. A. R. Hoare, a British scientist, and described by him in a widely read 1969 paper.[8] The word is taken from the verb *assert*, meaning in effect, to make a claim, state a position, or insist on a reality. An *assert* is a condition imposed on the object under test. An *assert* can be a precondition, a post-condition, or both. As commonly implemented, an *assert* is a condition that returns a value of *true* or *false*, but other logic is also employed, such as *null* or *not null*, *equals*, and *same* or *not same*.[9] If the object is working correctly, the condition should always be true at the point where the assert is placed.

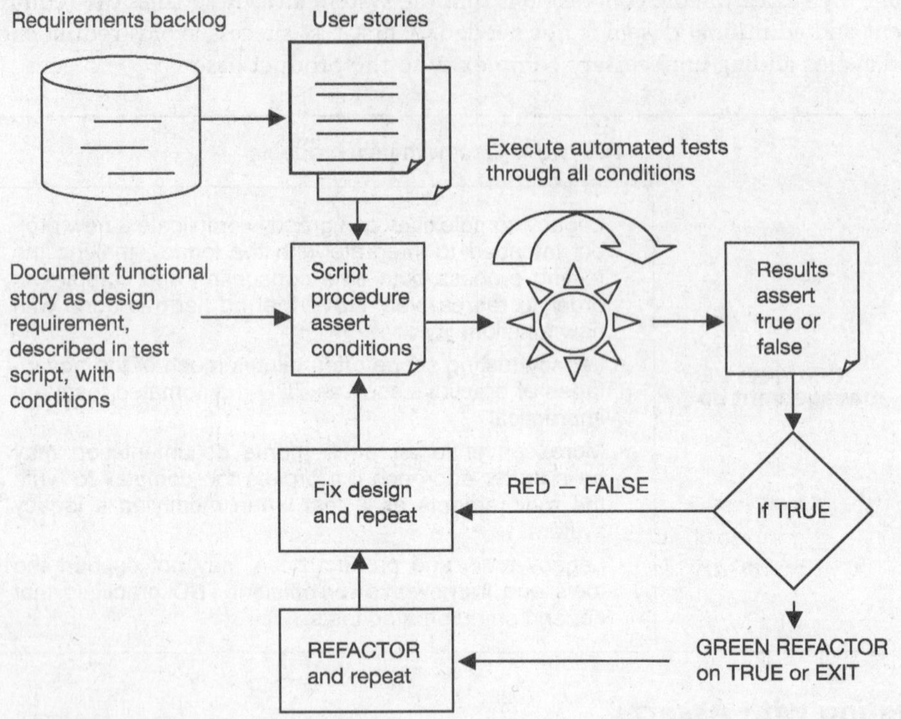

Figure 4-1 The TDD cycle

Testing with scripted asserts involves a three-step protocol. Figure 4-1 illustrates the concept.

1. Assert a precondition, then execute Step 2
2. Operate and execute the object procedures, then check the post-condition assert
3. Assert a result or post-condition—if the logic returns the expected result, the test passes

As an example, consider the functional description of a test for customer e-mail addresses in the customer database:

Customer e-mail address test

Set up the customer master data with e-mail addresses

Assert true: Every customer record has a valid data entry for an e-mail address.

Operation: In the test script, call the system object that verifies e-mail addresses. Verify that every customer record has a data entry of the form <alphanumeric variable character> @ <alpha variable character>. <alpha trigraph like COM, EDU, GOV, ORG, NET>.

Assert true: Return a 1 for each record examined that passes verification; 0 means the test fails—the system e-mail verification object does not exist or does not work, or the customer master data is incorrect.

Note: the precondition must be set up before the test is run. In this case, the setup loads e-mail addresses into the customer database.

Advantages of TDD

TDD addresses six big problems in achieving quality outcomes:[10]

1. *Scope creep:* Agile methodologists value simplicity.[11] In this sense, *simplicity* does not mean the *absence of complexity*; it means *the absence of unnecessary design* or *unnecessary scope*. Avoid design anticipation—so-called hooks—for requirements that ultimately never materialize. Avoid unnecessary redundancy and do not duplicate preexisting capabilities
2. *Coupling and cohesion:* Coupling and cohesion are properties of architecture. System coupling refers to interdependencies among components—the degree to which a change in one module affects the functioning or performance of another. For example, the chapters in this book are loosely coupled; changing figure and table references in one chapter has almost no effect on other chapters. Loose coupling is achieved by having the reference system start over at each chapter boundary, and by minimizing cross references between chapters.

   Cohesion is about consistency and similarity that promotes affinity. Systems with cohesion have common and consistent properties between modules that enable things to stay together and work together smoothly. Affinity could be procedural, temporal, logical, sequential, etc. The properties of this book are cohesive, chapter-to-chapter—style, organization, definitions, and themes all have strong affinity.

   Typically, both coupling and cohesion are subjectively scaled: coupling is loose or tight, cohesion is high or low. A mark of high quality is high cohesion and loose coupling. High-quality systems—those with loose coupling and high cohesion—are easier to maintain, easier to verify and validate, and more reliable. Testing readily identifies these properties. The fact is, it is much easier to write a test and get it to pass when the coupling is loose. A sure sign of tight coupling is that it is hard to write a test that passes! In this book, it would be harder to regression test the effect of a table-number change if the table numbers did not start over at each chapter boundary.

The effort to write multiple scripts is less if cohesion is high; all scripts are advantaged by similar system properties from one module to the next. Proofreading this book is much easier because of its cohesion; all tables can be identified with a script that searches for *Table <number> <alpha description>*.

Coupling and cohesion

Coupling and cohesion are outcomes of structured design, and are largely credited to the work of Larry Constantine, a distinguished researcher at MIT and IBM.

Constantine formulated the metrics of coupling and cohesion in the late 1960s, presenting his work in 1968 to the National Symposium on Modular Programming.[12]

3. *Trust:* Design and implementations that work are trusted by the team; so also is the designer or implementer. Trust in product development reduces nonvalue inspections and drives integrity in the product base. Testing establishes trust. The principle is: *no addition to the product base is made until the test passes*. Constant integration, frequent system builds, and rigorous regression testing guards the testing quality. Feedback corrects ineffective protocols.
4. *Rhythm:* Red-Green-Refactor sets up a pattern of activity with a certain cadence that maintains a pace and productivity, and most importantly, guards against wandering off the track. Rhythm promotes progressive successes.
5. *Requirements management:* Test scripts document technical requirements derived from user stories and other business documents that envision project outcomes. At the lowest level, the script is the persistent record of the requirement, logging information such as who created, accessed, updated, or deleted the script requirement, as well as the dates of each transaction. But there is more to managing requirements than just keeping track. As already described, tests reveal unnecessary and redundant requirements, dependencies that can be eliminated or minimized, and features or functions that can be eliminated to reduce complexity and overhead. And, tests reveal inconsistent requirements that might disturb cohesion.
6. *Regression assurance:* One of the motivations for a test-oriented development is to improve the likelihood of successful integration of a new capability into the product base.

Architecture Impacts TDD

Architecture is a prerequisite for TDD. On one level, it is a tool to organize and coordinate business requirements among the many product components, revealing, at a high level, redundancy, inconsistency, and problems of coupling and cohesion. On another level, architecture is the top-level specification of the structure, performance, appearance, relationships, and the interactivity among elements acting as a system.[13] It describes the external behaviors, the look and feel, and the connection dependencies of the elements. Architecture provides the overall road map to the finished product, although there is not always a green field for architecture. It may be constrained by a legacy product base, distribution system, or manufacturing and supply chain system.

<table>
<tr><td rowspan="2">A project management tip</td><td>Architecture, but not too much architecture</td></tr>
<tr><td>• Albert Einstein once said, "Everything should be made as simple as possible, but not simpler." As applied to architecture, Einstein provided good advice.
• As simple as possible means avoiding fortuitous complexity, unnecessary redundancy, and couplings that create unnecessary dependencies.
• In agile speak, as simple as possible means designing for the present requirement and not second guessing where the customer may next find value.
• The phrase but not simpler means do not decompose to such small units such as tiny user stories so that essential cohesion is missing and the overall understanding is lost in a forest of details.</td></tr>
</table>

Test Planning Is Essential to Good Test Metrics

British Field Marshal Sir Bernard L. Montgomery, a military leader of World War II, once famously told his staff when planning for the invasion of Europe, "I don't read papers," referring to the heavy weight of the memoranda his planners were trying to foist on him.[14] Perhaps Montgomery was the lean thinker of his day! His statement did not mean there was not a need for planning or plans, or for others to read them; his statement simply meant that beyond a point, the fine print obscures. Test planning is a bit like that: to some level of detail, it is necessary to put plans down in black and white; beyond that, more detail probably detracts from effectiveness. Emergent protocols should be allowed to fill in the gaps.

Test Planning Essentials

The primary application of test planning as described in this section is for unit tests, integration tests, and acceptance testing, not TDD. TDD, as already noted, is a rapid-fire design rhythm for which the team should develop design metrics. Test metrics, on the other hand, require a test plan for context. Test planning requires standard definitions so that metrics convey the same information to all concerned. In other words, common definitions provide cohesion among planning elements.

Table 4-2 contains the definitions of the terms *script, scenario, condition, attempt,* and *instance* for the object functionality or system under test.

Table 4-3 holds definitions of the quantitative metrics of testing.

Table 4-4 contains the definitions for the project's tests.

Table 4-5 contains managerial topics in test planning.

Table 4-2 Test plan definitions—stories

Planning element	Definition
Script	• A step-by-step procedure using the unit, module, application, or product functionality that implements a business story. • Typically there is one script for one story, but it may make sense to have more than one script. • Each script has a success criteria or assert, although the criteria may have to be dependent on conditions. • Scripts can be code, procedural language for an automated tool, or natural language for a user to follow.
Scenario	• A specific version of the script that is made unique by the test conditions assigned to it. • Test conditions can be (a) business conditions, or (b) conditions—or states—of the product, the system, or the environment.
Condition	• The initial state of the unit, module, application, product, and the environment, to include real or synthesized data.
Attempt	• An event in which one or more instances are run.
Instance	• A specific trial or run of the scenario. Different instances are the same scenario at different attempts.

Table 4-3 Test plan definitions—metrics

Planning element	Definition
Pass	• The score given to an instance that meets the success criteria of the script
Fail	• The score given to an instance that does not meet the success criteria of the script
Fail with conditions, or pass with exceptions	• As in pass or fail, except that certain criteria were met and others were not
Pass rate	• The ratio of the total instances passed to the total instances run in an attempt

Table 4-4 Test plan definitions—tests

Planning element	Definition
Unit test	• A verification test of a specific unit; the lowest element in the product hierarchy
Integration test	• A test of more than one unit working together, to include a new unit integrated into the legacy product base
Regression test	• A test of the legacy product base after integration of one or more units to verify that the legacy has not been adversely affected by the integration
Acceptance or functional test	• A test with users that focuses on the functional performance of the product base with the objective of obtaining the user's approval to go-live with the product
Criteria or assert	• Results that must be achieved for a test to receive a passing score

Planning Test Flow

Here is an example planning exercise in terms of *who will do what* to see how all this fits together. The business and the developers or testers work collaboratively, step-by-step:

- Business users select functional stories and identify the business conditions for scripts to be written.
- Testers plan the number of scripts based on the identified stories.
- Testers group the conditions according to their natural affinity and plan how conditions will be applied to scripts to make unique scenarios.
- Testers evaluate coupling. Some changes in affinity grouping may be required to loosen the coupling.
- Project management and the team leader make assumptions about the pass and fail rates of scenarios, calling upon experience or other benchmarks.

Table 4-5 Test plan definitions—management

Planning element	Definition
Complexity	• A measure of the internal structure or a variety of outcomes of a unit, module, application, or product • A complex internal structure may return a simple outcome such as *1* or *0*, or a complex outcome, such as a data record set • Measured on an ordinal scale such as high, medium, and low; it is best if some objective standard defines each ordinate
Planning and set-up time	• The time and effort required to initialize an attempt
Reflection	• The time and effort expended to analyze and propose corrective actions after a specific instance; especially—but not exclusively—if the test receives a failing score
Fix-it time	• The time and effort expended to address the outcome of the reflection
Containment	• The concept of exploiting a loose coupling so that a unit, module, or other previously tested artifice remains unaffected by subsequent development

Pass and fail rates are estimated by assuming a flow of *run the test . . . measure results and fix failures; rerun the test . . . fix and rerun again if necessary*. All scripts are run once to see which pass. Those that fail are run again after diagnosis and repair of the system under test; if any failures remain, the failed scripts are run yet again after fixes are applied.

The test-fix-test sequence, which we call an attempt sequence, is particularly appealing to agile managers because it is outcome oriented—the focus is on passes and failures and eventually getting all to green. To illustrate the idea, and as a working assumption, we will apply the *30-50-20 attempt sequence* as explained in the following panel:

30-50-20 attempt sequence	
Example with 10 scenarios in 3 attempts	
Thirty percent of all scenarios pass on the first attempt.	• Three of 10 pass, seven of 10 fail and must be retested in second attempt. The passing rate is 30 percent.

Fifty percent of all scenarios pass on the second attempt.	• Seven first-attempt failures are rerun after fixes are applied; five pass and two fail, an attempt passing rate of five out of seven (71 percent) but also five of the original 10 pass on this attempt, or 50 percent.
The remaining 20 percent pass on the third attempt.	• Two second-attempt failures are rerun after fixes are applied; two pass and none fail on the third attempt for an attempt passing rate of two of two (100 percent), but two of the original 10 pass on this attempt, or 20 percent.

When combined, note that the 30-50-20 percentages equal 100 percent of the scenarios. In other words, everything eventually passes; this is one of the principles of agile methods.

Here is another example with different numbers and some additional insight:

- Suppose for a given script with all conditions taken into account, the team plans *25 scenarios.*
- Assume the 3-attempt *30-50-20* sequence is a reasonable expectation.
- *First attempt:* Plan to run the 25 instances and expect seven passes ($0.3 \times 25 = 7$) on the first attempt, rounding down to the nearest integer, leaving 18 scenarios failed.
- *Second attempt:* Plan to run the 18 scenarios expecting to get to a cumulative 80 percent passing rate ($30 + 50 = 80$ percent). This means 50 percent of the original 25 are forecast to pass on the second attempt. Rounding up to compensate for rounding down in the first attempt, expect 13 passes in the second attempt, cumulatively 20 passes ($7 + 13 = 20$) after the second attempt, which is 80 percent of the original 25.
- *Third attempt:* There are only five scenarios left that are forecast not to pass in either the first or the second attempt. Plan to run these five scenarios, and the model forecasts them to pass on the third attempt.

To summarize what has transpired, one script expands to a 48-instance testing scope:

One script with 25 scenarios will produce 48 instances ($25 + 18 + 5 = 48$) when rounded to a whole number. This is 1.92 times the number of scenarios that began the test. The 30-50-20 sequence is an effort and schedule multiplier on scenarios. The multiplier effect is actually 1.9, disregarding any rounding errors:

Multiplier Effect
Multiplier of first instances + multiplier of second instances + multiplier of third instances
= Total multiplier for instances in three attempts
1 + (1 − 0.3) + (1 − 0.3 − 0.5) = 1 + 0.7 + 0.2 = 1.9
For 10 scenarios
10 + 7 + 2 = 19

A project management tip	The pass rate is an effort multiplier
	• The test plan anticipates a pass rate spread over a number of attempts. • The consequence of different pass rates and multiple attempts is that the testing effort is multiplied. • If there are three pass rates corresponding to three attempts, then the multiplier effect is calculated: 1 + (1 − Rate 1) + (1 − Rate 1 − Rate 2)

Estimating Hours

To estimate hours for the test plan, more parameters are required:

- *Complexity:* For each object-under test, grade the complexity of its test script. Complexity, as always, is a judgment call based on experience and benchmarks. Although a complexity scale is often some ordinal rating like low, medium, high, or very high, a numeric scale is more useful for planning. Choose a scale, something such as a numerical binary sequence corresponding to the ordinals low, medium, high, and very high; choose a scale that provides reasonable range and separation between the ordinal values, like: 1, 2, 4, and 8, respectively. Rank all scripts by relative complexity compared to an objective benchmark. In any particular group of scripts, it is not unusual to find that not all complexities are represented. For instance, a particular group of scripts might have all complexities ranked as high (a numerical rating of 4) compared to the benchmark.
- *Tasks and hours:* For a low-complexity script, make an estimate of the hours and skills required to set up and test the script. This low-complexity estimate will be the baseline that is scaled for complexity. Figure 4-2 provides an example of the estimates.

Complexity is a multiplier of effort for every test preparation and execution task

Task	Script complexity multiplier, hours			
	Low 1	Medium 2	High 4	Very high 8
Set-up per scenario (assemble data, set-up initial conditions)	2	4	8	16
Execution of an instance	1	2	4	8
Reflection, per attempt, per scenario (analysis, root cause, fix proposal)	1	2	4	8
Fix-it per scenario between Attempt 1 and 2	2	4	8	16
Fix-it per scenario between Attempt 2 and 3 (the more difficult problems persist)	3	6	12	24

Figure 4-2 Complexity estimates of testing tasks

- *Test plan hours:* Multiply the data from Figure 4-2 and the 30-50-20 sequence for 10 scenarios given in the panel above. The multiplication result is given in the grid, Figure 4-3. Figure 4-3 shows the total hours for 10 low-complexity scenarios. For medium complexity, double all the totals in Figure 4-3; double again for high complexity, and then double again for very high.

Planning the Scorecard

The testing scorecard is much like a pipeline monitor, watching the flow of things as they go by. A pipeline requires a temporal dimension, so plan the baseline according to a calendar. As an example to illustrate the scorecard planning, assume the following project test case:

Test case

- *Scripts:* ten scripts, all subject to the same 30-50-20 passing sequence
- *Script complexity:* two low, five medium, three high, and zero very high
- *Scenarios:* five scenarios for each of 10 scripts, 50 total

The complexity multiplier for low complexity is multiplied by the attempt data for 10 scenarios, using the 30-50-20 attempt sequence and the hours per task given in other data.

Low complexity	Set-up hours	Execute instances hours	Fix-it hours	Reflection and lessons learned hours
Set-up for scenarios	2 × 10 = 20			
Attempt 1		10 × 1 = 10	7 × 2 = 14	7 × 1 = 7
Attempt 2		7 × 1 = 7	2 × 3 = 6	2 × 1 = 2
Attempt 3		2 × 1 = 2	0	0
Total	20	19	20	9
Grand total, 10 scenarios	68 hrs			
Grand total, 1 scenario	6.8 hrs			

The 30-50-20 attempt sequence, applied to 10 scenarios, gives the results used in the grid above.

1st attempt: 3 passes, 7 fails

2nd attempt: 5 passes, 2 fails

3rd attempt: 2 passes, 0 fails

Figure 4-3 Forecast hours by attempt

To plan a baseline, assume the following project situation:

Project assumptions

- *Staff:* six, and all are multiskilled.
- *Skills:* any staff member can work on any part of the test.
- *Efficiency and effectiveness:* no one works efficiently all day long, and for various reasons, no one is likely to work every day.
- *Labor loss:* the labor loss benchmark is 15 percent, yielding a 34-hour workweek for throughput planning purposes.
- *Staff-hours:* with the six-person team, there are 204 planning staff hours per week (6 × 34 = 204).

Calculate the staff hours demand. Figure 4-4 illustrates the demand based on the data in Figures 4-2 and 4-3, adjusted for five scenarios using the 30-50-20 sequence. Note, in Figure 4-4, the *Testing tasks* multiplier for low complexity, 4.8, comes from the calculations in Figure 4-3 for hours other than set-up; the multiplier is escalated for medium and high according to the factors in Figure 4-2.

Staff hours are a multiplication of complexity factors and task effort

Staff hours for testing example			
Complexity estimate with 5 conditions			
Item	**2 scripts low**	**5 scripts medium**	**3 scripts high**
5 scenarios set-ups	20 hrs = 2 × 5 × 2	100 hrs = 5 × 5 × 4	120 hrs = 3 × 5 × 8
Testing tasks	48 hrs = 2 × 5 × 4.8	240 hrs = 5 × 5 × 9.6	288 hrs = 3 × 5 × 19.2
Totals hours	816 hrs		
Total weeks @ 204/wk	4 wks		

Figure 4-4 Staff hours for testing example

Pipeline Grid

A tool for showing the four-week plan from Figure 4-4 is the so-called pipeline grid. There are three elements of information:

1. Baseline
2. Day-to-day working plan
3. Actual performance

Week-by-week and cumulative-to-date data are often shown. Figure 4-5 is an example grid. Assume the scorecard is reporting at the end of the first four weeks.

Example: Testing resources are ahead of plan after 3 of 4 weeks

Pipeline scorecard—3 of 4 weeks, 6 person team, effective hours after labor loss				
Item	**Week 1**	**Week 2**	**Week 3**	**Week 4**
Baseline	204	204	204	204
Baseline cumulative	204	408	612	816
Working plan	200	204	208	204
Working plan cumulative	200	404	612	816
Actual hours	195	200	210	
Actual hours cumulative	195	395	605	
Working plan—actual variance	5	4	−2	
Working plan—actual variance cumulative	5	9	7	

Figure 4-5 Pipeline scorecard 3 of 4 weeks

Effective hours, after adjustment for labor loss, are planned in the baseline and estimated for the working plan. Variances between the working plan and baseline require a strategy to converge the plans to zero variance. Actual hours are the hours recorded by participants for the work task.

However, solely looking at hours is only looking at resource consumption, a so-called input-input view that does not measure outcomes. Agile methodologists always focus on outcomes. Figure 4-6 integrates the 30-50-20 outcomes sequence with the hours. To simplify Figure 4-6 to present the main point, the setup tasks from Figure 4-4 are not shown, although a similar pipeline should be constructed for setup.

Testing resources are ahead of plan after 3 of 4 weeks, but passes are behind plan

Pipeline scorecard—3 of 4 weeks				
6 person team, outcomes in 30-50-20 sequence, 1.9 multiplier 10 scripts, 5 conditions, 50 instances 50 X 1.9 = 95 Total instances: 50 passes and 45 failures				
Item	**Week 1**	**Week 2**	**Week 3**	**Week 4**
Baseline hrs	204	204	204	204
Baseline passes/failures	10/9	15/14	15/13	10/9
Baseline cumulative hrs	204	408	612	816
Passes/failures	10/9	25/23	40/36	50/45
Working plan hrs	200	204	208	204
Passes/failures	10/9	12/11	15/13	13/12
Working plan cumulative hrs	200	404	612	816
Passes/failures	10/9	22/20	37/33	50/45
Actual hrs	195	200	210	
Passes/failures	10/12	12/12	14/13	
Actual cumulative hrs	195	395	605	
Passes/failures	10/12	22/24	36/37	
Working plan—actual variance hrs	5	4	−2	
Passes/failures	0/−2	0/−2	1/0	
Working plan—actual variance cumulative hrs	5	9	7	
Passes/failures	0/−2	0/−4	1/−4	

Figure 4-6 Pipeline with outcomes

Testing by Sampling Conserves Time and Money

Recall the discussion in Chapter 3 about drawing an inference from a sample. It often arises that not all data can be tested and not all conditions can be tested because of economic constraints or time constraints. After all, iterations last only a matter of weeks during which time testing must be completed. Thus, the time box imposes limitations, but quality must not be compromised. Ordinarily, every conceivable user load or network load, or every operating condition of the environment cannot be tested; nor can every user concurrency situation or every distribution circumstance be tested, and so forth. Nevertheless, these areas cannot go untested. Therefore, the project is led to setting up test experiments that examine only a few of the testable situations. From the few, an inference is drawn that the others, untested but otherwise similar, have the same attributes in the same proportion.

For example, in one published account, errors in production software run from one or two per thousand statements up to perhaps eight per thousand, whereas some other software has never revealed a defect in production.[15] However, it is unlikely that all the code in large systems was examined to precisely count the reported errors; it is likely there was only time and money to test a few of the conditions. This process is called *sampling*.

Salt-and-Pepper Story

Sometimes it is hard to sell sampling to a skeptical project sponsor who is an I'll-believe-it-when-I-see-it manager. Consider this salt-and-pepper story as a means of explanation:

Fill a large bowl with table salt. Each grain of salt represents an element that could be examined and tested for compliance; each grain is an opportunity for a good result or a bad result. Let the salt represent working elements, so any grain selected would pass a test. Now mix in some pepper in an amount that is small when compared to the salt. Observe that the grain size is the same size and shape, and that the pepper is similar in all respects to the salt with one exception: There is some error in the preparation of the element that causes it to be pepper rather than salt.

After mixing it up, the salt-and-pepper mix should be about the same throughout the bowl since there is no particular reason for errors (i.e., pepper) to collect one place or the other. In other words, the location of the pepper in the bowl (i.e., our system) is completely random. Moreover, the number of pepper grains in the system is not known. The count of the pepper grains is a random number—that is, the count of pepper grains is a number that we know only probabilistically. The count of pepper grains could be different each time the system is built. It is important that this system possesses the statistical property called *stationary*. Stationary means that for each build it does not matter when the system is examined; the number of pepper grains and the number of salt grains in a build are the same at all times.

With the system of salt and pepper in place, the testing task is to discover errors. It is tedious to count every pepper grain. Instead, we will estimate the count of the pepper grains in the bowl by drawing an inference from sample data.

Make the first sample with a small spoon, perhaps a half teaspoon. Count the pepper and the salt grains, and then return them to the system. Draw a second sample with a larger spoon—such as a soupspoon—and repeat the counting and restoration. Draw yet another sample with an even larger spoon such as a ladle and again count the pepper and salt, being sure to return the sample each time before taking the next sample so the system is returned to the same condition for each examination.

In the first small sample taken with the half teaspoon, there were few pepper grains, even none at all. But with the soupspoon sample, there was probably a different pepper-to-salt ratio than was seen in the half teaspoon. However, as the sample got larger from soupspoon to ladle, observe that the ratio of salt to pepper did not materially change even though the number of salt and pepper grains in the sample was dramatically larger.

Now add more salt and pepper to the bowl. It does not matter how much, but be sure the proportions are about the same as in the original mix. Adding more salt and pepper adds more opportunities. The population in the bowl is now larger. After mixing the added salt and pepper, take another ladle and count the salt and pepper. Notice that the pepper to salt-and-pepper ratio did not materially change from those taken before the population size was increased. From these observations, there are some interesting conclusions:

- *Sample size:* Once a sample is large enough, the actual size of the sample is immaterial to discovering the ratio of the defects to the acceptable units in the system
- *Population size:* The size of the population is immaterial so long as it is much larger than the sample size
- *Defect distribution:* Defects must be randomly distributed among the acceptable units

It is a good idea to draw more than one sample to be sure that the sample is indeed representative of the system. For instance, suppose some of the salt grains were moist so that the pepper did not mix in. In that case, the moist grains could not be assumed to be representative. One possible event is that one of several samples might scoop up the wet salt with no pepper; in that event, the proportion of pepper to salt in the sample is unrepresentative of the system. The best practice is to draw several samples and average the results, replacing the sample each time so that one sample does not influence the next. Multiple samples diversify the risk that any one sample is unrepresentative. Confidence will be much greater with the average figure than it will be with just one sample.

A project management tip	Sampling has advantages
	• Sampling is an economically prudent way to get a handle on the quality of the product at different points along the way. • Do not wait till the end to sample; be agile and sample iteratively.

Salt and Pepper in the Real World: Step-by-Step Sampling

Here is how it usually works in the real project world. The task is to test some attribute of the object-under test. There is a large population of these attributes, and in the early going, some defects will occur.

Table 4-6 provides the step-by-step procedure for a sampling test:

Table 4-6 Steps for testing by sampling

Action Step	**Commentary**
Determine the attribute to be tested	• Example: Assume a developer is testing the functional response to a date entry in the form of mm/dd/yyyy
Establish the test conditions for a script of test steps	• Dates should be accepted from the years 2000–2100
Develop a scenario to execute the script according to the conditions	• A script inserts various dates and also varies the format
Determine the size of the population under test	• Count the number of days within the date limits and multiply by the format combinations • Example: 100 years between 2000 and 2100 • Expected population: 36,525 dates • Test each date in 4 formats: date-format combinations create 146,100 conditions in the population
Run the scenario for a number of instances to generate at least 1000 counts of the attribute	• Count the passes and fails • Compute the ratio of passes to passes + fails • Draw an inference about the likely untested defects in the whole population

Defining Confidence for Sample Results

The sample data provides information to draw inferences about the whole population. Recall that an inference is likely close to, but not exactly equal to, the real number. To be prudent, infer a range of values: rather than say that the defect ratio is specifically ten per one thousand opportunities, describe the defect ratio as likely in a range of values that includes ten per one thousand. But this raises the questions: how do we figure out the appropriate range limits, and with what confidence does the range encompass the real values? Fortunately, both range and confidence can be derived empirically from the sample data using some everyday rules of thumb that simplify the underlying mathematics. The simplifying assumptions are:

- *Population:* Assume the population is more than 100 times larger than the sample, and the population itself is large, so that the population is representative of the situation being tested—typically larger than 10,000 opportunities
- *Sample:* Assume the sample is large enough to be representative, no matter from where it is drawn in the population
- *Defect or condition:* Assume the defects in the population—more precisely, the conditions being tested for—are evenly distributed so that they will be proportionately in the sample the same way as they are in the population

The steps to come up with a range and a confidence figure are as follows:

1. Take samples and count the defects and measure the sample sizes; then calculate the proportionality of *defects* to the *sample size*—denoted *p*—in each of multiple samples.

   $$\left(p = \frac{\text{defects}}{\text{sample size}}\right)$$

   The number of samples is not too important; it can be as small as 1. However, one sample might be unrepresentative of the population; multiple samples provide an opportunity to develop an average sample that is more representative of that population.
2. Create histograms of the *p* calculations and the sample-size measurements. Observe the tendency of calculations and measurements to cluster about center values on each of their respective histograms; the center values are good estimates of the averages. Calculate the average *p* and denote average *p* as *P*. Calculate the average sample size and denote it as *S*. See this discussion illustrated in Figure 4-7.

At this point there is enough data to pick a confidence figure and calculate the range that goes with it, or the other way around. It is customary to pick a confidence, and one of the most common is 95 percent. The interpretation of a 95

The histogram of *P* (and similarly for *S*) shows clustering around an average value and an overall shape similar to a bell curve, thereby enabling simplifying assumptions to calculate relevant statistics

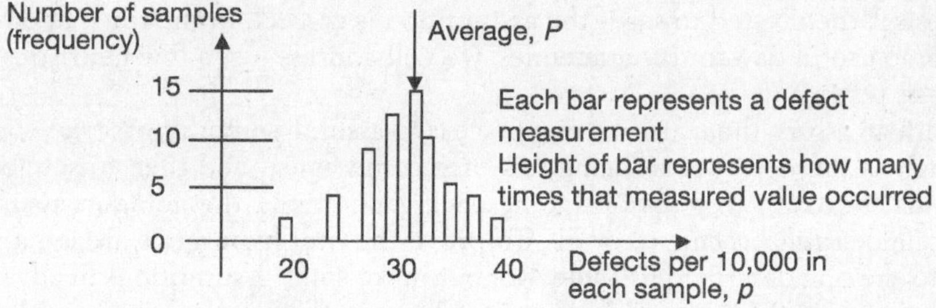

Average P = (sum [height of bar x defects, p]) / (total number of samples)

Figure 4-7 Proportionality estimate

percent confidence range is that 5 percent of the time, the real population values are likely outside the range. However, information is not available that would determine how far outside the range the real population values fall or whether they are above or below the range limits.

For a 95 percent confidence, estimate the confidence range from the sample information using this simplified formula:[16]

Range for 95 percent confidence =

$$\pm 2\times\sqrt{\left[P\times\frac{(1-P)}{S}\right]}$$

Example:

- Defect rate (average) calculated = $P = \frac{30}{10{,}000} = .0030$
- $1 - P = 0.997$
- Sample size (average) calculated = $S = 10{,}000$
- Range = $\pm 2\times\sqrt{\left[\frac{0.003\times 0.997}{10{,}000}\right]} = \pm\frac{11}{10{,}000}$
- 95 percent confidence interval is from 0.0019 to 0.0041, 19 errors in 10,000 to 41 errors in 10,000, with an average of 30 errors in 10,000

Testing a Hypothesis Builds Confidence

There is another way to approach sampling, and that is by constructing a hypothesis. A hypothesis is an assumption made about the object-under test. The hypothesis is then tested to see if the assumption is correct. In the spirit of developing some useful day-to-day guidelines, we will address just a few heuristics for hypothesis testing.

As with an assert, the usual starting place is to assume something is true, something such as the defect ratio being less than some figure, and then to set about confirming the truth. For reasons going back generations, the going-in assumption is called a *null hypothesis*, or H_0. To prove the null hypothesis, design a test similar to the one described in Table 4-6, but make some assumptions in advance about the outcome. For example, there could be sufficient experience with the team's design process to form a reasonable null hypothesis stating that defects are expected to be about 30 per ten thousand opportunities. Anything substantially more or less than the hypothesis is a signal that something unusual has occurred.

Type 1 and Type 2 Errors

The team can make two unfortunate errors:

1. The Type 1 error is what happens when the project team runs the test, gathers and analyzes the data, and then decides the null hypothesis is not true, when in fact it is. In the case under discussion, the test data might suggest that defects in the population are much different than assumed, when they really are not. This situation is a Type 1 error. Example: Perhaps a clump of pepper was sampled, thereby making the estimate of defects too pessimistic.
2. The Type 2 error is the other way around. The data suggests all is well, when it is not. Example: Perhaps a clump of salt was sampled, thereby making the estimate of defects too optimistic.

Take note that the cost of making a Type 1 or Type 2 error is not the same for each. Naturally, care should be exercised in each case, but usually the cost is high for one and correspondingly lower for the other.

A project management tip	Type 1 and Type 2 errors
	• The cost of a Type 2 error, posed as believing all is well when it is not, is potentially more costly than the more conservative Type 1 error.

Zone of Acceptance

Not only do the experts have to hypothesize the assumption, they have to also numerically estimate or specify the zone of acceptance. The zone of acceptance is the range within which the null hypothesis is considered true. For example, suppose the null hypothesis is that the design process typically yields 30 defects per 10,000 opportunities. A zone of acceptance might be from 20 to 40 per 10,000 opportunities. Any measured defect rate between 20 and 40 means the process is performing as expected.

In the agile space, the zone of acceptance is empirically determined from the initial iterations. Hypothesis testing need not impose defined process control on adaptive and evolutionary methods. However, the quality implications of the zone of acceptance may bring other stakeholders into the picture, such as marketing or product support. The zone of acceptance is going to establish an objective quality standard for the test results. In a word, the zone of acceptance is a specification for how tight *good* is.

Hypothesis Example

Suppose the experts estimate that the processes and practices employed, jointly with the complexity of the product design, should yield defects at $\frac{40}{10,000}$ or 0.04 percent on average. This figure is the team's benchmark, and it is the null hypothesis. The team makes a judgment about quality and decides on a deviation of $\frac{10}{10,000}$ as acceptable. Table 4-7 provides the various parameters:

Table 4-7 Null hypothesis

Parameter	Value	Commentary
Process expectation	$\frac{40}{10,000}$	• The null hypothesis • Benchmark supported by processes and practices
Quality allowance	$\pm\frac{10}{10,000}$	• Tolerance adopted by the team
Zone of acceptance	$\frac{30}{10,000}$ to $\frac{50}{10,000}$	• If there are measurements outside the zone, then the process or the measuring technique is suspect • *Too good to be true* is just as suspect as *much worse than expected*

Summary and Takeaway Points

The chapter theme is that *agile methods rigorously test to prove quality is designed-in*. Demonstrating quality through testing builds trust with the sponsor, the stakeholders, and the customer. Quality means the product will work and satisfy when put into production.

In the XP methodology, a recommended practice is test-driven development (TDD). TDD is applicable to any agile methodology. TDD is a means to document requirements, begin the design effort, and establish a Red-Green-Refactor rhythm.

Good test metrics for unit, integration, and acceptance testing come from good test planning. Test planning is about estimating the number of scripts, scenarios, and instances and estimating their pass and failure rates. Scorecards keep track of actual pass and failures compared to baseline forecasts.

Not everything can be tested. There are schedule and economic limitations. Samples can be used to infer quality results in the larger population. Confidence limits establish trust with the customer and sponsor.

Sometimes it is useful to posit a hypothesis and then test to see if it is true. Sometimes the results are too good to be true. Such an outcome is a tipoff to look more closely at technique and measurements. In spite of testing results along the way, the ultimate test is integration into production and the vote of customers about their satisfaction.

Chapter Endnotes

1. Having a set of general rules that frame day-to-day tactics that adapt to the situation is an idea that comes from the study of *emergence*. Emergent processes and systems are those that can make changes in the input-to-output transformation so that outcomes are more in line with expectations based on input conditions. Emergence requires feedback from output to input and a means to incorporate the feedback to affect a better outcome. See Anderson, *Agile Management for Software Engineering*, 11–12.

2. Kent Beck, the father of XP, is the innovator most associated with TDD, although there are others—Ward Cunningham, Ron Jefferies, and Martin Fowler—who have been instrumental promoting TDD with developers and project managers alike.

3. See Beck, *Test-Driven Development: By example*, 11. See also Fowler, *Patterns of Enterprise Application Architecture*, 95.

4. Martin, *Mocks Aren't Stubs*, MartinFowler.com, January, 2007. For additional insight, see Walther, "TDD Tests are not Unit Tests," StephenWalther.com.

5. Covey, *7 Habits of Highly Effective People*, 95, Habit 2: Begin with the End in Mind.

6. User stories are short, small business scenarios that are functional descriptions of a user's need. In the iteration planning meeting, participating users tell the stories. These stories form a backlog for the development iterations. See Cohn, *User Stories Applied: For Agile Software Development*, 4.

7. Beck, *Test-Driven Development: By Example*, x.

8. See Hoare, *An Axiomatic Basis for Computer Programming.*

9. Astels, *Test-Driven Development—A Practical Guide*, 62.

10. Kent Beck has written about the first four problems discussed in the text. See Beck with Andres, *Extreme Programming Explained: Embrace Change*, 2nd ed. 50–51.

11. See the XP values defined by Kent Beck in Beck with Andres, Ibid, 18. The reader is reminded that system, product, application, deliverables, and outcomes are all used interchangeably to give generality to the discussion.

12. Stevens, Myers, and Constantine, *Structured Design*, 13 (2), 115–139.

13. Paulish, *Architecture-Centric Software Project Management*, 5.

14. D'Este, *Decision in Normandy.*

15. Beck, *Test-Driven Development: By Example*, 120.

16. Downing and Clark, *Statistics: The Easy Way*, 235.

5

Developing the Scope and Requirements

Agile methods encourage requirements to change as often as necessary to ensure that the customer receives the best value for the resources committed.

> *A requirements paradox: Requirements must be stable for predictable results. However, the requirements always change.*
>
> *Niels Malotaux*

Agile methods trade on the concept of being adaptive to changing customer needs. The scope evolves as the customer is exposed to each product release and gives feedback, thereby influencing the next increment's design. Taken holistically, feedback, reflection, and next-iteration influences present unique challenges in scope definition and requirements management. Traditional cause and effect plan-to-product relationships are fuzzier and less specific. Actual outcomes are more dynamic over time than are plan-driven project development lifecycle (PD-PDLC) point solutions—that is, the natural volatility of requirements is felt with higher fidelity than what is allowed by the requirements freeze imposed by a big design up front.

The planning responses for scope and requirements are profound: the business case holds the product vision in a top-level framework with rather less direction than customary about feature, function, and performance; scope is planned incrementally, allowing for and encouraging evolution. Planning occurs in shorter and more time-sensitive frameworks called rolling waves, a planning concept discussed in Chapter 6. Development cycles—called iterations or sprints—are governed by a few rules that regulate requirements: The most important point to grasp is that volatility is managed on a scale from *high and allowable* at the project level to *stable enough for developers to work* during a specific development iteration. Requirements governance is a lesser task for project managers. Indeed, successful agile project managers accommodate the different role central authority plays in evolutionary and adaptive methodologies.[1] The role becomes modulation and containment of exuberant and aggressive customers while allowing, encouraging, and facilitating innovative interactions—consistent with the business-case framework—that arise from high-performance customer-developer teams, a topic in Chapter 8.

Emergent and Adaptive Methods

Adaptive methods have the property of *emergence*—the outcomes generally have more range and complexities than would be predicted by the simple combination and application of practices and project rules that govern development teams.

The range and complexity arises from feedback—a form of reflection—which gives the process of transforming input into output nonlinearity and a circular dependency. Output depends on input, but then input depends on including output effects, which requires the whole process to adapt to the mix of input and output in circulation.

This circular dependency with *adaption* forming a *closed loop* system is markedly different from the traditional closed loop linear system. The mission of linear systems is to accurately and predictably transform input to output with high fidelity; in effect, follow the plan!

Not so with adaptive feedback systems. The mission of adaptive systems is to make outcomes satisfying to the system agents who are all the active participants in the system processes. If the feedback is properly phased—that is, timed to arrive back at the input at a helpful moment—and if the interaction of all the participants is aimed at a common objective, systems with adaptive feedback can converge on high-quality results.[2]

Perhaps more so with agile methods than with any other methodologies, the hand of the customer moves the scope lever. The scope lever is one of four principle levers—the others are schedule, investment, and quality. Schedule and investment are given in the business case; investment is simply the limit on funding, a cap on affordability, and a resource to be distributed among iterations as the value proposition evolves. The business case milestones set the top-level schedule; milestones express business timing and set the project value in the context of a calendar. Quality is a lever with little range of motion, is provided at a uniformly high standard, and cannot be compromised without jeopardizing trust with the customer.

The Most Affordable Scope Is a Best Value

Agile projects value maximizing customer satisfaction over minimizing the variance to a plan. When scope, investment, schedule, and quality are put together in a best-value formulation, scope is the most flexible, but with a flexibility that is contained within limits of architecture, feasibility, and funding demand. To be sure, outcomes must make a worthwhile difference for the customer and put the enterprise in a better position, but within a budget cap. After all, someone has to pay for the project!

Best Value Defined

Best value means getting the greatest satisfaction for the invested resources.

A best-value outcome is the lowest cost for what is delivered, even though what is delivered might not conform to the original vision. Indeed, best value may actually be *more scope* than envisioned, but at an exceptional and affordable investment.

A best-value outcome is the most value-added outcome achievable. *Most value-added* means the project is maximally lean about operating expenses and resource consumption. It also means that the difference between the value of preproject ideas and opportunities and the value of useful products and services post-project is maximized. Revisit Figure 2-2 for a pictorial of this discussion.

A project management tip	Best value is the answer to scope
	• Even though scope is flexible, stakeholder expectations might be more rigid. • The best answer for satisfying stakeholders is to always provide the most benefit for the investment made—to maximize the value returned.

Scope Defined

Scope is all the things we *must do*, all the things we *want to do*, and all the things we *actually do.*

The capture tool for scope is the work breakdown structure (WBS). The WBS clarifies dynamic boundaries between teams, iterations, and releases as the solution evolves. Within the WBS is all the scope—as planned just-in-time—but not more than all the scope! Scope on the WBS respects the rules of governance.

There are some *must-do's* that influence scope: *Must do's* as a matter of governance and *must do's* as a matter of custom and expectation. Projects must adhere to standards that have become generally accepted practices; processes and protocols must be applied in a manner that is consistent with certifications; and projects must meet the unspoken demands of the market that over time have become routinely expected—demands for reliability, availability, compatibility, responsiveness, and ecofriendliness, to name a few.

Vision Is the Beginning

One cannot precisely mandate how to envision a product goal anymore than one can legislate imagination. Transforming visionary ideas into goals—real end states that are achievable—is a work of art, a bit of process, and a dose of applied leadership. The story usually begins as, "I had this idea one day . . .," however, imagination is but step one.

Envisioning

Envisioning is an investment in ideas. The common understanding is that an unformed or immature idea is given richness and detail, conformed to the value system of the enterprise, and then made actionable by a project team. A filled-in business case is the capture vehicle for envisioning. Recall from Chapter 2 that in the business case, a high-level business story describes the need. A product vision is offered. A concept of operations, albeit of low fidelity, identifies the community of users and those that support them by roles and their needed features and functions. Value is given specificity by the investment budget and milestones.

To envision beyond the business case, add depth and breadth to the business story. Consider these three steps:

1. *Assemble the agile team and interview the visionary:* Begin building executive and customer relationships. Involve everyone on the team to leverage multifunctional experiences. Get as much of a picture, in any and several forms, as possible—verbal, written, and the unspoken gesture. Take advantage of a person-to-person encounter to absorb the fullness of being present together—environment, responsiveness, and attitude; establish credibility with probing questions; be open to novel ideas and compelling motivations.[3]

   Search for the beginning. The *big idea* may have come as an epiphany, but more likely, it evolved over time by means of many informal conversations, and only then was shaped by influences from the media, market, and friends. The opportunity may be the fortunate confluence of technology availability and market receptiveness. Perhaps the idea is a reaction to successful competitors, external threats, or some other *push*. Opportunity and creativity might be unleashed because of public policy; or there could be a great national imperative that demands innovation.

In *Winning at New Products,* Robert G. Cooper writes, "... the game is won in the first few plays.... The seeds of disaster [are] often sown in the early phases ... [arising from] poor homework, lack of customer orientation, and poor quality of execution ..."[4] Cooper goes on to list 11 ways to get and absorb good ideas, but the first three are the most helpful:

Developing good ideas

1. Identify a focal point to bring all the ideas, information, and interviews together.
2. List all the contributing sources that could add value to the idea formulation.
3. Engage both the customer and users!

2. *Explore ideas:* Spin them about in a 360° view. What do they look like from the points of view of the customer, user, supply chain, sales, marketing, and product support? Draw, diagram, or write down the ideas from each and look for affinity and common ground. One piece of advice: *If you cannot draw it, you cannot write it!*
3. *Do a Kano analysis of features and functions:*[5] Kano analysis is done on a Kano chart, a graphical tool for portraying product features and functions in relation to customer satisfaction.

Envision with Kano Charts

As shown in Figure 5-1, the chart has four quadrants separated by horizontal and vertical axes. The horizontal is the product axis and the vertical is the customer axis. Features and functions that lie along the horizontal axis have no particular customer appeal. Customers are indifferent to these but they are still required by standards and conventions.

Opportunities and threats describe the four quadrants. The upper-right quadrant is the *ah-hah!* space. In the upper-right quadrant there is high customer satisfaction and a unique product value. The lower left is just the opposite: missing product value and correspondingly poor customer satisfaction. The two remaining quadrants are the middle ground between customer and product value.

Kano analysis provides further insights:

- Features that lie along the horizontal axis require a continuous investment but return little in customer loyalty; customers expect them in every product so they rarely provide any discriminating value.
- Features in the upper-right quadrant are usually high-value, high-investment opportunities. But as competitors recognize the attractiveness and provide similar offerings, these features decay towards the horizontal axis over time.

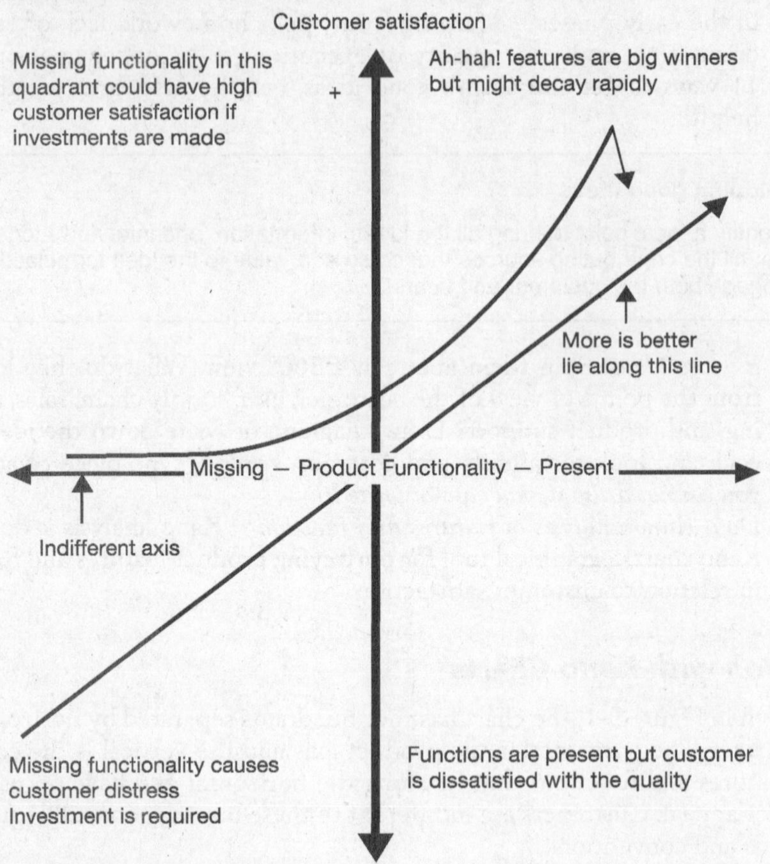

Figure 5-1 Kano analysis chart

- Features that are missing—as identified in the lower-left quadrant—become a must-do investment to catch up with evolving expectations of the market. Investments in this quadrant are a form of me-too investing that simply levels the field for discriminators or disqualifiers.

An Agile Partnership with the Customer Is Built on Rights and Responsibilities

The essence of the agile mindset is an unshakable focus on getting it right for the customer. *Getting it right* about scope and requirements requires forming an effective give-and-take relationship with the business and the user community to discern deliverables that are simple, timely, and targeted to hit the value mark.

Karl E. Wiegers, a well-respected specialist in project requirements, posits a bill of rights and responsibilities for the customer-project team partnership. For the customer, he cites 10 rights and 10 responsibilities.[6] Among these are several that are directly on point with the agile community, paraphrased as *the customer has a right to expect*.

Customer Rights
The customer has a right to expect: • The project team to speak the customer's language. • The project team to treat the customer with respect and maintain a professional collaboration. • To be presented with the opportunity to make adjustments and changes. • To receive a system that meets both quality and functional needs.

But the customer has responsibilities as well.

Customer Responsibilities
The customer has the responsibility to: • Invest their time and energy to educate the project team about the business and its requirements. • Make timely decisions that will maintain the work flow. • Establish priorities to organize work effectively. • Communicate changes as soon as they are known.

On the other hand, the project has rights and responsibilities. It is pretty much a flip of the customer list. The team has a right to expect that customers will exercise their responsibilities. For example, expanding on Wieger's list:

Team Rights
The team has the right to expect that customers will: • Commit to close and personal participation on the agile teams in a timeframe conducive to good progress. • Put to immediate operational use the incremental deliverables. • Complete evaluations of new releases in a timely manner. • Respect the backlog freeze during the iteration development.

Team Rights (continued)

- Respect the line between a functional requirement and a design specification; the former is the customer's responsibility and the latter is the project team's responsibility. Respecting the line is the ageless tension between the *what* and the *how*.
- Be honest about the so-called wicked problem if it arises. A *wicked problem* is one that seems to have no specification—the problem statement is back-fitted from a solution.[7]

Wicked Thinking

Wicked problem solving has a natural affinity with agile methods, because to solve a wicked problem, the analyst thinks iteratively rather than linearly—somewhat like a spiral—and generally begins with the end in mind. Try to imagine the desired end state first, and then work back to what the requirements must be.[8]

Wicked thinking arises when there are many interlocking issues and competing stakeholders for which there seems no obvious point of entry. All resolutions seem to conflict with something else.

Problems such as these also arise when constraints constantly change, thereby introducing new conflicts and dependencies that force the solution to change as well.

Wicked problems are a constant test of whether any specific outcome is ever really an answer. A sure sign of the wicked problem is constant spinning about on an issue.

There Is a Process for Requirements

The literature of projects is rich with guidance for developing detailed requirements, not only for software, but also for all manner of engineering disciplines. In plan-centric methods, some call developing requirements *structured analysis*, some call it *requirements engineering*, some simply call it *the requirements process*, and others may not have any name at all. Taken all together, there are literally dozens of practices hosted in one methodology or another.[9]

Agile methods go about requirements in more natural language—the language of themes, scenarios, and stories, much like the way this book is put together with major themes at each chapter heading and lesser themes to discriminate major sections. Agile methodologists begin with the top-level themes—business stories in the business case—which are then built out into use cases that are then dissected into user stories and ultimately into TDD scripts.

How to Write Requirements for Software

IEEE 830:[10]

In a word, the guidance for writing software requirements for a PD-PDLC, normally taken to be IEEE 830-1998 *Recommended Practice for Software Requirements*, is not usually applied to agile methods, primarily because 830-style requirements are product-focused lists of functions and features—a return to Deming—rather than a customer and user focus on why features and functions are needed—an embrace of Juran's trilogy.

There is danger in 830-style requirements because in practice they are more *push* than *pull* in the lean sense of the words. There is a tendency to list many requirements that have marginal day-to-day usefulness since there is minimal means for customers to express priorities in the traditional PD-PDLC.

Use cases:

Use cases originated in the so-called Rational Unified Process. Use cases are supported by many tools and aides; the text style can be very lean and agile. Use cases are strongly recommended in the Crystal family agile methods.

The main feature of the use case is the scenario, a generally complete story of user need. Scenarios are very applicable to agile methods, as discussed in Chapter 4.

It is easier to maintain coherence with architecture using a higher-level and more complete description like a use case.

User stories:

User stories are vignettes of scenarios. User stories originated as an XP practice as a means to express functional requirements. User stories can be identified by decomposing use-case scenarios.

Recommendation:

In this book, we recommend use-case scenarios and user-story vignettes to document user functional requirements.

Begin with a Framework

The business case, vision of the solution, and customer partnership are the prerequisites for building-out requirements. There are six steps:

1. Adopt the business story and product vision as the pinnacle of a requirements framework.
2. Assemble summary-level low-fidelity use-case scenarios that identify the user community, user roles, and user processes, the operating conditions or states, and the needed feature function and performance. The summary scenarios become the project-level backlog.
3. Parse the project backlog into planning-wave backlogs according to customer priority, technical feasibility, and sequencing governed by architecture. Planning waves are time horizons, each one more distant. Scope is allocated to each planning wave; each scope allocation is progressively

less detailed and more loosely defined for the waves farther out in time. Planning waves are discussed in Chapter 6.

4. As each wave comes up for planning in detail, parse the wave backlogs into iteration backlogs, again taking into account sequencing, feasibility, and business priorities.
5. During the iteration planning session, as discussed in Chapter 6, decompose the use-case backlog into user stories. Prioritize the stories and implement those that fit the team's capacity for one iteration time box. Those that do not fit are reallocated to the next backlog.
6. After each iteration, release, and wave, the requirements backlog is restacked according to priority. Apply governance to introduce new and materially changed requirements.

Figure 5-2 illustrates the discussion.

Framework Practices

The steps described in Table 5-1 guide overall agile requirements processing. By tailoring and adaption, the 5-1 steps are applicable at any level of the framework as shown in Figure 5-2.[11]

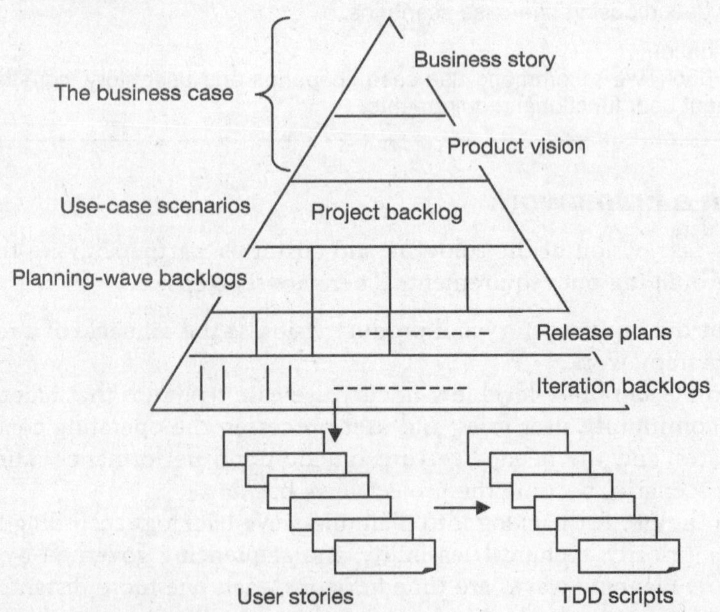

Figure 5-2 Requirements framework

Table 5-1 Framework practices

Process step	Commentary
Gather requirements	• Seek, identify, and gather requirements by interviewing stakeholders and accessing other relevant business and regulatory materials ranging from small to big-picture details. • Be conversational; many requirements are latent, only surface through conversation and discussion. • Probe for functional and nonfunctional requirements to include performance, environmental, regulatory, quality, and other needs. • Select interview candidates from sales, marketing, users, service and maintenance, supply chain, and other infrastructure support, as well as ancillary groups such as training and HR.
Organize according to attributes	• Organize requirements by affinity and hierarchy, and possibly by categories such as high risk, interface, user, etc. • Set an initial priority among requirements. Since agile methods encourage requirements to vary to fit demand, priorities will also. • Examine feasibility, affordability, and consistency with architecture and legacy demands. • Prototype and model, especially if approaching significant risks where a spiral front-end process is effective. • Estimate complexity as a figure or merit until detail estimates are made in the iteration.
Make a record of every requirement	• Index cards for user stories and class-responsibility-collaborator (CRC) class models, etc.; are expedient but temporary. • Commit requirements to a template managed by a database; the database enables tracing and tracking requirements to stories and vision. • If using TDD from the XP methodology, document requirements at the lowest level with a test procedure.
Verify and validate	• Verify completeness, compliance, accuracy, and testability of the solution by answering the question, *Are these the requirements to do the job right?* • Validate to answer the question, *Are these the requirements to do the right job?*
Manage changes	• Develop and employ a protocol to elicit changes, manage validation, and manage priorities. • Develop and employ a governance program as an integral part of change management.

Successful Interviews

Talking to executives, customers, sponsors, stakeholders, and users is the one best way to find out what is on everybody's mind. Sometimes a casual conversation works best, providing opportunity to absorb the general atmosphere of the situation—something Alistair Cockburn calls communication by osmosis. Other times, it is more appropriate to structure an interview.

There are many helpful references for interviewing for needs and wants.[12] They can be distilled to a few commonsense guidelines, as given in Table 5-2.

Table 5-2 Guidelines for interviewing for needs and wants

Action	Comment
Interview with a small team in a comfortable and familiar setting.	• Focus questions through one person. A second person helps with the conversation and observes nonverbal signs, and a third takes notes. • Adopt a familiar setting to remove distractions and thereby facilitate focus on the topic.
Prepare; have an interview agenda or outline and do homework to be subject-matter conversant.	• Share the agenda in advance, but let the conversation flow to unanticipated points or to points that are out of order. • Bring a subject-matter expert into the preparations, but minimize jargon unless commonly understood by the group.
Ask questions that cannot be answered with one word, being cautious not to lead the interview to a foregone conclusion.	• Engage in conversation. This is necessary to enrich the experience with detail and metaphor, fill out the value proposition, and find the limits of risk tolerance. • Capture the minutiae for fit later with the bigger concepts.
Follow up on the corollary or flip side of the question.	• Ask questions from many points of view. The 360-perspective is always revealing and useful for evaluating and setting priorities for items not on the critical path.[1] • Complete the circle of concept examination. What would the customer, competitor, or supplier say that differed from an internal stakeholder?
Search for the minimum, but seek the horizon.	• Find the simplest thing to do. Agile methods stress the importance of not doing everything at once, rolling out sequentially until the limits are reached. • Get a sense of the minimum, anticipate a plan for a bit more, and probe for the limits of the opportunity.
Remember the project balance sheet! Test for risk tolerance.	• Probe for an eagerness for upside opportunity, downside limitations, and triggers that are sensitized by attitude.

Teams Work with Stories, Models, and Prototypes

The detailed work on development requirements are done by teams. Development teams work at the last couple of layers illustrated in Figure 5-2. Analysis and examination of the backlog begins in a session called *Iteration-0*.

Iteration-0

The team prepares working materials, infrastructure, and the backlog in the first iteration, Iteration-0. The 0 signifies that the iteration produces no product. The two prerequisites to Iteration-0 are:

1. The top-level theme and business story has been developed following interview steps as in Table 5-1. Some methodologists call the top level an epic
2. The project-level backlog has been developed and parsed into planning-wave backlogs as illustrated in Figure 5-2

To execute Iteration-0, follow the steps in Table 5-3:

Table 5-3 Iteration-0

Step	Commentary
Assemble the team	• Ensure everyone, including the customer, participates
Organize information	• Topically organize all the information using white boards, sticky notes, or other means • Form affinity groups, typically by scenarios that are themselves a collection of stories • Create hierarchies to organize little ideas under big topics; create relationships between affinity groups
Interview for completeness	• Conduct more interviews to fill in the blanks and confirm relationships
Allocate requirements to iterations	• Allocate a set of requirements from the planning wave backlog to the iteration • Consider customer priorities, functional or technical sequencing, feasibility, and available technology
Create a story card	• If not using use cases and the UML, commit one testable requirement to a card or spreadsheet record • Add amplifying or clarifying information
Estimate complexity	• By group consensus, arrive at a figure of merit for the complexity and effort for each testable requirement
Create a burn-down list (SCRUM) or burn-up list (XP)	• List all requirements with attributes for who, what sequence, how much effort, what status—hours to finish
TDD	• If TDD is a team practice, commit the requirement to a test script

Use Cases, User Stories, Models, and Prototypes

Use cases, user stories, models, and prototypes are all tools to get a mind's-eye image of the requirement.

- *Use cases:* Alistair Cockburn, the godfather of Crystal methods, is a strong advocate for use cases. Use cases are ordinarily thought of as a model of the requirement, which can be presented graphically, pictorially, or in text. However, use cases also lend themselves to models supported by the Unified Modeling Language, commonly called UML.

Unified Modeling Language (UML)

UML is a tool that facilitates visualizing, specifying, constructing, and documenting system artifacts.[13]

UML provides a means to structure the case elements and allows for a scripted evaluation of the model for completeness, accuracy, redundancy, and efficiency.

UML has three building blocks: things, relationships, and diagrams.

1. Things are *structural* meaning nouns, *behavioral* meaning verbs, *grouping* meaning organizational parts, and *annotational* meaning explanatory
2. Relationships express associations and dependencies
3. Diagrams are graphical presentations of the language

A use case is a scenario. Recall from Chapter 4 that a scenario is a functional script with specific conditions. In the pecking order, use cases are more complex and involved than user-story vignettes are; several user stories are typically contained within a single use case. The use-case specification includes identification of human and system actors, the main scenario, and success criteria for the scenario. Pre- and post-conditions on the system and actors are specified—somewhat like specifying asserts—and triggers that initiate action are identified. Alternate situations, called extensions, are described. There might be other use cases related to the use case under discussion, referred to as *inclusions* or *extensions*.[14] The main scenario is the normal course of action; alternatives and error or contingency responses included by extensions. *Inclusions* are like subroutines in the main scenario. Figure 5-3 depicts a typical use case.

- *User stories:* Many agile methodologists write user stories on index cards and post them in a common area. Cards are decidedly low-tech to be sure, but posting cards is effective for common access. To scale up, electronic facsimiles are used, including spreadsheets.

  Obviously, the index card method imposes a limitation on content and detail—purposefully so. One or two sentences usually suffice for the story. The functional complexity is limited to that which can be developed in a

The use case explains the business story with an actionable scenario

	Use case: Place a product order
Business story	• An order placement clerk places an order for an item that is on a price list associated with an existing customer. • All customer account, sales credits, pricing, and product information fill the order automatically; the order is scheduled for fulfillment. • Acknowledgment is provided when the order is closed. Manual overrides are allowed.
Main actors	• Order placement clerk. • Order entry, pricing, and customer profile application.
Main scenario	• Order placement clerk selects *new order* to pull up a blank order entry screen and enters customer identification number. • Order header fills automatically from the customer's account profile. • Clerk enters product identifiers and quantities on an order line. • Product accessories and options are configured automatically. • Pricing and billing information is filled automatically. • Order is scheduled for fulfillment. • An order acknowledgment with confirmation is produced when the order is submitted. • Sales credits are posted automatically to account sales team.
Initial conditions	• Customer account is set up in the customer database. • Product is configured in the inventory system. • Price lists are configured for the customer-product combination.
Success criteria—minimum	• An order is confirmed.
Success criteria—nominal	• An order is confirmed, scheduled for delivery, and priced according to the customer's account.
Trigger	• Purchase order from customer.
Extensions	• If pricing is not available for the selected product, pricing application provides alert to screen. • Clerk is allowed to price the order on-the-fly. • Clerk is empowered to override pricing. • Clerk is empowered to override options and accessories. • Clerk is empowered to override sales credits to sales staff.

Figure 5-3 Use case example 07012009

matter of a few days. Amplifying detail is written on the back of the card or on companion cards. User-story detail is enriched by conversation with the end user at the time a developer begins work. Subsequently, the developer documents design-level detail with test scripts.

One suggestion for a simple story outline is: Actor <*name*> acting in role <*role label*> according to action <*action verb*> with attributes <*skills, security, time of day, etc*> has expectation <*result of action*> because <*motivation for action, reason for storyline, or dependencies or triggers*>[15]

User Story
An *order management associate* acting in the role of *order entry clerk* according to action *select customer* with attributes *order placement and pricing authority, customer account identifier, and customer profile* has the expectation that *order header will fill automatically* because *customer profile information is automatically linked to order header.*

- *Models and prototypes:* Models and prototypes are facsimiles of the end product. Models can be everything from a text description, UML diagram, and user-interface screen mockup to a formal mathematical model, structured diagram, or prototype code. Prototypes are commonly thought of as an actual working device, albeit in a low-fidelity implementation, or an implementation using shortcuts and temporary structures to support the demonstration. Some project managers resist prototypes as throwaway, but refactoring can salvage much of a prototype. Table 5-4 lists the common models encountered.

WBS Is a Tool for Organizing Scope

The tool of choice for organizing top-level scope described in the business plan is the WBS. The WBS in its simplest form is a list of all the deliverables expected of the project, organized similar to a table of contents.[16,17] In a more elaborate presentation, the WBS may have a temporal dimension, organizing the table of deliverables by release, and may also include some of the major tasks that are associated with each deliverable. No matter how it is presented, the WBS is the summary of the business-case deliverables.

Assignment and Verification

The WBS has two management purposes:

1. It is a verification tool
2. It is an assignment tool

Table 5-4 Requirements model tools

Model	Description
Entity relationship diagram (ERD)	• Identifies each logical entity in the system and documents the logical relationship among them.
Data flow diagram (DFD)	• Shows the data flows, directionally, with triggers or stimulus between entities in the system.
Quality function deployment (QFD)	• Provides a related set of matrices that trace requirements through a decomposition and show some cause-and-effect relationship.
Class diagram	• Provides a template for a real object. • An object is a specific instance of a class according to the rules of the template. • Shows relationships between classes, listing the public and private procedures or operations of the class and data requirements of the class.
State transition diagram	• Shows the before-and-after state of a system and the triggering mechanisms to change the state. Initial conditions and postconditions are shown.
Dialog map	• Shows the interaction of the user with the system and the possible navigation paths with triggers and controls. • A *dialog map* is a form of a state transition diagram that mimics the nonlinear method of problem solving that people actually use while conversing. • Summarizes the rationale behind the decisions. • Clearly displays all open issues and action items.
Data dictionary	• Holds the definitions of the data elements in the system. • Typically includes all the attributes such as field size and field type as well as the business and system name and purpose of the data.

As a *verification tool,* the WBS is used to identify all *the scope* in the project and *only the scope* in the project—in other words, the boundaries—because project boundaries are often misunderstood. Sometimes there is even confusion about which deliverables are approved and budgeted.

As an *assignment tool,* the WBS is used to put project effort and scope in the right work stream, planning wave, and release. To get things parsed right and avoid awkward interfaces between work streams, waves, and releases, parent-child relationships are used to facilitate finding natural breaks in the work effort. Figure 5-4 is an example of a table-of-contents style of a WBS with the indenture marking parent-child relationships.

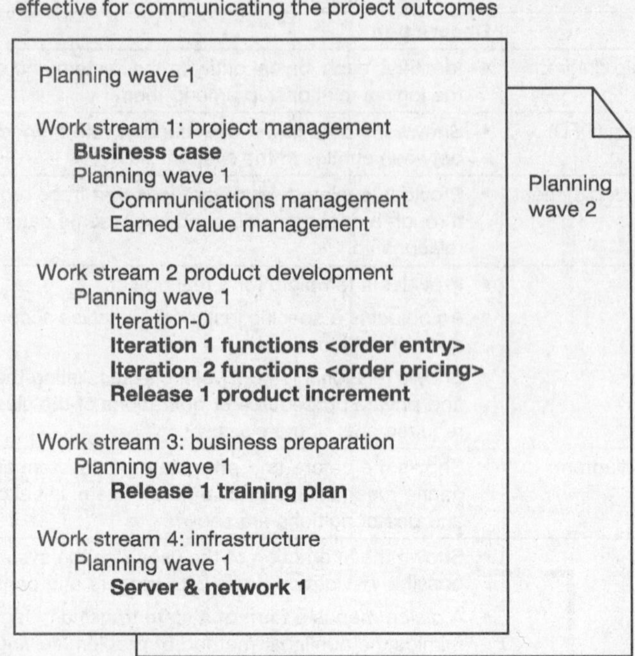

Figure 5-4 WBS ordered list

A recommended management practice is to marry the WBS with the project operating model. To do this, the WBS is shown in a matrix format. When shown with the WBS, the operating model is sometimes referred to as the organizational breakdown structure (OBS). Cross-points in the matrix mark where work intersects with the organization. The WBS-OBS matrix is denoted as the Resource Assignment Matrix (RAM). Figure 5-5 depicts the RAM.

Operating Model
The term *operating model* is used here as a synonym for the organization chart of the project. In many contexts, *organization chart* connotes reorganization and administrative control, whereas the operating model is the way people work at the moment for the project objective. *Operating model* also stands for the roles, responsibilities, and relationships of individuals in the project operation, even if not full-time or administratively assigned.

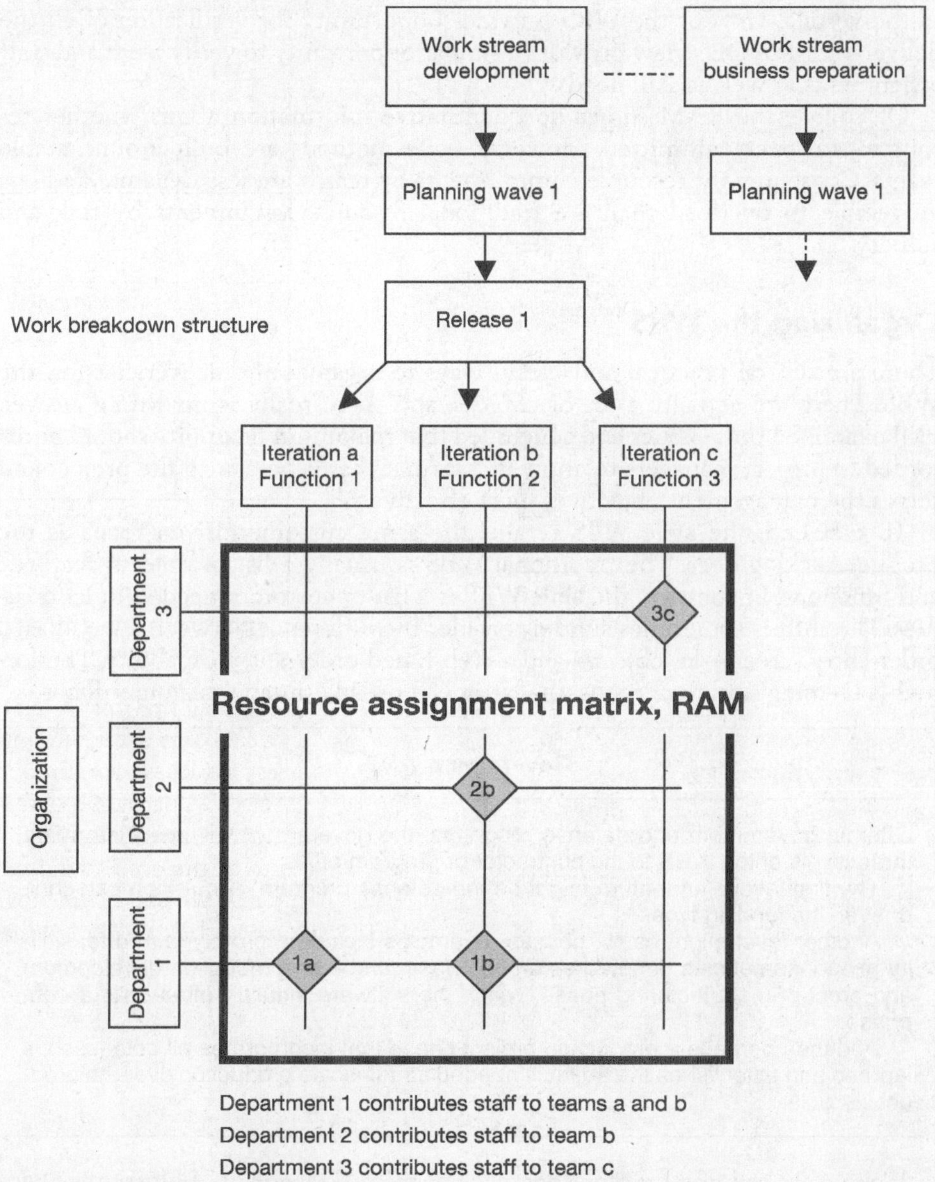

Figure 5-5 RAM version of WBS

Functional managers looking horizontally across the RAM immediately see all the work assigned to their staff from each work stream, wave, or release. Just as the vertical view of the WBS provides opportunity for verification of all the deliverables, the OBS view provides a similar opportunity to verify team and staff assignments as well as skill needs.

Of course, the RAM shows no quantitative information about whether resources are over committed. However, agile methods are built around stable teams. Consequently, resource commitments by teams are less dynamic and less vulnerable to overload than are traditional resource assignments by task and activity.

Organizing the WBS

There are several practical and useful ways to organize the deliverables on the WBS. There are actually a lot of choices, and there really is no wrong answer. PMI examined these issues and concluded that maximum flexibility should be afforded to project managers to apply in a format that is best fit to the project and serves the management objectives most effectively.[18]

To that end, the agile WBS retains the same customer-driven focus as the product backlog does. The traditional WBS is usually a list of objects, features, and functions. In contrast, the agile WBS is a list of customer-needed functionalities. The shift is sometimes subtle; consider the difference between a web-based order-entry screen—an object—and a web-based order-entry capability. The former is Deming's product focus; the latter is more like Juran's customer focus.

Government WBS

Often in government and defense programs, the government will specify the first three levels of the WBS to the contractor or program office.

The first level of indenture might be the defense program, acquisition category, or even the funding type.[19]

Another level might be for phases. Examples include a prototype and feasibility phase, sometimes denoted as *alpha phase*; and a preproduction development and proof-of-manufacturing phase, which the software industry often calls a *beta phase*.

And then perhaps a production project phase that incorporates all beta lessons learned and establishes the artifacts needed for full-scale production over the product lifecycle.

If there are temporal dimensions, such as releases, Figure 5-4 illustrates a way to include them in the WBS. The planning wave, sometimes called the planning horizon, is one such dimension. A wave is a unit of time typically three to six months in duration that is divided into several releases, within which the big-picture requirements are relatively stable. Chapter 6 describes planning waves in more detail. Suffice to say that each planning wave offers the opportunity to readdress the project plan.

The example WBS in Figure 5-4 also shows work streams. All projects of a nontrivial scale will have some work-stream structure. Typically, these are:

- Project management and the program office
- Design, development, and test; sometimes validation is completed by an independent system-test work stream
- Business preparation, to include business change management, user and support training including sales and marketing, as well as post-release product support and operational design required for restructuring the enterprise if that is a project objective
- Infrastructure and construction, to include new facilities, networks, major tools and supporting systems including information systems, manufacturing capabilities, and distribution and post-deployment support
- Product preparation, to include preparing marketing, sales, and rollout plans

Other functions may be a work stream onto themselves or they may be folded into another work stream. For example:

- *Architecture and system engineering:* Engineers or developers with architecture and system engineering skills are often placed in the project office to provide project-wide visibility, but at other times they are folded into individual teams to deal closely with product architecture, infrastructure, or construction and manufacturing.
- *Documentation management:* Document managers support development of user instructions and information, warranty services, and field maintenance and service bulletins. If it is a government project, some documentation will be mandated and might require specific data management by a responsible project officer.
- *Sales and marketing preparation:* Teams might support development of marketing artifacts, sales methods and tools, and other materials and programs for product promotion.

A project management tip	WBS and the project work streams
	• The operational part of the WBS begins with the work streams. • The upper administrative levels, such as major phases and planning waves, often are not shown.

Manage Scope Emergence with the Planning Horizon

Even though the business-case product vision, business story, and top-level architecture provide a working framework for deliverables, scope details emerge iteration-by-iteration, unplanned beyond the descriptions given in the project backlog and deferred until developers are ready to address a specific backlog. Central planning gives way to just-in-time planning. Project timelines give way to incremental timelines. Scope is allocated and adjusted according to customer priorities for each increment. The principal increments are defined by the project milestones from the business case; the planning horizon encompassing one or more releases; and the development iteration, one or more of which make up a release.

Detail specification is reserved for relatively short time segments, the longest of which is the planning horizon—a matter of a few months. Beyond the horizon are only fuzzy estimates—some would say guesses—anchored by the top-level architecture.

Over the Horizon with Architecture

Architecture provides scope cohesion from one horizon to the next; as such, architecture should be largely invariant from one horizon to the next. Architecture serves as a framework to which many applications, functionalities, and user features can be fastened; it describes the topology of the system, product, or process.[20] Topology describes hierarchy, interconnectedness, and whether nodes are reached by point-to-point, hub-and-spoke, or some mesh circuitry. Architecture provides the protocols or rules by which elements of the system tie together. It gives form to requirements and tells whether the product is built in layers, tiers, or subsystems. Architecture gives guidance on how loosely coupled components can be, and how cohesive they need to be for good maintenance and operability.

A project management tip	Architecture brings out the best
	• Architecture is the means to bring cohesiveness to disparate requirements. It provides form, shape, and connectedness. • Coherence amplifies individual effects by harmonizing alignment. Coherency wrought by architecture can provide the *ah hah!*

Architecture establishes boundaries, especially the boundaries between interconnected services. In fact, there is an entire body of knowledge around service oriented architecture, formally known as SOA.[21] But the architecture of electronic connectivity has created ambiguity where there was certainty. The question becomes: Exactly where is the business-to-business boundary when there are all manner of documents, service requests, and responder data flowing between nodes?

The architecture of modern systems has introduced enormous security concerns into business and personal domains. Now there must be careful attention to the scope of authentication and authorization, encryption and disguise, solicitation and misrepresentation, intrusion to what used to be sanctuary, and all manner of Trojan horses.

Rolling Wave

All these ideas for managing scope over multiple horizons collect under a concept called *rolling-wave planning*.[22,23] The metaphor is one planning period rolling into another like waves rolling onto a beach, the next wave being planned as the current wave is completed. Each planning period is called a planning wave. The objective is to allow evolution and change to be rolled forward into the next wave so the changes can be incorporated into the product execution plan for that wave.

The wavelength is different in each project. The usual planning wave encompasses more than one release. As a practical matter, the planning wave is a matter of months, about three to six. The idea is that a three-to-six-month horizon is about as far as anyone can see with the confidence necessary to do planning.

Requirement Priorities for Planning Waves

Setting priorities is really about managing impact. The effects of the really important things should be felt first. Stephen Covey writes in his acclaimed book, 7 *Habits of Highly Effective People*, about importance and timeliness. He constructs four quadrants using *importance* and *timeliness* as axes.[24] Covey's idea is shown in Figure 5-6. In a stable project, problems in Quadrant I, *most important-most urgent*, should not come up often. On the occasion when they do, lower-priority work is deferred to free up resources to resolve issues.

Covey's advice is to put real management effort toward Quadrant II, *most important-not urgent*, prioritizing away from Quadrants III and IV to whatever extent possible.

Of course, deciding what scope is important and urgent is often no small task. A good practice is to apply one of three priorities to all requirements since user stories and use cases are too numerous to prioritize individually:

- Priority I: *Minimum must-have* requirements that provide the customer with beneficial and essential features and functions that do not completely satisfy. Some of these might lie along the horizontal axis of the Kano chart; others might be in the upper-right Kano quadrant.

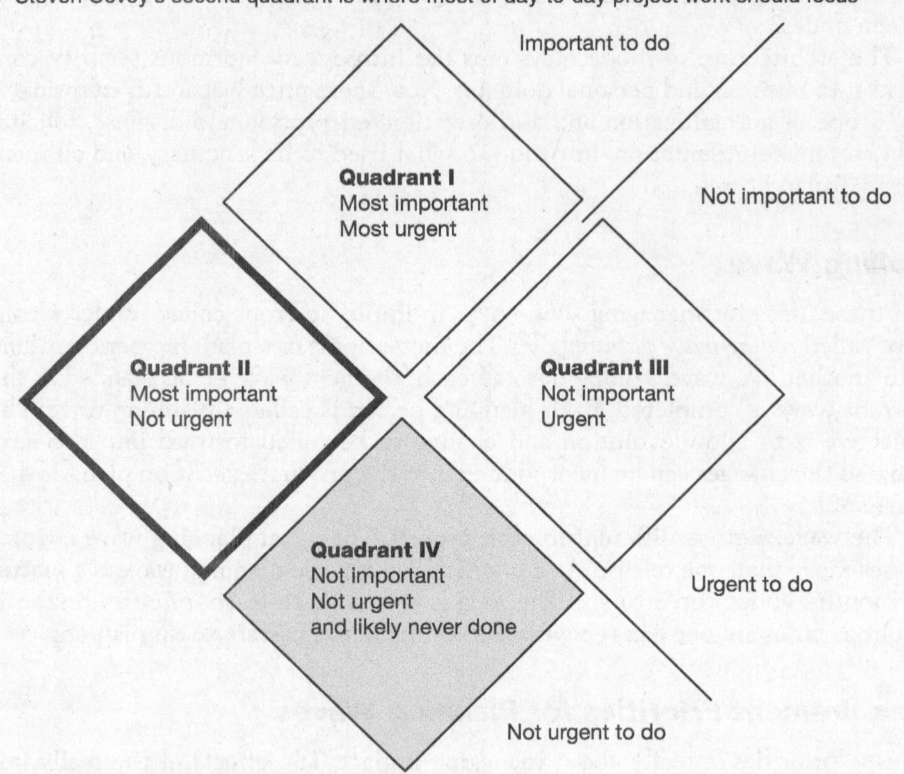

Figure 5-6 Covey's four quadrants

- Priority II: *Useful and wanted* requirements that are the nominal center of what the customer has in mind, perhaps driving much of the benefits. Requirements in this priority are important for benefits, but perhaps not time sensitive. Benefit realization pushes these requirements to the second priority.
- Priority III: *Not essential to the baseline functionality,* yet serve as useful refinements. They add convenience, unique and discriminating features, and improve efficiency, but may only contribute to benefits at the margin. Importance is minimal and there is no time urgency. Some of these might fall into the lower-left Kano quadrant. If missing, they affect customer satisfaction, but if present they do not drive customer attraction.

Unimportant requirements are not prioritized. They will not be implemented except when it becomes necessary to do so for regulatory and certification compliance. Many of these will lie along the horizontal axis of the Kano chart.

Predictability with Planning Waves

An objective of segmenting the project timeline into planning waves is to obtain predictable results, wave by wave. It is not really possible to take on larger projects that have significant investment unless executives and sponsors can be assured of benefits and investment recovery. Planning waves are a strategy for scaling agile methods to the complex scope of larger projects, and for addressing the three scope priorities discussed above. The steps to plan a predictable wave are listed in Table 5-5.

Figure 5-7 shows how the wave planning looks laid against a timeline with customer milestones as the delimiters on releases.

Table 5-5 Planning a predictable wave

Planning step	Commentary
Respect the customer's timeline	• Determine the release schedule based on milestones in the business plan. • Releases to production depend on the customer's ability to absorb change and apply the deliverables. • Releases are made up of iterations. Iterations are typically time boxed to a few weeks.
Allocate team capacity according to priority	• Allocate no more than about two-thirds of the iteration capacity to Scope Priority I, leaving one-third as slack. • If the planning risk tolerance is more conservative, back off to half. • Allocate the remaining capacity to Priorities II and III.
Fit requirements to available capacity	• Estimate the complexity of requirements. • Create a backlog based on the capacity available to handle the estimated complexity.
Plan a buffer between iterations	• Assume some overrun will need to be absorbed by the buffer.
Plan a release from the iteration schedule	• Plan a release around the business-case milestones. • Respect the customer's input regarding importance and urgency. • Take into account technical feasibility, functional sequencing, and dependencies with other teams and work streams.

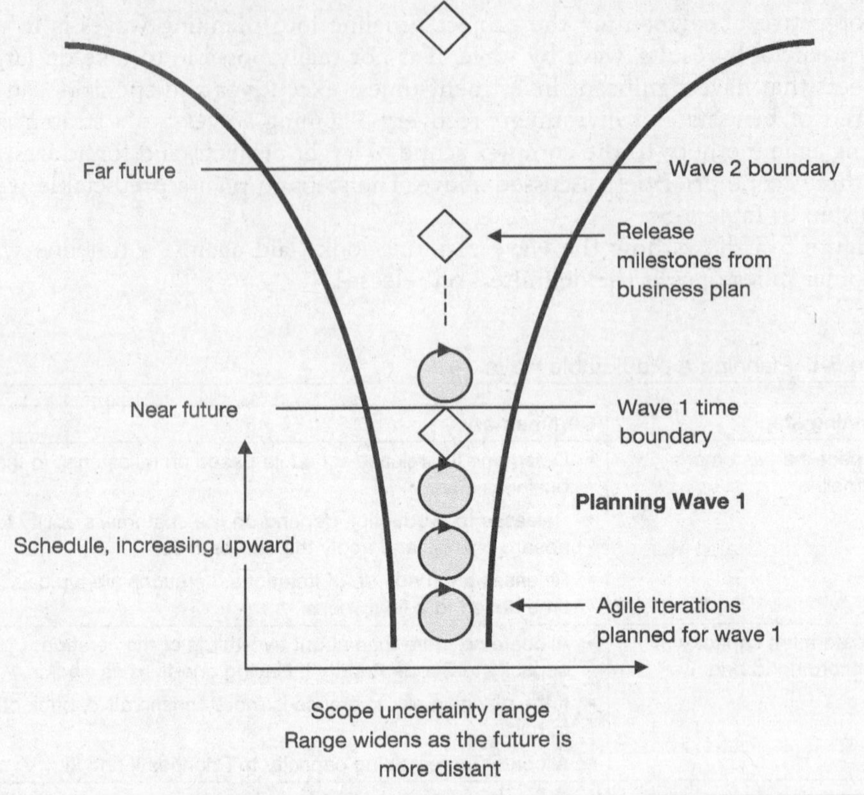

Figure 5-7 Wave planning

Summary and Takeaway Points

The theme of this chapter is that agile methods encourage requirements to change as often as necessary to ensure the customer receives the best value for the resources committed. A best-value outcome is the lowest cost for what is delivered, even though what is delivered might not conform exactly as originally envisioned.

> Best value means getting the highest satisfaction for the invested resources.

Requirements begin with the vision of functions and features provided in the business case. The first step for the project is to interview the visionaries and others who have product knowledge. The interviews fill in the details not written in the business case. Iteration-0 is the planning session to process the interview data, fashion the backlog for the project, and set the initial priorities.

The work breakdown structure is a useful tool to keep all the deliverables organized. In simplest form, it is a list of everything within the scope of the project that is expected by the sponsor and needed by the customer.

The point of agile methods is to be adaptive and responsive to changing requirements. The consequence is that the look ahead is not too distant. The management response is to plan for only short segments of time, reevaluating after each segment of activity is completed. A planning horizon is the longest of the short segments of time—about three to six months. In this period, a wave of activity is planned consisting of a number of releases, with each release consisting of a number of iterations.

Change is encouraged. Providing best value is providing the most valuable outcomes possible within the capacity to respond to ever-changing priorities and needs.

Chapter Endnotes

1. Ollhoff and Walcheski, *Stepping in Wholes: Introduction to Complex Systems,* 86.

2. Adaptive feedback systems, sometimes called *complex adaptive systems* (CAS), have been studied extensively in social and biological systems. The term *CAS* was coined at the Santa Fe Institute by Dr. John Holland et al., noted academics in the field. Complex adaptive systems are nonlinear; their outputs are not weighted sums of their independent elements, as given in the classic linear equation:

$$\text{output} = a \times \text{input} + b$$

Where a is a weighting and b is an initial condition or bias. Traditional use of feedback is to improve linearity and to faithfully follow, transform, or reproduce inputs. Linear feedback systems are described in Hellerstein, *Feedback Control of Computing Systems,* 5. CAS produce output based on agents and agent processes interacting in seemingly unpredictable ways, adapting to circumstances, but bound by rules set down by governance. Such output is often called *emergent*: the interaction of simple rules and parts creates very complex systems and responses. For an introduction to CAS, see Ollhoff and Walcheski, *Stepping in Wholes: Introduction to Complex Systems,* Chapter 20; Holland, *Emergence: from Chaos to Order,* Chapter 3.

3. See McQuaririe, *Customer Visits: Building a Better Market Focus,* 21–24 for an excellent reference for executive and customer visits.

4. Cooper, *Winning at New Products,* 121.

5. Goodpasture, *Quantitative Methods in Project Management,* 8–13.

6. Wiegers, *Software Requirements,* 26–34.

7. Conklin and Weil, *Wicked Problems: Naming the Pain.* This is one of several works by Jeffery Conklin on the subject of problem solving and wicked problems in particular.

8. Issue-based information system (IBIS), is a methodology for working on wicked problems. A construct called a QIA is used: question, idea, and argument. The *question* is about the desired end state. *Ideas* are offered about how to get there. The *argument* weighs advantages and disadvantages of each idea. The process envisions first a great diversion and then a conversion to an agreed approach, followed by endorsement and implementation.

9. The major standards bodies for the international community, specifically ISO and IEC, and in the United States, EIA and IEEE, have numerous standards for requirements engineering in various disciplines. In software for example, 12207 is the ISO, IEEE/EIA, and DoD standard for software lifecycles. IEEE/EIA 830 addresses software requirements and is a compatible implementation standard for 12207 compliance. Other groups, like the Software Engineering Institute, have practice guides for requirements engineering. Similar standards extend to quality engineering, and all manner of engineering for networks, hardware, safety, environmental, and many others. [International Organization for Standardization (ISO); International Electro-Technical Convention (IEC); Electronics Industry Association (EIA); Institute of Electrical and Electronics Engineers (IEEE); U.S. Department of Defense (DoD).]

10. For more information on requirement methodology tradeoffs, Michael Cohn's text provides insight. Bear in mind Cohn is a proponent of user stories, not use cases or 830-style requirements; Cohn, *User Stories Applied for Software Development*, Chapter 12.

11. For more information, the reader is referred to SEI at Carnegie-Mellon University, www.sei.cmu.edu, *Requirements Engineering;* Wieger's *Software Requirements*, Chapter 3; Sommerville and Sawyer, *Requirements Engineering: A Good Practice Guide*, 11.

12. See McQuarrie, *Customer Visits: Building a Better Market Focus*, Chapter 4; Wiegers, *Software Requirements*, Chapters 7 and 8; Kulak and Guiney, *Use Cases: Requirements in Context*, Chapter 4.

13. Booch, Grady, Rumbaugh, and Jacobson, *The Unified Modeling Language User Guide*, 14, 17–26.

14. Cockburn, *Writing Effective Use Cases*, 2–6.

15. Another similar outline for human users is given by Kelly Waters on his website www.agile-software-development.com in the form of "As a <user> I want to <goal> so I can <reason>".

16. The PMI Project Management Body of Knowledge includes a practice standard for the work breakdown structure. In the U.S. Government, the guidance handbook MIL-HDBK-881A has been the guidance document until 2009 when it was announced by the Under Secretary of Defense for Acquisition, Tech-

nology, and Logistics in a memorandum of January 9, 2009, that it would be replaced by a standard mandating WBS practices in defense programs.

17. Goodpasture, *Quantitative Methods in Project Management*, Chapter 3.

18. Berg and Colenso, "Work breakdown structure practice standard project," 69–71.

19. The defense budget is divided into major budget programs; for example, budget Program 6 is research and development. Projects of large scale are called *programs* that are then given acquisition categories, largely according to a dollar scale. Appropriations are made for specific purposes and allocated by public law. Some of interest to project management are research-development-test-evaluation, procurement, operations and maintenance, military construction, and others.

20. In this book, words are used interchangeably to represent the project outcomes: *Product, system,* and *deliverable*. The outcome could be tangible, such as a consumer product, or intangible, such as a service. The project outcome could be a new process applied internally in the enterprise. Except in the most trivial of cases, most outcomes depend on being part of a system, whether legacy or new-to-the-world. In this sense, consumer devices like telephones are systems.

21. Service oriented architecture (SOA), proposes that business activities are packaged as services and are called upon by users to deliver services in standard ways. SOA spans organizational boundaries, both business-to-business and between and among business units in an organization.

22. Goodpasture, *Quantitative Methods in Project Management*, Chapter 7.

23. Goodpasture, "A risk perspective: Rolling wave planning is a bet," 48–53.

24. Covey, *7 Habits of Highly Effective People*, 150–183.

Table Endnote

1. The critical path is a scheduling concept. In a series of project tasks, it is the path from inception to completion that is longest, ultimately determining the length of the overall project. *Any slip along this path causes the end date to slip.* Slips to tasks outside the critical path have little to no effect on the end date.

6

Planning Cost and Schedule

Adapting plans and estimates to changing customer needs and maximizing value at an affordable cost are the planning imperatives for agile projects.[1]

Planning is everything. Plans are nothing. No plan survives contact with [reality].

Field Marshall Helmuth Graf von Moltke

A few activities dominate almost every aspect of project management, whether for agile projects or others—planning and estimating on the one hand, communicating and executing on the other. Managed properly, the ideal project trajectory hits within reasonable error bounds of targeted cost and schedule while satisfying customers to the maximum extent possible. Taken together, planning, estimating, communicating, and executing are a big stage. This chapter takes up planning for cost and schedule.

Plans are not altogether objective, taking into account as they do values, conventions, and business imperatives of the enterprise. But even without complete objectivity, plans are an effective tool to provide the rationale and evidence that stakeholders require for committing resources. But to be credible, evidence needs backup in the form of estimates. Estimates we define as the objective results of analysis and melding of historical performance with judgment about future achievement. Estimates are the subject of Chapter 7 where they are discussed in detail.

It's Agile! Why Plan?

If there are no plans, any outcome is acceptable; if there are no plans, there is nothing to estimate; without estimates, there is no reason to measure. Without measurements, there will be no benchmarks, no improvement, and no answer to the questions of *where are we?* and *what are we doing?* In fact, without a plan, anywhere and anything will do.

So the team needs a plan, but a plan consistent with the role of the project manager to facilitate and motivate performance—not to direct the team's day-to-day activities.[2] Look back to Principle 5 of the Agile Principles given in Chapter 1:

> **Agile Principle 5**
>
> Build projects around motivated individuals.
>
> Give them the environment and support they need, and trust them to get the job done.

The operative phrase here is *to get the job done*. What job?

- It is the job described in the business plan and in subsequent project plans, albeit lean plans consistent with the Agile Manifesto
- It is the job as interpreted in near real time by the functional user
- It is the job that evolves over several iterations and is adapted to the emergent value proposition

Empirical process control, emergent solutions, nonlinear methods, customer-driven value—with all of these unplannables, is it possible to make a useful plan? Yes, the agile team can be coached to converge on an acceptable solution within a reasonable range of possibilities. Some governance and project management are needed, just enough architecture is required, and a planning framework called *rolling wave planning* is necessary for adaptive plans.[3]

Agile Plans Adapt

Agile projects are expected to adapt repeatedly in close proximity to the need. The working assumption is that the complexities of intangible requirements and systems preclude knowing enough to write a complete plan at the outset. Much like the wicked problem, the solution will ultimately define the need. Furthermore, the team is expected to modify practices appropriate to the evolving product, mentored by the project manager and other subject-matter experts.

Plans must adapt if for no other reason than because planning is the creative and innovative part of management. Planning is thinking; planning requires thoughtful consideration about an intended course of action. And planning is where many of the discriminating *ah-hah!'s* emerge. Planning creates a focus, forces creativity to be committed, and adds order to what might otherwise be chaos.

In plan-driven project development lifecycle (PD-PDLC) methods, planning absorbs many resources—it is hard to do in the first place, and once done, detailed plans are even more consuming to maintain so that they retain their relevance and value. In reaction to the experience of the PD-PDLC, the Agile Manifesto steers the other way. Discussion, debate, and conversation are valued over documentation, but documentation is not absent, only minimized to improve effectiveness.

A project management tip	Plan sufficiently
	• Caution is advised—adopting too literal of an interpretation of the Agile Manifesto may lead to underplanning, insufficient to properly represent the project to the stakeholders and provide guidance to the teams.

Planning the Balance Sheet

Consider again the project balance sheet introduced in Chapter 2. The business plan is represented on the left side. The plan not only provides the goal and the product vision, but specifies the investment and lays down milestones for beneficial outcomes. In effect, the business side of the project balance sheet is about targets and goals—targets for cost, schedule, scope, and benefits.

Even for relatively simple Level 0 plans, it is very likely that the business planners are indifferent—perhaps even unwitting—about how practical and achievable their plan is. At least initially that is why the project balance sheet inevitably shows a gap between the business objectives and the project's capacity and capability to meet those objectives. The business may constrain too many variables fixing milestones, scope, and budget. If one variable is most important, then other variables must forcibly adapt. If one of the other variables is not within the control and discretion of the business, then those that the business can control must forcibly adapt.

As an example, industry tradeshows are milestone inflexible—their dates cannot be moved, but the scope for presentations at the tradeshow can be adjusted. And another: consider a project to submit a competitive proposal that includes a product demonstration—the proposal cannot be late, but some product demonstration detail can be deferred until negotiations take place. Remember the millennium: the year 2000 could not be moved to accommodate a late project, but some program modifications could wait one or two quarters past January 1 before a date issue became problematic.

It is necessary for the project to respond to the business plan; first with estimates and then with its own plan that operates with those estimates. A project without a plan leaves the project vulnerable to impracticalities that may be embedded in the business plan. Following the wisdom of Fred Brooks, hunches are not a plan and are no defense if events do not unfold favorably.[4]

A project management tip	Planning is more important than the plan
	• The best use of the plan is to establish the correct starting direction and provide a framework to guide the teams to the next horizon. • With the first unforeseen difficulty, some aspect of the plan will have to change. That is the time the planning experience will pay dividends—when alternatives are required.

Not One Plan

The thing about planning agile projects is that there is not one plan, but many plans, and the plans change frequently. By doctrine, plans are simple in structure and amenable to updating. The planning is distributed over time and among teams as the need arises. Plans will often be just spreadsheet or database templates with certain information filled in. Scorecard templates and a dashboard are lean and useful means to convey the information and support team planning meetings.

Recall Figures 5-2 and 5-4. At each level of the framework and WBS, there will be one or more plans. There will be a business plan as described in Chapter 2, and there will be plans for the work streams, the planning waves and releases, and the team iterations.

These plans will not be implemented simultaneously; most will be deferred until just-in-time. Planning detail will be influenced by project management, customer input, subject-matter experts, and the governance process described in Chapter 8.

Work Stream Plans

Master plans for each work stream on the WBS are derived from the business plan; master plans are adapted horizon-by-horizon. The planning horizon is a time box of sorts applied to the release schedule. All planning conforms to the concept of rolling waves from one horizon to the next. As one horizon is achieved and the next appears, another set of plans are cast.

The project manager maps major business milestones to the work streams. Work-stream milestones are the most important release dates. They frame the planning horizons for product going live to production. Recall Figure 5-7, wave planning, which is adapted to the work-stream planning horizons and shown in Figure 6-1, business case milestone planning horizons. It is evident from Figure 6-1 that the uncertainty of each work stream is not the same; the product development work stream has the most far future uncertainty, reflecting the uncertain influence of customers on the scope of delivered features and functions. On the other hand, project management has relatively little uncertainty, reflecting that the work of project management is insensitive to variations in scope details.

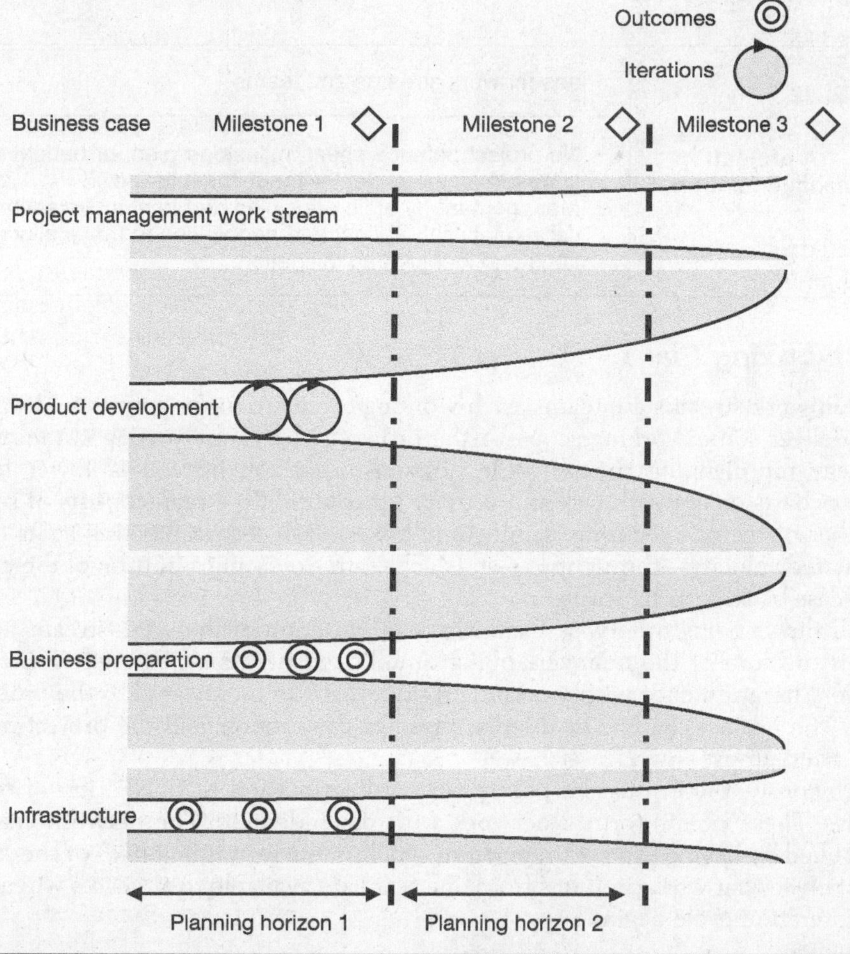

Figure 6-1 Business case milestone planning horizons

A somewhat similar approach is followed to come up with a budget plan for each work stream. Developing the budget at the work-stream level is tantamount to developing the project balance sheet for each work stream. The left side of the balance sheet is developed first and is provided top-down by the business. Investment is usually allocated proportionately to the work streams according to a value judgment by the business. As explained subsequently, other methods may also be appropriate. The right side of the balance sheet is usually built from estimates arrived at by looking at facts and forecasting future performance. Right–to–left side gaps are addressed between the project manager, team leads, and stakeholders.

A project management tip	Plans for work streams and teams
	• No project balance sheet, milestone plan, or budget is imposed on the project without consultation. • Management by agile principles requires conversation, iteration, collaboration, and negotiation to make allocations and identify gap mitigation.

Time-boxing Plans

Within work streams are teams, each working on iterations or sprints to develop and deliver some working scope to the product base. Time boxing is the main strategy for planning the schedule horizon-to-horizon instead of lower level Gantt charts or network task and activity schedules.[5] So a plan consists of some number of teams executing within time boxes, each team operating at its own estimated velocity—throughput—and each team executing a portion of the business-case backlog as its scope.[6]

All things being otherwise fixed, the total duration of the work-stream timeline is the sum of the nonoverlapping time-boxed iterations. By Agile Principle 4, every iteration ends with working product that can be released to the product base. The project can end at the discretion of the sponsor and the project manager after almost any release.

Obviously, there must be points of coordination and reconciliation of team efforts. These points form a network with dependencies. The network can be simplified by having each team perform synchronously in time boxes of the same duration so that work products from one team are available to all teams when the next iteration cycle begins.[7]

Labor Plans Team-by-Team

Given a time-boxed duration and a velocity benchmark team-by-team, a labor plan can be derived for each team and iteration within a planning horizon. These team-iteration labor plans identify individuals, skills, and time commitments. When there is more than one team, key individuals may have to be shared. Multiply the labor plan commitments by the chargeback rate[8] for each resource to obtain the labor-cost plan.

When planning individual commitments, care must be exercised because each team's velocity is sensitive to its cross-functional makeup, its experience skill-by-skill, and its membership—not too few and not too many. The training and experience of the team as a self-organizing and collaborative body, as well as the environment and tools, also affects velocity.

Daily Plan

Each day begins by putting together a daily plan. Teams do this for themselves. The project manager provides facilitation. Each team member contributes a few simple sentences identifying what he or she will work on that day and what accomplishments he or she expects. The plan is reviewed at a morning daily stand-up meeting. The meeting is time boxed to allow each member just a few minutes to talk about his or her personal plan. Every team member is expected to participate and to speak to his or her day's plan. Solutions are not discussed, but if there are needs for special-topic meetings, then these are arranged.

At the end of the day, the results of the day are checked into the product control system. The product base is rebuilt each day whenever practical.

On some teams, an end-of-day stand-up meeting is also held. It is similarly time boxed; it is not a solution meeting. Its purpose is to assess whether the daily plan was successful and to identify impediments and barriers for the project manager to address.

Summary of Plans

Table 6-1 contains an abstract of the discussion:

Table 6-1 Summary of plans

Plan	Commentary
Business plan	• Usually only one required; see Chapter 2 • The business plan establishes the major *business milestones* that are put on a calendar by the project manager • The business plan sets an *affordability cap* for project funding
Work-stream plan	• A *flow down of the business-plan* milestones and budget limits to the work stream according to the WBS • Flow down is controlled by estimates made by the project management staff and team leaders • *Planning detail is rolling wave* in style, reevaluated at each planning horizon
Team plan	• A work assignment plan for the iteration based on the allocated backlog and the team velocity benchmark
Team-network plan	• A plan that shows the points of coordination and dependency among teams working in parallel on the same project
Daily plan	• The working plan for the day developed by each team member for their own activities

Make Agile Plans for Agile Projects

There are many ideas about how to plan for agile projects. This section begins with the idea that plans should be unobtrusive and respectful of self-management principles. We conclude by noting that agile plans envision a rhythm and pace that promotes sustainable productivity.

Principle of Subsidiary Function

Agile methods follow the *principle of subsidiary functions*, which holds that no central authority should do what a subordinate entity can best do for itself; authority that is not specifically enumerated is delegated to subsidiary or subordinate units.

Principle of Subsidiary Function
The concept of subsidiary function, also called subsidiarity, was formally developed by the Roman Catholic Church in the nineteenth century to differentiate responsibilities between the Vatican and other units of the church. First published in the encyclical *Rerum Novarum* of 1891 by Pope Leo XIII, the principle has been extended and widely applied in both government and business. For more information, visit http://en.wikipedia.org/wiki/Subsidiarity.

There are rights and responsibilities that come with this principle. The central authority has a right to expect responsible behavior of its subordinate, but retains the right to verify performance—to trust, but with verification—and intervene to impose corrective action. The subordinate unit has a right to expect a degree of autonomy with reasonable inspection and verification, so long as the subordinate acts responsibly. The subordinate has a responsibility to act in its own interests and in the interests of the central authority, taking care to not over-optimize at a low level.

When the subsidiary function principle is extended to project planning, the first agile planning criteria is that it should not be unnecessarily obtrusive; an agile plan should not direct, prescribe, or otherwise limit maneuverability or activity beyond the establishment of acceptable norms and conventions. In other words, planning is to be done by the most competent and responsible decentralized project unit. As a practical matter, what it means is that the hierarchy of plans shown in Table 6-1 is to be respected.

Voice of the Business in Plans

Agile methodologists respect the fact that the business speaks for both itself and the customer through the business plan. The business is the recognized authority on the project's value proposition, and from that authority come the top-level milestones that frame all other plans. The teams can challenge these milestones, but the teams cannot unilaterally set them aside.

Agile plans accept conventions, standards, and practices that collectively are the organizational culture. The business may require conformance to outside regulation and adherence to certain models of behavior. Team behavior may have to conform to various maturity models. These and others will influence and color project planning.

Cone of Uncertainty

Agile planning is not immune to business attitudes about risk; in part, risk shapes the funding and affordability limits of the project. Risk attitude, embedded in a concept called *utility*, affects both the topside-funding cap and the limits of financial support for unforeseen difficulty.

Agile planning estimates need not be too exact at the outset since the project body of knowledge is too uncertain to justify and support precise estimates. When we say uncertainty we mean risk without foreknowledge of risk events and mitigations; but as the project progresses, our knowledge changes—uncertainty morphs into knowable risks that in turn either materialize or are mitigated. Project managers who have studied risk and uncertainty are familiar with the concept that risk is opposite the amount at stake. That is, before any real work is done, the amount at stake—the amount still available to the project manager—is at a maximum, but certainty about cost, schedule, and deliverables is at a minimum. As time unfolds the backlog is burned down and the amount at stake shifts from uncommitted to committed; only then does uncertainty transform into point solutions, thereby reducing residual risk. Only then are more exact estimates justified and meaningful. In fact, unjustified precision can be misleading to those who are unfamiliar with the so-called cone of uncertainty.[9] Figure 6-2 is a pictorial of the idea.

Cone of Uncertainty

Dr. Barry Boehm is credited with conceiving the cone of uncertainty and with showing its applicability to complex systems—although he did not use the phrase *cone of uncertainty* in his texts.

Boehm presented his concept as cost-size uncertainty versus project phase in his book, *Software Cost Estimation with COCOMO II*. His data was shown symmetrically around a nominal cost-size; the data showed a maximum variation of four-to-one above and four-to-one below the nominal value.

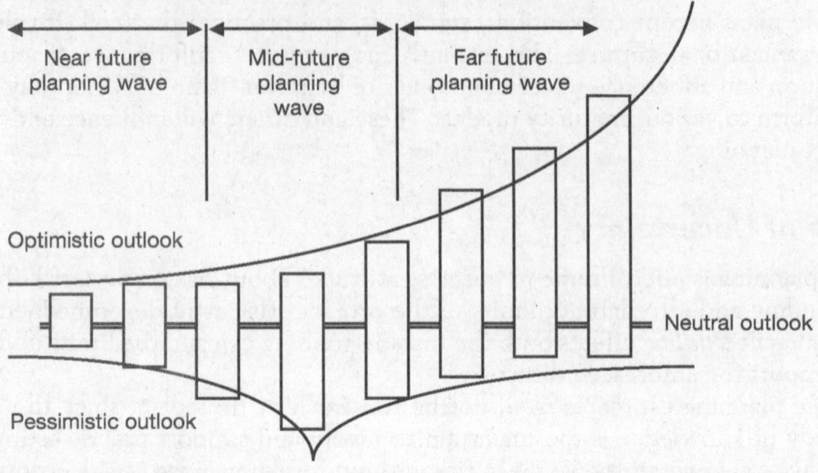

Figure 6-2 Cone of uncertainty

In the representation shown in Figure 6-2, different from Boehm's approach, uncertainty is represented above and below a neutral axis. There is an opportunity to underrun the cost—the optimistic outlook—as well as to overrun, as in the pessimistic outlook. The asymmetry depicts the nature of project estimates—they are more often too optimistic about the distant future rather than too pessimistic. On the other hand, the picture changes as the distant future becomes near term. Optimism transforms to pessimism as more detailed and precise knowledge of the immediate future is increased. So, it would be better to represent the optimistic underrun opportunity as less possible than would be the overrun opportunity. The changing attitude from optimism to pessimism is represented by the asymmetry above and below the planned value. Figure 6-2 shows an asymmetrical cone-like figure representing both a varying range of uncertainty and the idea that optimism and pessimism changes over time.

An inspection of Figure 6-2 shows that in the very near term, there is enough information to prove that optimism and pessimism are overall more constrained and about equally distributed about a nominal attitude. As the horizon moves out, pessimism grows as the uncertainties set in, but then in the far future, there is a general optimistic feeling that solutions can be found. For agile planners, Figure 6-2 is a heads-up: risk attitude changes over the lifecycle of the project. Plans reflect attitude; business plans will be optimistic; corresponding rolling wave plans will be more pessimistic, but then iteration plans will turn more neutral. The project balance-sheet gap will flux as the timeline matures.

Some care should be taken when applying the uncertainty cone. Projects do not automatically conform to the cone. As Steve McConnell has observed, there is nothing about uncertainty that will clear itself; specific actions must be invoked to cause opaque ideas to become transparent.[10] Agile projects respond in two ways:

1. Customers are embedded to give immediate interpretation to the requirements
2. Frequent deliverables provide opportunities for a wide array of users to experience the product and to weigh in with comments

Planning Throughput

Agile managers focus on outcomes rather than on activities. Unlike activity planning, which is the centerpiece of the PD-PDLC, outcome and throughput planning is the centerpiece of agile methods. In fact, there is an entire science around the concept of *throughput accounting* that focuses on the value difference—the value added—between project outcomes and preproject ideas and opportunities.[11] There are two estimating parameters that are controlling, and each can be known only within a statistical certainty:

1. Complexity of the user stories in the backlog
2. Velocity of each team

Complexity is figure of merit—a dimensionless number that is used as a multiplier to make one complex object stand out from another. For example, we say object *A* is two times as complex as object *B*—the number 2 being the multiplier. Complexity multipliers are applied to units of scope. As a multiplier, complexity escalates the effort and time required to develop a unit more complex than the baseline unit.

Velocity is the throughput of the team measured in units per scheduled iteration. Units are increments of product developed and completed by a team in the calendar duration of one development iteration. Velocity depends on team size, member competencies, team cohesion, and environment effectiveness.

As an example of how these two parameters work together, assume a team has a throughput of 40 units of scope in four weeks. The production could be 40 individual baseline units, but in another situation, the production might be four units of complex scope, each with a complexity multiplier of 10 on the baseline unit.

To be prudent, each of the parameters should be weighted for risk. After all, the accuracy of the parameters is limited to a range of certainty. There are statistical rules of thumb to make risk adjustments that are useful and practical day-to-day. Some have already been discussed, to wit: the fact that most naturally occurring phenomena acquire symmetry around a mean value over the long term;

the risk weighted average converges to the center of a symmetric distribution of values.[12] In the short run, however, the likely distribution is decidedly asymmetrical, skewed either toward optimism or pessimism.

Distribution rule of thumb

The project rule of thumb is that distributions of very near-term estimates are usually symmetrical—more pessimistic than optimistic in the midterm, and more optimistic for far future estimates.

Within one iteration, a confusing situation often arises: when asked if they can develop within a certain time limit, many developers will often answer yes—an optimistic response. But when asked if they can deliver earlier, the same developers will often say no to giving up any schedule—a pessimistic response. Statistically, this can only mean that distributions of outcomes would have to look like those in Figure 6-3. Note the expected value of each distribution in the figure. Recall that the expected value of a distribution is a weighted average of all the possible outcomes. In the two asymmetrical distributions, the small contribution of the long tail pulls the average a bit toward the tail and away from the most likely value at the peak of the distribution. In the top figure that represents the far future, it is more likely that less effort is needed—an optimistic outlook on effort. As the future becomes more near term, the outlook actually becomes more pessimistic because information becomes available, although just enough to cause concern instead of enough to understand the needs. There is some fear of the unknown. Gradually, information is developed in the near present. Usually, about as much is known about the things that could go well as is known about the things that could go wrong. The distribution becomes more symmetric.

Planning Schedule Losses

Have you ever stopped to marvel at how the last minute or two of a basketball game can take 10 minutes to play? How efficient is that? Even measuring over the longer term, the whole game can easily take three times the amount of time shown on the play clock—20 minutes of playing time often consumes one hour of wall-clock time. The fact is, the strategy and mechanics of the game dictate a certain *loss* against the wall clock.

Projects experience this loss as well. The project play clock will seem slower than the wall clock. For instance, people get sick, take personal time, take vacation to refresh and recharge, and need refreshment time during the workday. Over the long run, it is reasonable to assume a 15 percent labor loss in the labor plan. On an eight- or nine-person agile team, the impact of that 15 percent loss is equal to the impact of operating one-person-down almost at all times.

Distributions of outcomes versus probability of occurrence change according to quality of information available to developers

Probability*

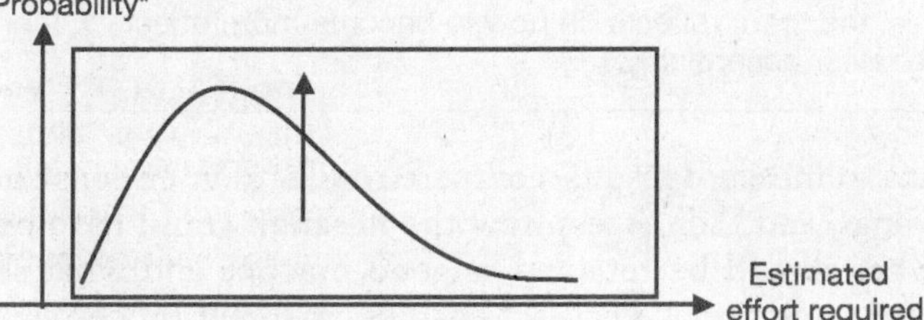

In the far-future, estimates are optimistic, focusing on opportunity, and indicating a lesser effort estimated

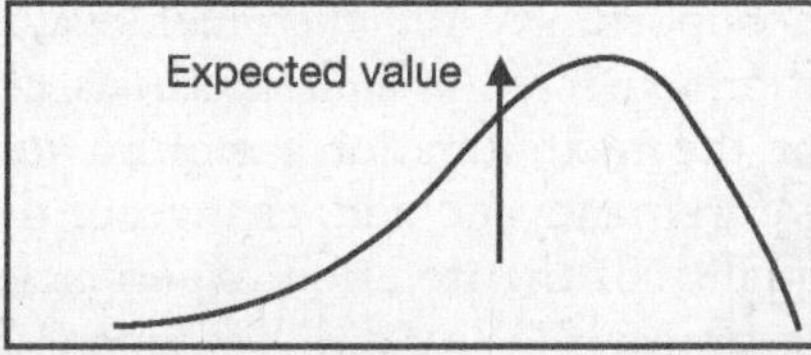

In the mid-future, estimates are more pessimistic, focusing on partial information that becomes available, surfacing some concerns about what remains to be known

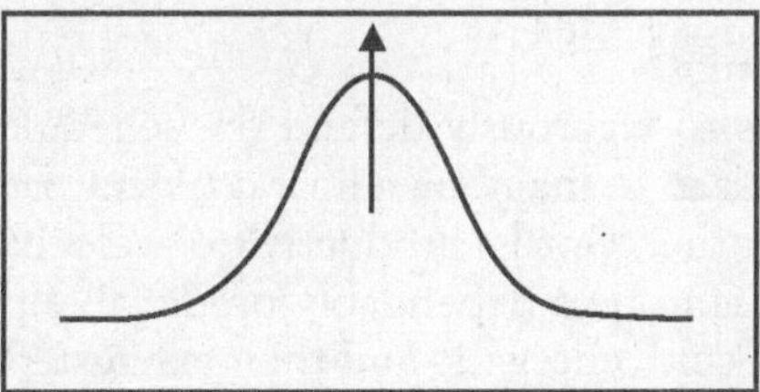

In the near-present, estimates are more clustered around a nominal value, indicating nearly complete information and equal estimates of things that could go right and wrong

* Strictly speaking, the curves shown are probability densities; to obtain the probability of estimate, compute the area formed by a rectangle of small *X* times small *Y*, *X* being the horizontal

Figure 6-3 Developer's distributions

Planning for Ag-PDCA

The sprint or iteration time is really about the *plan-do* part of the agile PDCA cycle (Ag-PDCA). *Do* means to execute until done; that is, when the *plan-do* part of the cycle is complete, an increment of product has been fully tested as an integrated unit with the product base. After the *plan-do* phase, go on to the *check-act* phase and synchronize with other teams as given in Principle 12.

> **Agile Principle 12**
>
> At regular intervals, the team reflects on how to become more effective, then tunes and adjusts its behavior accordingly.

Check-act means to measure results, compare results to intentions and expectations, report findings, and then assess how the iteration could have been done better. Evaluate what should be retained as good practice and what should be improved for the next iteration. Check-act enables emergent processes and practices because the team is influenced and changed by experience and feedback.

The *check* portion provides an opportunity for customer evaluations to be analyzed. With the product evolution expected in agile methods, *check* provides a fuzzy front-end opportunity for the next iteration's requirements planning. There is opportunity to restack requirements and add, change, or delete existing requirements. Reflection on the quality of the iteration experience is a lessons-learned opportunity. Ask why five times: [13] "Why did X happen? *Because of Z.* Why did Z happen?" And so on. From the five answers, fashion a team response to improve the next iteration outcome.

Rhythm of the Schedule

One objective of agile methods is to vigorously defend the schedule's rhythm to prevent the last-minute press, but also to maintain a near constant pace that can be sustained almost indefinitely. In other words, productivity—velocity—should be nearly constant, a parameter that is to be a dependably predictable planning metric. If the team runs hot and then cold, energetic and then exhausted, the velocity figure will be meaningless. Predictable velocity is needed to forecast Ag-PDCA cycles on the schedule grid. Look back to Chapter 1 to the Agile Principle 8:

> **Agile Principle 8**
>
> Agile processes promote sustainable development. The sponsors, developers, and users should be able to maintain a constant pace indefinitely.

One of the helpful consequences of Principle 8—*maintaining a constant pace nearly indefinitely*—is that there is a certain rhythm to the work pace of the project. Elsewhere, the rhythm of Red-Green-Refactor is explained. And to be sure, if the rhythm is off a few beats, it will be easily felt by hurry-up-and-wait, unscheduled downtime, and other nonrhythmic responses. Constraints imposed by stakeholders and outside authorities may upset the rhythm. Maintaining the rhythm by managing constraints is project management's task.

Agile plans take a page from the Theory of Constraints, and the concept of the drum-buffer-rope made popular by the research of Eliyahu M. Goldratt.[14] To maintain rhythm, Goldratt posits the drum as the source of the beat. In the agile project, the Ag-PDCA cycle is the drum. The buffer is just that—a time buffer to absorb unforeseen events so that the beat—the Ag-PDCA cycle—can be maintained. Workflow is the rope that ties it all together. Workflow authorizes cycles to begin and end and authorizes releases to production.

Summary of Planning Ideas

Table 6-2 puts all the ideas together.

Table 6-2 Summary of planning ideas

Planning feature	Commentary
Principle of subsidiary function	• A central and higher-level organization has a responsibility to refrain from intruding on its subordinate when the subordinate is competent and capable • By extension, plans must not direct and specify the actions of subordinate units • High-level units have a right to expect responsible planning by subordinates • Subordinates must responsibly plan and estimate their activities with sufficient detail, making intrusions by superior units unnecessary except for verification and validation
Voice of the business and customer in plans	• The project respects the business as the business-case authority and for the interpretation of both the business and customer need; specifically the milestones that support the value proposition and the affordability cap • Showing respect does not enjoin the project from challenging the business to carefully weigh its demands
Cone of uncertainty	• A good plan respects the concept that uncertainty is greatest when the least amount of effort has been expended in the project • A good estimating practice is to adopt standard estimating ranges at different points of maturity in the project • Transparency—increasing certainty—is not automatic; specific plans must be put in place to drive out the unknowns
Planning for losses	• A long-term 15 percent labor loss is a conservative planning parameter • On an eight-person team, a 15 percent labor loss is almost equivalent to losing one fulltime person from that team
Planning for Ag-PDCA	• The plan-do-check-act cycle encompasses all agile team activity

Table 6-2 (*continued*)

Planning feature	Commentary
Planning risk adjustments	• No estimate should be provided as a single-point estimate unless it is the expected value of a possible outcome distribution • Every estimate should be presented as having a range for which there is a confidence that the true value will be within the range
Planning throughput	• Throughput is governed by the complexity of the user-story backlog and the team velocity • Throughput is the product finished and ready for production produced by a team in the duration of one iteration • Throughput accounting evaluates the value-added of the team's effort
Rhythm of the schedule	• A good plan provides assurance of pace; in part by the strategic placement of buffers and in part by the adherence to the doctrine of identically repeatable cycles

Time Boxes Are the Building Blocks of Schedules in the Agile Space

In the agile space, schedules are accumulations of time-boxed iterations or sprints, framed by business milestones from the business plan and rolling wave planning horizons, all affixed to a calendar.

Timelines and Calendars
As a matter of terminology, we distinguish between a timeline and a schedule. A timeline is measured in units of time but has no reference to a calendar. When a timeline is affixed to a calendar, it becomes a schedule.

Time boxes are planned to synchronize not only with business milestones but also with the activities of other teams working similar time-boxed iterations. High-level network schedules tie together the major dependencies between teams. Within the team, the team leadership assigns schedule-constrained work to team members. Trend lines and work-remaining calculations forecast progress over the course of the iteration.

A project management tip	Scheduling in the space
	• The most important point to grasp is that schedules are constructed from a number of fixed-duration cycles, somewhat like building a train from many same-length freight cars. • Each cycle contains the same number of calendar days, has nearly constant throughput, and all are networked in finish-to-start in precedence. • Scope is constantly adjusted, making scheduling adjustments possible to fit the time-boxed cycles precisely. • The total duration of the schedule is capped by the time required to execute the requirements deck or by the funding available to sustain teams working.

One way to display the agile schedule concept is with a grid as shown in Figure 6-4. The gridlines align with development and planning wave cycles. Some number of cycles produces a release either on a business-plan milestone or on a milestone planned by the work stream. Each grid space is buffered to absorb small variations in performance; the final release milestone is likewise buffered to better ensure on-time delivery. If there are dependencies between one or more teams, those dependencies are felt at the grid boundaries.

Milestones from the Business Plan

The business plan is the top-level milestone plan. Schedules are nested in the same hierarchy as plans, as given in Table 6-1. So, the place to begin is with the business case, Level 0, 1, or 2. Milestones are given top-down to the project. In each case, Level 0, 1, or 2, the project accepts and respects business drivers that determine when capabilities are needed. An agile business case does not intrude on the prerogatives of the project manager and the team leads to set tactical schedules, so the schedule detail in the business case is not more than business milestones.

Some milestones may have calendar-specific event dates that carry a very definite value; other milestones are simply made relative to project kickoff. They are scheduled after receipt of order.

At Level 0 there are few milestones, perhaps no more than one or two, and likely these will be established and validated as part of the business-case governance process. Governance is collaborative by design and intent, so there will be an opportunity for the project team and the product owner or business representative to discuss, negotiate, and agree to the business milestones. Such socialization of the schedule is integral to reducing the gap on the project balance sheet to a manageable risk.

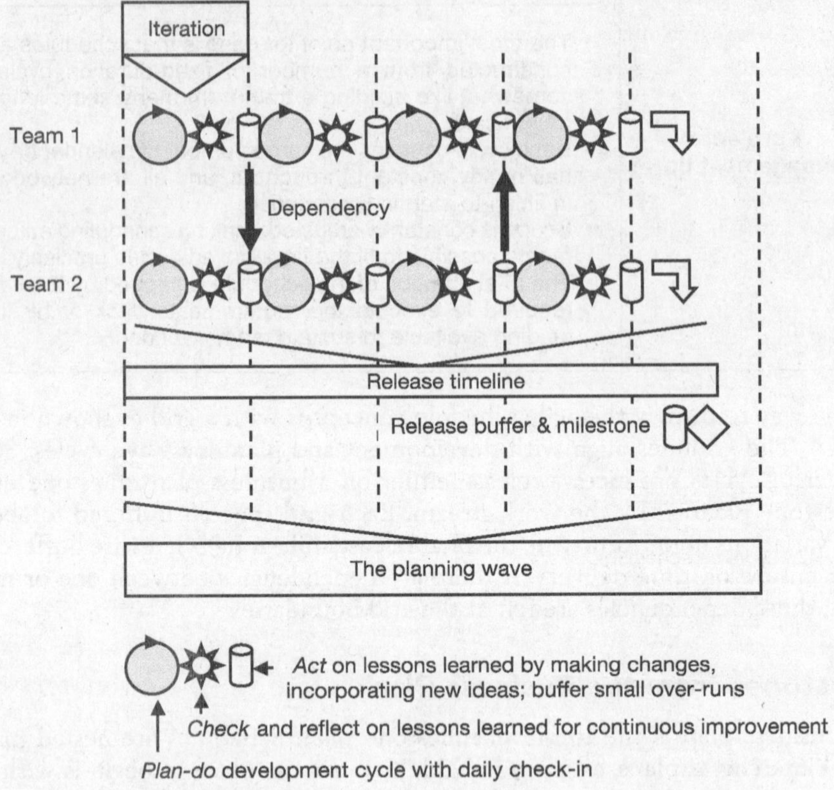

Figure 6-4 Agile schedule grid

At Levels 1 and 2, projects are much more complex than they are at Level 0, but the process is conceptually the same. At Levels 1 and 2 there may be competitive alternatives that each need to go through a decision analysis process, part of which will be an analysis of schedule possibilities.

Planning the Work-Stream Schedule

The classical approach to planning a schedule is to first plan the timeline and then put it to a calendar. The steps for developing the timeline are well documented in many standard project management texts.[15] The material in Table 6-3 contrasts the conventional and agile approaches.

Table 6-3 Work-stream planning

Conventional planning step	Agile planning step
Develop the WBS down to a work-package level of a few weeks' work	• Decompose the business-case product vision into major capabilities for each planning wave and release based on customer priority and benefit plan
Sequence the WBS deliverables—do the foundation before the walls, etc. Caution: Keep it simple!	• The primary sequencing comes from priorities set by the customer or user during planning for waves and then releases within waves • Architecture and technical feasibility determine fundamental sequencing, such as foundations and walls
Determine the dependencies among the WBS deliverables and modify the sequencing if necessary	• Dependencies may happen at a high level between teams and are adjusted after every release
For effort-driven schedules, estimate each task's effort and normalize to the number of individuals according to an effort per day metric For duration-driven schedules, estimate the affordable duration, and then compute the effort required to affect the duration	• A fixed effort is assigned to each team • The number of teams is derived from throughput demands to meet business milestones
Apply durations to the ordered-sequenced list to make a timeline using dummy tasks for buffers	• Schedules are built from time-boxed iterations • Each iteration is characterized by units of throughput—product that can go to production • The schedule is derived from the summation of the iteration durations needed to produce all the product • Detailed planning is apportioned among planning horizons
Apply the calendar to the timeline, blacking out nonwork days	• The calendar is driven in part by the business plan, in part by the derived durations, and in part by the rolling wave planning process

Planning the Iteration, or Sprint, and Release Schedule

The release timeline is comprised of a number of iterations connected in tandem strings; some tandem strings will be in parallel to each other and will join results, thereby forming a network. The critical path in the release network is buffered with a time box to add assurance that the release event will be as scheduled.[16]

Figure 6-5 shows a typical release schedule with network interconnections and a critical-path buffer at the milestone. Note that the release schedule is a number of plan-do-check-act cycles. To be prudent, the release cycle has at least one buffer for the release event, but other buffers are appropriate where tandem strings join.

Whenever two or more strings join at a completion milestone, or join as the predecessor iterations of a successor iteration, there is a chance for the timeline to shift to the right.

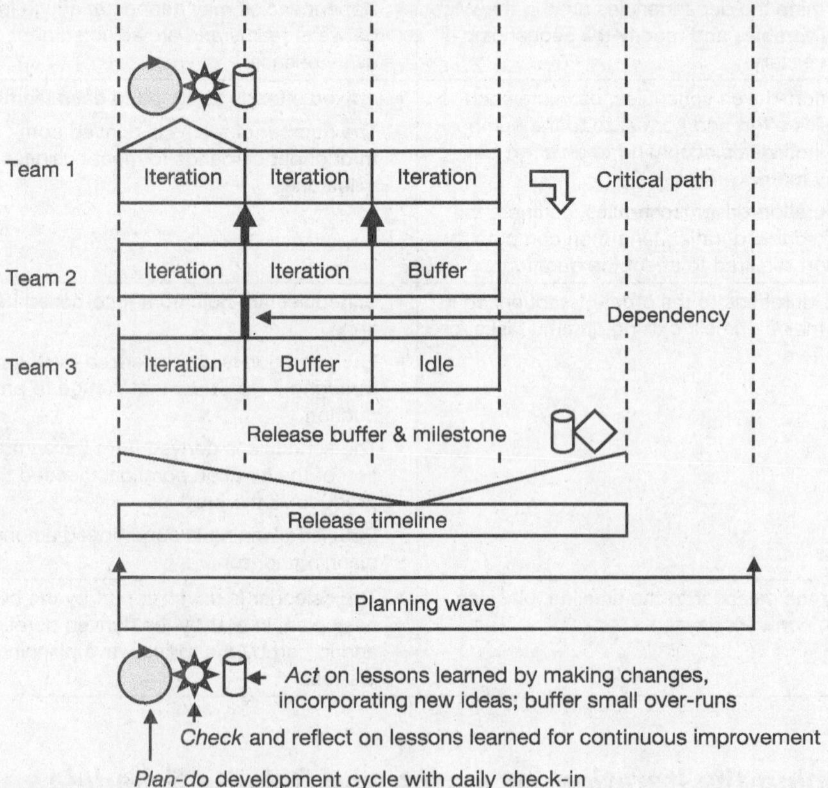

Figure 6-5 Release network diagram

Shift-right Phenomenon
There is a chance that at a milestone joining paths will cause the schedule to slip to the right. This *chance* is the risk of simultaneity; it is calculated as the product of the probabilities of all the joining paths, given that they should finish all at the same time. The mathematics represents the concept of nested opportunity spaces. Each path's opportunity—that is, success—is limited by the simultaneous opportunity (success) of its neighbor. Example: 95 of 100 successes by one path only provides 95 opportunities for a second path to simultaneously succeed instead of 100 that were available to the first path. If, for example, the iterations all should finish within the prescribed time box with probability very high, say 0.95, then the probability of making the milestone with three joining paths is equal to 0.95 × 0.95 × 0.95, or 0.86. To raise the milestone probability to 0.95, the schedule must move to the right by adding a buffer before the shifted milestone. The size of the buffer should be large enough to catch the most likely overrun.

The shift-right phenomenon is also known as *merge bias*. The name connotes the fact that there is a bias towards the schedule shifting when paths join. The problem arises if one or more joining paths are tardy. In that event, the schedule will slip to the right awaiting the tardy iteration to finish. Now of course, with rigid time boxes bounding each team's work, a tardy iteration should not happen. By design and by doctrine, all time-boxed iterations finish on the prescribed timeline. However, mindful of von Moltke's observation that no plan survives contact with reality, a prudent practice is to provide a small buffer on the off-chance that an iteration goes a bit long. In the extreme case of some calamity where it appears a team is not converging to a finish, the project manager is expected to step in and stop work.[17]

A project management tip	Getting to *done* at milestones
	• In general, regardless of where placed, buffers protect the integrity of the milestone schedule. • Of course, many Level 0 projects will be a much-simplified network of perhaps only one tandem string of iterations or sprints. • All projects, regardless of level, should buffer the release event.

Take note that the release event is not a point in time but rather an iteration in itself wherein a number of go-live production tasks are executed. Depending on accepted conventions and the nature of the product base—whether internal or external—and the support structure for the product, the go-live iteration could be quite varied. Go-live could be anywhere from a simple script that loads and links files to a quite complex iteration requiring dedicated, careful planning with the business, infrastructure managers, and application developers. To be lean and efficient, develop a go-live template that is repetitively used from one release to the next.

How long should an iteration be? There is no fixed prescription, but each methodology has its own recommendation. A principle of agile projects is that releases should be frequent. Take note of Principle 3:

> **Agile Principle 3**
>
> Deliver working software frequently, from a couple of weeks to a couple of months, with a preference to the shorter timescale.

Putting aside any truly Covey-like Category I *most important-most urgent* imperatives that would drive the schedule—or for that matter any immovable milestones—Schawber, for one, recommends fixing a SCRUM sprint to 30 consecutive days on the calendar, or 30 days on the wall clock.[18] Refer back to Table 1-6, comparison of agile methods—process, for recommendations from all the methodologies.

One way to approach planning is to schedule backward: work back from a practical length of time for a planning horizon, a period of time in which detailed planning can occur comfortably with reasonable confidence. This period is no longer than three to six months. As an example, assume 17 weeks as the baseline planning wave horizon. It would be good if the customer, whether internal or external, had several bites at the apple during the planning wave. Therefore, a release each month would be good if the customer can absorb change that quickly. If not four, then three releases should definitely be planned.

Planning the Spiral

Spirals are easy to visualize but tricky to plan. Planning any nonlinear timeline is complicated in that the elapsed time itself accumulates linearly—it does not circle about and fold back on itself. Obviously, it is made harder because tools based on databases and spreadsheets do not handle nonlinear timelines well. In Chapter 1, the *Spiral in a Linear World* section provides guidance on how to go about this. In a word, unwind the spiral and plan it as though it were linear, assuming a certain number of iterations about the spiral based on a judgment about the risks that require examination before the project launches into the mainstream with the first construction iteration.

Every spiral needs an exit strategy—actionable criteria for success so that the opportunity to move to the mainstream project methodology is recognizable. The exit criteria can certainly be objective and built around a satisfactorily performing prototype, but the criteria may also be a judgment call whether enough successful prototyping has been done.

Planning for Architecture and Nonfunctional Deliverables

Architecture is present in every project whether formally acknowledged or not. A good practice is to make the architecture visible and effective for guiding the product development. Consideration of architecture will certainly appear as part of the governance process for the business case. At Level 0, many projects will conform to an existing architecture. At Level 1 and 2, and especially at Level 2, consideration of new architecture may be very prominent.

Architecture is best developed by a team effort. The architect, if there is an individual in the project operating model with that portfolio, as well as other subject-matter experts, mentors and coaches the teams. Agile Principle 11 is noteworthy:

> **Agile Principle 11**
>
> The best architectures, requirements, and designs emerge from self-organizing teams.

As previously discussed, *Iteration-0* is the time to put in place system components that have no direct customer value. Nonfunctional requirements should not delay the development iterations needlessly, especially for nonfunctional needs that might be sequenced later in the project lifecycle. Nonfunctional deliverables often accompany the functional products delivered to the customer and often they are a prerequisite to the development of the functional product. The nonfunctionality deliverables are often on the horizontal axis of the Kano chart as discussed in Chapter 5. Nonfunctional needs include all manner of infrastructure to include computers, networks, storage, security protocols, manufacturing setups, tools and jigs or templates, scorecards and dashboards, and many others.

Summary and Takeaway Points

The theme we developed in this chapter is that *adapting plans and estimates to changing customer needs and maximizing value and at an affordable cost are the planning imperatives for agile projects*. Cost and schedule are derived from ever-changing requirements. After each iteration, new estimates adjust the operating plan. After each iteration, a comparison is made to the business milestones and cost-affordability limitation.

Plans respect the principle of subsidiary function; plans set up the project rhythm and pace. The main planning principle conforms to agile Principle 3: *Deliver working software frequently, from a couple of weeks to a couple of months, with a preference to the shorter timescale*. There are many plans appropriate to agile methods, even though agile methods are not plan-driven. The first plan is the business plan; it is flowed into the work streams. Individual iteration plans are made at each iteration planning session. The time box is the main planning building block. Daily activities are time boxed; iterations are constrained to a time box, and releases are comprised of iteration strings synchronized to business-plan milestones.

The planning wave is the time when detail planning is meaningful. A planning wave is usually in the range of three to six months. Within each wave, releases are planned on a frequency governed by the ability of the enterprise to absorb change.

The spiral is often a good front end to an agile methodology. Spiral practices evaluate feasibility risks and easily pivot to other methodologies. Planning the spiral is accomplished by unwinding the spiral and making an informed judgment about how many spiral segments will be needed.

Plans enable the innovation and inventiveness that is the mark of agile projects. In the absence of plans, any direction or any result is possible, but customers are unlikely to be satisfied.

Chapter Endnotes

1. Paraphrased from Malotaux's, "Timeline, Getting and Keeping Control over Your Project," a whitepaper that was originally prepared for the Annual Pacific Northwest Software Conference, Portland, OR, 2008.

2. Recall that the project manager is called the *SCRUM master* in the SCRUM methodology.

3. Anderson, *Agile Management for Software Engineering,* 9–10.

4. Paraphrased from Brooks', *The Mythical Man-month*, 21.

5. The Gantt chart is a bar chart with individual bars representing activities. The length of the bar is the scheduled duration for that activity. The overall timeline of the project can be computed by summing the nonoverlapping bar segments. Dependencies between bars are not usually shown. The chart is named after its inventor Henry Gantt, mechanical engineer and industrialist, who introduced the chart in the 1910s. Gantt was a college roommate and professional associate of F. W. Taylor, the father of Taylorism, who is discussed in other chapters.

6. Velocity is an XP term and a measure of throughput that is applied generally to all agile methods: Objects actually put into production.

7. A time box is a prescribed length of time for a set of multifunctional activities. Scope is modified to fit the time box, not the other way round. The daily stand-up meeting is done with a time box. Each development iteration and planning wave is time boxed.

8. The chargeback rate is the rate per unit of time that the individual is charged to the paying organization. The rate may be the base salary or the salary lifted by a factor for benefits, or it could be a rate that includes a lift for both benefits and overhead. In some organizations, and particularly if contracted, the chargeback rate may be a standard cost. A standard cost is a fixed rate by labor or

job category regardless of the person's paid-out compensation. In some cases, the standard cost is greater than the actual compensation, and in other times, it is not. Other practices may use a rolling average of actual compensation as the chargeback rate. Standard cost is sometimes computed as a rolling average.

9. Boehm, *Software Engineering Economics*, 311, presents Figure 21-1, which illustrates estimation accuracy versus project phase. The figure is cone-shaped, but Boehm does not use that wording in his text. The estimation accuracy by phase diagram is reproduced as Figure 1-2 in Boehm et al, *Software Cost Estimation with* COCOMO *II*, 10.

10. McConnell, *Software Estimation: Demystifying the Black Art*, 35–40.

11. Anderson, *Agile Management for Software Engineering*, Chapter 2.

12. Readers can prove this phenomenon for themselves by histogramming various phenomena in the project. There will tend to be a clustering around a central value.

13. "5-Whys," developed by Sakichi Toyoda of Toyota Motor Corporation.

14. Goldratt and Fox, *The Race*, 179; Goldratt and Cox, *The Goal: A Process of Ongoing Improvement*.

15. Project Management Institute, *Project Management Body of Knowledge*, Chapter 6.

16. Recall that the critical path is the longest connected path through the network. See Goodpasture, *Quantitative Methods in Project Management*, 187–192.

17. Schwaber, *Agile Project Management with SCRUM*, 136. According to Schwaber's Sprint Rules, SCRUM masters stop work when the sprint appears no longer to be viable. A subsequent planning meeting is called to evaluate next steps.

18. Ibid, 8.

7

Estimating Cost and Schedule

There are no facts about the future, only estimates.[1] A good agile estimate accounts for the complexity of intangibles and the uncertainty of requirements.

> *It is very difficult to make a vigorous, plausible, job-risking defense of an estimate that is derived by no quantitative method, supported by little data, and certified chiefly by the hunches of the managers.*
>
> *Dr. Fred P. Brooks, Jr.[2]*

Estimates, by definition, are the objective components of plans; estimates are the analytical results obtained from examining proposed activities. Many elements of information make up an estimate, but as Dr. Brooks has admonished in the opening quote, perhaps none are more important than the facts—the certainties—about past performance. Plan-do-check-act is the cycle. To *check* is to assemble the facts; to *act* is to use the facts to the best advantage of the next cycle. Estimates, on the other hand, speak to future events, and there are no facts available regarding future events. The future can be described only probabilistically. Managers may hypothesize that the cost or schedule will hit a planned value, but more realistically the hypothesis should be to hit within limits of a range, not a point value with certainty. *Invariably, the most vexing thing about estimates is their propensity to be mistaken for facts, or worse—a commitment!*

Every project manager has experience managing both cost and schedule, and all know that one affects the other, meaning that cost and schedule are interdependent so their plans and estimates are intertwined. For reasons to be discussed and as would be expected, labor cost tracks effort very closely. As effort increases, so does its cost in about the same way—double the effort, double its cost, at least to a first approximation. But effort does not have that same effect on the schedule. To be sure, the schedule often extends when effort goes above plan. What project manager has not heard of Brooks' Law?[3]

Brooks' Law

Adding manpower to a late software project makes it later.

Since Brooks proclaimed his law in 1975, many analysts have examined the behavior of schedules as more individuals are added into the project mix. From their work, much empirical evidence is now available to support forecasting. Some of that information will be used in the material that follows.

The Character of Estimates Affect Predictability

Next to requirements, estimates are probably the most influential factor on the predictability of the project outcomes. In the agile methodologies, estimating is a team activity. The team both comes up with the estimate and lives with the estimate. The project manager and other subject matter experts coach the estimating process and provide benchmark data and other information requested by the team, but mostly the estimate is the product of teamwork.

Agile estimates

The first principle of estimating for agile projects is to estimate for outcomes, not activity.

Agile teams are managed for throughput and outcomes, not for activity. Estimating outcomes surfaces the ageless tension between good-faith effort and completion. Completion is a commitment to produce a measurable and valuable outcome; good-faith effort is a commitment to work diligently and thoughtfully. It is acknowledged that every project includes some activity that is a good-faith effort, in effect a level-of-effort. Project management itself is more a level-of-effort than a completion. The point to grasp is that because activity is only a means and not the end, and the *end* is the only thing valued by customers, agile estimating shifts to the end items that are useful and wanted.

The traditional activity-oriented Gantt charts and activity networks give way to scheduling time-boxed iterations and releases. Instead of being activity-centric, the end game is to apply throughput as effectively as possible. As previously established, throughput and backlog complexity are the two parameters that govern team production. If it is hard or even impossible to imagine all the requirements, it is equally hard to imagine the efforts needed to implement the requirements. These issues are summarized in two words: *Complexity* and *uncertainty*.

A project management tip	Complexity and uncertainty
	• *Complexity* is quality described by how many ways units can interact, a measure of how many unique states a system can be in, and how many responses one stimulus causes. • *Complexity* is what transforms a cost-to-benefit opportunity into a cost-to-consequences threat. • *Uncertainty* is what is unknowable until just-in-time. • *Uncertainty* is risk without knowledge of an unfavorable event or neutralizing mitigation.

Estimates Become Commitments

Every project sponsor asks for estimates—estimates of required funds resources, estimates of major milestones if they are not given, and estimates to support other scorecard key performance indicators. But it is rarely a green field. Usually the sponsor already has numbers in mind: numbers for benefits—how much and when—and numbers for an investment budget. But do the numbers fit the product vision? Are all the constraints and demands consistent and not self-conflicting? Managers estimate and plan to answer these questions, because not knowing sometimes leads to unfavorable consequences instead of benefits.

Care must be taken. Every project manager knows that estimates do not stay estimates very long. Even if the sponsor has used the word *estimate*, more often they are thinking, *do not exceed*, or *tell me what it's going to cost and when I am going to get it*. And the farther up the chain the estimate is forwarded, the more it loses caveats. Unfortunately, all too frequently estimates become commitments almost as soon as they are uttered. Knowing this, prudence demands that the estimates be fact-based and reasonably adjusted for risk to set a proper confidence interval. Following agile principles, the best way to convey understanding and resolve differences is face-to-face with the business. Even so, there will likely be a residual gap between the project plan and the business plan. When the residual gap is close enough, the project manager moves on, accepting some risk. What risk? The risk that by adapting to opportunity, iteration by iteration, the means will be found to achieve business objectives and satisfy the customer. Close enough is often as much accuracy as a project needs; *close enough* is agile.

Understanding Complexity

To get a handle on complexity requires some understanding of its properties. Complexity has no better than an imprecise definition. Indeed, there are dozens of definitions. However, to simplify matters we say that it is the known, knowable, and possibly unknowable interactions of a large number of system elements. Complexity can also mean redundancy; more than one system element is capable of handling a function. However, it may not be known or knowable which element acts at what time and under which conditions. It can also mean unnecessary design and functionality asked for but not actually used. Complexity is not the absence of simplicity. The simplest system that is minimally satisfactory may be complex, but the corollary is true: Simplicity is the absence of unnecessary complexity.

Complexity puts systems on the edge of chaos, meaning that relatively minor stimulus could create unwieldy and unpredictable outcomes. Complex systems have high entropy, meaning that complex systems can acquire or be in many states—some more stable than others—and not all known to developers and testers. It is influenced by the N^2-effect discussed in Chapter 11, whereby the number of interactions between elements increases nearly as the square of the number of elements. Even a small N, say 20, means almost 400 ways for an interaction to occur, and each of these has conditions, triggers, and subsequent effects.

The systems we are concerned about have many elements, in fact very many elements, more than any one person can keep in mind. Extended to their interdependencies, the numbers can be overwhelming. As discussed in Chapter 4, complexity colors testing, quality assurance, and post-product support.

Warren Weaver describes systems of interrelated elements as having organized complexity.[4] Organized complexity means that over time, certain interactions will dominate; their properties can be observed, tested, and measured. Other interactions, although possible, happen so infrequently that they are operationally inconsequential. For these there is not a good return on investment to justify discovery, observation, testing, and measurement.

Complexity complicates estimating—there is probably no news here. Key estimating parameters, like velocity, are subject to uncertainty arising from unforeseen interactions among the solution elements. Interactions with legacy systems bring many more elements into play, driving the N^2 effects harder, and making testing much more complicated. Simple automated unit tests are less revealing; integration with the installed base, always more complicated than unit testing, becomes an ever-larger factor in throughput. Allowing for the unforeseeable requires discounting throughput, much like discounting future benefits for unforeseeable circumstances. In the agile domain, complexity is an economic issue and a throughput issue. The more complex the backlog, the more time is needed for a given throughput to burn off the backlog. Time, in turn, affects the present value of benefits and the operating expenses of the project. Tradeoffs between good, better, and best will be required.

Ideas about Complexity
Entropy and chaos are ideas about complexity that have some application to the discussion. Entropy is a quality measure of order and disorder, and thereby measures the number of stable states. Systems with a very large number of states, particularly including states that are hard to even know about, have high entropy. Chaos is a measure of the sensitivity of the system response to input changes. A system that is *chaotic* has dramatic yet predictable responses to small changes in the input conditions.

Estimates Fall within a Range

All estimates regardless of methodology are by definition probabilistic, meaning that actual outcome is not known with certainty but is likely contained within a range of values. As an example, a developer might estimate that an object requires 100 hours + 20, − 10 hours, meaning that the range is from 90 to 120 hours.

Within the range, the various numerical possibilities do not all have the same probability of occurrence. For example, 120 hours is within the range; but even though this value is possible, developers may feel that 120 hours is improbably pessimistic. The value with the greatest probability is the *most likely* value. It is the most likely outcome if there were only one chance to develop the object. The most likely effort might be 100 hours. But if there were several objects to estimate, then some consideration must be given to all the possible outcomes in the range.

One way to take all possibilities into consideration is to average all the possibilities, but a simple arithmetic average assumes all values in the range are equally likely even though they are not. A better estimate is obtained when the information about probabilities within the range is taken into account. So rather than simply adding all the values and dividing by the number of possibilities, do this: Take the number of possibilities as a pool of points; from the pool assign points to each value in the range according to your judgment about its probability. Multiply each range value by the points assigned and sum the value-points products. Then, as before, divide the sum total by the number of points. The result is a risk-weighted average called the *expected value*. The expected value is that one number that best represents the whole range of possibilities from 90 to 120 hours. An example is in the panel. Note that the expected value is less pessimistic than the average because the weighting diminished the contributions of the end points—90 and 120—and gave emphasis to the more likely values of 100 and 105.

Example: Risk-weighted Average

- Number of values: 6
- Range values, in order: 90, 95, 100, 105, 110, 120
- Simple average value: $\frac{1}{6} \times (90 + 95 + 100 + 105 + 110 + 120) = 103.3$
- Range value probabilities as a proportion of a pool of 6 points, in order: 0.25,0.75, 2.0, 1.75, 1.0, 0.25
- Summation: $(90 \times 0.25) + (95 \times 0.75) + (100 \times 2.0) + (105 \times 1.75) + (110 \times 1.0) + (120 \times 0.25) = 617.5$
- Expected value: $\frac{617.5}{6} = 102.9$

Another issue regarding the range presents itself in that the range is not absolutely bounded—the possibility exists for the real outcome to fall outside the range. The word to describe how well the range represents the real outcome is confidence. *Confidence* is the quality metric regarding the likelihood that the real value will actually be within the estimated range. For example, one confidence estimate regarding the likelihood that the real outcome will be less than 120 hours but greater than 90 hours might be 90 and 80 percent, respectively. This means that:

- Out of 100 available similar project development opportunities, 90 instances should take less than 120 hours; in 20 instances, the effort might take less than 90 hours
- Only 10 of those 100 opportunities might exceed 120 hours, although 80 of the 100 instances should exceed 90 hours

Figure 7-1 illustrates this confidence estimate discussion. The figure shows many measurements or estimates that cluster about a center value. The estimates near the center value are more probable than are the estimates farther out and near the tails. The bell curve is a depiction of probability versus the range value. The other curve is the *S* curve, which is a depiction of accumulating probability from 0 to 1. Confidence is expressed by the probability accumulation from one range point to another.

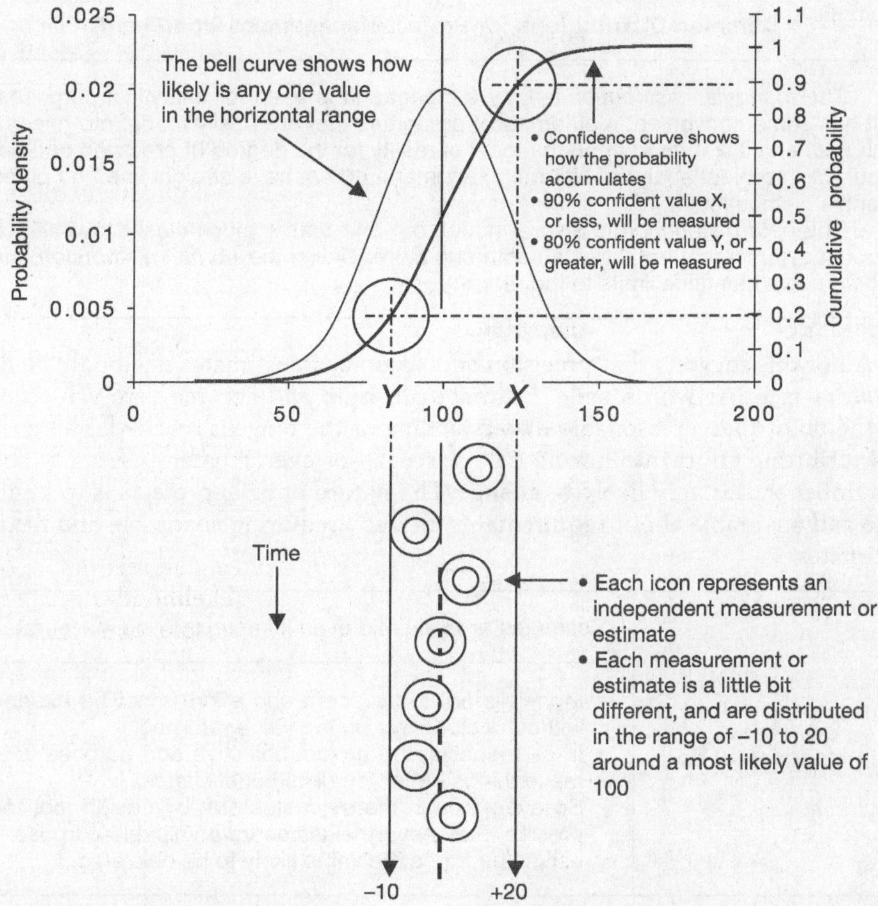

Figure 7-1 Confidence estimates

Common Distributions for Project Management

To be a little more precise about matters, the probability curve in Figure 7-1 is a probability density function (PDF) that shows how dense or intense the probability is at any point in the range. Obviously, the center is the densest.

The most common and familiar PDF is the *normal curve*, better known as the *bell curve*.

But there others that are common in project management. The two that show up often are the *triangular distribution* and the *beta distribution*.

Common Distributions for Project Management (*continued*)
The *triangular distribution* is only a model and is used for analytical purposes. It has some convenient mathematical properties that are easily made into rules of thumb, and it is a *good enough* model of reality for the degree of precision and accuracy in project analysis. Natural phenomena do not have straight line and plane angle distributions. The *beta distribution* is also a model, but one that is much closer to reality. It is not symmetrical but it has smooth curvature. Unlike the *normal distribution*, the *beta curve* has finite limits to the range.

All of this suggests that precision and accuracy in estimates need only be *good enough*—in other words, agile. Estimate precision and accuracy are valued only to the point that a reasonable understanding of the range is reached. There is no point putting effort into having a 98 percent—or even greater—certainty about a number that is very likely to change. The nature of agile projects is to be flexible and adaptable about requirements, thereby requiring adaptable and flexible estimates.

A project management tip	Estimates are valuable even if imprecise and inaccurate
	• Money is not to be spent and effort is not be exerted without a close eye on the value returned. • In all respects, the project objective and purpose is to make things better for all its beneficiaries. • So even though the estimates are, by design, not too precise, they nevertheless serve a valuable purpose—estimates frame the value likely to be delivered.

Drivers on Cost and Schedule Estimates

The backlog, the productivity of teams, and the number of teams working largely drive cost and schedule. Here are the most important points:

Drivers on cost and schedule

- Team productivity is only stable for a planning wave; thereafter, circumstances may change.
- Estimates are deferred until just-in-time based on a detailed examination of the backlog.
- Estimates are then extended to subsequent iterations in the wave, understanding that the *check-act* portion of the iteration cycle will affect requirements backlog and require refinements of the estimates.

The highest uncertainty is the number of actionable requirements and their complexity. The project backlog is the beginning point, but teams expect the backlog to be changed during the course of the project. There is usually no reliable forecast for the degree of expected change.

On the other hand, time boxes are fixed and deterministic. All teams expect low turnover and are populated within a small range from 7 to 12 members. Each team has a throughput capacity—velocity—that is estimated or known by benchmarking within a reasonably small range. Confidence in the expected value of velocity is high.

So the estimated schedule, and to a large extent the estimated cost, is driven either by the number of time-boxed iterations required to liquidate the backlog, or by the number of iterations the sponsor chooses to afford. The material in Table 7-1 summarizes these ideas:

Table 7-1 Summary of complexity drivers on cost and schedule

Parameter	Strength of influence	Cost and schedule effects
Estimated number of requirements at the user-story level	• High on cost • Moderate on timeline	• Directly drives the total number of units of throughput needed to liquidate the backlog • Each unit has a cost • Each unit is developed within an iteration
Estimated complexity of individual requirements	• High on cost • Moderate on timeline	• Directly drives the total number of throughput units needed to liquidate the backlog • Each unit has a cost • Each unit is developed within an iteration
Estimated velocity—units of throughput per unit of time	• High on cost and schedule	• Directly drives the timeline and overall cost • The range of the velocity estimate affects the predictability of the iteration success

Environmental factors that influence estimates are summarized in Table 7-2:

Table 7-2 Summary of environmental drivers on cost and schedule

Parameter	Strength of influence	Cost and schedule effects
Number of members in the team and the mix of skills, experience, and cohesiveness	• High influence on velocity	• Performance above or below expectation affects velocity • Labor loss of 15 percent is a good practice metric for projects lasting seven months or longer
Availability of favorable environmental factors such as colocation, tools, coaching, and infrastructure support	• Moderate influence on velocity	• Environment affects team performance
Dependencies with other teams and work streams	• Low if properly sequenced and buffered • Not included in the velocity estimates	• Dependencies affect the ability of an iteration to begin as planned • Interteam dependences may affect the order of delivered functionality without affecting overall cost and schedule
Critical path or noncritical path	• Not every iteration is on the critical path	• Resource scarcity of subject-matter experts affects the delivered scope • Opportunity may arise to make up the shortfall in scope without affecting the schedule, but at a cost • If the iteration is not part of the critical path, it may be starved of a required resource, and might miss the scope objective

Scope, Complexity, and Velocity Drive All Estimates

Estimating in the agile space focuses on three parameters:

1. Number of requirements in the backlog
2. Complexity of requirements
3. Team velocity

From these three, the timeline and cost can be estimated. As each planning wave matures, the estimating begins again for the next wave that rolls in.

Mainstream Estimating Practices

Table 7-3 lists estimating practices that are mainstream in the industry:

Table 7-3 Mainstream estimating practices:

Practice	Commentary
Top-down allocation	• Not so much an estimate as a value judgment, a budget of time, dollars, or both is spread proportionally among features and functions according to the customer's attitude about importance and urgency.
Similar-to, or analogous	• The estimate is taken from the cost history of a similar system, product, or task. • The estimate is adjusted for drivers that may have changed such as inflation, environment, and specific requirements that are no longer relevant. • New requirements are estimated proportionally to their nearest analog.
Parameter or model driven	• The estimate is taken based on multiplying units by a parameter, like dollars per page by the number of pages. The parameters come from historical benchmarks. • Models such as COCOMO II are populated with parametric data, various multipliers are applied, and the results of many parametric factors are summed into a final result.[1]
Stick-built bottoms-up	• Each element is individually evaluated for the likely cost; similar-to estimates, parameter estimates, models, and simulations may be combined with detailed evaluations, analysis, and prototyping to build up an estimate from the lowest nondivisible element.

Cost and Duration Are Derived!

Chapter 6 discussed the planning process for agile projects beginning with the business plan. The top-level business milestones and affordability targets originate in the business plan. However, that is the business side of the project balance sheet. The corresponding cost and schedule estimates made by the project fill out the other side according to these two important points:

1. Schedule duration is derived by applying available throughput to the business case scope, *and continues to be derived after every iteration!*
2. Cost is derived from the effort to meet requirements as in all methodologies, but the agile twist is that *requirements are never frozen;* the requirements deck remains open for nearly the whole duration of the project.

In the big picture, requirements are changeable as the product master seeks a best-value solution. Obviously, an open requirements deck means that cost and duration are always in play, ultimately limited by the cap on affordability established in the business plan. Duration is not estimated in the manner that is customary in plan-driven project development lifecycle methodologies because requirements are only incrementally stabilized for each iteration.

A project management tip	Cost and duration
	• Plans change with each iteration. • Cost and schedule duration are derived from the total throughput required to work down all the requirements. • Requirements, however, are not fixed; in the agile methodologies, the customer, whether internal or external, is encouraged to constantly interpret what is needed. • So, the cost and duration are not fixed, but the stakeholders get to vote after every release whether to continue.

Building an Estimate: Meter and Scale

To build an estimate, focus first on the elements from Table 7-1, which require estimating or benchmarking: *requirements complexity* and *velocity*. The fundamental approach to estimating is built on two principles:

1. Diversification reduces risk
2. Benchmarks provide a safe port in a storm

To diversify the risk that an estimator may be wrong, engage many independent estimators. Direct each expert to look at the same problem at the same time and provide an estimate. Then combine all the independent estimates in some agreed way to arrive at a consensus.

To incorporate benchmarks, compare your effort with an understood standard, making adjustments for unique circumstances. Four elements are needed to diversify and benchmark:

1. A process for independent evaluation by more than one estimator
2. A process and a means to combine estimator results to get a consensus estimate
3. A process to compare and make adjustments to a benchmark
4. A relative-weight scoring system for complexity

These elements are further expanded:

Process for evaluation and consensus: A recommended process for independent evaluation with combined results is called *wideband Delphi*. Wideband Delphi will be described in subsequent sections.

Compare and make adjustments: A good benchmark will be a unit of scope already completed and in production about which the team has a good understanding. Make proportional adjustments for functional and feature complexity, the state of requirements as they were going-in, the environment that prevailed, the experience and cohesion of the team at that time, and the customer involvement.

Scoring system: A scoring system will have two elements:

1. An unambiguous definition of what to score
2. The scale and meter for the score

There are many ideas about what to score: Business stories, scenarios and themes, use cases, and user stories—all of these and any of these are candidates. The important point is not which to pick, but to pick one and thereafter be consistent and repeatable!

The meter—the metric or unit of measure—can be any of many possibilities. The common list is function points, feature points, story points, or standard or *ideal* days. These are not measures of activity; they are measures of product produced.

A project management tip	Activity versus product
	• Do not fall into the trap of focusing estimates on activity. • What is needed for a unit estimate is the effort to be expended within a prescribed time box to produce one unit of product at an estimated level of complexity.

For purposes of discussion and illustration, we will focus on the story point. Story points are not particularly better than the others, but in the spirit of *pick one!* story points are our choice. There is no dimension assigned to a story point—the meter is a dimensionless number. There is no exact definition to a story point, but we have defined a story point for the purposes of this book:

Story Point
A story point is a quantity of effort to develop one unit of product with minimum relative complexity; in effect, *a story point results in a unit of outcome.*

In this sense, we think of an iteration delivering so many story points of outcome. The more a requirement is valued in story points, the more scope and complexity is represented. Effort tracks points with a 1-to-1 ratio—double the points, double the effort.

To calibrate the effort of one story point, the team firsts agree on granularity—the grain of the requirements decomposition. Too fine a grain loses cohesion; too large a grain obscures detail. Deciding the grain is a judgment to be considered, debated, and agreed to by the team. Once the requirements have been decomposed, the team selects an example of the simplest requirement and also one that seems about midpoint in complexity. Then, the simplest requirement is assigned the lowest value of points on the scale and becomes a benchmark for lowest complexity. Similarly, the midcomplexity requirement is given a midscale value. The actual numerical values are completely dependent on the scale chosen.[5]

The scale is the number of points assignable. Scale is simply a means to establish the relative difference between units. The scale could be the numbers from 1 to 20, or from 10 to 200; the actual scale is irrelevant to the results. An important idea to keep in mind is that it is generally accepted that people effectively can cope with an order of magnitude—1 to 10, up to perhaps 1 to 20. Beyond that range, people find it very hard to meaningfully assign different values.[6] If an object being estimated does not seem to fit within the range, then the object is judged very complex and thereby out of range. In this case, a best practice is to decompose the very complex object into less complex components and estimate them as a collection.

Quick Example of Story Points

Here is a quick example of how this works; process steps and data are shown in Table 7-4, Estimation example, and continue in Table 7-5, Managing estimates.

Once estimates are made, it may be required to reprioritize and resequence stories to optimize a benefit stream or fit effort within the limits of a time-boxed iteration. A summary of steps is given in Table 7-5.

Estimating in this manner is more an art than a science. The first one or two iterations may be off a bit if there is not a good benchmark going in, but accuracy will correct itself after the first couple of iterations as the teams go through self-inspection, reflection, and adaptation to measured results.[7]

Estimating Velocity

In the foregoing example, it was assumed that the team had benchmarked itself to a throughput of 20 story points per iteration, ±2 points. There are a few ways to establish this benchmark:

- If the team has been together for a while, then past performance on other iterations is the best indicator
- If the team has not been together or if the environment has been frequently changed, then the team could execute a practice development or run a simulation on a couple of stories to benchmark their performance

Table 7-4 Estimation example

Example step	Commentary
Benchmark team throughput	• Assume there is one team working that has benchmarked its velocity—team throughput—on similar projects at 20 story points per iteration, ±2 points, for a range of 18 to 22
Set a throughput goal for the iteration	• The team elects to take on 17 points of the highest-priority work • By selecting only 17 points rather than 18 to 22, the team takes into account that a buffer is needed to guarantee success • A buffer provides an allowance for the user to have some flexibility to interpret requirements during the iteration
Count requirements in backlog for the first iteration	• A candidate set of requirements for the iteration backlog has been assembled according to priority • By a simple count, the selection is about 20 percent of the total backlog
Estimate complexity	• By a means yet to be described, the overall requirements backlog and the candidate iteration backlog complexity have been estimated • The estimated complexity of the selection is 25 story points, ±3 points; too much for this team for a single iteration • The iteration backlog will have to be reprioritized to only 17 story points

Table 7-5 Managing estimates

Example step	Commentary
Product master sets priorities	• The product master sets a priority for the requirements in the iteration backlog • The product master selects a backlog that fits the throughput capacity of the team
Project manager estimates project duration	• The project manager also makes estimates: 20 percent of the total requirements deck has an estimated scope of 25 points • Assuming that representative selections were made, infer that the total deck is five times larger: 125 points, ±15 points • To burn down 125 points, ±15 points , using one team, it could take as many as nine iterations, calculated by $\frac{125 + 15}{17}$ iterations, and taking the next highest integer • On the other hand, after the first couple of iterations, the team may conclude that 17 points is not aggressive enough; the team adapts to experience and the figure is raised to 20 points per iteration • The impact on the project is profound: The total duration might be reduced by two iterations

- The team lead and the project manager might agree that the team is similar to other teams for which there is a good benchmark. After the first couple of iterations, the team will find its own mark.

Estimating Complexity

When making estimates, consistency is valued more than accuracy for the first couple of iterations, because with a consistent approach continuous improvement is possible. Consider these two points:

1. The same people should do the estimating each time. The experiences and biases of the estimators will have a large influence on the outcomes. Agile methods count on adaptive correction to smooth things out, but such adaptation requires the team to stay together and to be consistently involved in all estimating.
2. The same estimating tools or practice should be used, because again there are biases in any practice that can only be neutralized over time and with experience.

There are several alternatives for scale. The more popular alternatives are given in Table 7-6. Two of the three scales shown are nonlinear. The purpose of the nonlinearity is to force some separation between complexity estimates. In other words, it is more meaningful to say something is twice or three times as complex

Table 7-6 Popular estimating scales

Scale	Commentary
Linear	• A linear scale from 1 to 10, all the integers available as a possible complexity score • Does not directly *help* separate course grades of complexity between low, medium, and high • However, grouping as shown is an effective way to use the linear scale: low 1, 2, 3 . . . medium 4, 5, 7 . . . high 7, 8, 9 . . . very high 10
Binary	• A binary scale from 1 to 32, the sequence being 1, 2, 4, 8, 16, 32 as the only possible complexity scores • Helps separate course grades of complexity by only allowing the specific values in the scale
Fibonacci	• A Fibonacci scale from 1 to 21, the sequence being 1, 2, 3, 5, 8, 13, 21. In this scale, each number is the sum of the preceding two numbers • Some like this scale better than the binary for separating complexity values, but it is a judgment call • The Fibonacci sequence is used in many types of analysis but, in the context of requirements complexity, its properties are not materially superior to the binary scale

as something else is than to say something is 1.25 times as complex. Accuracy need only be *good enough* for the team to do its work; too much precision is unwarranted. For these reasons, either the binary or Fibonacci scales are used most often.

An Estimating Process: Delphi and Poker

Estimating tools provide assistance to the estimating process. To see how they are used, we will apply them to the *estimate complexity* step in the scenario given in Table 7-4.

A tried-and-true approach is called the Delphi method. The Delphi method was developed in the 1948 by the Rand Corporation to address uncertainties surrounding emerging defense technologies. In a more up-to-date variant, Barry Boehm and John Farquhar expanded and made popular study work done in 1970 by Farquhar. Farquhar's study compared the accuracy of the Delphi estimates with estimates of the same problem from simple group collaboration. Boehm and Farquhar arrived at a process they called *wideband Delphi*, which itself has been more recently adapted and updated by other practitioners.[8] In any variant of the Delphi method, the gist of the matter is that each team member estimates independently. A process of consensus building provides a means to arrive at a team estimate from all the independent estimates.

In a conventional Delphi approach, a facilitator gives each estimator information about the estimation task; there may be preliminary discussion with the facilitator to understand the issues. The estimator works independently and privately to arrive at an estimate. Privacy ensures that the estimator is not influenced by the reputation and biases of the other estimators, or off-put by any personal loyalties and organizational politics. After the first round of estimates, the facilitator works privately with each estimator to understand their point of view; the facilitator provides each with the benefit of the other estimates, albeit anonymously. Estimators are allowed to reconsider and change their estimate based on the new information. The process continues until the facilitator has enough information to recommend an estimate. There is no requirement stating that all estimators agree with the estimate taken away by the project manager.

Delphi in Systems Design
In high-reliability systems, independently developed redundant programs can be employed to vote on a proper system response to a stimulus. This is a form of a Delphi methodology applied to system design. The theory is that if a wrong answer is found in one version of the program, other redundant but independent versions will not have the error and will collectively out vote the one incorrect representation.

In its original form, Delphi is inconsistent with agile principles. Agile principles require public collaboration between team members. On the other hand, simply averaging the answers of a simple collaboration has some structural problems. For instance, in a simple average, one outlier can skew the average. And there are the intangibles to consider. By force of personality, one aggressive estimator can bias the whole team to a single point of view.

Wideband Delphi is the middle ground between Delphi and simple collaboration. It is slightly different from its parent; the *wideband* label comes from increased communications and collaboration added to the more private Delphi method.

Here is how wideband Delphi works: the project manager calls the estimating team together for an initial collaboration and group discussion. Information from the WBS and other sources is provided. Each estimator then works privately and independently on the first estimate, but subsequent rounds of reestimation are collaborative with each estimator given an opportunity to explain their estimate. The process ends when the group develops a satisfactory consensus.

In a popular implementation of wideband Delphi for agile projects, a game called *agile planning poker* is played.[9] Each player holds a hand of cards with all the numbers from the scale. Typically, either the binary or Fibonacci scale is used but, as we know, the scale is largely immaterial if applied consistently from one team to the next.

In the first step of the game after an initial discussion with the facilitator and after being dealt a hand, each player makes their first estimate by turning over their cards. To make it closer to the way real poker is played, everyone shows his or her card at the same time. In part, the simultaneous turnover of the card is to avoid estimators changing their estimate after viewing the other cards.

In the second step of the game, just like in any variant of wideband Delphi, the team discusses the estimates. Usually, only the extreme estimates are discussed to save time. Following the first play and the group discussion, a second hand can be played, or the team might have enough information to arrive at a consensus without playing a second hand.

In a study of planning poker versus just a simple average of the estimates, the researchers found that poker estimates, after completing the game, were less optimistic and generally more accurate than a simple arithmetic combination of independent estimates.[10]

Staffing Effects on Estimates

A useful rule that has emerged from those who have studied Brooks' Law in real situations is that, although the schedule does extend when effort is added, the sensitivity is much less than a 1-to-1 ratio. Empirical results show that the schedule extends approximately by the cube root of the effort increase. Doubling the effort likely increases the scheduling duration only by a factor of 1.27.[11]

However, Brooks envisioned adding effort in a way that would increase team size, thereby threatening team cohesion and impacting communications because of the N^2 problem. In agile methods, team sizes are fixed except for the occasional addition of a subject-matter expert on a temporary basis. Therefore, the way to add effort is to add whole teams. Certainly, another team will complicate communication and collaboration with all other teams, but the impact will not be as personal as making existing teams larger.

In conventional project management with activity-driven network schedules, leveling the workload of individuals is always a difficult task. In agile methods, this problem all but goes away since the basic building block is a team and not an individual. Team workload is designed to be nearly constant so that pace and productivity are maintainable over a long period. There will be exceptions for special talents in short supply that must be shared across teams, but the problem of resource leveling is greatly diminished.

Even without increasing effort, schedule can be impacted by the way resources are deployed—that is, the way teams are applied to requirements. The fact is that just as Brooks debunked the man-month by showing that effort and calendar are not interchangeable because of sequencing constraints and indivisible tasks, the same is true when scaled up to the team and iteration.[12] Everything else equal, the schedule always extends when otherwise independently acting resources become correlated by dependencies. This we know intuitively and by observation, but there is also a mathematical basis for the phenomenon as explained in the text box. The mitigation choices are few: planned-in time buffers for each team to finish their work and thereby not delay the start of the next development cycle; and planned-in complexity to allow for logical sequencing required by architecture, functional dependencies, and technical feasibility.

Interdependence Causes Things to Spread Out

When independent parallel or tandem activities become interdependent, their interdependence is like either an intersection or a union, in effect either an 'AND' or an 'OR' respectively.

The opportunity space of the union or intersection will be different than the individual activities and generally more encompassing, best evaluated in practical situations by simulation or models.

Summary and Takeaway Points

There are no facts about the future, only estimates. A good agile estimate accounts for the complexity of intangibles and the uncertainty of requirements. A good estimate melds the facts from history with a judgment about likely future outcomes.

Every good estimate is really a range of possibilities, some very likely and others not so likely. Range is made more meaningful with an estimate of confidence.

There is no magic bullet or algorithm that substitutes for judgment and consideration when facing the complexity of intangible requirements. Experience shows that the myriad of interactions hide many effects until the product is tested, sometimes until it is first used. This is where the power of incremental development and delivery comes to bear: complexity is best addressed in digestible chunks amenable to planning in waves and estimating in segments that can be stabilized for development.

In the agile space, estimates are focused on outcomes within a planning wave. A convenient surrogate for estimating purposes is a vehicle such as story points. Story points express a unit of delivery at a benchmarked complexity. More complexity means more story points.

Velocity is a measure of throughput: how many story points one team can produce in an iteration. If the backlog is many complex requirements, then the story points producible in one iteration will only cover a few requirements, and the other way around.

In the end, estimates provide the objective evidence needed by planners to reassure stakeholders and establish trust with customers.

Chapter Endnotes

1. The quotation is a favorite saying of Dr. David Hulett, given to the author in 1997 during an engagement assessing the risk of a millennium project.
2. Brooks, *The Mythical Man-month*, 21.
3. Ibid, 25.
4. Weaver, *Science and Complexity*.
5. A detailed example of the relative points estimating approach as applied to a non-software project is given in Goodpasture, *Quantitative Methods in Project Management*, 84–97.
6. Cohn, *Agile Estimating and Planning,* 52. For authority, Cohn references the 1997 work of Thomas Saaty, a renowned researcher in the field of decision-making and analysis. Saaty calls his body of work the Analytical Hierarchy Process (AHP); See Saaty, *The Analytic Hierarchy Process.* Saaty has documented his work in many papers. For example, see Saaty. *Decision Making with the Analytic Hierarchy Process,* 83–98, in which Saaty uses the linear scale of 1 to 9 to demonstrate the assignment of values to decision elements.
7. For a more comprehensive discussion of story points and velocity, see Cohn, *Agile Estimating and Planning,* 35–40.
8. Boehm, *Software Engineering Economics,* Chapter 22. The method is summarized on pg 335. Farquhar, *A Preliminary Inquiry into the Software Estimation Process*. See also a good explanation for practitioners. Stellman and Greene, *Applied Software Project Management*, Chapter 3.

9. Planning poker was first written about in a short paper by James Grenning. It was then made more popular by authorities such as Mike Cohn. See Cohn, *Agile Estimating and Planning*, Chapter 6; Grenning, *Planning Poker, or How to Avoid Analysis Paralysis while Release Planning.* Now, commercial and online versions of the game are available.

10. Molokken-Ostvold and Haugen, *Combining Estimates with Planning Poker.*

11. McConnell, *Software Estimating: Demystifying the Black Art*, 223. The cube root of 2 is approximately 1.27, meaning 2 = 1.27 × 1.27 × 1.27 to a pretty close approximation. The equation for schedule duration increase is:

$$\text{new duration} = \text{old duration} \times (\text{new effort/old effort})^{1/3}$$

12. Brooks, *The Mythical Man-month*, 17–19.

Table Endnote

1. COCOMO is an acronym taken from the phrase COnstructive COst MOdel, emphasizing the model's focus on the construction phase of the project. COCOMO II is a follow-on model to the original COCOMO 81 developed by Dr. Barry Boehm and his associates in 1981. As given by Boehm, et al., on page 3 of the reference, COCOMO II was developed partly in response to the growing popularity of object models, off-the-shelf software packages, the demise of batch processing in lieu of more lean methods, and the employment of iterative, incremental, and agile methods. See Boehm, et al., *Software Cost Estimation with COCOMO II.*

8

Teams Are Everything

Small teams that are faithful to frequent, incremental releases, and capable of self-organization, are the performance-unit building blocks of agile methods.

Problem 1: The people on the projects were not interested in learning our system.
Problem 2: They were successfully able to ignore us, and were still delivering software, anyway.

Alistair Cockburn

There has always been a place for lone eccentrics: brilliant and unpredictable, innovative, and occasionally delightful in their genius. But the essence of agile methods is teamwork. And why not? Patrick Lencioni writes, ". . .teamwork is the ultimate competitive advantage. . ."[1] And, not only teams, but teams of professionals with multiple skills who can act redundantly and work collectively.

And more good news: agile teams will not be working alone. Teams will be surrounded by a generous number of stakeholders, people positioned up and down the supply chain. There will be members of the marketing and sales teams, executives, post-production support, and others who have both an interest and a stake in the outcome. All will offer help and support, a few will be deeply committed, some will set constraints, and others will cause delays—perhaps unwittingly—so all around there will be help.

But there are reasons to pause. It is hard work to develop the kind of teams that work well in agile methods: teams that are self-leading, self-organizing, and march productively to their own drum. And there are unique circumstances: the customer is embedded with the developers. The impact of having the product master embedded in the midst of team operations can be profound: instant interpretation, timely feedback, and a single voice. But sometimes close is too close! The line between technical and functional requirements becomes blurred; the stability required to meet tight iteration time boxes is disturbed. A compelling personality might unduly bias decisions.

Teams Are Formed from Social Units

People are naturally sociable. People draw comfort, security, strength, and reinforcement both from others around them and from networks they join. For evidence, look at the popularity of electronic networking. Not only is there widespread participation in social networking, but business networking has also gone electronic. In businesses and organizations of all types, the sociability of people enables successful teamwork.

Groups as the Genesis of Teams

In a manner of speaking, family is the first group we join. Family members learn about networking and learn to network. They learn behaviors that enable group participation. As a group, family members communicate, exchange information, support group activities, and bestow rewards.

For a group to form there must be opportunity and motivation for interaction among the participants, but a crowd is not a group, nor is a cocktail party. To have a group, there must be:

- A common purpose that attracts members either to join and stay.
- Some division of responsibility and some distinguished roles such as leader and functional contributor.
- Accepted norms for behavior and participation.
- Defined operating processes.
- A set of protocols for reward, discipline, or sanction. These protocols provide a means for attaching incentives to group membership and for dismissing undesirables.[2]

Attitudes about territory, space, and identity shaped by culture and experience affect behavior within groups. Everyone has his or her own tolerance for closeness and a need for a place to call his or her own—a phenomenon called territory dominance. But there is personality dominance also. Dominance must be settled before a group can act effectively. Group membership sharpens feelings about self-identity: *Who am I and how do I fit in?* People immediately sense those who have *command presence* and who are going to emerge naturally as leaders. When we address virtual teams in this chapter, some of the issues of identity and space will take on new meaning.

Groups are not teams; however, forming a group is often the first step in forming a team. And populations, partnerships, bureaucracies, associations, and committees are not teams. Teams are different from all of these. And some *teams* are really not teams at all. For example, business executive *teams* are frequently criticized for behaving more like a group than like a team. The problem with executive teams is dominance: teamwork is inhibited by unsettled dominance of person and territory—the power and influence that comes from organizational position are not easily set aside.

Partnerships, Bureaucracies, and Populations
• Partnerships are shared-risk and shared-reward relationships; partners operate independently but pool their outcomes for a common reward. • Bureaucracies are hierarchical command-control structures that organize resources in parent-child relationships. But mutual support up and down the chain is often begrudged and is present only because the command regimen requires it. Nevertheless, bureaucracies are the model of choice when organizing large populations. • Populations and associations are farther still from the idea of a team. In most cases, they also lack the structures of a group or bureaucracy. People are members of associations by choice, choosing according to a few common attributes such as a professional affinity. • Committees can be teams of course, but often a committee is just a small-scale bureaucracy, wherein the members do assigned tasks with only a modest commitment to the larger goal.

So, what is a team?

Team Defined
A team is a social structure wherein all members individually and mutually collaborate toward the achievement of a common goal that is possible only by the committed and collective contribution of all members.

In the agile space, a team is a *performance unit*. A performance unit, viewed from the outside looking in, is a single entity with operational capability described by a performance specification. *Velocity* is the performance metric, defined as the amount of constant-quality throughput that is produced over the course of one iteration.[3] From a management perspective, a performance unit is an encapsulated body with a defined throughput; its mission is to transform backlog into valuable product.

A project management tip	The team as a little black box
	• A team can be characterized almost as an object, encapsulated by team boundaries. • Encapsulation creates a little black box. • The little black box has public and private procedures, a defined means to get things in and out, and a predictable, repeatable performance.

In Chapter 7, the entire estimating regime rests on the concept of a team as an integrated performance unit. The capabilities of individuals are secondary because working collaboratively and collectively diversifies the variances found in individual performances

Teams from Groups

Teams are not the most natural social formation: many people are uncomfortable with, or skeptical of, teams and working on a team. We all know from our common experience that teams do not just happen. Tuckman's *forming-storming-norming-performing-adjourning* behavior model remains relevant since its introduction in 1965.[4]

Bruce Tuckman's model[5]
• Forming: The team meets and learns about the challenges and opportunities. • Storming: Different ideas compete for consideration and adoption. • Norming: Behaviors are adjusted to make teamwork productive. • Performing: Collective, collaborative work-styles reinforce the work of each member; conflicts are about solutions, not people. • Adjourning: The task is completed and the team's work is archived; the team members are dismissed to their operational units.

The first step is to form a group. Once a group establishes some basic stability, teaming begins—storming and norming in the Tuckman model. The team inherits properties of the group, properties like common purpose or charter, roles and responsibilities, and rules for personal behavior. But reaching a state of performing requires extending the group parameters in several important ways:[6]

- Define a compelling, unambiguously identifiable, and measurable team mission.

- Establish standards for personal achievement, commitment, and accountability. Energy is to be directed toward outcomes and not toward individual competitions.
- Set an expectation that the team must succeed for each person to be successful.
- Require work to be collaborative and collective; most deliverables require the integration and application of multiple skills.
- Develop leadership from within the team. A strong hierarchical leader is not always necessary to organize and manage the work if teammates can comfortably share leadership responsibilities.
- Develop methods and processes within the team, but adopt and adapt them from the standards and conventions of the enterprise.

Principles and Values Guide Teams

Reaching a high performance level requires member-to-member cohesion—a willingness and commitment to stick together and see the job through. Team cohesion, sometimes called unit cohesion, depends on shared values and beliefs and commonly accepted principles for day-to-day guidance. In a truly cohesive team, the individual so believes in the welfare of the team that individual loyalties become team loyalties. Cohesion sustains the will and commitment to the mission and to the organization.[7] But much is required; people must subordinate their individual competitiveness, must be receptive to critique and help, and must join in with others, surrendering a bit of privacy, self-centering, and positional power and authority. *S1 high-task* directive management gives way to leadership by relationship: collaborative, bidirectional listening, facilitating, and supporting.

Situational Leadership

S1 through S4 are the tags for the four situational leadership styles promoted by Hersey, Johnson, and Blanchard.[8]

S1 is high-task direction projected onto low-capability followers.

S2, S3, and S4 are less directive and more delegating, assuming a correspondingly greater competence and motivation of followers.

Perhaps most important, the success of self-organizing teams—those that are given license and latitude to satisfy the customer rather than to follow a prescription—depends on internalization of team values and principles.

Values that Make Teams Work

Certain values make teams work because they go to the heart of interpersonal relationships: trust, commitment, accountability, continuity, simplicity, clarity, and certainty.

- *Trust:* Trust is believing that others will act not only in their interests but also in yours. It requires an exchange of power, and power exchange is only enabled by honesty, openness, and a track record of dependability and accountability. "Trust lies at the heart of a functioning, cohesive team. Without it teamwork is all but impossible," writes Patrick Lencioni. In fact, among the five main reasons for team failure, he lists lack of trust as number one.[9]

  In the absence of trust, there can be no team, so bureaucracies are built instead. Bureaucracies are inherently oriented to structure, substituting positional power and prescribed command and control for trusting relationships.

  One must be free of fear in order to trust. Freedom of fear implies safety in both personal and professional relationships. Safety makes it possible to be vulnerable and consequently willing to join with others for strength and resolve. In fact, *personal safety* is one of the seven principles of the Crystal method and is repeated in the Humanity Principle of XP. As defined by Crystal's Alistair Cockburn, personal safety is a step toward trust; personal safety is freedom from the fear of reprisal. Trust, building on safety, is in part giving power over your person to someone else and being comfortable with the power transfer.[10]

  Virtual teams have their own special circumstances that impact building trust. In spite of many separations—time, distance, location, and organization—trust is just as important as if members were co-located.[11] Trust requires mutual identity—there can be no trust among strangers. There must be effective communication to assess safety and establish the parameters of the power transfer. Communication depends first on language and second on culture. Culture affects understanding of the meaning and the intent of words and deeds—when does no mean no; is a nod agreement, an understanding, or just politeness? Culture affects how we convey purpose and priority—does an e-mail attach the same importance as a phone call, and does a phone call mean there is personal rapport? Consider this example: to some, mistakes are evidence of reaching, striving, and going for the near unattainable; to others with a different cultural outlook, mistakes are evidence of poor planning and execution. For some, only facts are trusted; for others, intuition and vision are more valued.

A project management tip	Track records build trust
	• Only time and opportunity to build a track record between the virtual members will resolve mistrust.

- *Commitment and accountability:* Teams value the sincerity and integrity of the commitment and willingness to be held accountable. Who has not approached a team assignment with skepticism, reluctant to join a personal fate with the fate of the team, or harbored a suspicion that more will be asked than given? A real team is *norming* when members offer and pledge unwavering commitment to the team objective. A real team is *performing* when members are willingly open to the judgment of others, agreeing that success is defined by a joint performance.
- *Continuity, simplicity, clarity, and certainty:* Teams value continuity, simplicity, clarity, and certainty of purpose and method. To have clarity and certainty presumes little or no confusion. Effort, ingenuity, and energy are directed to intended results and are not dissipated by spinning wheels, changing direction, and adopting the flavor of the day. Simplicity is the absence of unnecessary complexity, yet the simplest solution may still be complex.[12] Continuity means that from one moment to the next, change is under control.

Table 8-1 captures the ideas so far discussed.

Table 8-1 Summary of team values

Value	Commentary
Trust	• A willingness to be vulnerable to and accepting of the performance and commitment of others as they act in your joint interests
Commitment	• A pledge to apply all possible effort, energy, and ingenuity to the successful completion of the goal
Accountability	• A willingness to be judged by others and an acceptance of a personal responsibility for the completion of assigned tasks
Continuity	• An exhibition of a condition wherein things remain essentially the same until changed for reasonable and justifiable reasons, subordinating change to the completion of the team goal
Simplicity	• The absence of unnecessary complexity
Clarity	• The absence of confusion
Certainty	• The absence of unmitigated risk

Principles for Successful Teams

Principles are the guidance for daily work. Principles channel energy and activity directionally in accord with values. Taking principles to heart is a prerequisite to affect teaming in an agile self-organization model. Table 8-2 lists the universal principles that every team should adopt:

Table 8-2 Principles for successful teams

Principle or guideline	Commentary
Teams are the best structure to execute complex interdisciplinary projects	• Multifunctional teams accept and embrace complexity, disorder, and uncertainty more effectively than individuals working alone because of mutual support for problem solving and opportunity for group creativity
No team will be chartered without a compelling purpose and mission to accomplish actual work	• A compelling mission is the most effective motivator for cohesion and commitment
Communication and collaboration will be frequent and without reticence	• Teams are only better than groups of individuals when teammates achieve synergy • Synergistic results require communication and collaboration on a timely basis while there is still opportunity to incorporate advice
Teams will be made small, but encouraged to network for scale	• Larger teams require internal structures and authority figures to manage the scale • Small teams can have the effect of large teams by networking and committing to joint objectives
Team assignments will be made with staff disposed to commitment and accountability	• Assignments made only on the basis of position and availability are discouraged • Assignments focus on completing the compliment of technical, functional, and decision-making skills • Assignments recognize that high-performance people are not plug-compatible replaceable
Time and activities to promote trust will be planned into the project timeline	• Strangers do not trust • Virtual teams need more time and specific opportunity to overcome factors unique to the displacement of team members
A safe working environment will be provided	• Safety is the first step to trust • Reprisals for speaking out will not be tolerated, a role as nemesis will be accepted

Table 8-2 *(continued)*

Principle or guideline	Commentary
Team members will be encouraged to actively listen, give the benefit of the doubt, respond constructively, and acknowledge others' achievements[1]	• The *golden rule* of team behavior
Team results and measurements will be evaluated for collective achievement	• Individuals are valued for their skill and ingenuity • Collective achievement is valued for its best value fit to customer expectation
Rewards will be applied to collective performance before individual performance	• The performance of the team is paramount; it transcends the performance of individuals
Self-organized teams will be granted a measure of autonomy to select their leaders and formulate their processes	• Self-organized teams can actually work without a leader, with a leader selected by the team, or with a leader role that is rotated[2] • Processes should conform to enterprise conventions to ensure the validity of all assertions and claims made to certifying bodies • Cost, schedule, and scope are managed external to the team in agile methods

Teams Are Building Blocks in the Agile Project

The team is the operating unit around which the project plan is built. A team is an active performance unit characterized by its ability to develop new product. Recall that *product* is the surrogate for whatever it is that the team produces, whether tangible or intangible, whether for internal use or external application.

The team is the performance unit that earns value and adds value to the project backlog, bringing reality to the product vision. The team is the primary operating expense of the project; it consumes most of the available investment. The pace of teamwork is the main schedule driver. Time on the calendar is primarily an accumulation of time boxes.

Operational Effectiveness

The throughput benchmark is the primary operational characteristic of the work product team. Benchmarks are track records of proven, effective performance. To be an effective, high-performance unit, the team must train together, stay together, and work together. Continuity of membership and consistency of practice are the only ways to get a reliable fix on the productivity of the team.

Effective operating units are composed of professionals who share the values and accept the principles given in Table 8-2. But teams absorb the culture of their host organization. Enterprise values come first. If the enterprise is performance-oriented and places a high value not only on timely, high-quality production but also on effective interpersonal skills and knowledge sharing, then so will its teams. The likely corollary is that it will be harder to instill an appreciation for operational effectiveness when the values and principles given in Table 8-2 are not shared by the parent organization. If members are drawn from multiple enterprises as in the case of virtual teams, then a commonly shared value system may not exist. It will have to be synthesized for the team from the contributions of members.

Operating Model of the Agile Team

> **Operating model**
>
> In the context of a value system, an operating model is the meld of the people, process, and technology chartered as a team to do work.

The operating model of the agile project team conforms generally to the parameters described in Table 8-3.

Teams depend on the project manager for establishing and maintaining a project environment and for managing the relationship with the stakeholders. The material in Table 8-4 explains the project management role with respect to the team-operating model.

Customers and end users assist the team during each sprint or iteration, as explained in Table 8-5.

Teams in Networks

Increasing the number of working teams increases capacity, but teams working within a network enables capacity with complexity. There will still be sequencing constraints, as there is no network that can enable nine women to have a baby in one month. But architecture elements can be parsed among teams in a network. Dependencies can be coordinated. The branch structure of networks enables decomposition of backlog and recomposition of product.

For agile project purposes, a network is a lattice-like structure with nodes, branches, and components. The node is the location of a component—team or system. The branch is the relationship or interface between nodes. Relationships depend on how the architecture and the WBS is divided and then allocated to

Table 8-3 Operating model of the agile team

Operating principle	Commentary
Teams are small, typically 6 to 8, but could be as large as 12	• The project manager facilitates the formation of the team • Subject-matter experts that are needed only part time are identified by the team and recruited by the project manager from the resource pool • An initial team may send its members to other teams to seed those teams with the knowledge of the product base required to maintain coordination
Team leadership and management is determined by the team	• Leadership is empowered by the team members themselves. The leaders may be elected and may be rotated from iteration to iteration • Management planning, coordinating, communicating, and reporting need not be vested in one individual • Teams are self-organizing; each team member assumes a part of the management workload • A team representative is required to participate in team-of-teams network coordination and to be a consistent point of contact for the project manager, product master, and other outsiders in the project environment • The team-of-teams representative typically has a leadership role and is empowered to make decisions • The team leader ensures that effective processes are adopted, a clear and compelling goal is set, and means of accountability and measurement are in place and functioning[3]
Team processes, practices, and rules are established by the team	• Each team may operate a bit differently; however, every team must operate consistently in order for the throughput benchmark to be meaningful • Processes must conform to the normal conventions of the organization in order to not invalidate claims and assertions required for certifications • Each methodology has its own set of rules and recommended practices • Adopting the rules and practices and enforcing discipline is a collective activity driven by commitment and accountability • Discipline is inversely related to formal control; the more self-discipline, the less formal control is required • Processes address technical and managerial practices; the team is accountable for measuring and reporting progress, assessing problems, forecasting risk, and determining mitigation • Project scorecards and dashboards are respected by the team • Virtual teams require processes for communication and coordination
Teams benchmark for productivity	• The objective of agile teams is to produce work product frequently at high quality • A productivity benchmark is necessary to have a predictable throughput • Each team is responsible for establishing and maintaining a reliable benchmark

Table 8-4 Project manager role

Operating principle	Commentary
The project manager coaches the team	• The project manager is not a directing authority over the team in the style of a manager enforcing a plan • The project manager is the manager who is responsible to the stakeholders for the business case • The project manager coaches the team to ensure all mechanics are in place, all conflicts are being managed, all nonperforming members are corrected, and all measurements and performance records are timely and accurate • Scorecards and dashboards are reviewed for completeness • If there are only one, or a few teams, the project manager facilitates the daily meetings and other meetings where a facilitator is appropriate
The project manager supports the team	• The project manager is the project-level risk manager, responsible for keeping the gap closed, or nearly so, on the project balance sheet • Constraints, roadblocks, and commitments of stakeholders and customers are managed by the project manager • All resources and environments required by the team are acquired, assembled, and deployed by direction of the project office • If there are several teams operating in a network, the project manager coordinates network activity • Cost is typically managed outside the team by the project manager • Rewards and compensation plans are administered by the project manager
The project manager manages conflict, performance and administration	• In the event the team can not resolve conflict, the project manager steps in • In the event the team fails to perform, the project manager can stop work, dissolve or reorganize the team, or take other measures as required • The project manager forecasts performance, reports results, and manages cost, scope, and budget with the sponsor • The project manager is a participant in the governance council

teams. Relationships form the channels between teams that facilitate cross-team communication, collaboration, and coordination.

The interconnection of branches and notes expresses logic. In the case of a project network, logic expresses relationships among teams designing, developing, and producing project deliverables. No timeline, calendar, or durations are

Table 8-5 Customer role with the team

Operating principle	Commentary
Product master interprets requirements	• In the SCRUM methodology, the customer representative is called the product master • The customer has a responsibility to provide a product expert—one or many depending on scale—to interpret requirements and validate test results • The customer has a right to see and evaluate product development at an early enough stage that correction and adjustments are possible
The customer establishes the value proposition	• The voice of the customer speaks for the value proposition of the project beginning with the business case • A primary task of the customer is to set priorities among features and functions competing for resources • Urgency and importance are the say of the customer; feasibility, architectural consistency, structural sequencing, and affordability are the say of the technical and management staff
The product master is committed to team success	• The product master is the one customer who is committed and accountable for the user input to the product development • For agile teams to be effective with relatively short iterations, the team has a right to expect that a committed customer or user will be at-the-ready, embedded in the team if possible, but always available on very short notice
The product master speaks for the customer community	• The product master represents the customer community • In large scale projects, the customer community may be organized into one or more teams by functional needs • The project master helps the project manager coach the customer community for a coherent picture of requirements

required to construct the network. If actual timing requires lead and lag buffers beyond the buffers in each iteration, then they are added as whole iterations.

Figure 8-1 illustrates the discussion.

Mind-shifting to Agile Networks

Most of the discussion about agile projects has not assumed a network operating model. One team working diligently from one iteration to the next can accomplish much. But sometimes one team cannot get it done in time. A schedule that is too long might morph calculable risk into incalculable uncertainty. A project stretched too long might endanger the whole benefit stream. A lengthy project is the antithesis of agile: rapid response intended to be faster than the cycle of business and markets.

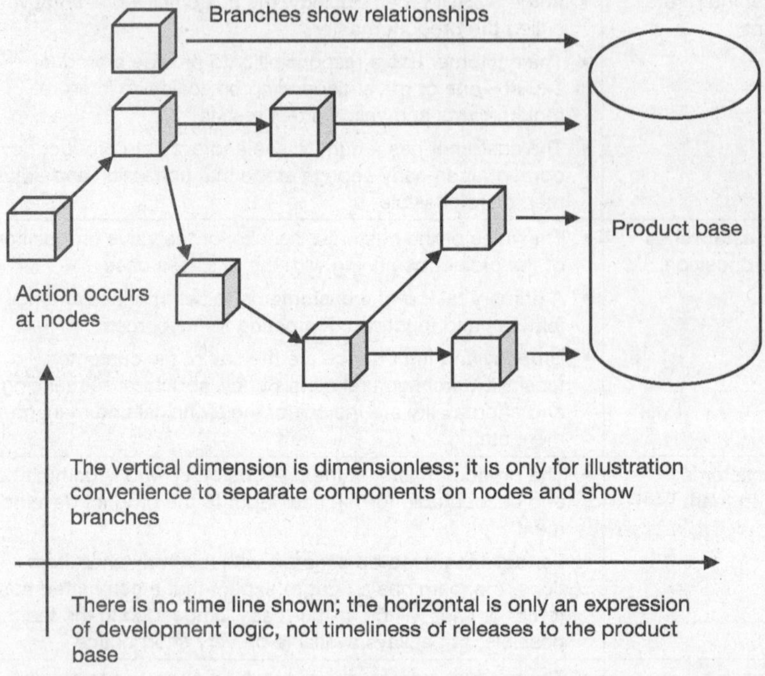

Figure 8-1 Generic network

The remedy is to apply more resources to ramp up development and delivery capacity. But making teams larger is problematic. Communications—the lubricant of team productivity—is adversely affected by the addition of more team members. Experienced project managers know that adding more people also adds more person-to-person bidirectional communication links—Karoline needs to talk to Emma as well as everyone else that is added, and everyone needs to respond to Karoline and Emma, as well as the others. In fact, the number of links increases by nearly the square of the number of teammates—or the *N^2 effect*, discussed in Chapter 11.[13] Other frictions of coordination and cohesion are likewise amplified. Being mindful of Brooks' Law—*adding more people to a late project makes it later*—managers hesitate to ramp existing, ongoing teams with additional staff. The operating model with a better chance of success is to add more small teams and network the results.

For agile projects, there is a mind shift about networks; networks are about team-to-team relationships, not about developer task-to-task relationships:

> **Agile network**
>
> The network is not about tasks and activities; it is about linking performance units and their outcomes.
>
> The network is about objects, not tasks. The network is a team of teams.
>
> The usual tasks shown on a plan-driven project development lifecycle (PD-PDLC) activity network are moved inside the team boundaries. The team is the performance unit—not the individual.

So, the networked schedule is a connection of team time boxes, with production objects as the central focus, and a schedule grid. Time boxes—a team working for a fixed length of time—are affixed to the time grid; releases and planning horizons are synchronized with the grid. A pictorial of the schedule grid is given in Figure 8-2.

Performance within the network depends on the performance of each team; individual performance is encapsulated within the team structure. As already established, the team's performance is benchmarked and predictable; the risk to the team of any individual is mitigated by diversifying among team members. The main tools of diversification are redundancy, multifunctional skills, and collaboration.

Network Logic

Any network is a presentation of logic. The generic network pictured in Figure 8-1 and the team schedule pictured in Figure 8-2 are no exceptions. Logic captures two ideas:

1. Some deliverables are independent and have no dependency on others. For these, the team's starting point in the network is arbitrary, perhaps only dependent on the importance and urgency expressed by the customer. The logic can be fast-tracked by working independent teams in parallel.[14]
2. Some deliverables have interdependencies. The interdependencies can be complex or simple. By simple, we mean each team develops it own increment to the product base and depends only on other teams to properly integrate their efforts with the product base—the principle of *do no harm*. In a simple dependency, there is not a functional precedence between teams, but there is a need to be always working with the latest product base so that regression tests validate proper integration.

   By complex, we mean there are sequential constraints between teams. Not only does the outcome of one team directly drive the outcome of another with finish-to-start precedence, but also the network logic respects

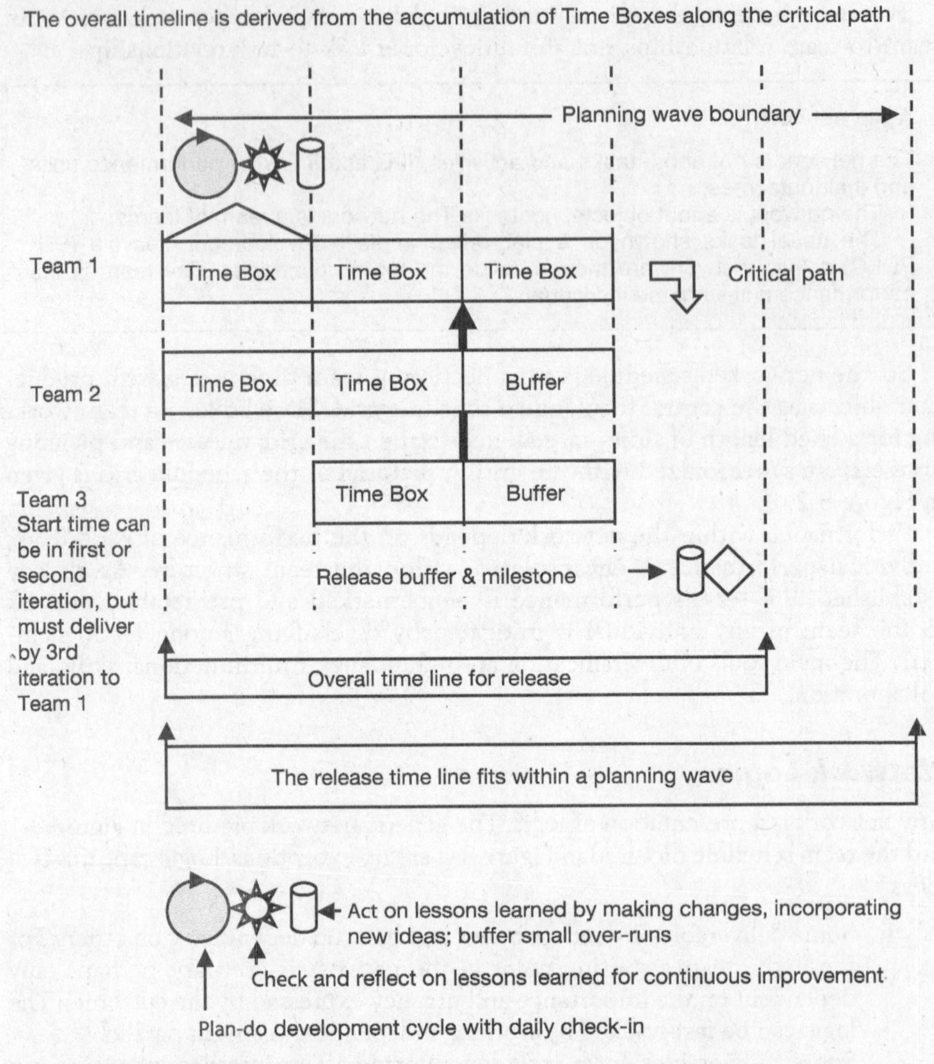

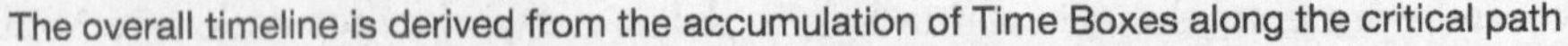

Figure 8-2 Generic team schedule

sequencing. With a sequential constraint it is impossible to rearrange sequence order and it is impossible to speed things up—that is, *crash* the schedule—by adding more resources earlier.[15]

Look back to Figure 8-1 to see both simple and complex logic concepts illustrated for Teams 1, 2, and 3. Team 3 can start in either the first or second iteration cycle; there is no dependency that fixes the start time. However, Teams 2 and 3 have a dependency with Team 1 at the outset of the third iteration cycle.

Although networks can be shown in more than one form, all share certain attributes given in Table 8-6.

Managing the Team Network

To manage a network in agile space, respect for Principle 2 is required.

> **Agile Principle 2**
>
> Welcome changing requirements, even late in the development. Agile processes harness change for the customer's competitive advantage.

Begin by constructing the team network diagram for the project logic. Allocate project backlog to each node according to customer priority and sequencing constraints. Then, develop a spreadsheet scorecard to integrate the accomplishments of each team at each node. Figure 8-3 is an example.

Table 8-6 Schedule network attributes for agile methods

Attribute	Commentary
The schedule is a uniform grid	• The grid is based on the duration picked for iteration time boxes • Release dates are synchronized to the grid • Planning horizons are fixed to the grid
Buffers reduce shift-right risk	• Buffers absorb variances in velocity that might force a team to deliver late • Total duration is buffered to absorb additional iterations needed to satisfy customer demands
A critical path is identifiable	• The critical path is the path that determines the last release • All paths in the network may not be connected because of no identifiable dependency
Velocity is not rigidly fixed	• Velocity has some distribution around an expected value • Simple triangular distributions are assumed for individual teams
Total duration of the schedule is derived	• Total duration is derived from schedule logic, overall complexity, and the throughput available to liquidate the complexity
Teams can have simple or complex dependencies on one another	• Simple dependencies means no sequential constraint with another team; complex dependency means there is a sequential constraint with another team

As with all scorecards, three elements of information are required:

1. Baseline measure; in Figure 8-3, the baseline is the storypoint production for each team by iteration
2. Operating plan that is the baseline adjusted for up-to-date information
3. Actual accomplishment

Calculations of variances to the baseline and operating plan are shown in Figure 8-3 and are:

$$\text{variance} = \text{plan} - \text{performance}$$

Production efficiencies are shown in Figure 8-3 and are calculated as:

$$\text{efficiency} = \frac{\text{performance}}{\text{plan}}$$

From the network logic, develop a spreadsheet resource plan that can be coordinated with functional managers that provide the team resources. The resource assignment matrix discussed in Chapter 5 is the beginning point for the resource plan.

Team-of-Teams

The team-of-teams is a means to coordinate team activity and product deliverables within a network. Typically, a network is constructed for each workstream.[16] Figure 8-2 is an example network for the development workstream.

The team-of-teams operates like a management working group. As a working group, it has these attributes:

- An unambiguous charter intended to coordinate product teams within the network.
- A timeline for operations that spans the timeline of all product teams.
- An imperative to meet every day, but to keep deliberations within a prescribed time box.
- A self-organizing and shared leadership.
- A set of self-designed processes for evaluating product team performance in the network.
- A membership from all the product teams and the project management office. With the consent of all members, and being mindful of the daily time box, stakeholders with a particular affinity for the network may be involved. For instance, a key manager responsibility for infrastructure, tool support, or perhaps even vendor management.
- A commitment to open, honest, and safe communications.
- A dashboard for general communication.

The team scorecard for STORY POINT production, measured at the end of each iteration, shows early velocity is not up to the planned baseline—there is recovery of the velocity, but not enough to make the planned scope at the first release milestone

	Planning Wave 2										
	Release 1										
	Interation 1			Interation 2			Interation 3			Release 1	Variance to release
	Team 1	Team 2	Team 3	Team 1	Team 2	Team 3	Team 1	Team 2	Team 3		
Baseline	50	55	50	50	55	50	50	55	50	465	
Operating plan	48	50	45	50	53	48	52	55	50	451	14
Actual performance	48	48	45	50	50	48					
Variance to baseline	2	7	5	0	5	2					
Cum variance to baseline	2	9	14	14	19	21					
Efficiency to baseline	96.00%	87.27%	90.00%	100.00%	90.91%	96.00%					
Variance to ops plan	0	2	0	0	3	0					
Cum variance to ops plan	0	2	2	2	5	5					
Efficiency to ops plan	100.00%	96.00%	100.00%	100.00%	94.34%	100.00%					

Figure 8-3 Team scorecard

The team's administrative assistant publishes a daily agenda. Not only does the administrative assistant manage the agenda, but he or she also updates the dashboard and handles other communications and coordination with the membership.

A project management tip	Steering the workstreams
	• On projects with multiple workstreams, each workstream will have a network. There will likely be points of coordination required between workstreams. • For such coordination, the project manager will have a working group chartered to steer the workstream efforts. • This working group sometimes goes by the name of *steering committee* after the character of its work. • It meets weekly by common practice. • The workstream team-of-teams is the resource pool for the steering committee. Stakeholders are often invited.

Some Teams Work; Others Do Not

Accepted doctrine is that agile teams recruit their members; staff is not arbitrarily assigned by resource managers. And agile teams are coached, not managed. The coach may be a professional agile methodologist specializing in coaching, or the coach could be the project manager.

Agile teams are self-organized and are afforded considerable latitude to get the job done. Teaming sounds great. Why doesn't it work every time?

Why Teams Don't Work

There is a serious body of thought around the idea that teams do not work, do not work well, or do not work in many situations. Many have studied dysfunctional and failed teams and situations where teams cannot seem to succeed. The findings are worth examining for lessons learned.

Teams in Corporate America
In fact, teams as multifunctional performance units only came along in American corporate life since the late 1960s. In many ways the team is a reaction to the overwhelming size and impersonal character of the corporate design that evolved from early twentieth century Taylorism. Taylor's ideas, already addressed in Chapter 1, are the seeds that drove bureaucratic design to its pinnacle, featuring multilayered enterprises that treated people as plug-compatible parts. Look only to the popularity of the cartoonstrip Dilbert™ to see the evidence. A more extensive read on the history of teams is found in Robbins and Finley's *The New Why Teams Don't Work: What Goes Wrong and How to Make It Right.*[17]

Problems begin with people as individuals. Many people are not naturally predisposed to teamwork in contrast to individual contributor work. Many who share the deep-seated cultural value that every person is a uniquely talented individual resist anonymity and subordination. Others who are fiercely and individually competitive find it difficult to accept restraints and constraints, and to put aside their own competitiveness for the greater good.

Teams are about how to organize small numbers of people, and so this is one of the first things that can go wrong. Teams are made too large. Anything larger than about a dozen requires overhead structure, management tiers, and bureaucracy to hold the team together in some kind of organizational suspension.

Apart from wrong-sizing the team, there are other management miscues:[18]

- Boundaries are too often left fuzzy—confusion is a productivity killer. Are all members clear on the team's mission, goal, and scope, and what is out?
- The mission is not made compelling; people are not naturally attracted to the purpose and goal. Constant encouragement and reinforcement is needed to overcome boredom and disinterest.
- Team members too often are selected by making the easy choices; often by position and availability. Instead, selection should be by rigorous evaluation based on skills and commitment.
- There is no allowance for a nemesis member to neutralize *group think*. Group think is a simple idea but a grave threat. Commonly held beliefs and biases become enshrined almost as axioms, crowding out alternatives and counterpoints that might be more productive and beneficial.
- The team membership is allowed to turn over too rapidly, diluting cohesion and squandering productivity built on personal relationships.

Researchers Harvey Robbins and Michael Finley have also looked at why teams don't work. They add these reasons, among others:[19]

- There is a bad decision-making process or there are inadequate decision-making skills.
- Even when guided by good decisions, teams habitually execute them poorly.
- The team includes difficult people; talented eccentrics that cannot abide sharing and collective teamwork.
- There is competition among members that often leads to secrecy and compartmentalization, quite opposite to collaboration.
- There are empowerment uncertainties, awkward and untimely decision chains, and confusion about roles, rights, and responsibilities. Empowerment requires great trust and a faith in the decision making and loyalty of the empowered.
- Many personnel issues are left unresolved, not the least of which is compensation and reward. The question, *What do I have to give up?* is not satisfactorily addressed.

With the litany of problems in the lists just given, is it any wonder that some question if teams can work, do work, or should even be a part of the operating model?

Why Teams Can Work; Why They Do Work

In the main, teams *can work* because they are social units compatible with the socializing instincts that all people have to be around like-minded people. And teams draw people in who are attracted to a compelling purpose. But, not too big a team: no one particularly likes the impersonal nature of *big*. Smaller is more personal and familiar; smaller is closer to the action; smaller is very reinforcing, made so by the opportunity for rapid feedback. Caution is advised: the values and principles discussed in this chapter need to be genuinely woven into the fabric of the enterprise, not just layered on for the moment. Anything short of honesty will impact trust and threaten safety.

Teams are a fortunate consequence of making organizational models flatter, spurred onward by the hugely influential theories of Michael Hammer and James Champy to reengineer the corporation.[20] One development in business management from the reengineering movement of the early 1990s was acceptance and faith that small multifunctional teams operating as nearly autonomous units can accomplish remarkable things.

Teams *do work* because small multiskilled performance units are ideal for addressing the unusual complexity and uncertainty that attends even small-scale software systems. Scale may require a team-of-teams, and even workstreams each with teams-of-teams. Teamwork fits the proven way to address large problems: to decompose them into the simplest forms for construction, and then recompose the product increments to achieve the product vision. It is perhaps fortunate that the sophistication and capabilities of performance teams have come along at a time of enormously intricate and pervasive systems that envision huge complexity existing in very small and increasingly very mobile platforms.

People Are Not Machines

Perhaps the best point to make is the one made by Crystal's Alistair Cockburn when he declares that people are nonlinear, both in their behavior and in their performance—nonlinear, meaning a little stimulus might produce one result but a little more might cause either regression or acceleration.[21] It could even be argued that in addition to being nonlinear, people are a bit chaotic. Systems with chaos have unpredicted responses to stimulus, their state changing over time in a seemingly random way. In systems, chaos is more a matter of an observer not being aware of cause and effect; in people, it is more a matter of irrationality at odd moments.

SCRUM and Crystal Clear, and to a lesser degree XP and EVO, declare people to be unique and not person-for-person interchangeable. To this point, agile managers make it a priority to recruit team members rather than risk assignments made by well-meaning involved-but-uncommitted managers.

Declaring people unique is certainly a repudiation of Taylor's job description and profiling practices. Taylor believed with proper job definition and supervision that any qualified person can fill a role. Seeing every person as unique is also a repudiation of the resource-planning model behind the PD-PDLC. The PD-PDLC resource model is built on the premise that the organization model can be filled with average, qualified staff members according to a resource plan.

How does agile manage staffing? First, get the right people. Approach each person separately to ascertain his or her fit to the team. Specific profiles are not as important as filling out redundancy, ensuring all functional skills are covered, and establishing that candidate individuals are fit for teamwork.

Second, be true to Principle 5, *trust motivated people to get the job done*, and Principle 8, *plan for a steady and sustainable pace*. A compelling mission and commensurate reward, in the context of a safe and effective environment, will be motivating. But then do not exploit motivation to the point of staff burnout. Approaching burnout, both nonlinear and chaotic behavior is an ever-present risk. Planning a sustainable pace requires paying attention to labor loss—an amount of time that takes away from the normal working time.

Third, diversify the skill base of the team by having more than one person available who is capable of handling a particular task. Cross train among jobs on the team so that more than one person can run a script, examine a database, or fashion a user interface. Switch job responsibilities, such as writer, tester, or verifier, from one iteration to the next. Cross-evaluate performance between team members.

A project management tip	People are not machines
	• People are most effective when they are comfortable with the culture. • Culture is the body of values and principles that we believe in and the guidance for the actions we believe is right, honest, fair, and ethical. • Teams have a culture. Forming a team is in part recruiting staff with a cultural commonality. • Every team should have a process for evaluating fitness and mitigating the unfit.

Conflict Resolution

Handling conflict effectively goes a long way to mitigating why teams do not work. The body of knowledge about conflict resolution is deep and wide, covered in many standard texts on project management, and addressed by many who have studied teams.[22] A few points regarding agile teams:

- *Accepting new members:* Agile teams are expected to stay together throughout the lifecycle of the project; not adjourning and handing over to new teams formed for later planning waves. Over time, turnover is expected, but only modest turnover because of the strength of unit cohesion. With turnover, team productivity will require recalibration; in the short run, productivity may suffer. New members require time to form effective relationships with teammates who have bonded through a shared experience. New members will not be plug-in replacements; more likely, their skills will differ from those who have left the team. It is expected that some realignment of roles and responsibilities will follow staff changes. It will take some time for realignments and relationships to fully mature.
- *Trusting new relationships:* Trust must be earned, and earnings take time. A look to Stephen Covey is appropriate: everyone comes into a relationship with a small deposit in their trust account.[23] People naturally assume an optimistic outlook when meeting people they respect. No one will be invited to join a team as a stranger. The objective of the new arrival is to build up his or her account balance. Each new team member should be accepted on this basis: he or she can be trusted until proven otherwise. Each new member must appreciate that regaining lost trust is very difficult, and even more time consuming than was establishing trust in the first place.
- *Competitiveness on the team:* Building complex systems is a competitive business, and the people who do it are competitive. But, intuitively and practically, competition breeds privacy and secrecy. There can be no effective collaboration if things are too compartmentalized. Communications and collaboration are the oil of team processes, and without them, frictions build into conflict and tension. Coach the team to replace secrecy and privacy with collaboration and trust.
- *Not a team player:* Some people cannot abide teamwork and never will. They cannot be won to collective work by trust and safety. They are constantly at odds with team values and principles. Presumably, they would not be knowingly recruited; presumably they would not be assigned to a team by a knowing manager. Nevertheless, teams find themselves with nonplayers, usually because they have an exceptional skill that is in high demand and short supply.

- *Virtual teams:* Virtual teams have their own unique conflicts. Virtual teams are not culturally integrated; members are far apart and miss the personal gesture. Socialization and bonding with teammates is largely absent; the social component is mostly local. Conflict arises out of misunderstandings which have their roots in values, language, culture, and purpose. A good practice is for virtual teams to meet face-to-face during the forming stage. If this is impractical, then a limited personal representation is next best—an exchange program. Although teleconferencing and videoconferencing are important technologies, almost nothing replaces personal touch.

Incentives and Compensation

The simple rule is to build rewards, incentives, and compensation around team achievement, not personal achievement. As simple as it is, such a rule goes against the grain of almost all compensation practices in modern enterprises. Human resource departments, procedures, and principles are built around serving the individual, not the team. Almost any team-level compensation and reward is going to be an exception to policy, and therein begins the job of project management. Most projects and teams are rewarded in cash or kind for performance:

- Spot awards for extraordinary performance in unusual or unplanned circumstances
- Performance awards based on successful releases
- Retention rewards for key individuals, conditioned on acceptable performance by the person and his or her team

The more troublesome compensation problems arise for business members assigned to the team. Senior business people are usually compensated variably with bonus, commission, and incentive packages. How, then, are those persons to be compensated for time away from a variable compensation opportunity? The answer is usually found among these formulations:

- *Commissioned sales staff:* For the dollar component of compensation, pay project compensation based upon the recent track record of commissions smoothed over a reasonable period of time. For the nondollar component, such as credit toward sales trips, the credit can continue to be awarded based on project compensation, or the salesperson can be awarded the trip in the role of sponsor or coordinator based on successful performance on the project.
- *Bonused managers:* If the product master has a bonus that is based on macro parameters, such as enterprise performance, the bonus can continue unchanged. Personal performance bonuses can shift to project performance.

A project management tip	Compensation and reward
	• A fair and transparent compensation plan is unquestionably part of making team members comfortable with moving from a functional environment to a team environment. • Money speaks, and if attached to team performance, it speaks loudly to the value placed on teams by the enterprise. It will partly resolve the oft unspoken question, *What am I giving up?*

Virtual Team

The virtual team is a special case for agile projects. Virtual teams enable skilled personnel who cannot physically co-locate to work together. In some cases, a virtual team may extend the affordability of the project. In other cases, it may bring technologies within reach that are otherwise unattainable economically. And, the virtual team may be able to bridge disparate boundaries within enterprises and among partners, suppliers, and others in the supply chain.

A number of barriers must be overcome to gain these advantages. A common purpose must be compelling to all team members. What is inspiring to one may be ordinary or unappealing to others. A means of establishing trust must be found and communications protocol that will facilitate the ever-necessary collaboration is needed. A measurement, reward, and celebration system that is culturally compatible in multiple sites is also required.

> **Cultural influences**
>
> At a semiconductor plant in western European, team members were overheard exclaiming to their American coaches, "We don't want T-shirts and coffee cups!"

Delegating and trusting leader-follower relationships, encouragement of self-management and self-organization, and peer review accountability are not ubiquitous. American culture tolerates challenge to superiors, tolerates the antigroupthink nemesis, accepts and encourages flat organizations, and actively discourages discrimination in all forms. But other cultures have other values and respect these matters differently.

So, in spite of ever more effective and efficient electronic networking capabilities to overcome time and distance, the human factor remains paramount. The important parameters on everyone's list are these: [24]

- Time and distance—in spite of electronic communications—produce offsets and discontinuities in creativity, construction, production, and in the flow of thinking.

- Lifestyle, culture, language, and distance inhibit rapid deposits in Covey's so-called trust account requiring extra time, effort, and opportunity to overcome the barriers and the inertia. Newton's First Law applies: if otherwise undisturbed by an extra and determined effort, things will continue along unchanged and unimproved.[25]
- Identity is disturbed. People have a physical space and a local identity. But then they are expected to have a virtual identity and to be present in a virtual space. In some cases, there could be stresses where two identities must be managed in near real time. Physical space can be made private; virtual space is more open and more vulnerable. These differences may cause tension or a distraction, all contributing to incoherence.
- When is time-off? Some virtual teams can take advantage of the world clock and work continuously. But that means problems, issues, and events occur around the clock. Is a 24-hour workday really compatible with Principle 8 to plan for a sustainable pace?

A project management tip	Virtual teams
	• Virtual teams can and do work, but the issues identified in *Why teams do not work* are amplified and made more acute. • Plan additional effort to mentor and coach for success. • Assume that team velocity will be lower than a similarly staffed co-located team until the virtual team gains experience working together.

Matrix Management Manages Resources in the Agile Space

There are several operating models for projects; they can be agile and otherwise. The *PMBOK® Guide* illustrates the most common models in Chapter 2, Project Life Cycles and Organization.[26] Of interest to project managers with agile teams is the matrix because it has the potential to impact the concept of a long-life performance unit team.

Matrix Attributes

A management matrix is a two-sided grid with project responsibilities on one side and functional responsibilities on the other. Cross-points represent the intersection of shared responsibilities.

A project management tip	The matrix introduces conflict
	• Matrix management introduces deliberate conflict. • Competition at the cross-point is the source of conflict. • Organizations that are weak in conflict management should avoid the matrix.

The cross-point may also represent the intersection of *two bosses* for an individual team member. Each boss expects loyalty, commitment, and accountability—a tall order for most. Conflict mitigation requires general managers to decide: is the project or the functional organization to have primacy? Sometimes it is a pretty tough call; the business of business must go on. In the agile space, there can really be only one practical answer: the performance team must have priority to have a meaningful benchmark for throughput.

By common convention, the project is represented on the top side of the matrix with vertical columns arrayed under the project office. The functional organization is represented on the left side with horizontal rows extending from the functional managers. Figure 8-4 illustrates the discussion.

To develop a matrix when starting a new agile project, make a list of all the management responsibilities for both the project and the organization. Then, allocate the responsibilities to each side of the matrix according to the operating model. The operating model usually takes one of two forms, but the first model is preferred because all the project responsibilities roll up to the project manager:

1. The functional manager is a resource supplier, taking responsibility to provide people to the project.
2. The functional manager becomes a contractor to the project. The functional manager assumes responsibility for team performance; essentially forming performance teams that are contracted units to the project office.

With thoughtful allocation, the same responsibility does not show up on both sides of the matrix. Thus, responsibilities do not overlap, so why should they compete and create conflict? The answer is disparate missions: *the mission of each side is different, and, thus, the priority placed on the joint intersection by each side is different.*

On the one side, the project mission is to meet an iteration timeline. All hands must be present. On the other side, as an example, the functional mission may be staff development. The functional manager may have a key performance indicator, with compensation attached, to ensure a minimum number of hours of skills training within a budgeted timeframe. A team member, caught in the middle at a cross-point cannot be in two places—the project and the training. A tiebreaker is needed.

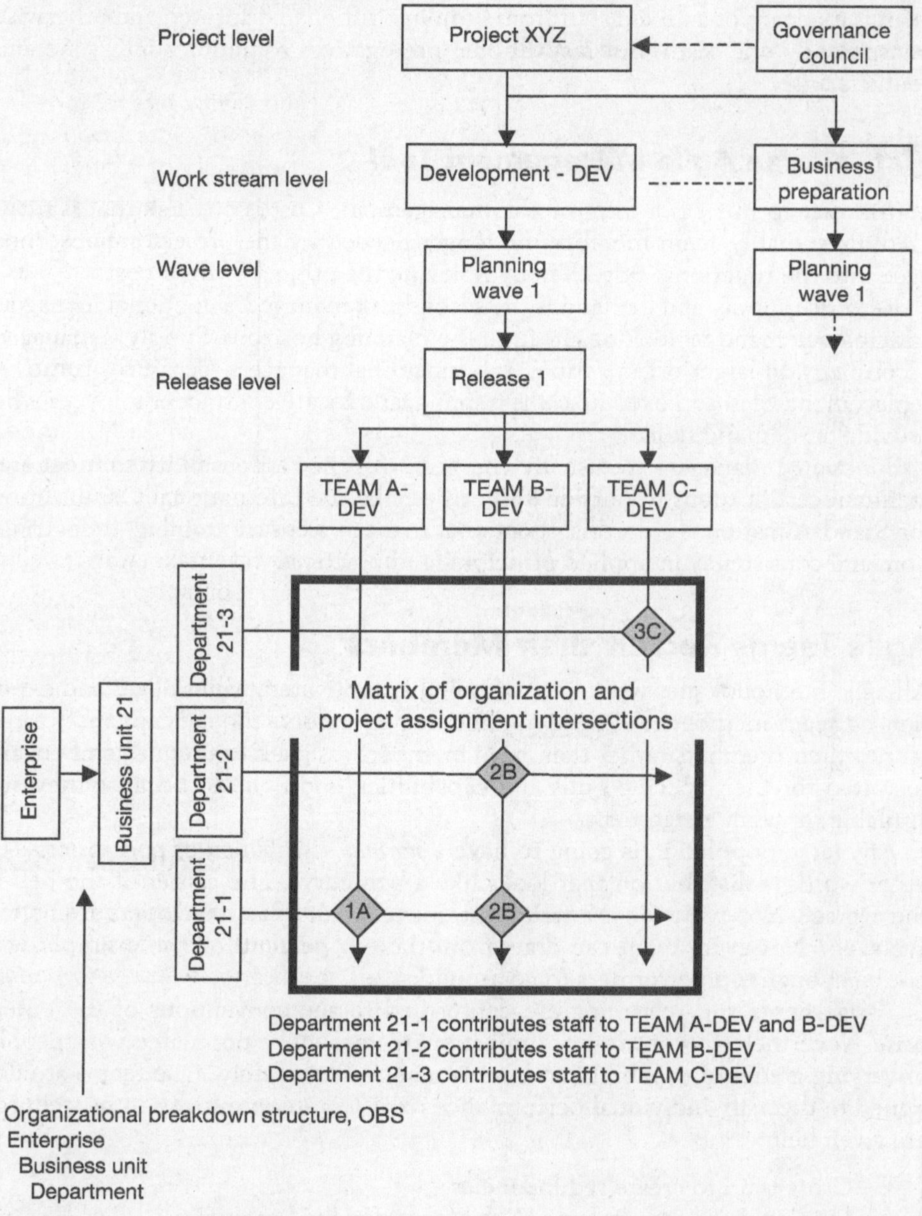

Figure 8-4 Generic matrix

The situation just described is made all the worse if each side of the matrix is a different institution. For example, in some contracted situations, a performance team is made up of a mixed staff from both institutions, co-located and otherwise transparently one team. But institutional prerogatives sometimes intervene and conflicts arise.

Matrix as an Agile Management Tool

Matrix management is a form of risk management. Cost is one risk that is managed. Presumably, team members no longer needed by the project are absorbed back into the functional side, thereby relieving the project of their cost.

Resource supply and demand is the second risk managed. Functional managers anticipate demand by looking ahead to the planning horizons. Supply is managed accordingly. In larger organizations, the functional managers recruit for turnover replacement, plan and execute skills training, and locate contract employees who provide on-demand skills.

Functional managers are usually charged with the responsibility to meet and maintain certifications to outside authorities, like the International Organization for Standardization. To do this, functional managers ensure training, indoctrination, and consistency in applied principles and practices.

Agile Teams Recruit their Members

All agile methodologies work best with highly motivated, well skilled, and experienced team members. All agile methodologies endorse the concept that teams recruit their members rather than have members assigned to them. Members are recruited for their specific skills and capabilities, and not just because they are available for team assignment.

Any large population is going to have a *normal distribution* of performers—in other words, a distribution that looks like a bell curve. The center of the bell is the average. Not everyone is a stand-out. Indeed, half of all developers are below average![27] Not every team can draw from the top percentiles; there simply will not be enough top performers to go around.

Assignments and recruiting are conformed to the conventions of the enterprise. Nevertheless, even after optimization, teams will be populated with people of varying grades of capability and performance. Fortunately, agile teams are designed to diversify individual performance risks. Common mitigation procedures are given below:

- Cross-train to create redundancies
- Employ pair-programming to reinforce designed-in quality
- Conduct peer reviews to catch problems and inconsistencices early

- Benchmark velocity to get a handle on the actual performance; rebenchmark after experience with the first few iterations
- Buffer the iteration plan for unforeseen variances
- Plan for labor loss

A project management tip	Not everyone is a superstar
	• Plan for reality; everyone is not a top performer. • A committed effort often overcomes skill shortfalls; see *David and Goliath* and the record of the 1980 U.S. Olympic hockey team.[28]

Summary and Takeaway Points

The theme in this chapter is that small teams, capable of self-organizing, and absolutely committed to frequent and incremental releases, are the performance-unit building blocks of agile methods. A team is a social structure wherein all the members individually and mutually collaborate toward the achievement of a common goal—achievement that is only possible by the committed and collective contribution of every member.

Every team has a set of values and principles, but the most important is trust. Without trust that your teammates have not only their own but your interests in mind, there can be no truly collaborative and collective teamwork.

In the agile space, teams are a building block and a performance unit. The principle performance parameter is velocity, the measure of throughput.

To achieve scale, teams are formed into networks. A team of teams manages the network and ensures coordination and collaboration among teams.

Some teams work and some do not. Apart from trust, the main impediment to successful teams is the lack of a compelling mission and the lack of clear boundaries for action and results. Teams that work do so first because there is trust, and second because their members believe in the mission and are supported by the enterprise.

Incentives and compensation should be at the team level. Team compensation is at odds with most human resource principles that compensate at the individual level.

In larger organizations, some form of a matrix is inevitable. The matrix coordinates the project mission with the functional management mission.

In the end, teams work and produce superior results. Agile methods are made possible because of the superior work that is done by teams.

Chapter Endnotes

1. Lencioni, *The Five Dysfunctions of a Team: A Leadership Fable*, vii.

2. Sherif, Muzafer, and Sherif, *An Outline of Social Psychology*, 143–180.

3. A similar concept that a team is better thought of as a unit of performance, although not in terms of velocity and agile methods, is described in Katzenbach and Smith's "The Discipline of Teams," 81(2):111-120, which reports on the run-up studies leading to the publication of their book *The Wisdom of Teams*, 1994.

4. Tuckman, "Developmental Sequences in Small Teams" 384–399. Tuckman subsequently revised the theory adding a fifth stage, *adjourning*, in a 2001 reprint of the 1965 article in *Group Facilitation: A Research and Applications Journal*, Issue #3, Spring 2001.

5. Wikipedia, "Forming-Storming-Norming-Performing."

6. Katzenbach and Smith, *The Discipline of Teams: A Mindbook-Workbook*, 4.

7. Henderson, *Cohesion, the Human Element in Combat*, 4.

8. Hersey, Blanchard, and Johnson, *Management of Organizational Behavior*, 173–174.

9. Lencioni, *The Five Dysfunctions of a Team*, 43, 195.

10. See article "Personal Safety," provided by Alistair Cockburn at http://alistair.cockburn.us/Personal;plsafety, an excerpt of: Cockburn, *Crystal Clear—A Human-powered Methodology*, 28.

11. Kimble, Li, Barlow, "Effective Virtual Teams through Communities of Practice" Research Paper 2000/9, 5.

12. Beck with Andres, *Extreme Programming Explained*, 18–19.

13. The number of unique communication paths between N individuals is given by the formula $N \times (N - 1)$. When N is large, this formula is effectively N^2. For example, if there are five people on the team, named *A, B, C, D,* and *E,* then there are 20 independent paths that can be used to communicate among the five parties. *A* can talk to *B, C, D,* and *E,* and *B, C, D,* or *E* can talk back to *A,* just to identify eight paths. But add three people to the team, and there becomes 56 ways to communicate! A little friction in each communication path will add up quickly and dissipate team productivity.

14. Project Management Institute, *A Guide to the Project Management Body of Knowledge (PMBOK® Guide)*, 155–156.

15. The classic example of a schedule that cannot be crashed is "nine women cannot have a baby in one month." See also The Project Management Institute, *PMBOK® Guide*, 155–156, and Brooks, *The Mythical Man-month*, 16–18.

16. In this book, the term *team of teams* is reserved for the management team required to coordinate the network. However, some practitioners refer to the network as the *team of teams*. See Ambler, "Roles on Agile Teams: From small to large." http://www.ambysoft.com/essays/agileRoles.html. Ambler also refers to the team of teams as the *large agile team*. However, in the SCRUM methodology, the *team of teams* is referred to as the *SCRUM of SCRUMs*, and defined as

the team that "...coordinates multiple working teams on the same project." See Schawber, *Agile Project Management with SCRUM*, 44.

17. Robbins and Finley, *The New Why Teams Don't Work*, 4–8.

18. Coutu, "Why Teams Don't Work," Interview with Dr. J. Richard Hackman, May 2009.

19. Robbins and Finley, *The New Why Teams Don't Work*, 49, 88, 130, 131, 185, 186, 188.

20. Hammer and Champy, *Reengineering the Corporation: A Manifesto*, 34–52.

21. Cockburn, "Characterizing People as Nonlinear First Order Components," HaT Technical Report presented at the Fourth International Multiconference on Systems, Cybernetics, and Informatics.

22. An excellent treatment for project managers is given in Harold Kerzner's classic textbook *Project Management: A Systems Approach*, Chapter 8. Conflicts in teams from the point of view of general management are well treated in Robbins and Finley, *The New Why Teams Don't Work*, Chapter 11.

23. Covey, *7 Habits of Highly Effective People*, 188–190.

24. For an excellent overview in report form, see Kimble, Li, and Barlow, "Effective Virtual Teams through Communities of Practice," Research Paper 2000/9. In book form, an excellent reference is Haywood, *Managing Virtual Teams: Practical Techniques*, 5–10.

25. Paraphrased from the writings Sir Isaac Newton who published his laws of classical mechanics in *Philosophiæ Naturalis Principia Mathematica*.

26. Project Management Institute, *A Guide to the Project Management Body of Knowledge (PMBOK® Guide)*, 28.

27. A *normal curve* is symmetrical about the average. One half of the total population is above average and one half is below.

28. Malcolm Gladwell has a remarkable analysis of effort versus skills in his piece entitled, "Highly Effective Underdogs," 40–49.

Table Endnotes

1. Katzenbach and Smith, *The Discipline of Teams*, 111–120.

2. Dyer, et al. *Team Building: Proven Strategies*, 22.

3. In the SCRUM method, the team itself is one of the only three roles, along with the product master and the SCRUM master; there is no specific endorsement of the team leader role. However, having designated representatives to a *SCRUM of SCRUM session* is recognized as a means to scale up to multiple teams. See Schawber, *Agile Project Management with SCRUM*, 6, 121.

9

Governance

Governance brings order and empowers innovation, leveraging the power of the enterprise for project achievement.

> *We always overestimate the change that will occur in the next two years and underestimate the change that will occur in the next ten. Don't let yourself be lulled into inaction.*
>
> *Bill Gates*

Governance and agile methods may seem like an oxymoron—but not so. A means to govern is essential for orderly project functioning. Without governance, the advantages of adaptive and evolutionary methods could be overwhelmed by functions bolted together haphazardly and rendered operationally ineffective, expensive to maintain, and disadvantageous to customers and stakeholders. Agile practitioners agree that governance is necessary. Indeed, a look through the web yields numerous papers, blogs, and websites that are dedicated to promoting agile governance. Agile methodologists have gone so far as to build in governance practices. As an example, at the team level, the daily time-boxed stand-up meeting is a governance mechanism. This meeting regulates the daily activity and points resources to problem areas in need of resolution. And another: once requirements are committed to the iteration backlog, they are not allowed to change. Stabilizing requirements for the short term regulates the iteration scope.

A governance program should be purposeful about maximizing the business potential of a project while at the same time dedicated toward minimizing the risks to business performance. A governance program should enable and promote innovative and imaginative solutions but deter behavior that strays too far from norms. In short, a governance program exists for five reasons that are in effect the *governance mission statement*:

Governance mission
1. To oversee and approve investment on behalf of business beneficiaries. **2.** To codify decision-making rights to enable teams to have autonomy and freedom to maneuver. **3.** To enable and promote innovation, evolution, and technical excellence within the framework of architecture and operating norms. **4.** To be the ultimate arbiter of risks that affect both business performance and accountability. **5.** To provide accountability for compliance to mandatory standards.

Governance Is Built on Quality Principles

Four principles guide an effective governance implementation:

Governance principles
1. Governance should be applied proportionately to the amount at stake. **2.** Governance should provide clarity for mission and purpose, scope boundaries, decision-making authority, and decision rights. **3.** Governance should respect the principle of subsidiary function: governance should not intrude into the management of functions that are best left to functional and project managers. **4.** Governance must be lean, timely, and responsive, respecting agile principles to provide enough, but just enough oversight and control to accomplish the governance mission.

Consider a couple of points:

1. Governance can be the vehicle to moderate supervision and flatten bureaucracy. This is accomplished by conveying rights to teams so they can make their own decisions.
2. Governance can bestow rewards for disciplined behavior. With discipline, trust follows, and trust enables self-determination.

Trust is an absolutely necessary condition for lean governance. Without faith in the actions of others, there is an inclination to add many resources and process steps to check and inspect. The best leaders are trusted by their followers, and the best teams are trusted by their leaders. Leadership inspires inquisitive minds to question the status quo and to search for a better way; leadership motivates innovation. A trusting organization is a *safe* organization. A real benefit of trustfulness and discipline is the safety to go about doing really innovative and interesting tasks.[1] In the agile space, *safety* extends boundaries; wider boundaries often brings new discovery and challenging opportunity within reach, adding to competitive returns.

Governance Empowers

In its best form, governance empowers action and endows decision-making rights to project management and team leaders.

Leverage empowers: put a little in and get a lot out. All governance systems leverage enterprise power on behalf of projects. This is never truer than it is when the working with the business-case budget. Innovative products and services that feature technical excellence and effective customer service—those in the *ah-hah!* quadrant of the Kano chart—typically return many times their investment. Governance legitimizes activity—that is, spending and resource commitment, research and development, and continuous improvement—in all sectors of the balanced scorecard. Do not lose sight of the fact that funding sources are always in the hands of executives and stakeholders. Executives and stakeholders both sanction and constrain projects; they will loosen their purse strings and provide investment for projects thoughtfully presented, professionally managed, and objectively governed.

Decision rights empower: The unambiguous right to make a decision is conveyed by policies. Governance conceives and enforces those policies. As odd as it sounds, governance can actually get the organization out of the way by clearly pushing decision making to the project.

Governance clarifies direction among conflicted constituents. Constituent conflicts and confusion constrain action. All concerned parties have interests they instinctively protect, and they promote only those projects that serve their interest. Governance provides objective arbitration to achieve balance among parties.

Purposeful decisions enable effective project management. Confusion saps power; it is inevitable that there will be choices that are overlapping, contradictory, unaffordable, or inconsistent. But effective governance provides decisions that clarify, instruct, and direct action.

Leadership empowers: Governance bodies practice situational leadership tailored to the circumstances at hand. Leadership in all forms motivates, inspires, and encourages action. Under the auspices of the governance council, there can be funding and support for research and development, prototyping, experimentation, and modeling. New ideas can be given early exposure and risks can be managed and contained within reasonable limits with methods and practices such as the spiral model described in Chapter 1.

Some Mechanics Are Necessary

Some governance bodies, policies, standards, and certifications are inescapable. Familiar examples: financial governance given by GAAP or the Sarbanes-Oxley standards; and information technology governance rendered by voluntary compliance with CoBIT or ITIL; and quality certifications monitored by the ISO.[2] These agencies and policies are decidedly not agile! However, careful application of their more valuable recommendations avoids bigger problems downstream.

Governance for agile projects is at the discretion of the organization; governance can be as little or as great as the risks demand. Governing bodies provide a service to constituent managers. It is really up to those managers to decide how much oversight is enough to protect their interests.

Operating Elements

To make governance work effectively, four operating elements are needed:

1. A policy model for effective dissemination of direction and guidance
2. A management framework for deciding among alternatives and objectively making best-value decisions
3. A protocol for exercising decision rights and situational judgment
4. A mechanism or regimen for accountability that satisfies the oversight responsibilities of business councils and senior managers

Each of these four elements is expanded for discussion in the sections that follow.

1. Policy model for governance

Policy makes effective governing possible. Without a policy regime to provide guidance and boundaries, managers fill the void and make it up along the way. A business may be able to operate in a policy vacuum, but to do so means setting precedents with every major decision. Experience has shown that it is more effective to do these things:

- Establish only those few policies that are necessary to bound behavior
- Establish the policies in advance of their need
- Establish polices at a high level
- Allow specific extensions and interpretations to fill in the operating detail

A good policy is brief, unambiguous, operationally relevant, readily available on-demand, and capable of being extended operationally. As given in Table 9-1, effective policies are supported at the highest executive level. A framework holds all the policy instruments. Policies are actively deployed according to a deployment plan; compliance is actively tracked.

Table 9-1 Policy attributes

Policy feature	Meaning and intent
Charter	• At its highest level, policy should be chartered and endorsed by the organization's senior executive • Policy is incumbent on all by flow-down through the organizational structure
Framework	• All functional domains should have a policy library of governing documents • Dependencies among and across domains should be identified and managed in a policy cross-reference
Deployment	• A communications and deployment plan should be developed and implemented • Policies should be easily available to all constituents by organizational network or otherwise
Compliance	• Compliance measurement and accountability should be actively managed
Operational relevance	• Policy must be maintained; policy must change as business and the business environment change • Business units should extend high-level policy to incorporate operating detail • In the spirit of continuous improvement, a means to receive feedback and act upon good ideas should be provided; policy recipients should be encouraged to make policies clear and unambiguous

As an example of policy take a look at Table 9-2.

	Decision policy for the project manager
A project management tip	• *The simplest policy for decision making is*. . . always make a best-value decision based on the collective value of the risk-weighted factors. • When deciding among alternatives, pick the alternative that informs the business most favorably, even if there is suboptimum result for the project.

2. A management framework

Governance is management executed outside project boundaries that protects objectivity and independence. Objectivity and independence establish fair play and trust in decision making.

Management is provided by a council—a governance council—established and empowered by the organization's executive management. The governance council may also include an independent architecture council charged with maintaining coherent architecture for the systems and products being governed, and a business preparation council that represents users, customers, and stakeholders.

Table 9-2 Policy example

Policy component	Meaning and intent
Subject area	• Information technology assets
Policy statement	• Applications, systems, infrastructure, and data are to be shared among business units to maximize their business value • Stand-alone exceptions are allowable with approval • Stand-alone renegades are to be actively discouraged
Policy objectives	• Improve business operational efficiencies by reducing the cost of business unit interoperability and functional coordination • Mitigate business performance and compliance risks from uncertified systems and data • Provide for disaster recovery, ensure integrity, protect confidentiality of systems and data • Assure reliability and availability of business systems
Application and dissemination	• Applicable to all business units • Disseminate to all managers and team leaders • Make available on the company intranet
Compliance	• Mandatory for all systems and data except personal desktop applications not intended for official use • Compliance to certified by managers annually

The mission of the governance council—along with any related councils—is to be the operating executive for the five-point governance mission. Day-to-day, the council examines each business case and makes project go-no-go decisions in context with the organization's goals, strategies, and conventions. Chapter 2 discusses the information content of the agile business case at three levels and discusses the interaction of approving authorities with the business case process.

To be lean, the governance council may involve only one or two persons for Level 0 business cases. Decision making at Level 0 is amenable to being regulated by electronic workflow; such flow-control systems save time and money and preserve decision-making records. At Level 1 or 2, more elaboration is needed. Recall the principle that governance is applied proportionately to what is at stake: total investment, customer impacts, benefit realization, and business performance.

The staff assigned to the governance council reflects the mission particulars. The number of staff is less important than their skills and authority. Like team members, council members should be recruited for their acumen—their business knowledge, customer familiarity, comfort with technology, and an analytical mindset. The council cannot be tone deaf to politics. Political skills will be necessary to enforce decisions and gain constituent support.

Most governance councils are event-driven, meaning that they act when an event requires attention, rather than meet on a regular schedule. In the spirit of agile methods, governance councils time box their deliberations.

The governance council is responsible for a governance framework. The framework provides the services and functions given in Table 9-3.

Table 9-3 Management and policy framework for governance

Framework component	Commentary
Mechanics and services	• Provides a means to publish, approve, maintain, and access objects; primarily documents. • Provides a document repository. Manages check-in and check-out. • Provides web-based documents—typically policies and decision documents—routed for approval by workflow, and accessible on an internal website after approval. • Makes it easy to access policy and decisions by searching internal web.
Policy support for business case	• Defines and establishes parameters for Level 0, 1, and 2 case. • Enforces business case submittal, approval, and maintenance with workflow. • Defines and establishes the approving authorities and the workflow for approval.
Verification of project compliance	• Enforces tripwire functions that track compliance to policy requirements.[1] • Makes it easy to comply, track, and report compliance by data entry and retrieval by web forms.
Verify other functional compliance, e.g., IT and finance	• Enforces policy compliance according to policy directives. • Utilizes functionality to publish, approve, maintain, and access. • Makes it easy to comply, track, and report compliance by data entry and retrieval by web forms.
Security and integrity of policy library	• Manages access and modifications to content according to security policy and practices. • Enforces authorization, authentication, rights and privileges to create, read, update or modify, and delete documents.

3. *A protocol for decision rights*

Effective governance embeds its decision-making instructions and limitations in a protocol. Decision-making protocols lay out the rights, responsibilities, and rules for everyone involved in decisions.

Decision rights specify *who* can be the decision maker, *what* they can decide, and *how much* resource they can commit in various circumstances. Three examples:

1. *Sponsor rights:* Sponsors approve the business case. Decision rights are conveyed to the project sponsors for each of the three business cases—Level 0, 1, and 2—according to the investment, impacts, and benefits anticipated at each level.
2. *Project management rights:* Project managers govern performance, accountability, and achievement. Project managers are given rights to affect performance, insist on accountability, and intervene to correct inefficient and ineffective practices.
3. *Team rights:* Teams govern requirements and day-to-day practices. Performance teams are conveyed decision rights for selecting requirements for the backlog, setting priorities, and sequencing features and functions for production. Teams regulate their own practices and decide which are applicable and appropriate to the situation.

Rights come with responsibilities. The decision maker is responsible for:

- Following the decision-making rules of the governance regime
- Making decisions in timely fashion
- Supporting the team that executes the decision
- Taking responsibility for results

Protocols are rules-based. Rules impose order; rules enable decision making at a distance. Table 9-4 lists some of the more common rules:[3]

Table 9-4 Decision-making rules

Rule	Commentary
All decisions respect the value proposition of the project as a given in the business case	• It is acknowledged that the voices of the business and the customer are heard in the business case • Funding limits, milestones, and product vision come from the business case • The balanced scorecard is felt through the business case; it represents each sponsor's commitment to the project
Decisions that support outcomes are favored over decisions that support achieving a plan	• Satisfying the customer is higher in priority than is meeting the specifics of a plan
All decisions will be ethical, lawful, and conform to regulatory and policy structures	• Each decision maker is responsible for the quality of the decisions made

Table 9-4 *(continued)*

Rule	Commentary
All decisions will be evaluated for risk; downside possibilities will be within the decision rights of the decision maker	• Every project decision involves risk; financial risks are customarily evaluated with discounted cash-flow methods • The downside of risk—how bad it could be—must not exceed the authority of the decision maker
Decisions among alternatives that are otherwise equal will be decided in favor of best value for the enterprise	• Best value always includes a consideration for the customer

Decision makers have been mentioned many times. Table 9-5 addresses the questions of *what do they decide?* and *what business case level is affected?*

4. A mechanism for accountability

Being accountable means taking responsibility for results. Good results require, among other things, compliance with governance direction and guidance. The best evidence of compliance is customer satisfaction with product outcomes.

Table 9-5 Decision makers

Decision makers	What do they decide?	What business-case level is affected?
Executive team	• Highest-level strategy and goals • Capital and expense funding above Level 1 • Personnel decisions with strategic impact • Business-to-business relationships that affect high-level strategy and goals • Next steps based on strategic benchmarks	• Level 2 always • Level 1 when key to executive strategy and goals
Governance council or architecture council	• Consistency with legacy business practices, legacy systems, and forward-looking roadmaps • Strategic technologies, new product direction • Strategic steps based on scorecards and benchmarks • Portfolio sequencing • Priority of limited resources	All levels

Table 9-5 *(continued)*

Decision makers	What do they decide?	What business-case level is affected?
Functional managers	• Resource commitments to new activity • Change management to absorb new outcomes • Next steps based on scorecards and benchmarks	All levels
Project managers	• Estimate for new or changed activity • What processes and measures will apply to each team-level activity • Next steps based on scorecards and benchmarks	All levels
Team leaders	• Estimate inputs for new or changed activity • What processes and measures will apply to each activity within the team • Which resources are applied to each team activity	All levels
Subject-matter experts (SMEs)	• Tactical steps to be taken to solve a specific problem	All levels

However, investment must be recovered and other beneficiaries must be served. Achievement of key performance indicators (KPIs) on the balanced scorecard is the next best evidence of accountability for results.

Outside agencies that convey certification require proof of compliance. Audits to gather information from scorecards, dashboards, workflow records, and other artifacts provide proof of performance.

In the next section of this chapter, we will address compliance in more detail.

A project management tip	Accountability to the business case
	• Effective accountability metrics always incorporate a *results measure.* • Avoid measures of input consumption and activity such as dollars and hours; focus governance on outcomes and beneficial results.

Governance Verifies Compliance

Although compliance is only one point in the governance mission, one test of any governance paradigm is how well compliance is verified. In the agile space, results come periodically and incrementally. During the *check-act* part of the Ag-plan-do-check-act cycle, there is opportunity to audit compliance to standards, regulations, and conventions, and analyze achievements on scorecards and dashboards.

Scorecards and Benchmarks for Results

Scorecards are snapshots of achievements. Scorecard data is temporal, meaning *time-sensitive*; for governance purposes, data snapshots at milestones usually suffice to show whether governance objectives are being achieved. For example, some scorecard information depicts performance against benchmarks established by the governance council to guide project performance.

Dashboards are information portals that provide not only the temporal scorecard but also stationary information. Some stationary information such as when and how standards are deployed may be useful for certifying compliance.

The architecture council may require technical benchmarking when there are risks identified with technology feasibility, infrastructure performance, or architecture. Technical benchmarks are usually embedded in a process called *technical performance measures* (TPM). TPM envisions periodic measurements of technical achievement, comparison of achievements to benchmarks, and then actions to mitigate variances. Team productivity figures, quality measures, and product performance results are typical technical benchmarks. Agile projects lend themselves to benchmarking and TPM because frequent deliveries offer many points of evaluation, provide data to support trend lines and forecasts, and build progressively towards the TPM goal. There is ample time to build a cumulative experience over a range of circumstances that enrich the results.

Lean Scorecard for the Black Box

In thinking about the utility of a scorecard for business-case governance, recall the black-box model of a project: the project is fully encapsulated; there is no visibility to the internal mechanisms. The box has input to accept resources and triggers, output to provide results, and other ports to accept governance controls and environmental support. See Figure 9-1 for the visualization of this concept. There is one subtlety to note: in a plan-driven project development lifecycle (PD-PDLC) rendering of a black box, the input and outputs would be business and project-planned values; in the Ag-PDLC rendering, the input and output to and from the business are expectations as described in the business plan. The actual consumption and achievement are project facts. In effect, Figure 9-1 is an alternate presentation of the project balance sheet.

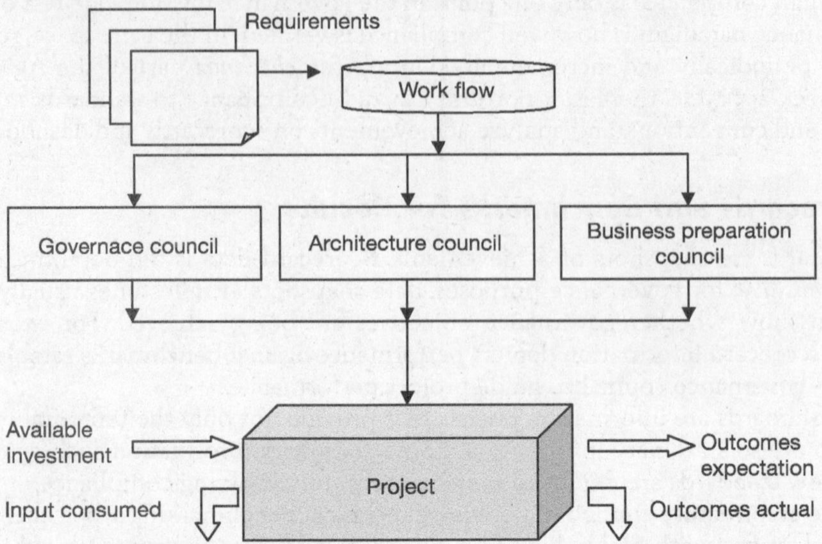

	Scorecard	Milestone			
Source	**Metric**	**1**	**2**	**3**	**4**
Business	Investment available	10	15	15	12
Project	Funds (input) consumed	9	15	16	12
Calculation	Funds variance	1	0	−1	0
	Funds efficiency	111%	100%	94%	100%
Business	Outcomes expected	5	7	7	6
Project	Actual outcomes	4	7	8	6
Calculation	Outcomes variance	−1	0	1	0
	Outcomes efficiency	80%	100%	114%	100%

Figure 9-1 Project black box with governance

At each input and output, there is expected and actual performance. Among these four data elements, variances and efficiencies can be calculated. Recall that a variance is a difference between two data elements; efficiency is a ratio of two data elements.

As a quick example, take a look at the scorecard given in Figure 9-1. The units of measure are arbitrary, but in most cases, they will be dollars on the top half and story points on the bottom half.

The top half of the card is similar to a PD-PDLC measurement; calculations in the top half are measuring consumption in the black box. Without the data in the bottom half, there is no way to know if the project is churning or producing results. The data in the bottom half of the card shows results. It is instructive in a real project to compare top and bottom half variances and efficiencies to continuously improve forecasting and benchmarks.

When looking at efficiencies, the objective is always for the ratio to be 1.0 or greater, meaning that expectations are met or exceeded. Now, 100 percent is a tough benchmark to achieve. For any number of reasons, there are often *losses* that drag the efficiency below 100 percent. After each iteration and release, during *check-act* reflection, reasons for efficiencies and variances are examined for opportunities for improvement. Table 9-6 illustrates the applicability of scorecards, dashboards, and benchmarks according to business-case level.

Table 9-6 Measurement tools by business case

Decision makers	Scorecard KPI or TPM	Dashboard balanced scorecard metrics	Benchmark
Executive team	Not usually reviewed	Level 2	Level 2
Business council or architecture council	Level 2	Level 1, 2	Level 1, 2
Functional managers	Level 0, 1, 2	Level 1, 2	Level 1, 2
Project managers	Level 0, 1, 2	Level 1, 2	Level 0, 1, 2
Team leaders	Level 0	As applicable to the team	As applicable to the team
SMEs	Sometimes reviewed for TPMs	Not usually reviewed	Not usually reviewed

Summary and Takeaway Points

Our theme is governance brings order and empowers innovation, leveraging the power of the enterprise for project achievement. A governance program should be purposeful about maximizing the business potential of a project while at the same time, dedicated to minimizing the risks to business performance. It should encourage innovative and imaginative solutions but deter behavior that strays too far from the norms of the enterprise. In short, a governance program exists for five reasons:

1. To tie an investment to business value and results
2. To codify decision-making rights

3. To enable and promote innovation, evolution, and technical excellence within the framework of architecture and operating norms
4. To manage risks that affect business performance and accountability
5. To provide accountability for standards compliance

Four principles guide an effective governance implementation:

1. Governance is to be applied proportionately to the amount at stake
2. Governance should provide clarity for mission and purpose, scope boundaries, and decision-making authority and rights for approved projects
3. Governance should respect the principle of subsidiary function: governance should not intrude into the management of functions by subsidiary operating units
4. Governance must be lean, timely, and responsive, respecting agile principles to provide enough, but just enough, oversight and control to accomplish the five-point governance mission

To make governance work effectively, four operating elements are needed:

1. Policy model
2. Management framework for deciding among alternatives and objectively making best-value decisions
3. Protocol for exercising decision rights that empowers decision makers to exercise judgment about estimates and to objectively decide among facts
4. Mechanism or regimen for accountability that satisfies the oversight responsibilities of business councils and senior managers

Scorecards and benchmarks provide the data for verification. Every governance system closes the loop on results. After all, obtaining results that benefit the customer and the enterprise is the motivation to regulate performance.

Chapter Endnotes

1. The concept of a safe organization is an important concept in the so-called human-powered methodologies called Crystal methods. See Cockburn, *Crystal Clear—A Human-powered Methodology*, 28.

2. The Generally Accepted Accounting Standards (GAAP) in the United States is administered by the Financial Accounting Standards Board. Sarbanes-Oxley refers to the U.S. law that sets standards for reporting and certifying the accuracy of financial reports. See also COSO, a preferred model for Sarbanes-Oxley compliance; Control Objectives for Information and related Technology (CoBIT) is a set of governance practices for information technology administered by the IT Governance Institute. Information Technology Infrastructure Library (ITIL) refers to the IT practices developed by the U.K. government. The Interna-

tional Standards Organization (ISO) is dedicated to promoting quality under the umbrella of ISO 9000 standard, among others.

3. Adapted from the author's work in Goodpasture, *Managing Projects for Value*, 39.

Table Endnote

1. A *tripwire* function is a condition set by the governance council that will cause some governance action to kick in if the condition becomes true. The tripwire could be set around a financial parameter, a milestone, or some functional need. In some cases, a tripwire could be set around a scorecard from the customer.

10

Earning Value

Agile projects earn value by delivering product incrementally, periodically, affordably, and according to the priority of the customer.

> *If the customer is not satisfied, he may not want to pay for our efforts. If the customer is not successful, he may not be able to pay. If he is not more successful than he already was, why should he pay?*
>
> *Niels Malotaux*

In the agile space, value is always business and customer-centric; agile doctrine accepts that the business and customer are their own best authority on what is important to them. In the agile space, value accumulates over time—functionalities and features are added to the product base release by release according to priorities and benefit demands that are reevaluated by the customer iteration by iteration. Value accumulated is value earned; agile projects add to earnings as the project backlog is burned off.

Agile Rule for Earned Value
Each release is a value earning; without a go-live to production, there is no earned value.

Customers, Users, and the Business

To simplify matters, the terms *customer*, *end user*, and *business* are used interchangeably on the basis that the business represents the customer interests with high fidelity.

The business includes the sponsors and stakeholders. Sponsors have a direct responsibility for the business case; stakeholders have a responsibility for the balanced scorecard.

Customers are beneficiaries of the project; customers can be internal and part of the business, or external. Users are functional experts. Users are part of the customer community, but many customers who set the value proposition are not users.

Defining Value

Many qualities called *value* are very much in the eye of the beholder—*esteem value* that pleases rather than performs, and *use value* that satisfies because functions work and perform as intended. Generally speaking, value satisfies when quality exceeds price—that is, outcomes meet or exceed expectations and the price seems fair. And, there are objective measures:

- *Investment value:* the lowest possible cost to produce a satisfactory deliverable
- *Benefit value:* the present value to the business of the benefit stream paid for by the customer, internal or external
- *Best value:* the monetary worth to the customer of a deliverable that simultaneously provides high esteem value and functional satisfaction; not necessarily a low cost value but what the customer is willing to pay to have the benefit[1]
- *Free-value:* a variant of best value; free means getting the product for essentially a zero price; in the best case, the producer still makes money, but not directly from the end-customer

Value Distinctions

- Are investment-value and best-value distinctions without a difference? No, the investment value of a simple order entry function may be $100K to develop—and more each year to maintain—but to the customer, the simple order-entry function may be a best value at no more than $20K.
- To bring investment value into alignment with best value requires economy of scale.
- Economy of scale is a means of recovering the development, production, distribution, and maintenance costs incrementally from many customers.

Value Distinctions (*continued*)
• Benefit value is the present value summation of all best value transactions. • Free: When the marginal cost of production is all but zero, as it is with much software, producers can literally give away the product, charging only a very small distribution fee or access fee; or charging nothing at all to most and something nominal to a few for a premium product; or charging a third party for an *association*, as for example advertising.[2]

Investment value is a balance of myriad quality dimensions and project affordability. Recall from Chapter 3 the many attributes of quality, among them fitness to form and function; fitness to timeliness and cost; fitness to operational need; and satisfaction of wants, needs, and esteem. The product must be good enough in its many dimensions, but it need not be so good that it is not economically viable. Hasn't everyone heard, "Better is the enemy of good"?[3] Balancing value needs and project affordability is a mixed bag because the subjective qualities of value are constrained objectively by cost.

Best value is attained when quality exceeds price and benefit value exceeds investment, investment being all the resources needed to realize the product. In a word, sponsors, stakeholders, and customers are satisfied when they receive their money's worth, whether investor or buyer. *Quality-exceeding-investment is the most fundamental definition of value-added, value earned*. It is the foundation for the shift from cost accounting to throughput accounting; and from cost accounting to earned-value accounting, all to be discussed later.

For the business and customer alike, value satisfaction is entwined with expectation—given an opportunity, value is attained when outcomes meet or exceed expectations.[4]

Value means
• There is something worth paying for • Quality exceeds the resources invested • Outcomes exceed the expectations

Even when not dimensioned in dollars, value comes at a price, the discussion of *free* notwithstanding. Nevertheless, an ageless definition of value is, "It is what the customer is willing to pay for." The corollary is simply this: if no one is willing to pay, then the value is not commanding or compelling.[5]

Accounting for Value

There are three ways to account for value: cost accounting, throughput accounting, and earned-value accounting. The focus in this chapter is on earned-value accounting because earned value is about outcomes for customers in relation to available investment from executives. Thus, earned-value accounting is a practical bridge between executives, customers, project managers, and financial officers.

Cost accounting is the traditional way to count beans. Its focus is on minimizing the operating expenses of development and production in order to earn back the cost of capital. Value is attained if these three conditions are present: operating expense does not exceed the operating budget; the net present value of project expense and benefit cash flows is positive; and the economic value added of cash commitments is also positive.

Throughput accounting focuses on the value added by the team to the baseline value of the preproject opportunity. Throughput, previously defined, is the product produced in one development iteration. In agile projects, the throughput parameter is velocity, measured in story points per iteration.[6] In other words, throughput and velocity are rates of production. The preproject opportunity has some inherent value. For example, there is some value in new ideas conceived but unimplemented, legacy capability existing but unchanged, and bug lists prioritized but unaddressed. The inherent value motivates the business to make some investment to define the opportunity, figure out the benefit possibilities, identify the stakeholder community, and begin to move down the *V* shown in Figure 2-2. Once things get underway and project releases begin, value is earned. In monetary terms, the earnings are essentially the present value of the benefit stream associated with the release. Earnings first recover the initial investment; the balance of earnings adds value to the initial investment. A throughput accountant calculates the value added, and the cost accountant calculates the marginal return on the invested expense. Figure 10-1 depicts the discussion.[7]

From the discussion and Figure 10-1, take note of the different ways operating expense is handled. In the agile project the majority of operating expense is the labor cost of the teams; additionally, there are infrastructure expenses, tool licenses, and the like. Once optimized, expenses are nearly a fixed cost to the organization in this sense: when the team finishes one iteration, it goes on to the next; when the project is completed, the project teams go onto the next project. Labor is only marginally variable over the long reach. However, cost accountants usually categorize all operating expense as a variable project expense; throughput accountants ignore operating expense when calculating the value-added, since they view operating expense as a nearly fixed expense.

Earned Value Is Earning Back the Investment

Earned value is a straightforward concept that has been around since commerce began. In simplest terms, earning value is giving the customer their money's worth. In agile projects, customer value earning accumulates from incremental product releases.

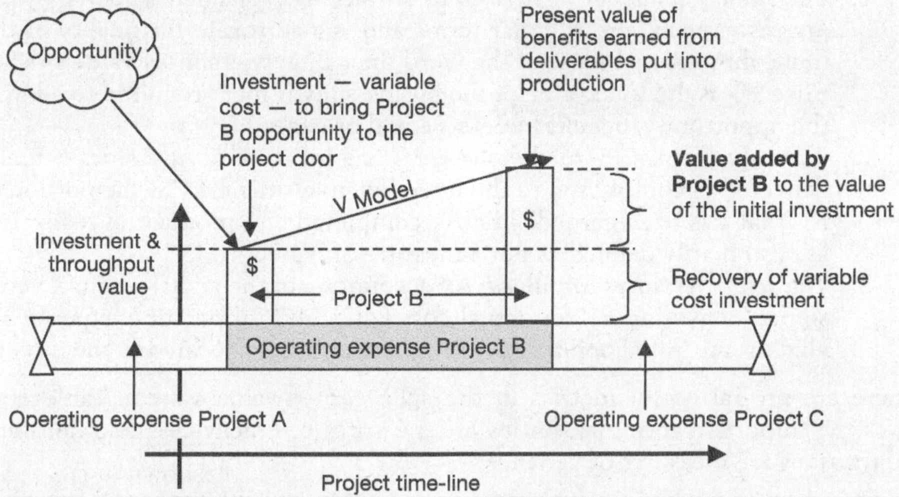

Figure 10-1 Throughput value

Business benefits are derived from customer value, but benefits accumulate over time whereas customers perceive value right away. In other words, there is a relationship between an outcome for the customer and a benefit for the business: at the moment of release, there is a product in production, the customer is satisfied, there is a benefit forecast, but the business benefit is unrealized—for the time being, it is a benefit on paper only. Over time, benefit forecasts become benefit realities; benefit accumulation continues until the entire opportunity has been earned. In this chapter, earned-value accounting deals with product delivery and benefit forecasts. Benefit realization is the subject for Chapter 12.

In project terms, earned value means planning for an outcome and then achieving it, applying only the intended resources. When the project is completed and expectations are met, the entire value is earned—all requirements are rendered in production and equated to benefits.

Agile methods change the bookkeeping a bit, but by Agile Principle 1, delivering value is at the top of the list:

> **Agile Principle 1**
>
> Our highest priority is to satisfy the customer through early and continuous delivery of valuable software.

Three Components of Earned Value

Conceptually, an earned-value system has three measurable components:

1. *The value planned or forecast to be earned:* The planned value (*PV*) expresses expectation in dollar terms and is a surrogate for quality in the multi-dimensional sense of the word since quality is simply value at a fair price. *PV* is the total value of the business investment required to address the opportunity; benefit forecasts equal or exceed (*PV*).
2. *The value earned:* Earned value (*EV*) is a measure of outcomes actually delivered in comparison to the intended investment. *EV* is the portion of *PV* that has been earned—that is, completed and production ready. *EV*, as customarily defined, is not a measure of benefits.
3. *The actual resources consumed:* An accounting of the actual resources consumed delivering *EV*, or actual cost (*AC*). *AC* is operating expense, including any initial opportunity investment that is allocated to the project.

There are several useful metrics in the agile earned-value system. Table 10-1 gives the important formulas. Ratios are measures of efficiencies; additions and subtractions are measures of variance:

Earned-value Labels and Acronyms
Other acronyms are used in the earned-value systems, although the current EIA standard 748B (2007) uses *PV*, *EV*, and *AC*. Since the earned-value system was introduced in 1967, the Department of Defense used another acronym set, but the use of that set was ended in 1996 with the adoption of EIA 748. This older acronym set and the comparison of the older defense earned-value system to EIA 748 are explained in Fleming and Koppelman.[8]

An EV Example 1

As an example of how this works, consider this business case:

The $100K Product Business Case
• $100K is to be invested in a product development. • In one planning horizon, three releases are planned for $25K, $25K, and $50K worth of features and functions. • The releases are at milestones M1, M2, and M3, respectively. • Collectively, these dollars and dates are called the performance measurement baseline (PMB).

Table 10-1 Agile earned-Value arithmetic

Formulation	Commentary
$\frac{EV}{PV} \geq 1$	• The ratio is a measure of value achievement efficiency • The ratio shows how efficiently the earning plan is being executed • Delivered value should always meet or exceed expectations for quality, feature, function, and performance • If the ratio falls below 1.0, then deliveries are not meeting expectations
$\frac{EV}{AC} \geq 1$	• The ratio is measure of resource efficiency; specifically, the project balance sheet efficiency between the business and the project • The ratio shows how efficiently the investment is being converted to deliverable value, dollar for dollar • The value of deliveries should be equal to or greater than their investment • If the ratio falls below 1.0, then one dollar invested is returning less than one dollar of value • Investment is owned by the business; operating expense is owned by the project
$EV - PV \geq 0$	• The difference is the schedule variance, a measure of being ahead or behind schedule • A positive difference is a favorable schedule variance; 0 difference means exactly on schedule
$EV - AC \geq 0$	• The difference is the cost variance, a measure of being under or over cost • A positive difference is a favorable cost variance; 0 difference means exactly on cost

Assume the following is how the project performs at each milestone.

At M1, the PMB scorecard is evaluated:

M1 Results

- Cost accounting reports that $35K has been spent, $10K more than the $25K that was planned.
- Project management reports that the intended features and functions due at M1 were delivered and put into production.
- Project administration reports investment efficiency, EV/AC, is below expectation. Inception-to-M1 period efficiency is calculated as:

$$\frac{25}{35} = 0.71$$

- Team members reflect on lessons learned at M1; efforts are made to improve the investment efficiency to 1.0 or greater.

The project team works onward to M2.

At M2, the PMB scorecard is examined again:

M2 Results
• Cost accounting reports that $25K was spent as planned in the PMB for the period from M1 to M2, adding to the $35K spent getting from inception to M1, so total actual cost is now $60K rather than $50K as forecasted. • Project management reports that again the team is successful in delivering all the required features and functions at M2. • $40K remains in the unspent budget, and $50K remains in the undelivered value. M1-M2 period EV/AC efficiency improved to: $\frac{25}{25} = 1.0$ • Accumulated efficiency is: $\frac{50}{60} = 0.83$

The team continues on to M3.

At M3 the PMB is given another look:

M3 Results
• The team is once again successful, delivering all the required components. • Some investment efficiency was realized: $45K was spent delivering $50K of value getting from M2 to M3. • The spending cap has been exceeded: $35K at M1, $25K more at M2, and $45K more at M3 for a total of $105K. • M2-M3 period EV/AC efficiency improved to: $\frac{50}{45} = 1.11$ • Accumulated efficiency is: $\frac{100}{105} = 0.95$

Project summary:

Table 10-2 summarizes the value attainment for this project.

An EV Example 2

In the case just described, investors added to the pot and covered the extra cost to deliver the whole opportunity. It does not always work that way. In the agile business case, the cost is often capped at an affordability limit.

Table 10-2 $100K product PMB scorecard

Milestone	Project results	Commentary
M1	• Efficiencies: $\frac{EV}{PV} = \frac{\$25K}{\$25K} = 1.0$ $\frac{EV}{AC} = \frac{\$25K}{\$35K} = 0.71$ • Variances: $EV - PV = 0$ $EV - AC = -\$10K$	• The project is overrunning cost $EV - AC < 0$, but is on schedule $EV - PV = 0$ • Value is being delivered efficiently, $EV/PV = 1$ but investment is not earning value efficiently, delivering only 71¢ for each dollar invested • There is a risk expectations will not be met • The affordability cap may be reached before all the value is delivered due to the investment inefficiency
M2	• Cum efficiencies: $\frac{EV}{PV} = \frac{\$50K}{\$50K} = 1.0$ $\frac{EV}{AC} = \frac{\$50K}{\$60K} = 0.83$ • Cum variances: $EV - PV = 0$ $EV - AC = -\$10K$	• The AC for the period from M1 to M2 is $25K, exactly as planned • Investment efficiency is back on plan; no additional ground has been lost on this parameter • Project remains on schedule but over on cost • Investment efficiency for M1 to M2 was 1, raising the cumulative metric from 0.71 to 0.83 • The risk remains that expectations will not be met, but the risk has been moderated because the investment efficiency is off track
M3	• Efficiencies: $\frac{EV}{PV} = 1$ $\frac{EV}{AC} = \frac{50}{45} = 1.11$ • Variances: $EV - PV = 0$ $EV - AC = -\$5K$ • Overall scorecard $\frac{EV}{PV} = 1$ $\frac{EV}{AC} = \frac{100}{105} = 0.95$ $EV - PV = 0$ $EV - AC = -\$5K$	• Investors added $5K to the pot in order to complete the project • All the value was earned and earned on time, but at a cost that exceeded expectations • The project satisfied customers but disappointed investors by 5 percent

Here is the same case, but reworked to the new reality of capped resources.

Background:

Recall that at M1, changes were made to improve efficiency. By M2, efficiency had improved from 0.71 to 1.00 during the M1-M2 period, although the cumulative efficiency improved only to 0.83.

At M2, \$40K remains in the unspent budget, but \$50K remains in the undelivered value.

New operating plan at M2:

The team and its embedded customer reach a decision to reset priorities. The customers help the team pick out the highest-priority requirements that are affordable with the remaining \$40K budget. At M2, taking advantage of the improved EV/AC efficiency, 1.11, achieved in the M1-M2 period, the M2-M3 iteration is replanned with that metric:

$40K × 1.11 = $44.4K of the highest priority scope
is planned for delivery, although only $40K is to be
spent delivering $44.4K of value

Table 10-3 shows the business case results at M3.

Some may find it curious to think of measuring schedule performance by the EV unmet at the milestone, rather than measuring by days behind the PMB schedule as laid out on a calendar plan—days behind the PMB calendar being a concept called *earned schedule*. The EV schedule metric reflects a focus on results rather a focus on input, although a fair criticism is that a dollar-based EV schedule metric will eventually show a zero variance if all the EV is earned even if the project is late on the calendar. However, recall that days and dollars are simply input to the project process. The development process transforms these so-called

Table 10-3 Second scorecard for \$100K product

Milestone	Project results	Commentary
M3	$\frac{EV}{PV} = \frac{\$94.4K}{\$100K} = 0.944$ $\frac{EV}{AC} = \frac{\$94.4K}{\$100K} = 0.944$ $EV - PV = -\$5.6K$ $EV - AC = -\$5.6K$	• $\frac{EV}{PV}$ <1; expectations for product value were not completely met • \$5.6K of value remained unattained although 100 percent of the investment was consumed • $\frac{EV}{AC}$ <1; investment efficiency was less required • *EV – PV* shows that the project is behind schedule by \$5.6K, having yet to deliver \$5.6K of value • *EV – AC* shows that the project remains in a cost overrun status even though the project has ended without spending more than the allowable investment

raw materials into finished product. In the end, the most meaningful measure is about what the process produces.

Earned Schedule
Earned schedule is a relatively new calculation in the earned-value space, having been brought to prominence in 2003 by Walter Lipke in a paper entitled *Schedule is Different* published by the Project Management Institute in their magazine entitled *The Measurable News*, Summer 2003: 31–34. Rather than calculate schedule variance as the difference between the PV and EV at a point in time, earned schedule calculates the time difference between EV measured at a point in time—a point called the *earned schedule*, ES—and the time on the PMB calendar when the EV should have been earned, a point called the *actual time* (AT).

A project management tip	Earned value focuses commitment
	• Agile doctrine reinforces commitment to results and thereby directly aligns with earned-value methods. • Proponents of earned value methods, whether in the agile space or not, have always been strongly committed to a results focus.

EV Forecast

One advantage to looking at results in context with history is that trends become apparent. From the examples, it is evident from looking at the data at M1 that the project was either at risk for completing the opportunity by M3, or at risk for needing more investment.

Quantitatively, at M1, the information was available to forecast how much the investment efficiency had to improve in order to completely fulfill the opportunity. The reasoning goes like this:

- At M1, there is no schedule variance; however there is a cost variance that threatens completion of the product.
- There is also an investment efficiency shortfall. If the investment efficiency remains at 0.71 with no improvement, then each remaining investment dollar will only produce 71¢ of value. $65K remains in the budget at M1 and $75K of value remains to be delivered. The normal EV forecast is that by M3, only $46K = $65K × 0.71 of the remaining value will be delivered, divided as ~$18K at M2 and ~$28K more at M3. The total value delivered is forecasted to be $71K—the sum of $46K and $25K value earning at M1—$29K short of expectation (numbers have been rounded).

- To complete the opportunity within the affordability cap, investment efficiency must be raised from 0.71, measured at M1, to $1.15 = \frac{75}{65}$ for the overall project at M3. Moving a metric by 44 points from 71 to 115 is no small matter.

There is yet another EV scenario for this project situation. If the customer and team cannot arrive at a reasonable use of the remaining $40K available at M2 to move onward to M3, *then the project ends at M2*. No partial credit is given and no partial tasks are undertaken in agile methods. In other words, the $10K overrun at M1 threatens $50K of value to be earned and delivered at M3. Figure 10-2 shows this graphically.

It is worth noting that the forecast is only possible if there if a baseline to measure against and about which to make forecasts. Recall that the PMB is defined in terms of outcomes and value to be earned. It is only possible to have a baseline within the planning horizon for which the baseline information is reasonably valid.

Value Is Earned at Every Agile Release

Earned value mechanics are straightforward and easy to apply. Here is how they work, using the same acronyms already defined:

- As depicted in the examples already given, earned value is an output measure. In the agile space, accumulated output is throughput times the number of iterations. Recall the discussion of throughput in the context of story points. Story points are a unit of production. Each team is benchmarked for its throughput—the number of story points it can put into production.
- PV is the number of story points planned for delivery in one time box.[9] Throughput, in the form of story points, is nearly a fixed number. Throughput is sensitive to team cohesion, skills, and environment, but these things are fairly fixed and stable, team by team. What is not fixed is the complexity of the requirements and the number of requirements. Complexity affects the total number of requirements that can be satisfied in one time box. In turn, complexity and the sheer size of the requirements deck, understanding that the size of the deck will change during the course of the project, affects the total number of time-boxed iterations that are necessary to complete the opportunity.
- EV is the actual number of story points put into production.
- AC is the cost of running the team for one time-boxed iteration; at the project level, AC also includes any other investment made directly for the project's purpose. For the most part, each team has a nearly fixed running rate cost—the cost per iteration—since the team complement changes very slowly and the majority of team cost is labor cost.

Project earning, graphically portrayed, forecasts a $50K shortfall in earned value because of a $10K cost problem in the first iteration

Milestone 1 status:
On schedule, $25K of value earned, but $10K over on cost
$75K of value remains, but only $65K of budget
Projection is that project will not complete last $50K of value; no partial credit is given

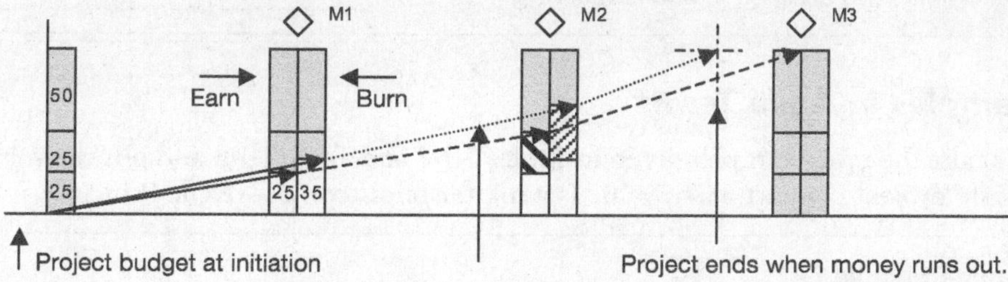

If investment efficiency of 25/35 = 0.71 continues

Milestone 2 status:
On schedule, $25K of value earned, but still $10K over on cost
$50K of value remains, but only $40K of budget
Projection is that project will not complete last $50K of value; no partial credit is given

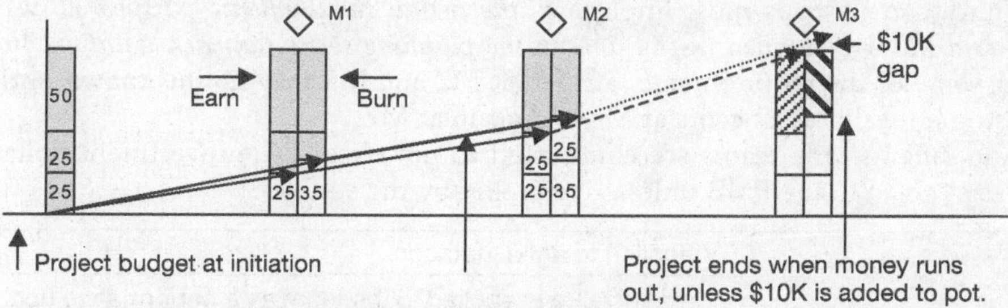

Investment corrected to 25/25

Figure 10-2 Project earning forecasts

$$\text{Cost per unit of throughput} = \frac{\text{Cost of running the team}}{\text{Throughput capability of one iteration}}$$

Example:
Throughput capability of one iteration = 50 story points
Cost of running the team for one iteration = $12K

$$\text{Cost per unit of throughput} = \frac{\$12{,}000}{50} = \$240 \text{ per story point}$$

Throughput example
Fifty low-complexity requirements can be satisfied in one iteration if each is rated at 1 story point. If the requirements are high complexity, 10 story points each, then only 5 requirements are satisfied in one iteration.

Examples in Agile Terms

Let's take the two examples given in Tables 10-2 and Table 10-3 and put them in an agile project context. First, value is a matter of outcomes—Agile Principle 7:

Agile Principle 7 Working software (product) is the primary measure of progress.

Second, in order for these examples to be workable in an agile methodology, M1, M2, and M3 would all have to be within the same planning horizon. It makes no sense to try to project the PMB over the horizon of a planning boundary.

Third, and perhaps most important, *the actual requirements satisfied at M1, M2, and M3 are planned just-in-time in the planning session of each iteration*. Indeed, some of the requirements satisfied at M2 and M3 may not be known until a customer evaluation occurs at M1 and again at M2.

And, finally, agile teams are committed to not exceed the investment dollar values as given in the PMB unless given relief by the sponsor.

A project management tip	EV applied to agile methods
	• Earned value is applied to the team as a performance unit, not to individual tasks. Recall the discussion of performance units in Chapters 7 and 8. • A major difference between earned value in a traditional plan-driven project development lifecycle (PD-PDLC) and an Ag-PDLC is the difference between valuing task and valuing completions to production. • EV concepts can work within an agile team; EV is handled by burn-down and burn-up charts.

The first example in Table 10-2 is recast this way for the events leading to M1:

Agile Project Background
• At M1, the PV is 100 story points that are planned for delivery at a cost of \$25K, \$250 per story point according to a project benchmark. • By benchmark, two teams are required to provide the 100 story points; it is assumed that teams are benchmarked identically at 50 story points per milestone period. • By calculation, the loaded cost to run each team for one release is \$12.5K. The loaded cost is simply the number of units of labor in one team-release times the dollar rate for each unit.

The teams are now prepared to go to work and reach M1. The embedded product master has established the requirements priority from the backlog. Work begins. The scorecard is examined at M1:

M1 PMB
• When M1 arrives, the scorecard of each team is examined. Both Team 1 and Team 2 have each produced and delivered 50 story points into production. One hundred story points total. • However, Team 2 had to augment their team with a subject-matter expert for an unplanned cost of \$10K. • The AC at M1 is \$35K; the PV is \$25K, and the EV is also \$25K. Investment efficiency is 71¢ per dollar.

Now, planning ensues to reach M2: The situation leading to M2 is similar to that at M1, except that no extra subject-matter expert is needed—a fact that will restore the investment efficiency to 1.0 for the period from M1 to M2. However, the problem remains about how to make up the extra \$10K consumed in the first period. \$75K of value—300 story points—remains to be delivered, but only \$65K remains in the budget, potentially a miss of $\left(\frac{300 \times (75 - 65)}{75}\right) = 40$ story points. A productivity gain to reduce the cost of a story point from \$250 to $\left(\frac{\$65K}{300}\right) = \$216$ is needed, a tall order!

There are relatively few options. The team complements are cohesive units; it is a bad idea to add new members to the teams late in the project in violation of Brooks' Law. In the long run, productivity—that is, velocity—is amenable to changes in tools, training, staffing, and environment. But in the short run, to raise velocity, the most likely payoff is look for synergy opportunities between or within teams that would give a boost to productivity.

Continuing with the example after M1:

From M1 to M2
• Assume the teams work from M1 to M2 at the baseline velocity. In that event, at M2, \$25K is earned for \$25K of AC. Remaining PV is \$50K and remaining budget is \$40K.

Planning session at M2 to reach M3:

Planning M2 to M3

- \$50K of PV remains. \$50K of PV is 200 story points at the baseline velocity.
- Assume the embedded customer resets priorities at M2 to improve velocity getting to M3.
- The M2-M3 velocity is reestimated. An 11 percent improvement is forecast; the new figure is now 111 story points for each \$25K of cost.
- 200 story points can now be liquidated with:

$$\$45K = \left(\frac{200}{111}\right) \times \$25K, \text{ but only } \$40K \text{ is available}$$

- The investor agrees to add \$5K to the pot, bringing the total to \$45K for the M2-M3 period.

However, the cost of running one team for one iteration is \$12.5K.

- There is not enough money for four full iterations:

$$4 \times \$12.5K = \$50K$$

only \$45K is available, but only \$45K should be needed.

- Either a couple of staff members will have to be dropped—unlikely given the need to improve productivity by 11 percent—or all iterations will have to be shortened by:

$$10\% = \frac{5}{50}$$

Is it really possible to improve velocity in a short period by reworking requirements? To a small extent, yes. Velocity is not cast in concrete; it is susceptible to small variations in collaboration, functional interpretation, and the overall requirements mix. To be able to honestly forecast improved velocity, the embedded customer and all team members must work to find small improvements.

At M3, the PMB is examined for the last time:

PMB at M3
At M3, 200 story points are delivered at a cost of \$45K planned as follows: • Each iteration in the period M2/M3 is shortened to a cost of \$11.25K, although with 11 percent higher velocity. • $\$11.25\text{K} \times \frac{111}{\$25\text{K}} = 50$ story points each

The results are the same as in Table 10-2.

Agile EV Comparison

Table 10-4 summarizes the major differences between earned-value practices applied to agile and traditional methods.

Table 10-4 Earned-value comparison—planning

Ag-PDLC practice	PD-PDLC practice	Commentary
• The total dollar value of the opportunity is given in the business plan by the investment commitment and the total affordability cap	• Same as the agile project	• The business plan expresses the value proposition of the business, even if all the detailed requirements are unknown
• Value is planned only over the duration of the current planning wave	• Value is planned for the whole project upfront	• By Agile Principle 2, requirements are encouraged to change even late in the project
• The PWB is only for the current planning wave	• The PWB is for the entire project and for the entire opportunity	• The PWB can only be set for the segment of the timeline where the requirements are stabilized
• Requirements are not specifically valued, since requirements change between iterations	• Requirements are valued in the sense that the WBS holds all the deliverables traceable to requirements	• It is presumed that the embedded product master on each agile team will direct the team only towards valuable, important, and timely requirements
• The outcomes of teams are valued	• Each deliverable on the WBS is valued	• The total value earned is the throughput of the total number of appearances of unique team-time boxes in the network

Table 10-5 compares the measurements made in a traditional system and the agile practices:

Table 10-5 Earned-value comparison—measurements

<table>
<tr><th>Agile practice</th><th>PD-PDLC practice</th><th>Commentary</th></tr>
<tr><td>• Performance measurements apply only to each planning horizon, one by one</td><td>• Performance indexes apply to the whole construction effort</td><td rowspan="2">• Performance forecasts reflect the difference between iterative and end-of-project methods</td></tr>
<tr><td>• Performance is forecast at the milestones within the current planning wave</td><td>• Performance is forecast for project completion, specifically estimate-to-complete and estimate-at-completion</td></tr>
<tr><td>• History is only modestly usable to forecast the future because requirements are going to change</td><td>• History is supposed to be a reliable trend setter for the future because the requirements are defined upfront</td><td>• The importance of history reflects the difference between adaptively satisfying the customer and following a plan</td></tr>
<tr><td rowspan="3">• A value measurement is never in dispute</td><td rowspan="3">• Value measurements are always in dispute</td><td>• In traditional systems, value measurements are made periodically, whether or not a task or work package is completed</td></tr>
<tr><td>• The amount of value of a partially completed effort is always a point of dispute</td></tr>
<tr><td>• In the agile space, value measurements are made at the end of the iteration when by definition, only completed product increments count in the value measurement</td></tr>
</table>

Plan, Do, Check, and Act at Every Release

The steps for enabling earned value in any methodology fit the plan-do-check-act cycle:

- *Plan:* decide what the value proposition is; forecast outcomes in a plan that becomes the measurement baseline, PMB
- *Do:* execute according to the plan
- *Check:* measure value earning after every *do*; forecast the impact of variances

- *Act:* plan course corrections based on lessons learned from *check* analysis and forecasts

Plan: Planning the Agile PMB

As seen in the prior examples discussed, there are certain prerequisites for establishing the PMB:

- A value metric, such as story points, that is outcome focused and representative of a unit of value when put into production
- A velocity metric that has been benchmarked
- A cost metric, such as the running rate for each team in either standard days or standard cost

Look back to the example just discussed: the velocity was benchmarked at 50 story points per $25K. The $25K could be *standard dollars,* meaning a standard chargeback rate. Alternatively, the velocity might have been quoted as 50 story points per 30 standard days, thereby taking dollars entirely off the table.

To put the PMB together follow these four steps:

1. *Scope the planning wave:* Assisted by the product master, select the likely backlog of requirements and set priorities. Estimate complexity and assign story points to each requirement. As an example: an estimate is made that the 200 highest-priority requirements are worth 1500 story points.
2. *Estimate throughput:* Using the velocity benchmarks, calculate the number of iterations that will be needed. At 50 story points per iteration, 30 iterations are needed to burn down a backlog of 1500 story points.
3. *Plan releases:* With assistance from the product master, determine the stories for release at each milestone; plan the number of iterations at each release. For example, a planning wave might arrange 30 iterations as three teams executing 10 iterations each, spread over three milestones: At M1: 3 teams × 3 iterations yields 450 = 9 × 50 story points. The same is repeated at M2; at M3: 3 teams × 4 iterations yields 600 = 12 × 50 story points.
4. *Set up the scorecard:* Fit the planning data to a scorecard, filling only the baseline. An example of the scorecard is given in Figure 10-3.

Agile EV Measurements

In the PD-PDLC implementation, there is often serious dispute about the value earned. Disputes arise because EV measurements are taken at the end of a reporting period, regardless of whether an outcome is completed; a judgment, subject to dispute, is made about the partial value earned. Not so in the agile methodologies. Measurements are only made at the end of iterations. Work is completed

Project scorecard is set up to record history and thereby give a heads-up for the next milestone
This scorecard is repeated twice, once for Release Milestone 1 and again for Release Milestone 2
At initiation, actual performance is 0, so variances are maximum values
All numbers are user story points put into production as functions and features

	Planning Wave N										
	Release Milestone 1 and 2 Plan										
Numbers in story point to production	**Interation 1**			**Interation 2**			**Interation 3**			**Release 1 & 2**	**Variance to release**
	Team 1	**Team 2**	**Team 3**	**Team 1**	**Team 2**	**Team 3**	**Team 1**	**Team 2**	**Team 3**		
Baseline PV	50	50	50	50	50	50	50	50	50	450	
Operating plan PV	50	50	50	50	50	50	50	50	50	450	
Earnings EV to production	0	0	0	0	0	0	0	0	0		
Actual performance AC*	0	0	0	0	0	0	0	0	0		
AC variance to baseline	50	50	50	50	50	50	50	50	50		
Cum AC variance to baseline	50	100	150	200	250	300	350	400	450		
Investment efficiency EV/AC	NA	NA	NA	NA	NA	NA	NA	NA	NA		
Earning efficiency EV/PV to baseline	0	0	0	0	0	0	0	0	0		
Cost variance EV – AC	0	0	0	0	0	0	0	0	0		
Schedule variance EV – PV to baseline	–50	–50	–50	–50	–50	–50	–50	–50	–50		
AC variance to ops plan	50	50	50	50	50	50	50	50	50		
Cum AC variance to ops plan	50	100	150	200	250	300	350	400	450		
Earning efficiency to ops plan	0	0	0	0	0	0	0	0	0		
Schedule variance to ops plan	–50	–50	–50	–50	–50	–50	–50	–50	–50		

*AC is measured in story points that a standard cost team should be able to produce. If additional cost in staff or resources are needed, then a proportional increase in the AC is made.

Figure 10-3 PMB scorecard example

or it is not; only the completed work counts. There is no customer value in the incomplete work, so no partial credit is given.

The measurements are relatively simple to take at every milestone:

1. *Measure the AC:* Add to the repetitive running rate one-time expenses incurred for special tools or for subject-matter experts. Note one very important difference about the scorecard that follows with previous earned-value discussion: the actual cost—the so-called burn—is measured in story points. The reasoning is as follows: a standard team with a fixed staff costs a certain number of dollars and is benchmarked to produce some number of story points. Cost can be accounted for in dollars or in the equivalent currency of story points. If additional staff is needed, then the staff cost is made proportional to some number of story points and added to the team's cost in story points, even though the throughput remains constant. If tools and other nonstaff expenses are needed, their cost is made proportional to some equivalent number of story points and added to the actual cost. In effect, a relative cost is used in the scorecards. Knowing the actual dollars and keeping track of actual dollars is not necessary unless it is convenient. However, in the end, all units on the scorecard must be similarly dimensioned so that the mathematics are consistent.
2. *Measure the EV:* Count the story points earned for the product increment in the release.

Scorecarding Value

The scorecard is illustrated in Figure 10-3. The AC and EV measurements are scored at each milestone and recorded on the scorecard. From the measured data, the values for calculated metrics are computed using the formulas in Table 10-2:

Earned Value Formulas

- Investment efficiency: $\frac{EV}{AC}$
- Earning efficiency: $\frac{EV}{PV}$
- Cost variance: $EV - AC$
- Schedule variance: $EV - PV$

The scorecard in Figure 10-4 illustrates the baseline PMB with example data.

Project Earned Value scorecard records history and provides a heads-up going into the next milestone
This scorecard is repeated twice, once for Release Milestone 1 and again for Release Milestone 2
All PV, EV, and AC numbers are user story points

	Planning Wave N										
	Release Milestone 1 and 2 Plan										
Numbers in story point to production	Interation 1			Interation 2			Interation 3			Release 1 & 2	Variance to release
	Team 1	Team 2	Team 3	Team 1	Team 2	Team 3	Team 1	Team 2	Team 3		
Baseline PV	50	50	50	50	50	50	50	50	50	450	
Operating plan PV	45	45	50	50	50	50	50	50	50	440	10
Earnings EV to production	45	45	50	50	45	50	0	0	0	0	
Actual performance AC*	55	50	50	55	50	50	0	0	0	310	
AC variance to baseline	−5	0	0	−5	0	0	NA	NA	NA		
Cum AC variance to baseline	−5	−5	−5	−10	−10	−10	NA	NA	NA		
Investment efficiency EV/AC	81.82%	90.00%	100.00%	90.91%	90.00%	100.00%	NA	NA	NA		
Earning efficiency EV/PV to baseline	90.00%	90.00%	100.00%	100.00%	90.00%	100.00%	0.00%	0.00%	0.00%		
Cost variance EV − AC	−10	−5	0	−5	−5	0	0	0	0		
Schedule variance EV − PV to baseline	−5	−5	0	0	−5	0	NA	NA	NA		
Cum schedule variance to baseline	−5	−10	−10	−10	−15	−15	NA	NA	NA		
AC variance to ops plan	−10	−5	0	−5	0	0	NA	NA	NA		
Cum AC variance to ops plan	−10	−15	−15	−20	−20	−20	NA	NA	NA		
Earning efficiency to ops plan	100.00%	100.00%	100.00%	100.00%	90.00%	100.00%	0.00%	0.00%	0.00%		
Schedule variance to ops plan	0	0	0	0	−5	0	NA	NA	NA		
Cum schedule variance to ops plan	0	0	0	0	−5	−5	NA	NA	NA		

*AC is measured in story points that a standard cost team should be able to produce. If additional cost in staff or resources are needed, then a proportional increase in the AC is made.

For Release Milestone 3, a 4th iteration is added for all teams, providing a capacity for 600 story points. Total story points delivered from all three releases are: M1: 450, M2: 450, M3: 600, total 1500.

Figure 10-4 Example measured PMB

Reporting Value Earnings

The scorecard is a good tool for project professionals, but not optimum for reporting to stakeholders and executives. A dashboard is more user friendly for top-level communication. Different degrees of abstraction can be used to hide detail. For example, red-yellow-green scores easily communicate the conclusion of an earned-value analysis without the burden of the underlying analysis. *Green* could indicate an EV forecast within some small range, perhaps less than five percent different from expectations, *yellow* could indicate a larger range of EV performance, perhaps within 15 percent of the intended performance, and *red* is anything larger.

In the first example given in Table 10-2, the project was first reported to be off course on cost by $10K out of a $100K budget. That would fit a *yellow* marking on the dashboard for cost performance. On value performance, at M1, the forecast is also yellow. Recall these facts:

- 100 story points were earned at M1
- 260 story points are forecast to be earned in the period from M1 to M3, given that the investment cap is not to be exceeded
- All things remaining equal, 360 story points is the forecasted outcome, leaving 40 story points unearned
- This forecast is that 360 of 400 story points in the opportunity will be earned, or 90 percent. So, the value performance is also *yellow*

Summary and Takeaway Points

The theme of this chapter is that *agile projects earn value by delivering value incrementally, periodically, affordably, and according to the priority of the customer*.

Value is a perception of the business; in the main, it is what drives the business to invest in the project. In simplest terms, earning value is giving the customer their money's worth. In agile projects, value earning happens as deposits are made in the customer's value account. Progress is only measurable as outcomes accumulate in production.

For earned-value measurements, requirements per se are not valued. What is valued is the production of the team in response to requirements, typically characterized by an outcome-oriented metric, such as story points. Other metrics are usable so long as they focus on outcomes and not inputs.

Efficiencies can be computed from earned-value information. Efficiencies provide the means to estimate the landing spot of the project. If close enough, no action is necessary.

In the end, the whole opportunity is earned if all the value is delivered to the customer for an investment within expectations, and with quality that satisfies.

Chapter Endnotes

1. Thiry, *Value Management Practice,* 10. Five value ideas are discussed: use, function, cost, exchange, and esteem. What Thiry calls *function value* is what the author calls *best value.*

2. For a provocative discussion of *free*, see Anderson, *Free, the Future of a Radical Price,* 3–6.

3. The original quote in French is "Le mieux est l'ennemi du bien," from Voltaire's *Dictionnaire Philosophique,* literally translated as, "The best is the enemy of good," extracted from http://www.famous-quotes.net.

4. Thiry, *Value Management Practice,* 7–10.

5. Goodpasture, *Managing Projects for Value,* 6.

6. The reader is reminded that this book integrates several agile concepts from different methodologies. A focus on output is ubiquitous. Velocity is an XP idea; story points, also from XP, is one of several ways to dimension throughput, but it is the dimension used throughout the book.

7. Anderson, *Agile Management for Software Engineering,* 15–20.

8. Fleming and Koppelman, *Earned Value Project Management,* 31, 32, Appendix II.

9. Story points are used here in the sense of an outcome. The exact requirement and the deliverable it engenders is abstracted to story points. However, any output metric could be used in the EV calculation.

11

Scaling Up and Contracting

Agile methods are scalable; within limitations, agile methods are amenable to the advantages of contracts and virtual teams.

> *We must not, in trying to think about how we can make a big difference, ignore the small daily differences we can make which, over time, add up to big differences that we often cannot foresee.*
>
> *Marian Wright Edelman*

Agile methods started out as a great way for small teams to manage their affairs and get quality work done. In fact, the Agile Manifesto and the Agile Principles seem optimum in just that way. But success on a small scale makes one wonder if agile methods can scale up to larger projects requiring multiple teams, virtual teams, or even contracted teams. Within limitations, the answer is yes.

Scale Amplifies Every Problem

All software projects are uncertain in scope and complex in their structure—that is the nature of dealing with intangibles. With a system of intangibles, it is hard to imagine all the scope, even scope on a small scale—but it is even harder to imagine how all the scope elements really work in context because there are so many interrelationships, and because imagination itself is not bounded or managed. And even though not all complex systems are large-scale systems, all large-scale systems are complex. Scale means large reach, breadth, and extent, typically addressing a broad customer community with a cacophony of input about how things should work.

Big Picture Issues

A summary of the macro issues of complexity and architecture that confront large-scale endeavors is given in Table 11-1:

Table 11-1 Big picture issues—complexity and architecture

Issue	Mitigation	Agile mitigation
Complex systems span hardware, software, and their integration	• Implement work specialization and division of labor[1]	• Identify professionals with varied work specialties and put them on the same team, seeking redundancy and synergy in the same team • Redundancy means teams need not work in assembly-line fashion with handoffs among members • Synergy is the leading indicator of cooperative and collective work
No one can keep the whole system in mind	• Document the top-level architecture	• Add an architect role to the project and teams • Diagram, or otherwise use models to document system architecture
Complexity has many points of influence and control, some of which self-conflict	• Disallow certain system states and chaos responses	• System engineer for safety and stability • Maintain a rhythm of Red-Green-Refactor to prove working designs and maintain high levels of quality • Teams must honor sequencing and regression testing • Rebuild the system often—daily if possible

Large-scale efforts cause tensions between teams. Teams are no longer independent; they must cooperate in networks and honor dependencies from team to team. Teams are required to yield some autonomy for the larger objective. The material in Table 11-2 summarizes these points and shows the general mitigations and extensions that are peculiar to agile methods:

Table 11-2 Big-picture issues—teams, customers, and business

Issue	Mitigation	Agile mitigation
Cost is very sensitive to the N^2 effect	• Relentlessly remove arbitrary complexity	• Manage the N^2 effect as part of the budget-cost gap on the project balance sheet • Make architecture maximally cohesive but minimally coupled to reduce friction in large systems • Automate tests to quickly evaluate design at least every day for unnecessary redundancy and complexity that drives cost and inefficiencies
Team-level optimizations conflict with bigger picture	• Architect from the top down to minimize constraints • Place incentives on enterprise optimization	• Reevaluate architecture after every release; make corrections and adjustments for the next release • Include architect in the team-of-teams
Customer and business priorities conflict with technical priorities	• Prioritize technical feasibility and logical sequencing ahead of customer needs	• Embed customers in development teams to improve information exchange and build trust in the development process • Manage priorities by a team-of-teams facilitated by the project manager and architect • Escalate priority unresolved disputes to the sponsor or governance council
Customer and business constituencies are large and self-conflicting with no anointed leader	• Seek top-level executive ownership of the customer and business community	• Set up coaching and mentorship for customers and businesses embedded in teams • Set up team-of-teams for customers and businesses to communicate and coordinate

Customer Scale

Very likely, the first hurdle to be overcome is defining the customer community. Large-scale projects inevitably reach many disparate constituents. Trying to find focus and a common purpose among them is hard enough; finding a group of product masters that can accurately and effectively represent all the customer, user, market, and sales issues is harder, often hampered by functional managers' real inability to commit resources to the project for the duration.

Mitigations for customer scale are situational. The executive team often must intervene to establish priorities. It is rare that day-to-day business key performance indicators are relieved to make way for the project, only adding to the conflicts between providing good people to the project and retaining good people in the business. As gaps are opened by assignment of staff to the project, it is inevitable that someone must take a risk, much like the effort to bridge the gap on the project balance sheet. There is no formula, no prescription. Each organization must make its own choices. However, agile methods are not effective without close customer attention; without customer integration on the teams, priorities and adaption are more likely to be technically driven, raising the specter of a technical project rather than a business project.

The N^2 Effect

Scale amplifies complexity exponentially; the simplest software systems are by nature complex, so large-scale software is extremely complex.[1] This phenomenon is known as the N^2 effect, named after the mathematical formula that describes how the number of interaction possibilities increases by nearly the square of the number of system components. Scale makes even small things seem larger and more complex; systems, networks, organizations, and environments are hard to imagine and keep in mind. The N^2 effect brings the difference between detail complexity and system complexity into picture. Detail complexity is about individual objects and effects. It may be possible for a customer or a developer to keep in mind hundreds of objects and object details, such as colors, buttons, fonts, fields, authorities, names, and so on. However, system complexity is about how these objects interact, and interact differently according to myriad conditions that change.[2] System complexity is much more difficult to imagine, much less keep up with. Therefore, even small increases in detail complexity leads to N^2 larger-system complexity. Thus, the need for simplicity—that is, the simplest complexity possible—is quite real since it is a high-leverage parameter on development cost, schedule, and post-release support. Figure 11-1 illustrates the interconnectivity phenomenon; Figure 11-2 shows how close the approximation is for N larger than 20.

Getting to Smaller

Critics note that neither the Agile Manifesto nor the Agile Principles address personal and organizational discipline, product and support architecture, or proven engineering practices, all necessary to do serious work on an enterprise scale. To be sure, there are elements of truth in what critics say.[3] They often charge that small team methods do not work well in the context of contracts; or when there is no co-located environment; or when there is no face-to-face contact and communication; or when teams are required to honor dependencies with other teams and projects. But there are mitigations for each of those charges.

Among correspondents, there are N × (N − 1) potential communication paths to exchange and acknowledge information, and to interface procedures

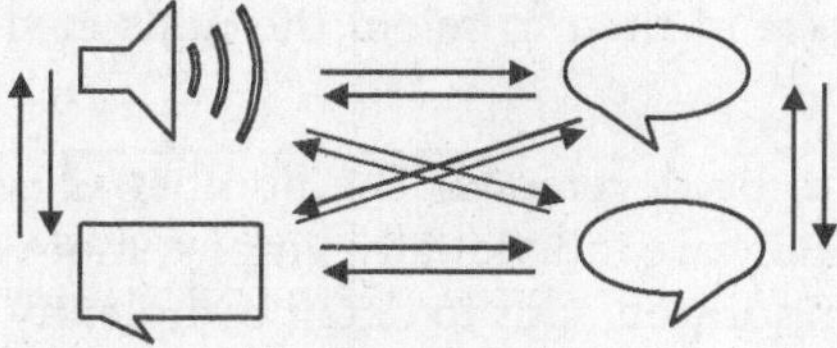

As shown above 12 = 4 × 3

Figure 11-1 The N^2 effect

For large N, the approximation of N × (N – 1) is N^2 as shown below in the curves for each that nearly overlay each other

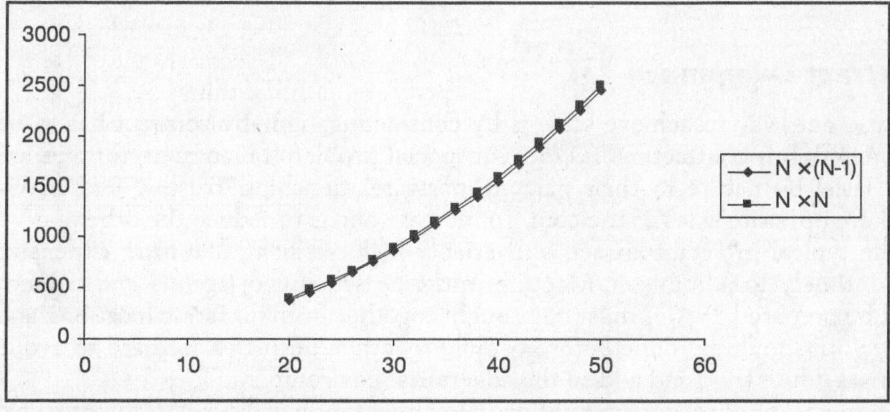

Figure 11-2 N^2 for large N

The trick is to translate scale into something that appears smaller and more manageable. In all too many situations, the friction of all the moving parts overwhelms the opportunity. This very phenomenon motivates deconstructing the system into smaller, nearly independent increments, exposing internal functions that might have been obscured, and defining object interfaces that are more easily manipulated than internal pathways and procedures. Even a mainframe computer expert like Fred P. Brooks, Jr. extols the virtues of incremental development in his twentieth anniversary edition of *The Mythical Man-month.*[4] When describing why EVO is successful as system-build methodology, Niels Malotaux writes that it is because a large number of small-scale efforts break up the complex development into manageable and predictable deliveries.[5]

So, while the proven mitigation to working with systems of large scale is to break them down into smaller units, to encapsulate or abstract the unit details to the smallest number of interface points, and then to rejoin the units at their interfaces, two problems remain:

1. There are now many small parts to be developed. The number of parts could be quite large, even though they are individually simpler, more understandable, and less risky. Decomposition adds to detail complexity.
2. The N^2 problem at the interfaces grows with the number of small parts, although the interfaces are simpler, more understandable, and easier to manage individually. In other words, internal system complexity that may be near chaotic is transformed into an interface system complexity that is predictable.

In a word, a large-scale system, even when decomposed, is still a lot of scope. There remains a need to be able to work on something larger than what one team can undertake.

Contract Dilemma

Because one way to achieve scale is by contracting, agile-by-contract has to be considered. But contracting has its own special problems. Contracts, for one, are adversarial by nature in their party-to-party relationships. Trusting and adversarial are opposite sides of the coin. To increase one is to reduce the other.

The typical project contract is invariably *high ceremony, low trust*, expensive and untimely to administer. Meetings must be scheduled; agenda and content must be prepared. Parties must be brought together from disparate locations, and homework should be done before coming together. Surprises are hard to avoid; surprises dilute trust and add to the adversarial environment.

Contracts require documentation. Documentation substitutes for personal real-time discussion, debate, and decision. It is hard to apply the agile idea of *just enough* when writing documents. Documentation tilts toward plan-driven; documentation requires that some things be thought through in advance and not left to just-in-time.

Person-to-person real-time embedded participation is the cornerstone of agile teams. It seems counter intuitive to substitute remote relationships for a real-time environment, especially if in a time zone around the world. Good documentation will be needed to carry communications beyond the boundaries of face-to-face. Do these things mean that agile methods are incompatible not only with contracts but also with virtual teams?

Networks Enable Large Scale

Some of the material in prior chapters addressed scaling practices of multiple teams working together on the same project. Table 11-3 gathers those ideas together:

Table 11-3 Summary of team scaling practices

Team scaling practice	Commentary
Multiple work streams	• Each work stream addresses some aspect of the project scope • Work streams can be dedicated to infrastructure, technology, product development, post-production support readiness, training, supply chain, project management, and others
Network of teams	• A network couples the activities of multiple teams to produce a collective outcome • Networks are employed when the productivity of one team is inadequate to satisfy the value proposition in a timely fashion • There may be teams that are somewhat more specialized than the multifunctional performance units
Team-of-teams	• The team-of-teams is the group responsible for coordinating and communicating activities among the teams on a daily basis • It may be necessary to form a steering committee to coordinate between work groups
Network buffer	• Buffers are periods of time for which no activity is scheduled • Buffers absorb unknown and unplanned events and activities • Buffers are the times that can be used for the schedule overrun of a team that needs a bit more time to complete its iteration • Buffer time is typically managed as a project resource by the project manager

Communicating in the Large-Scale Network

Networks facilitate a large number of people working on the same project. Networks have these attributes for structure and control:

- Nodes, where work gets done, having points of entry and exit for communications—typically a team, but a node could be a person in a virtual team
- Pathways and means to bind together nodes in a common community; and means to carry communication between nodes, regulated by protocols, some formal and some informal and unspoken
- Administrative tools to keep the network going, implement redundancy and workarounds for outages, and provide security, privacy, and access control

Networks are more agile than ever before: adaptive, informally lean, and operationally efficient. Recent societal changes account for many of the ways networks apply in the project context:

- Widespread access and adoption of instant messaging and wireless connectivity has given unprecedented pace and democracy to communications.
- The cultural acceptance of informality in business relationships has flattened the operating model and made it acceptable to skip echelon when communicating. Flatness encourages lateral relationships; lateral relationships speed communications and transfer information more accurately.
- The web and electronic networking have raised expectations that information should be readily available and easily accessed, used, and applied, and that feedback response should be nearly instantaneous. In system terms, there is now an expectation that the loop should close; action begets acknowledgement and follow-up in the network.

Although the Agile Manifesto states a preference for person-to-person communication over documentation, the Manifesto doesn't declare that documentation is unnecessary. The simple fact is that with a large number of teams, multiple work streams, and a large number of participants, the person-to-person dialogue necessary to communicate and distribute all the information about the system quickly becomes impractical. Accuracy, timeliness, and completeness are all put in harm's way. Documentation is more of a necessity. Indeed, documentation can satisfy many project agendas simultaneously. Jim Highsmith, one of the original 17 authors from the Manifesto group, writes that documentation supports collaboration and communication, enhances knowledge transfer, preserves historical information, assists ongoing product enhancement, and fulfills regulatory and legal requirements.[6]

Documentation is changing both in format and in utility—more and more documentation is electronic. Electronic documentation is leaner than its paper counterparts. Its very leanness enhances its value. It is quicker, easier, and cheaper to store, access, and distribute. It is also quicker, easier, and cheaper to maintain, but it is more vulnerable and more difficult to secure. Electronic documentation can be agile: adaptive, near-real-time accurate, and easily refactored.

High-scale projects require documentation for team operations. Examples of operational documents are architecture, product design, and test scripts and scenarios. Electronic templates are lean tools used to gather the ***minimum information elements*** (MIE). Document management systems that regulate access, versions, and privileges are effective and lean for keeping a library according to the conventions of the project that dictate which information elements can be simply comments in software code and which are to be committed to written documentation.[7]

However, much of the literature on agile methods expounds on the whiteboard and the virtues of story cards written on index cards.[8] As temporary expedients for personal group settings, there is probably no better, but results and conclusions need more permanence. Most teams do not retain the index story cards; except for the test script, there is no documentation of the requirement at the story level.

But when working in networks, portability of information must be considered. Physical war rooms, whiteboards, and index cards are for local use and consumption. In networks, electronic scorecards and dashboards are the preferred means to communicate widely, accurately, and with timeliness about information that is temporal, time sensitive, or of general interest.

Most projects will want to introduce a workflow process to regulate activity and to communicate the MIE for various actions. For example, feedback from users during acceptance testing is commonly gathered, analyzed, archived, and regulated by the workflow. Templates provide a way for users to enter the MIE; templated information is routed via a governance process, as discussed in Chapter 9.

Tactical information in the team network is provided by a number of artifacts:

- Templated architectural, technical, and functional designs and configuration data
- Project requirements backlog and the team's iteration backlog
- Progress charts consisting of the SCRUM burn-down list—a list of items completed and yet to be completed—or the XP burn-up list, a similar idea
- Trend charts of progress and earned-value calculations
- Other scorecards and dashboards

Work Dependencies in the Network

Working successfully in a network requires honoring the dependencies between the teams. Honoring dependencies means respecting everyone's time, finishing iterations as scheduled, and delivering scope as planned to avoid idle time until work can be resequenced for completion. The identification and coordination of these dependencies is the agenda of the team-of-teams.

Networks impose limitations on customers and users working on development teams. Customer and users working in a network give up some latitude to reset priorities and to introduce new requirements because priorities of other teams must be considered. Optimization at the team level gives way to optimization at the network level.

Virtual Teams Expand Throughput

A virtual team is one whose members are not all co-located. Indeed, the members may not be, and often are not, in the same organization, business unit, or time zone. Virtual teams are characterized by having membership with different environments and culture; membership that works at different times and locations; and membership that may have differing views of priorities and imperatives. Nevertheless, virtual teams are a way to expand the throughput of the network by incorporating members that cannot otherwise be present together.

Emulating a Real Team

Virtual teams often begin by emulating the behavior and circumstances of real teams. The first thought is communications. Real teams can handle a much greater N^2 communication intensity because much of person-to-person communication is nonverbal. In communication terms, nonverbal is a very high-bandwidth channel capable of communicating a large-information message instantly, although the message is often highly encoded and subject to inaccurate decoding. And even verbal communications are more easily digested if the context is understood simply by being present. It is much easier to sort out the cacophony of discussion if face and voice and context are put together.

Consequently, when planning for virtual teams, bear in mind that virtual teams do not have the luxury of infinite bandwidth; their more restricted channels tend to have less richness, lower volume, and volume that moves more slowly. There is a natural tendency to filter messages and only communicate the least complicated message. Electronic communications is the most available countermeasure—everything from a constantly open conference line, to instant messaging, video linkages, webinars, and a common dashboard that operates like a social networking wall are effective.

The impact of less communication on velocity is not intuitive. Some teams relish the hubbub of real-time communications, and others do not. Some miss the osmosis of casual communication as way to keep on top of things, and some prefer more regimented approaches. A good practice is to benchmark the velocity before beginning the first iteration. Even so, it may be necessary to accommodate velocity estimation errors in the first few iterations until feedback corrects practices.

Assigning Work to Virtual Teams

The iteration planning meeting is the agile mechanism for assigning work. All the team's complement attends. The same applies to a virtual team. The operational difference is that the whiteboard and index cards are replaced by an electronic whiteboard shared by a webinar application and an audiovisual conference.

Assigning work to virtual teams should follow this simple rule: partition work according to natural boundaries that minimize and simplify interfaces. Albert Einstein has been quoted to the effect, "Make everything as simple as possible, but not simpler." By this he advised that arbitrary complexity holds no value and may even contribute to inefficient and ineffective solutions. But oversimplification is also hazardous. The solution can lose cohesion and the bigger picture becomes so obscured that effective solutions are impossible to build from the too-small parts.

Tracking Progress and Identifying Problems

Two agile practices for tracking progress and identifying problems are earn-burn charts and trending graphs developed from the earn-burn data. Other progress-and-problem trackers are testing scorecards, pipeline scorecards,[9] and daily stand-up meetings.

Earn-burn Data

Earn-burn data is about how much resource has been expended, how much more is needed to complete a work unit, and how many work units have been completed.

In the SCRUM methodology, burn-down charts show these data. In the XP methodology, burn-up charts show the same thing but in the opposite direction.

SCRUM teams work to mark completed tasks off the chart; XP teams work to put completed tasks on the chart.

Burn refers to the effort; earn refers to completed work. Only completed work earns value.

Earn-burn within the team is an earned-value concept.

The daily stand-up meeting is affected by the communications that are unique to virtual teams. The less-efficient electronic channels may have to be compensated by extending the time box of the daily standup. Nevertheless, the usual rules that require everyone to speak and that limit those speeches to two minutes are still applicable.

Commitment and Accountability

Agile practices demand total commitment and accountability, both for personal and for team achievements; no less is expected of virtual teams.

Incentives and Rewards

It is obvious on the face that celebrations are more possible and more effective with co-located teams. In the virtual space, rewards are more personal and made specific to the situation, especially if virtual team members are physically challenged. In some situations, local functional managers take over some of the project manager and team-leader responsibilities to ensure proper recognition.

Agile-by-Contract Enables Scale

In one sense every agile project operates under the auspices of a contract because the business case is a contract in all but legal form. As it happens in all bilateral agreements, there are times when the sponsor-project relationship becomes challenging, the vision is not clear enough, or the gap on the project balance sheet widens unfavorably. The challenge becomes greater if it is decided to contract with a provider; now the relationship is expanded to sponsor-project-provider.[10] At each juncture, there is the possibility for misunderstanding, obfuscation—deliberately or unwitting—and misalignment of aims and means.

Contract Objectives

Why contract? There are several reasons, all of which are forms of risk mitigation and resource management:

- *Capability:* To gain access to people with skills and methods that are otherwise unavailable to the project
- *Feasibility:* To acquire deliverables from a lower risk source
- *Capacity:* To temporarily increase production when the need for long-term capacity does not yet exist

Contracting is motivated by a business calculation that a contract is more beneficial than do-it-yourself—there is a cost and there is a benefit, each to be calculated in light of risks. To pay off, the cost and benefit estimates must be realistic about the supplier's capacity and capability, and about the project's capability to convey needs and wants effectively to the supplier. Much can go awry. It is risky business to communicate through a contract channel about fluid and unknown requirements. It is also risky to assume the contractor can do a good job in the agile environment, or a better job than the project can do for itself. In short, there is nothing firm and fixed about a contract for technology work on complex undertakings. Be on guard to not make a risky proposition worse by contracting inappropriately. Here are important points to grasp:

Contract points to consider

- A contract in any form is a risk management tool; an objective of every contracted situation is to transfer the risk responsibility from one party to another.
- Every transfer of risk responsibility involves cost and benefit calculations.
- One party charges a premium to accept a risk; the other party pays the premium to have the risk transferred.

A project management tip	What makes a contract?
	It is generally understood that the following five elements need to be in place, either orally or in writing, before there is a legal and enforceable contract: 1. There must be a true offer to do business by the project. 2. There must be a corresponding acceptance of the offer to do business by the contractor. 3. There must be a specified consideration for the work to be performed. Consideration does not need to be in terms of dollars. 4. The supplier must have the capacity to perform as represented in their acceptance offer. 5. The statement of work must be for a legal activity; it is improper to contract for illegal activities.

Contracts through the Risk Management Lens

Risk is managed by both parties to the contract. Each follows a similar process:

- Identify risks
- Estimate and rank risks by impact
- Estimate and rank risks by likelihood
- Direct mitigation to the high-impact-with-high-likelihood risks first

A contract is another form of the project balance sheet: there is a business side, a project side, and a gap between expectations and affordability on the one hand, and capability and capacity to meet expectations profitably on the other. The gap is called risk.

> In the agile space the number one issue for risk management is unknown and unknowable requirements.

With only top-level visionary requirements specified, there is no scope specification that is actionable without customer or end-user interpretation. Consequently, there can be no detailed estimate of cost, schedule, or even of the methods and tools that might be required. Any contract that is written has to account for these risks and establish risk premiums accordingly.

Contracting in any form cannot eliminate project risk; contracting can only make project risk more manageable. There are choices: The project manager may choose to retain some or most of the cost risk and only transfer the performance risk; or, the project manager may choose to transfer both cost and performance risk. The risk premiums will be different according to choice—the more risk retained in the project, the lower the risk premium will be.

Even so, the project may not get what it expects. As an example, in a so-called fixed-price arrangement, the contractor may fail to perform, leaving the project with a schedule problem at the very least. The contractor may run into unforeseen feasibility problems, experience business failures elsewhere that affect the project, or be impacted by external threats such as changes in regulations or acts of God.

A project management tip	The competition to manage risk
	• Both parties when entering into a contract seek to minimize risk. • The contractor will be inclined to identify risks early on so that the risks can be covered by provisions in the contract: more money, more time, and assistance in various forms. • The project team will be inclined to seek performance guarantees and the means to reward upside achievement or to punish downside shortfalls.

Contracting Concepts for Cost and Results

Two concepts that underlie all contracted arrangements are shown in Table 11-4. One concept is around effort and results: the idea of *completion* as different from a *best effort*. The second concept is around cost responsibility: the idea of *fixed price* as different from *cost reimbursable*. Concepts of effort and results can be mixed and matched with different forms of cost responsibility to reduce risk and reward achievement:

Table 11-4 Contracting concepts

Contracting concept	**Commentary**
Completion vs. best effort	• When pledging *completion*, the contractor commits to a finished product; typically the price is fixed • When pledging *best effort,* the contractor commits to making a good faith attempt to fulfill all the requirements with quality work, but makes no commitment to a finished product; work continues as long as the contractor is paid for progress • *Best effort* is the better choice when feasibility is unproven, requirements are incomplete, or the strategic direction is uncertain
Fixed price vs. cost reimbursable	• Fixed-price contracts require the contractor to deliver a completed product at a price, including the risk premium, negotiated and agreed-to before work begins • Fixed-price contracts are *completion* contracts • Fixed-price contracts are the most lean to administer • Fixed-price contracts transfer all the cost risk to the supplier for which the project is charged a relatively high risk premium • Cost reimbursable or cost-plus contracts pay the contractor's cost, usually at the invoice amount, and also pay a fee calculated separately from cost • Cost reimbursable contracts transfer very little of the project's cost risk to the contractor and require only a contractor's best effort toward completing the work • The risk premium is very low, even to the point of no premium • Cost reimbursable contracts are not completion contracts • Cost reimbursable contracts are not as lean as fixed-price contracts; more administration and exchange of business data is necessary to be successful with cost reimbursable contracts
Time and materials (T&M)	• T&M is used to buy labor, usually by the hour, at a fixed price per hour; expenses, tools, and supplies are usually reimbursed at cost • There is no commitment to completion or even best effort; the contractor takes no project responsibility except to supply qualified people • A risk premium is built in to the hourly rate to cover the high cost of recruiting to fill turnover

Contracted Incentives and Rewards

Incentives and rewards motivate contractor teams just as they do with internal project teams. The common convention is first to apply incentives based on cost performance, and then based on value-added achievements. Some common arrangements are shown in Table 11-5. Figure 11-3 illustrates sharing between the project and the contractor.

Contracting in the Agile Space Shares Risk

Every project expects their contractor to perform with integrity, quality, and an adherence to ethical and lawful behavior—that is a given.

Table 11-5 Incentive contracts

Incentive program	Commentary
Fixed-price incentive (FPI)	• The contractor is given an incentive to perform within a price range rather than to perform to a specific price point • In the range between the target and the ceiling price, the project and the contractor share the price risk • Outside the range, either higher than ceiling or lower than target, the contractor assumes all risk • There is a lower risk premium built into the price, so the target price is typically lower than a fixed-price contract with a fixed-price point
Award fee contract	• The contractors fee is based on achievements on a number of parameters negotiated in advance before work begins, something like a balanced scorecard • An award fee is typically applied to cost reimbursable contracts, but can be an additional fee applied to fixed-price contracts
Cost reimbursable fixed fee (CRFF) and cost reimbursable incentive fee (CRIF)	CRFF: • A fixed fee, but with a reimbursable cost; the idea is that fee and cost are separable • Negotiated in advance as a fixed amount and paid regardless of the cost performance of the contractor • Since the contractor bears no cost risk, there is no risk premium built in • Modest and usually based on a reasonable return on capital employed, an economic value added argument CRIF: • Fixed fee incentive shares improved cost performance with the contractor; based on a sharing ratio, each dollar of cost savings is shared with the contractor

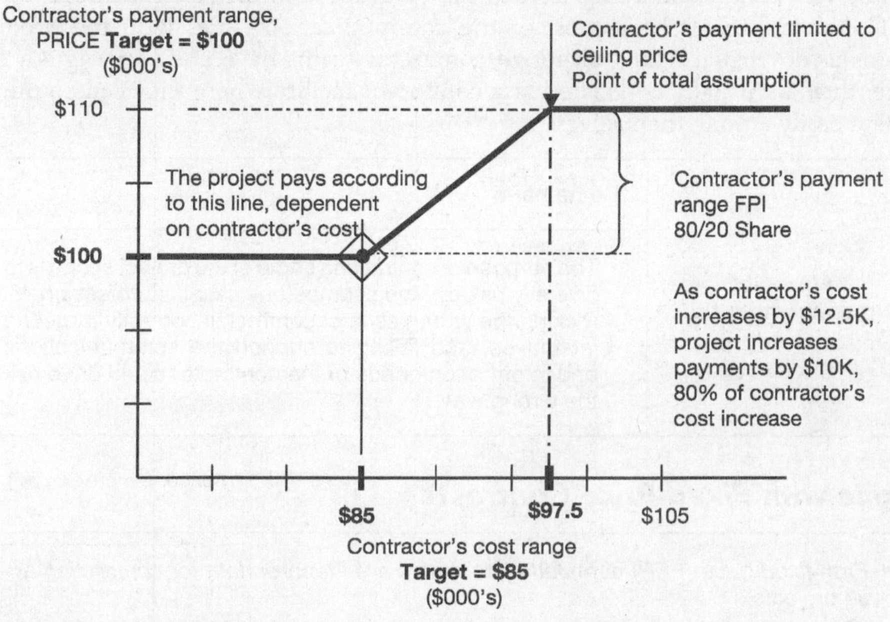

Figure 11-3 Fixed-price incentive contract

Contracts establish relationships and provide the means and methods to transfer knowledge, data, and priorities. In return, the project benefits from the contractor's work, and the contractor benefits from the business relationship.

Contracts rarely impose methodologies. Qualified contractors bring compatible methods and practice to the relationship; if contractors did not do this, they would not be selected as a provider. Contracts are a poor vehicle to transfer values and culture—the things believed in and thought to be the right things to do. Nevertheless, commitment and accountability are two values that need to jump across to the contractor. Fortunately, contractors often mimic what they observe, seeking to minimize differences by absorbing their best customers' style of work to some degree. And of course there is the carrot and stick: incentives and penalties are two means to get attention and drive behavior. Some caution however: W. Edwards Deming famously eschewed all slogans, exhortations, quantitative goals, and incentives. Since Deming, research has shown that incentives or penalties can affect behavior. But for either incentives or penalties to be effective, consequences must be obvious, there must be widespread knowledge and understanding of the possibilities, effects must be felt immediately and be relevant, and they must meet social norms for fairness and reasonableness.[11] The most applicable contract vehicle meeting these criteria is the award-fee contract because award periods can be very timely and award criteria can be adapted to the circumstances.

Contractor teams have most of the communication issues with the project teams as do virtual teams, although contractor teams have one very big advantage: they are usually co-located at a contractor facility where they can communicate easily among themselves.

A project management tip	Do no harm
	• The purpose of contracting some of the project scope is to diversify risk by hiring competent, capable professionals. • Picking the wrong style of contract, incorrectly targeting incentives, and failing to support the communications and information needs of the contractor could drive risk the wrong way.

Agile with Fixed-Price Contracts

- *Firm-fixed price (FFP) completion contracts are inappropriate for contracting agile projects.*
- Firm-fixed price completion requires an agreement on a price firmly decided up front for a set of unchanging deliverables; scope must be stable for a fixed-price determination.
- Conditions for FFP are not present in an agile project.

Even though FFP is inappropriate, there are alternatives. One workable strategy is to contract for one iteration at a time, each such contract being a work order. To reduce administration and make such contracts timely, a framework is created to provide basic contract services for the work orders. In this fixed-price work order scenario, the project team selects a set of requirements from the backlog and provides them to the contractor to evaluate and price. The project specifies a time box for the duration of the work order. The contractor is paid a fixed price upon work-order completion.

For a work-order scenario to be practical, the agile concept of the embedded user must be addressed in context of the contracted situation. One possibility is to send a user from the project organization to the contractor for the duration of the time box. If the contractor is nearby, this arrangement may work well. Another approach is to set up a dashboard and other access that provides an electronic emulation of being onsite.

Either approach creates tension with the contractor. Caution is needed; the rules of engagement for fixed-price contracting are that the project cannot be intrusive; the project is given only the very minimum oversight of the contractor's activity. There is no privilege to direct or advise the contractor's approach or methods. Further, there must be respect for the terms of the contract, or there could be chaos. The scope of the work order is fixed by negotiation; the user is on hand to interpret needs but not to change scope.

Another possibility is to preload the work order with an acceptance test scenario coordinated with the user in advance.[12] The scenario is written by the project team users; of course, it is written in advance of any coding by the contractor. The test scenario becomes a part of the work-order scope and a form of requirement specification.

FPI contracts are a possibility for those situations where customer interpretations, priorities, and urgency are understood to a degree that would allow for the reasonable estimation of a price range, bounded by a target price and a ceiling price. The range should be generous so that the impacts of numerous points of guidance from the user can be absorbed. To construct an FPI contract there are two prices to agree on:

1. The target price is the optimistic price based on everything going well. The contractor's profit is greater at the target price than it is at the ceiling price.
2. The ceiling is the most pessimistic price and allows for missed requirements and other risks to materialize and to be included. The contractor's profit is minimal or even nonexistent if the work is delivered at or above the ceiling price.

The project and the contractor share the cost between the target and ceiling, with the project typically taking 70 to 80 percent of the risk. At the ceiling price, the contractor assumes 100 percent of the risk for any further cost.

Cost Reimbursable Contracts for Agile Projects

Cost reimbursable contracts are designed specifically for the agile project situation. The rules of engagement expect and allow intrusion, redirection, and interpretation of requirements. Insofar as such actions increase cost, that increase is passed along to the project without risk to the contractor. However, there is no completion commitment. Performance risk is transferred from project to contract. All cost risk is retained by the project in the cost reimbursable fixed-fee arrangement; some cost sharing can occur in an incentive fee structure. In all forms of cost reimbursable contracts, there is little impetus for the contractor to control costs, although an incentive fee can boost cost control. In the simplest cost reimbursable form, a fixed fee is paid based on the contractor's expected cost of capital and a reasonable return on equity. However, as actual cost goes up or down from the original estimate, the fee does not. The fee is fixed once agreed to.

Incentive fees and award fees are very applicable to cost reimbursable contracts. Incentive fees are cost-sharing arrangements, with the project usually accepting the larger share. Award fees are parameter-based fees. A scorecard, not unlike the balanced scorecard, is agreed to at the inception of the contract. At periodic points of evaluation, a fee is awarded based on the scores attained. In the agile situation, the award period is typically one planning wave. The scorecard can be for functional, technical, or managerial parameters:

- Quality of features and functions as perceived by the customer
- Quality of the unit development as measured by the pass rate of unit and integration tests
- Responsiveness and accuracy of updating scorecards, dashboards, and other media to forestall surprises

Agile Time and Materials Contracts

T&M is the way to buy labor by the hour for the duration of a wave, usually by hiring independent contractors. Once a contracted developer is embedded in a team, the team's cohesion is of primary importance.

A project management tip	Work orders versus T&M
	• Work orders transfer more risk than does T&M. • T&M simply solves a staffing problem. • Work orders bring additional staff, a management team, and a commitment to completion with accountability.

Summary and Takeaway Points

The theme of this chapter is that agile methods are scalable; and within limitations, amenable to the advantages of contracts and virtual teams. To scale up requires some to give up on the autonomy and independence of the performance unit team. Several scale-up techniques are applicable:

- *Networks:* To ramp productivity to meet business objectives in a timely fashion, multiple teams are required. To be effective, teams work in networks, forming relationships and exchanging information.
- *Virtual teams:* To add staff from disparate locations that cannot be co-located for one reason or another, virtual teams are a solution. Virtual teams must overcome the disadvantage of not being co-located; they require accurate and timely communication, a dedication to overcoming

cultural differences, and assignment of work according to rational decomposition of requirements.

- *Contracts:* Contracts can be used to address risks of capacity, capability, and feasibility. Contracts transfer risk out of the project into other hands. However, contract situations have all the issues of virtual teams plus the overlay of the contract structure. Fixed-price contracting is inappropriate for agile projects. T&M or completion work orders—either fixed-price incentive or cost reimbursable—are workable contract frameworks.

Properly applied, scaling techniques do make it possible to extend agile methods beyond simple projects.

Chapter Endnotes

1. Interaction between components grows by approximately the square of the number of devices interacting, $N \times (N - 1)$. For large N, this formula is very close to N^2. This phenomenon explains why making teams larger becomes counterproductive after a point. A similar concept applies to any components that communicate, whether a software object or a subsystem.
2. Anderson, *Agile Management for Software Engineering,* 15.
3. Schawber, *Agile Project Management with Scrum*, 119–132, 147.
4. Brooks, *The Mythical Man-month*, 201.
5. Malotaux, *Evolutionary Project Management Methods,* 2.
6. Highsmith, *Agile Project Management: Creating Innovative Products,* 12.
7. McConnell, *Code Complete,* Chapter 19, 453–492.
8. Beck, with Andres, *Extreme Programming Explained*, 95.
9. *Pipelines* and *pipelining* are terms that describe the use of a scorecard to capture data that seems to flow by. See Goodpasture, *Pipelining your Project*, 37–43.
10. The terms *provider, supplier,* and *contractor* are used interchangeably to denote the entity that is doing the work governed by a contract. The project is the entity that does the contracting with the provider.
11. Geller, *The Psychology of Safety Handbook*, 195–197.
12. Cohn, *User Stories Applied for Agile Software Development*, Chapter 6.

Table Endnote

1. Division of labor is perhaps the oldest mitigation. Adam Smith saw the need to have work specialties, a division of labor so to speak, in order to get any but the simplest work done well with high quality, something that he wrote about in his eighteenth-century book *The Wealth of Nations.*

12

Benefit Realization

Agile methods start the benefit stream earlier, generating more valuable returns from frequent, incremental product deliveries.

Now this is not the end. It is not even the beginning of the end. But it is, perhaps, the end of the beginning.

Winston Churchill

There is no need to do a project if the business does not benefit. Simple stuff, but in the long run, a project's success will be judged more on the satisfaction of the beneficiaries than on the performance of the project. Look only to New Coke or the Apple Newton for examples of successful projects with unhappy endings.

Plan-driven project development lifecycle (PD-PDLC) methods often struggle with benefits realization, largely because everything comes at the end of the project cycle, and long after the opportunities are first identified. But the fix is in: agile shortens the delivery cycle, increases the delivery frequency, demands timely employment of deliverables, and facilitates feedback to drive improvements!

Benefits Are Part of the Plan

Every benefit plan begins with the business case and its business sponsor. The benefit plan addresses each beneficiary's rights and responsibilities, and the returns each should expect from a successful project. Persuasion of managers and executives to buy in to the benefits plan begins with the business case. Both the enthusiastic and the reluctant, whether visionary or opportunistic, are constituents of the business plan.

Chapter 2 covers the business case in detail, and the decision making that goes along with it. Recall that Level 0 is only a simple form handled easily by workflow; the suggested benefit is included in Table 2-8. There we see that Level

0 benefit measures are functional key performance indicators (KPIs) or balanced scorecard metrics. Level 1 is a bit more complicated because more is at stake. Table 2-9 extends Table 2-8; besides functional KPIs and balanced scorecard considerations, there are also P&L benefits at Level 1. At Level 2, serious benefit analysis is required; as suggested in Table 2-10, a revamped balanced scorecard may be required.

Benefits Manager

Post-project success may well rest on the business unit manager who is going to own the business results. *Ownership* means that the manager accepts responsibility to drive deployment within the business, although many stakeholders will be individually accountable for business results. The benefit manager's task is a bit like herding cats: someone needs to keep all the players moving in the same general direction. From each segment of the businesses' scorecard, there are key performance indicators affected by the project's impact. Examples abound, such as lower operating expense, increased revenues, better-trained and more capable staff, more satisfied customers, lower warranty costs, quicker call-center response time, better first-time maintenance fix rates, and many others.

There are likely to be many beneficiaries who are not stakeholders—beneficiaries such as customers who buy products and use services. And, there could be many others involved in post-project success who are functional participants doing their job—such as call-center operators who answer customer questions.

<table>
<tr><td rowspan="2">A project management tip</td><td>The benefit plan</td></tr>
<tr><td>• The benefits manager may have more influence on project success than the project manager.
• The benefit stream may have a lifecycle of years, whereas the project may last only a matter of months.</td></tr>
</table>

The benefits manager may not be a single person but rather a group joined by the common objective of making the project a success. In that event, the group needs a leader. For Level 2, the benefits leader may be an executive; for Level 1 the leader may be a senior manager. For Level 0, the benefits leader is more likely a functional unit manager.

Business Preparation Work Stream

It may seem odd to speak about convincing the organization to accept the project results, to employ them, and take advantage of their capabilities. But many projects require organizational change to incorporate outcomes; it is not news that change is difficult to accept, often resisted, and that benefits tied to change are the most difficult to realize. Change is not something that happens casually; it often requires inspirational and motivating leadership. And, it often requires the slog of day-to-day attention to a myriad of details that define and implement a road map.

Business preparation is often its own work stream. Business preparation is chartered to develop and implement post-project capabilities. The business may be required to hire staff, train or retrain existing staff, put new supply capabilities in place, prepare product support capability, and develop sales and marketing materials. Business preparation may also address compensation plans and balanced scorecard objectives, even P&L adjustments.

A project management tip	The rapid cycle of change for business preparation
	• The rapid cycle time of agile projects shortens the planning timeframes for business preparation. • Executing business preparation tasks must take into account agile principles: be quick, incremental, responsive, and adaptive. • Change is managed release-by-release. • A look over the planning horizon provides a heads-up for change to come, but the bottom line is that change comes very quickly with agile methods.

Avoiding the Big Bang

Unlike the *big-bang* plans of the PD-PDLC, agile methods make multiple releases to build acceptance and trust, and adapt to evolving need with each release. Change occurs incrementally: everyone's business data will not change overnight, everyone's job will not change on go-live morning, and all the moving parts that serve customers will not be changed and reordered in a stroke.

Even though many stakeholders, users, and customers will be involved over the lifecycle of the project, at any one release the number is likely to be smaller. For instance, not everyone will have their password changed at one time, not everyone needs to be trained within a few days of go-live, and the communications message to those affected can be more targeted and timely.

Driving for Benefits

There is no autopilot for benefits. Realizing benefits is hard work and requires dedicated attention. The first step is to actively work with the organization to find an attractive means to incorporate project results in the day-to-day routine. If the benefit plan extends over any length of time, then there will be changes in the business unrelated to the project. Business changes will disturb the planned benefits and require the plan to be modified to accommodate new benefit targets—remember: planning is everything, the plan is nothing. Recall from Chapter 10 that our definition of benefits is the flow of KPI results that begin with product delivery. At the moment of delivery as described in Chapter 10, the customer recognizes value, but no benefits have been realized. At that moment, benefits are a forecast. For dollar denominated benefits, the forecast is customarily risk adjusted by applying discounted cash flow (DCF) methods. Over time, as benefit forecasts become benefit realities, the business value of the project opportunity is earned. Thus, benefit realization is a matter of timing, and within timing, it is a matter of sequencing.

Sequencing for Benefits

Deliverables are sequenced at each release according to this ordering:

1. Foundational capability driven by technical sequencing and architecture constraints—that is, the walls before the roof
2. Functional capabilities that are highest in priority to the customer by importance and urgency
3. Functional capabilities according to their impact on benefit cash flow

Sequencing impacts benefits directly so the order of delivery is determined by the team, i.e. technical sequencing is determined by the product architect, and functional sequencing is determined by the embedded business user or analyst. Time is of the essence; the rhythm of releases is important for maintaining pace and momentum. With the rapid pace of agile projects—faster than the surrounding business cycles of strategic planning, quarterly P&Ls, and annual reports—only the most involved stakeholders will be able to affect benefit priorities, and they do this by committing resources as product masters and embedded users.

Ambassadors of Benefits

The embedded users and product masters are the ambassadors of benefits. They carry the business message to the project, affecting outcomes and priorities. They also interpret activity and report to their business chain about progress and problems. During business preparation, they more than anyone are capable of explaining outcomes to other functional users and customers. In many cases, the embedded users do the heavy lifting of evangelizing the benefits case.

The embedded users quickly become product experts. Their expertise is valued by functional managers and the stock of these individuals often rises. They are often deployed in temporary roles as coaches, troubleshooters, and even trainers. Indeed, if business preparation produces a train-the-trainer program, then users from the project, as subject-matter experts, often participate as trainers.

Adoption

Benefit tracking begins with the first release. Adoption may be slow. Because of the natural reluctance to change, embracing new capabilities may not be automatic. To encourage adoption, competing or legacy capabilities should be withdrawn as soon as practical. It may be possible to help adoption by having the first few iterations produce product increments that are naturally attractive and capable of creating a buzz.

There are, of course, early adopters who will eagerly grab new capabilities, especially technology capabilities rich in software features and functions, and especially those that are user-configurable. But early adopters are only one of five personalities in the body of knowledge known as *diffusion of innovations*.[1] The five are:

1. *Innovators:* Anxious to work with the product in a preproduction or beta status and take risks with immature product; usually very personable and networked individuals, well connected with technology, and able to handle a high degree of uncertainty
2. *Early adopters:* Opinion leadership eager to put product through its paces and be first on the block to have the advantage of a new capability
3. *Early majority:* Willing to adopt after visible proof that the bugs have been worked out and operational effectiveness has been proven
4. *Later majority:* Reluctant but willing, not too comfortable giving up what they know best
5. *Laggards:* Might never adopt and so drop out of the pool of users

Innovators often make their own decisions to engage using new ideas; they are often in at the beginning and may be drivers behind the original vision. Early adopters may wait for official sanction before taking up a new product; later adopters may be forced by decision makers to get involved. Regardless, Everett Rogers, one of the early academics in the theory of diffusing innovation, posits that everyone passes through a five-stage decision-making process, albeit on difference timelines.[2] Roger's paradigm is:

1. *Seek knowledge:* Seek basic information to become familiar and acquainted with a new idea, product, or service
2. *Accept persuasion:* Evaluate benefits in the context of personal use and application
3. *Decide:* Decide to adopt or reject
4. *Implement:* Begin to apply the product or service to the everyday routine
5. *Confirm:* Accept the product as a fully qualified alternative to the prior capability

In the agile space, this five-step process repeats with every release, although the steps begin to merge and the timeline is shorter as each release builds upon the past. The mission of business preparation is to smooth this decision process as much as possible; to prepare the knowledge base; and to prepare persuasive information so that moving to implementation and confirmation is as rapid as possible.

Handing Off for Benefits

Although agile methods avoid handoffs and rely instead on long-term commitments and multifunctional teams that carry on for the lifecycle of the project, the fact is that a handoff must occur between the project and the business. At some point the project will be completed, although in the agile space, a handoff happens at each release; project completion is a milestone at the last release.

Handoff happens when the project drops support for deliverables and the business begins support. Handoff is also marked by activating business scorecards and dashboards. Workflow is rerouted from the project to the business. The governance council continues its activity, but now the council works at the behest of the business rather than the project. Incentives and compensation agreements are activated. The balanced scorecard KPIs are started anew at the next business cycle.

Handoff may trigger other activity: there may be customer or user communications distributed, new or changed support procedures initiated, new supply-chain links activated, or even functional reorganization.

A project management tip	Passing the flag
	• The project-business handoff has some of the trappings of passing the flag from project manager to business manager. • Of course in the agile space, handoffs happen incrementally; there is no big bang at the end with celebrations and a change of command, so to speak.

Measuring Results Drives Improvements

Measurements begin with KPIs from the balanced scorecard:

- Decide what is to be measured—look to the business plan and the balanced scorecard. Reach an agreement with the project sponsor and other affected stakeholders about what the expectations are for improvements.

- Determine a means to measure and gather the data—be wary that an intrusion to make measurements may influence the measured value.
- Determine a baseline of the current state of the business—obtain buy in from all affected functional and executive managers for the baseline figures.
- Measure and gather data onto a scorecard—maintain awareness that one release may affect the benefits of another.
- Analyze the data, interpret results, and report information.
- Use benefit data to drive continuous improvement.
- Synchronize project-benefit data collection with business key-performance measurement cycles. Be wary of short-term transient effects that are unrepresentative of long-term benefits.

Measurements Scorecard

Releases influence what is measurable, modifying the possibilities with every production go-live. Consider a back-office application project for *order entry* as an example: perhaps after Release 1 there is a new capability for simple order entry; the operational efficiency of simple order entries is the measured KPI. At Release 2, perhaps additional functionality allows an order to be priced according to a contracted price list, changing operational efficiency of Release 1 simple order entry. In other words, separate functionalities can cause benefit cause-and-effects to become intertwined. After Release 2, there is a need to recognize that effects will be felt on the benefit stream associated with Release 1.

A project management tip	Regression applied to benefits
	• It is unlikely that benefit managers will be familiar with regression concepts; they may not anticipate benefit dependencies from one release to the next. • Coach the benefit managers about the effects of benefits from incremental and evolutionary methods.

To set up the scorecard, the bookkeeping should account for the release schedule, as shown in the example scorecard grid in Figure 12-1. In this figure, we see that for the *N*th business cycle—where *N* is a business quarter or year—there is a baseline performance measurement taken in a period before the first release. That measurement should accurately portray the state of the business before any effects from project outcomes. Subsequently, and after each release, additional

The benefits scorecard tracks benefit performance incrementally as the product base is updated by each release

Key performance indicator	Business cycle 'N'				
	Baseline period	Release 1	Release 2	Release 3	Ending wave 1***
	Baseline	Type 1 function	Type 2 function	Renewal function	Type 1, 2 & function
Operating efficiency*	88%	83%**	86%	94%	97%****
Headcount	201	212	205	189	189

*OE is the ratio of the operating results to the operating plan for period expense dollars
**OE follows headcount; no synergy from user/functionality interaction is evident
***Summary information for a dashboard
****Synergies improve OE more than just a headcount reduction

Figure 12-1 Benefits data collection

measurements are taken. Performance differences can be compared from release to release from the baseline to a release.

Transient Benefit Effects

Figures 12-2 and 12-3 show a common phenomenon: introducing a change may actually make business performance worse until it gets better. At Release 1, the introduction of the Type 1 function has adversely affected operating efficiency. Agile does not cause this circumstance, but may affect it in several ways:

1. The short cycles of releases may impact the ability of business preparation to properly initialize the business for the oncoming change. Training, communications, support, inventory, and distribution may have difficulty reacting in short cycles.
2. Frequent releases may have a pile-on effect as the next release comes shortly after the prior release. Users are unable to follow all the changes to make maximum use of the capabilities.
3. Incremental deliveries may require temporary business workarounds for functionality not yet delivered. Workarounds are first learned and then unlearned, causing friction and churn within the organization.
4. The development teams may have to deliver temporary functionality that becomes a throwaway. Temporary interfaces, workaround functionality, manual overrides, and other manual scripts may be required. These artifacts detract from value-added throughput and add to the support burden in the short run, even as they impact operational efficiency.

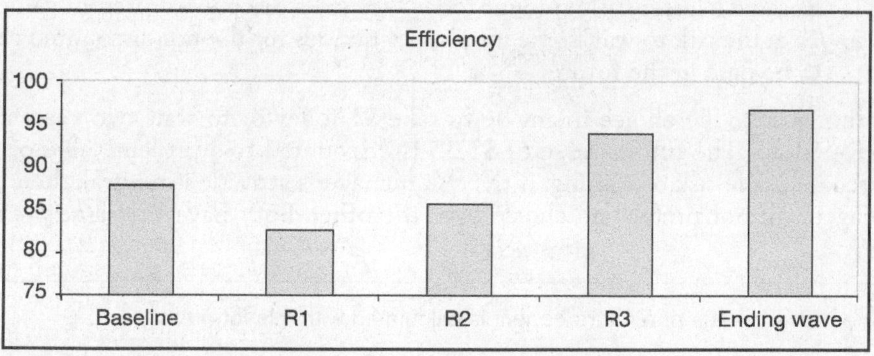

Figure 12-2 Business performance—operating efficiency

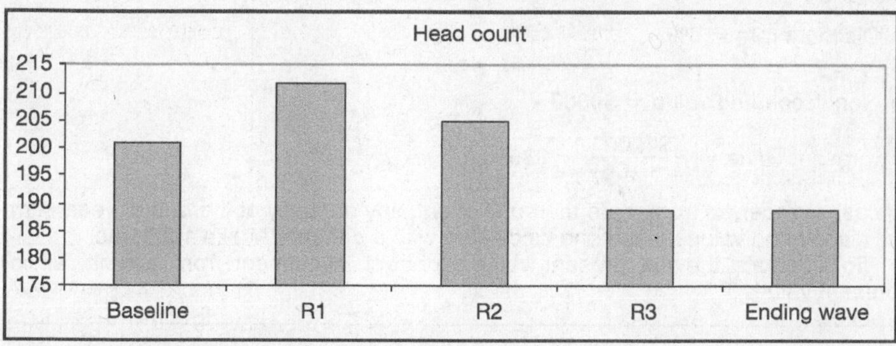

Figure 12-3 Business performance—headcount

Discounting the Future

In Chapter 2, the point was made that most financial forecasts take a discount for risks. After all, the future is only an estimate, not a fact. Discounts are usually taken over longer periods of time, typically years. Obviously, most projects will end well before the benefit period expires, even if benefits start early on as in agile projects. There are two popular discounting methods that fortunately arrive at the same evaluation for the cash value of a benefit stream: net present value (NPV) and economic value added.[3] NPV is probably more familiar, so it will be used to illustrate the business-case example that follows.

Working in present value offers a risk manager a choice:

1. Receive a lesser cash amount today—called a discounted present value
2. Take the risk to wait some number of periods for the nondiscounted cash to be paid in the future

In other words, the choice might be to take $1 today or to wait two years and receive $1.25. The future value of $1.25 is discounted to a present value of $1 to recognize the risk of waiting. If the risk manager's attitude is neutral, then the manager will not prefer one choice over the other. Both have the same *present value*.

The present value of a future benefit is calculated with this formula:

$$\text{The present value} = \frac{\text{nondiscounted value}}{(1 + \text{discount rate})^N}$$

where N is the number of periods from the present to some future time and the discount rate accounts for the risk of waiting.

Example:

- Discount rate = 6%
- $N = 2$
- Nondiscounted value = $4000
- present value $= \frac{\$4000}{(1 + .06)^2} = \$3560$

If cash is received from more than one event, say annually at the end of year, sum all discounted values, each one calculated with a different N, like 1,2,3, etc.

To calculate the net present value, subtract investment from benefit, all in present value.

In the example given, the risk manager is indifferent about receiving an immediate payment of $3560 or waiting two years for a $4000 payment. On a risk-adjusted basis, both sums have the same value. To illustrate the agile project case, consider the following project:

Project example

There are four functions to be delivered: F1, F2, F3, and F4.

- $12,000 is to be invested to develop the functions, $3000 per function, for which the payback from each is $1000 per year, year after year.
- Each function is delivered in its own release, and each release occurs every one-third year, or trimester.

- F1 is delivered at the end of the first trimester, and so the benefits from F1 are measured for the first time at the end of the second trimester. Each function is subsequently measured the same way, beginning in the trimester after its release.
- For comparison, the Ag-PDLC and a big-bang PD-PDLC are shown. In the PD-PDLC all four functions are delivered in the fourth trimester and benefits are measured for the first time in the fifth trimester.
- The discount rate is given by the enterprise financial officer as 6 percent.
- The net present value = benefit – investment. The project is paid for when the NPV ≥ \$0.

The project case is shown in the grid in Figure 12-4. Here we see the impact of incremental deliveries. The nearer-to-present releases are less risky because there is more certainty about the near future than there is about the far future,

The present value of benefits is accelerated by the early and frequent deliveries of agile methods

	Present time	**Future time, increasing risk →**					
Discounted benefit stream @6%							
		Year 1 trimesters			**Year 2 trimesters**		
\$1000 per function per year*	Net present value, 5 trimesters	1-1	1-2**	1-3	2-1	2-2	Grand Total
Function 1	– \$1755	Release 1-1	\$320***	\$315	\$308	\$302	\$1245
Function 2	–\$2075		Release 1-2	\$315	\$308	\$302	\$925
Function 3	– \$2390			Release 2-1	\$308	\$302	\$610
Function 4	– \$2698				Release 2-2	\$302	\$302
Agile	**– \$8918**						**\$3082**
Big-Bang PD-PDLC	**–\$10792**				**Release 2-2**	**\$1208**	**\$1208**

*Annual benefit from each function, 1/3rd paid each release period, \$333 before discounting
**The discount period is assumed to be 3 equal periods per year
***It is assumed that release 1-1 is at the end of trimester 1-1. In trimester 1-2 cell, \$1000/3 has been discounted for two trimesters, = 333 / [(1 + .06/3) * (1 + .06/3)]. The risk-weighted present value is \$320; the future value is \$333

Figure 12-4 Benefits discount schedule

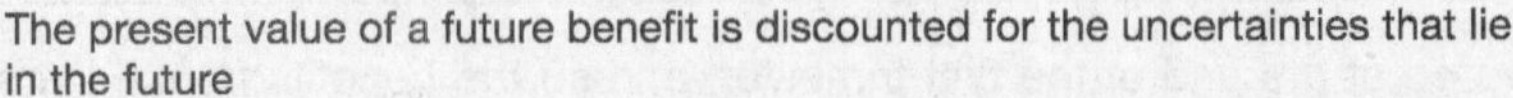

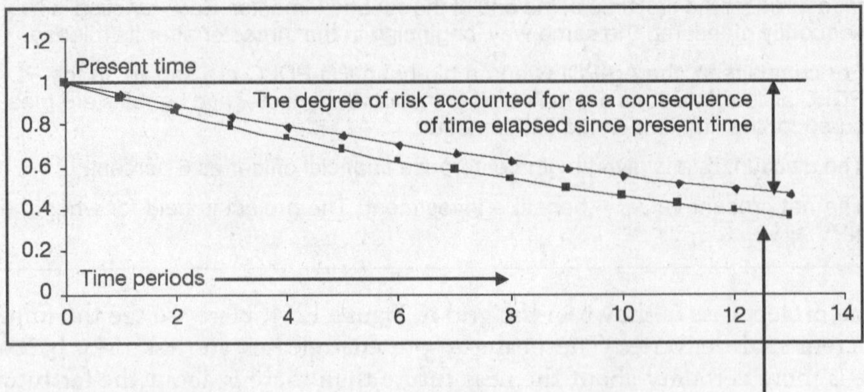

Examples: Lower curve is discounted at 8%; upper curve at 6%

Figure 12-5 Present value risk curve

all other parameters being equal. Figure 12-5 illustrates risk versus time. The discount factor incorporates all the risks to future benefits.

Refer to Figure 12-4. In the first row for Function 1, the net present value is given as −$1755 for benefits accumulated for five trimesters. A negative NPV means that the present value of the $3000 investment, as given in the project set-up panel, has not been fully paid back on a risk-adjusted basis. The NPV is calculated this way: The sum of the four benefit amounts in Trimester 1-2 through Trimester 2-2 is $1245. Using the formula for NPV given in the prior panel, calculate:

NPV Calculation

- Net present value = benefit − investment
- Net present value = $1245 − $3000 = −$1755

For comparison of the Ag-PDLC with the big-bang PD-PDLC, the last row in the figure assumes all incremental functions are delivered in the same trimester as the last of the agile increments; the discount rate is the same for all rows.

Look in the grand total column for the real effect. The benefit stream from the agile project for the same four functions is 2.5 times greater than the PD-PDLC in the fifth trimester. The early deliveries start generating benefits right away. This result is quite dramatic. It tells the story clearly that *a carefully planned and crafted benefit stream from incremental deliveries can generate benefits quicker than a benefit stream from PD-PDLC!*

The agile project will have a breakeven NPV in the fifth year, as will the PD-PDLC. In the long run, if both methodologies *deliver the same functions with the same quality*—not altogether a certain thing—there will be no material difference in the benefit streams; the agile financial advantage is all in the early periods.

Summary and Takeaway Points

In this chapter, we develop this theme: *Agile methods start the benefit stream earlier, generating more valuable returns from frequent, incremental product deliveries.*

The incremental nature is a big driver on the benefit plan. But no benefit plan will be worthy unless it is tied into the real business by a connection to the business scorecard. Moreover, benefits will not be fully realized unless someone takes ownership and drives for benefit realization. There is no autopilot for benefits.

There is an important role for a benefit owner acting as the benefits manager. Handoff is made from the project manager to the benefit manager, a bit of ownership passing with each increment. Because many stakeholders come into the picture release by release, the benefit manager's management challenge is to align all their interests as best possible. The incremental character of agile projects affects planning for business preparation, affects the measurement cycle, and presents opportunities to optimize the benefit stream for larger near-term returns.

Indeed, by taking a risk-adjusted view of the benefits, the early and incremental nature of agile projects can significantly amplify the benefit value during the project lifecycle. It might even be possible to make agile projects self-paying from the early and more robust benefit stream.

Chapter Endnotes

1. Rogers, *Diffusion of Innovations*, 23, Chapter 7.
2. Rogers, *Diffusion of Innovations*, 21.
3. Goodpasture, *Quantitative Methods in Project Management*, Chapter 5, 124–147. The equivalence of NPV and EVA is discussed in detail with examples beginning on page 143.

Appendix I
Methodologies

There is no point in being precise when you don't know what you are talking about.

John von Neumann

Practice details about each of the four methodologies featured in this book, SCRUM, Extreme Programming (XP), The Crystal Family—Clear and Orange—and EVO are described in this appendix that is complementary to the methodology quick-read provided in Chapter 1.

The SCRUM Methodology Is Management-centric

. . .SCRUM, a most perplexing and paradoxical process for managing complex projects.

Ken Schwaber

SCRUM is first a management regime; it is a mind shift from traditional project paradigms about how to organize work, apply talents, intimately involve the customer, and deliver quality to all the project beneficiaries. SCRUM is a management framework on which many different practices can be hung and linked into a project process. Among the four methodologies, SCRUM is the one most prescriptive about management concepts. SCRUM only suggests best technical practices and so SCRUM is applicable beyond the software industry where other practices could be embraced. Indeed, a variant of SCRUM in industrial projects began in Japan as described in Chapter 1. However, in this book, SCRUM is the software-centric methodology aligned with the Agile Manifesto. The following points are the main ideas in SCRUM, many of which are also shared with agile methods:

- Working product is the main measure of success and the main focus of team activity
- The customer is represented by the product master, the product master is embedded on the team, other users and customers are always very close at hand to offer near-real-time user evaluation and feedback
- Product should evolve incrementally as influenced by customers
- Working lean under empirical control is critical for the speed and nimbleness required to be agile
- Small colocated, self-organizing teams do the best work with the least invested effort
- Project managers add value by facilitating teamwork, clearing hurdles, and mitigating impediments to team productivity

SCRUM Metaphor

SCRUM did not start out as a software project management process. Indeed, SCRUM is relevant and applicable to projects of all character. Recall from Chapter 1 the early industrial products work done by Hirotaka Takeuchi and Ikujiro Nonaka. They envisioned the rugby sports analogy for the project behaviors they observed: in Rugby Union, the SCRUM is a formation of eight multi-functional teammates who link together in a common mission to gain possession of the ball and advance it to the goal. Getting to the goal *is not handed off from one squad to another*. Practices such as kicking and passing are not rigidly sequenced. The tactics of the SCRUM are situational and quite varied, but leadership always comes from within the team. Although there are coaches that provide a framework to operate within, the team is not centrally managed. The game dynamic starts over at each SCRUM possession, allowing for a near-real time assessment of strengths, weaknesses, opportunities, and threats.

Table I-1 is SCRUM according to Takeuchi and Nonaka and summarizes their ideas, which are still very relevant to agile project thinking.

Continuing with the sports metaphor, the coach plays the role of SCRUM master, and the fans play the role of product master. There are other parallels with agile methods in general and with SCRUM specifically:

- *Time boxes:* The game is divided into quarters or halves that are rigidly managed by time, equivalent to the sprints. Certain repetitive activities are rigidly time-boxed, such as time-outs.
- *Milestones:* The game itself is driven by a milestone at the end. This is in effect the release schedule.

Table I-1 SCRUM according to Takeuchi and Nonaka

Feature	Commentary
Built-in stability	• Management sets stretch goals and challenging requirements, but otherwise grants generous freedom and latitude to the implementation team
Self-organizing teams	• The team dynamic takes on the attributes of the entrepreneurial opportunity, setting its own norms and electing its own leaders • In Takeuchi's and Nonaka's words, the team is driven to a state of *zero information*, operating much less on prior knowledge and much more on the collective wisdom of the team as augmented by the customer • A team has successfully arrived at self-organization when it can operate autonomously, cross-fertilize itself with knowledge from its participants, and set its own goals that may in some cases transcend those of management
Overlapping project phases	• Project phases are not rigidly sequenced in finish-to-start formations with gated entry and exit and handoffs from one staff to another • Rather, the team carries forward, much like the rugby scrum, and overlaps are allowed and encouraged between phases
Multilearning	• Learning occurs in multiple ways: members in close proximity learn about the markets and customers and business from the embedded users; members learn cross-functionally from each other
Subtle control	• Management lays a light hand, allowing self-control while managing ambiguity, uncertainty, and roadblocks that might enable chaos • Measurements are made and reported but the overhead is subordinated to the objective of delivering value to the customer • Takeuchi and Nonaka list seven specific control mechanisms: 1. select the right people, 2. encourage suppliers to mimic the team behavior, 3. tolerate mistakes, 4. reward and incent performance, 5. encourage listening, 6. create an open work environment, and 7. manage the rhythm and velocity of the activity from one phase to the next
Organizational transfer of learning	• Embrace knowledge transfer outside the team to the enterprise as a whole to create more of reservoir of institutional knowledge and permanence of investment

- *Adaptive outcomes:* Although there is a goal and a strategy to win, the outcome—particularly the score—is not predictable with any certainty in spite of considerable resource commitment.
- *Game plan:* The game plan is the business plan architecture of the team's mission. Beyond the game plan, tactics are just-in-time and developed on the field by the team.

Contemporary SCRUM Methodology

SCRUM as it is popularly known is an adaptation of Takeuchi–Nonaka, specifically for the software industry. The leaders most associated are Jeff Sutherland and Ken Schwaber, but there are many others who did early work and continue to contribute to the SCRUM community. The main features of SCRUM are given in Table I-2, Table I-3, and Table I-4.

Table I-2 SCRUM human factors

Human factor	Commentary
Teams	• Work on SCRUM projects is done by small teams of about 5–10, perhaps up to 15 participants • Teams are self-organized • Teams are multidisciplinary and include more than the software sciences • Teams complete iterations without handoffs
Product master	• Products are sponsored by a product master who is responsible for the product vision and business requirements • *Product* is the surrogate for all the project's business outcomes
SCRUM master	• Teams are mentored and facilitated by a SCRUM master who is the SCRUM project manager • The SCRUM master is responsible for clearing the way and breaking down all the internal and external barriers, providing the subtle touch described by Takeuchi-Nonaka • When the team cannot resolve issues, the SCRUM master provides management

Table I-3 SCRUM practices

Practice	Commentary
Product or sprint backlog	• Backlog is the list of priority-weighted requirements awaiting implementation • Requirements from the product backlog are allocated to sprints and become sprint backlogs • The product backlog is continuously reevaluated at the conclusion of each sprint • Unsatisfied requirements are reprioritized back into the product backlog
User stories	• User stories are fleshed out and more detailed by face-to-face conversations with developers during the course of the development • In this sense, detailed requirements are just-in-time input for the development process • During the sprint, requirements are considered fixed

Table I-3 *(continued)*

Practice	Commentary
Sprint	• A sprint is 30 days on the calendar during which the team works on a fixed unit of scope that has been assigned to the sprint
Time boxing	• Time boxing is a practice whereby a given activity is limited to a prescribed time • Scope is variable in a time box
Daily stand-up meeting	• The team assembles each day for a short stand-up meeting, typically time boxed to 15 minutes • Each team member speaks • The SCRUM master facilitates • Outside stakeholders are not invited • Solutions are not discussed • The main topic is the daily work objective and any barriers to success
Refactoring	• Refactoring is a design and development practice • Refactoring means changing internal design to improve quality and conform to standards without changing external performance and properties • Refactoring is a practice that enables a quick-paced project with flow and rhythm

Table I-4 The SCRUM methodology

Method step	Commentary
0. A project is envisioned	• A project is chartered to meet a need, execute business strategy with the intended purpose of achieving a business goal • The goal encompasses a vision of the product, a community of users and stakeholders who will benefit, an investment plan, milestones, and a benefit plan
1. Requirements and user stories are collected into a product backlog	• Requirements for the project outcomes, whether a product or a process, are gathered in the form of user stories and prioritized by the product master • There is an expectation that the unallocated backlog will change over the course of the project
2. Sprint planning meetings map the backlog to sprint windows	• One or more sprint planning meetings map the backlog of customer and end-user requirements to a fixed-duration sprint • These meetings have the effect of loading the teams with their workload for a specific sprint • The product master and the embedded users on the sprint teams have full knowledge of the backlog allocation

Table I-4 (*continued*)

Method step	Commentary
2. Sprint planning meetings map the backlog to sprint windows (*continued*)	• Unlike plan-centered methodologies, specific outcomes are predicted and forecast at the sprint level and not at the project level • All outcomes conform to the product vision described in the business plan
3. The development sprint is executed	• The first allocation of the backlog to the first development sprint is most important • It is expected the backlog and user stories will be modified as the sprints deliver functionality and users become more aware of what they need and want
4. A close-out or lessons-learned meeting	• Feedback and a retrospective look at the sprint execution in near-real time to the completion of the sprint is necessary to correct faults going into the next sprint
5. Releases to production	• The outcome of a sprint may or may not go to production • As the backlog allocation is made, release-to-production plans are developed

Most SCRUM practices are common to all agile methods.

The SCRUM methodology is clean and simple, reflecting the strong emphasis on a light-touch central management and much faith in the development team to work effectively.

Figure I-1 illustrates the basic SCRUM sprint.

Extreme Programming Is Disciplined

XP is my attempt to reconcile humanity and productivity in my own practice of software development and share that reconciliation.

Kent Beck

In applying this methodology, project managers experienced in more traditional methods should draw some reassurance from the fact many of the practices will be familiar. However, there are some that are extreme: test-driven development (TDD) as discussed in Chapter 4 is perhaps the most extreme practice, although an early variant of TDD actually had its genesis back in NASA's early space programs. TDD is tied closely to another extreme practice: refactoring.

Refactoring, already introduced in the discussion about SCRUM, is a practice Beck now includes in incremental design. Of course, forms of incremental design have been around for decades in various forms, even in hardware development. Incremental design in agile methods includes evolution from increment to increment, following customer priorities rather than a big design up front.

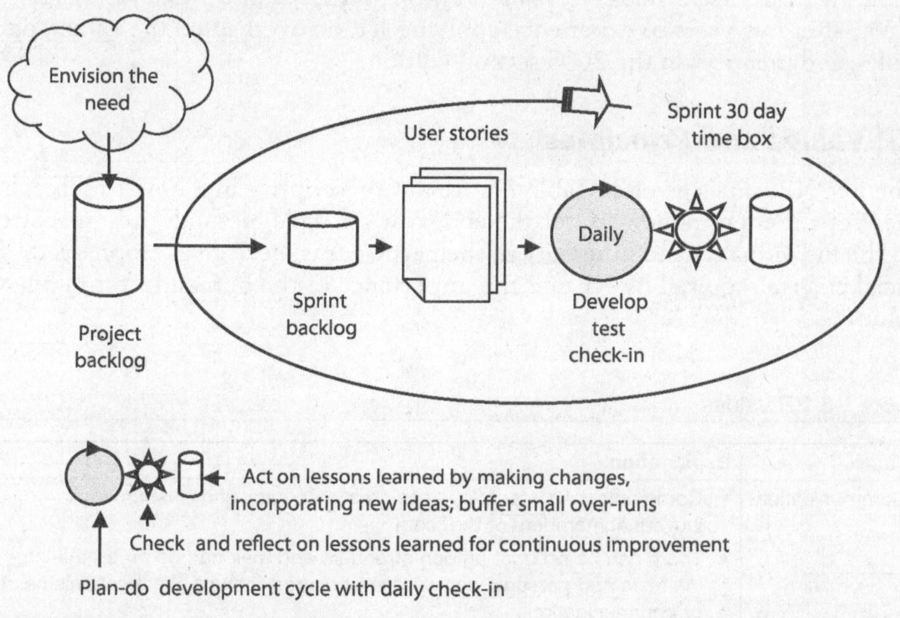

Figure I-1 SCRUM methodology

Pair programming is another practice that is extreme and somewhat counter intuitive to the programmer productivity ideas developed in the 1980s that stressed quiet, dedicated, individual workspace.

XP Differences

XP differs a bit in the supported practices from other agile methods, and its methodology is a little bit unorthodox, starting as it does from a test perspective. This concept, described in Chapter 4 and known to XP proponents as TDD, sounds quite strange to those schooled in structured analysis. In structured analysis, design begins by accumulating a complete requirements specification. But TDD begins with a test script that documents a low-level design requirement—albeit derived from a user functional story—in the form of a test, and verifies by test failure that the capability under design does not exist already in the product base.

Beck is assuredly one of the most public faces of XP, although he has had a lot of help: Martin Fowler, Ward Cunningham, and Ron Jefferies were all compatriots at the first XP application at Chrysler, and have seen been advocates for the methodology. First, to apply the methodology on an enterprise project, Beck's team more or less set the rules and practices. Beck provided a good overview of XP with his 1999 book, *Extreme Programming Explained—Embrace Change*.[1] Then, after five years of experience applying XP, he overhauled the values, principles, and practices in the 2005 second edition.

XP Values and Principles

The five XP values given in Table I-5 are not prescriptive in a how-to sense, but they set a mental framework for the endeavor. All agile methods put great stress on the individuality and humanity of the participants; Beck gives emphasis to the social change required by XP and the importance of the human factor in his XP values.[2]

Table I-5 XP values

Value	Explanation
Communication	• Communication is employed to create intimacy and trust among individual members of the team • There can be no trust among strangers and their can be no trust if interests and personal power are not shared through the mechanisms of communications
Simplicity	• Unwitting and unnecessary complexity is a hazard. Simplify to improve quality • Perhaps most important, do not get ahead of the customer by investing too much and too early in anticipated requirements • One example of unnecessary complexity is designing hooks for future needs that never materialize
Feedback	• Information about defects is used to improve the process • Each iteration is presumed to build upon the lessons learned from the prior iteration, and the lessons to be learned are brought to the team primarily by end users and others with operational knowledge and experience
Courage	• This value is less about personal bravery and more about speaking when action is necessary, confronting nemesis to resolve issues, and taking action in the face of criticism
Respect	• Respect is matter of extending personal courtesies between team members and about accepting the value of other's contributions in the spirit of a collective solution
Others	• Chosen by the team and the project as circumstances require

The XP principles given in Table I-6 are a treatise on many environmental and procedural effects that teams will encounter.[3] XP Principles provide guidance to practitioners that they can apply according to circumstances.

Table I-6 XP principles

Principle	Commentary
Humanity	• XP supports the idea of individuality and not staffing by plug-compatible replacements • Placing emphasis on individuality means making each person feel welcome in the team; each team member should have the opportunity to grow personally in the course of the project
Economics	• The project must maintain faith with the business case and the sponsors that line up the investment to fund the project
Mutual benefit	• Beck calls mutual benefit "The most important XP principle . . ." meaning that the project experience bestows benefits on sponsors, customers, and participants—in effect, a win-win for developers and users
Self-similarity	• Reuse good design and avoid reinvention and unnecessary redundancy
Improvement	• Nothing is perfect so there is opportunity for improvement in each iteration. However, project management, in consultation with the customer and governance units, makes judgments to contain exuberance moving from good to better to best
Diversity	• Multifunctional skills on teams reduce risk of any one team member not performing, suddenly unavailable to the team, or new problems crop up that require a diverse solution • XP assumes that any team member can work on any part of the solution
Reflection	• Think about how and why work is being done the way it is • After each iteration, there is planned time to take stock of what has happened and evaluate what should be retained and what should be discarded or improved
Flow	• Maintain a project rhythm and avoid periods of inaction and no production • In this respect, XP, like agile methods, embraces the idea of lean processes that value near-real-time steps over batch and queue; that value self-directed action over waiting for central decision making; and value continuous action that keeps team members involved in value add activity
Opportunity	• Opportunity is where business value is that can be transformed by project action into business deliverables that drive the benefit stream
Redundancy	• Like diversity, redundancy in the team staffing skills inventory guards against single point failures, but the same idea applies to product design and capability

Table I-6 *(continued)*

Principle	Commentary
Failure	• Failure, as in *not succeeding*, is allowed, even celebrated, as a learning experience
Quality	• Quality is more sacrosanct than the other project variables of cost, schedule and scope • Quality is the source of value for customers, and the value proposition is not to be compromised
Baby steps	• Baby steps is another way of describing incrementalism and the need to start with the easiest object that can be made to work; from this humble beginning, other more complex objects are added incrementally
Accepted responsibility	• All agile methods buy into the XP principle that each team member must accept a personal responsibility to be accountable for individual and team results • Somewhat like the resistance to assigned staffing, responsibility assignments are resisted; instead, team members are encouraged to seek responsibility

XP is, in the end, a methodology, although Beck himself downplays the idea so that maximum flexibility is afforded the team to apply practices that suit the circumstances. Practices are embedded in a process. The process envisions frequent production releases. Each release is composed of a number of time-boxed iterations that are similar in scope and purpose to the sprint described in the SCRUM method. But whereas the SCRUM sprint is 30 calendar days, the XP iteration can be different durations in different projects, but once the timeline is set, it is a constant throughout the project. Each iteration is scoped to produce some part of the requirements. The XP requirements are gathered as part of listening and interviewing done by the development teams during release planning. Requirements are documented as higher-level scenarios, then dissected into user stories, and ultimately turned into TDD test scripts. The scripts are the initial design step in the iteration, somewhat discomfiting to the traditionally trained. Another uncomfortable idea is that in its purest form (at least as exercised on a small scale), there is no methodology requirement for a system design that transcends the various releases. However, in this book, we frame all projects with architecture.

There are 24 practices, which are divided into a group of 13 most important practices and 11 corollary practices, as given in Table I-7 and Table I-8[4]

XP Process

There are two overriding process ideas in XP: to gain efficiency by being ruthless about disciplined practices and design simplicity, and to deliver customer

Table I-7 XP Practices—primary

Practice	Commentary
Sit together	• Co-locate everyone in a common environment so that the primary means of communication and collaboration is face-to-face discussion and exchange of ideas.
Whole team	• XP emphasizes that the team should be complete in all requisite skills to complete the development, but not just product developers—the whole team is multidisciplinary with functional and technical expertise.
Informative workspace	• Use visuals to communicate continuously, particularly low-tech visuals like whiteboards, index cards, sticky notes that can be constantly in view. The visuals should inform easily without a lot of time spent interpreting the meaning.
Energized work	• Do not work to burn-out; maintain a sustainable pace. XP emphasizes that there should be no crises management at the end; the pace should be sustainable nearly indefinitely. Thus, team members can come and go for short times with their place covered by the diversity of redundant skills on the team.
Pair programming	• Program in teams, sitting together and solving problems jointly. This is certainly in contrast with most conventional wisdom that programmers should work individually in private space.
Stories	• Plan using stories that are units of customer functionality. XP does not embrace use cases in the way that Crystal does, but it does embrace the need for embedded customers to express themselves in business terms that are then interpreted by the team into design requirements.
Weekly cycle	• XP, like all agile methods, envisions planning as being cycles nested within cycles. The weekly cycle is intended to wrap up a significant body of work before a rest period.
Quarterly cycle	• Business cycles are typically in quarters, and so the project must be cognizant of business cycles on which the project depends for funding and other approvals, and very often the rollout schedule as well.
Slack	• Build buffers into the schedule, as described in the planning chapters of this book, to ensure a minimum must have requirements set is delivered to production and to ensure that all time boxes finish on schedule and not hold up others.
Ten-minute build	• Design for short, frequent builds; if short builds are not possible, this circumstance is a leading indicator of complexity, possible legacy issues, and perhaps a too-coarse decomposition of requirements. • Furthermore, short build times are lean and thereby maximize value add testing and validation.
Continuous integration	• Maintain the product base rigorously so that everyone is working with the latest design. • It is critical for leaning the development that missteps due to sequencing errors and errors due to configuration mishaps are avoided.
Test-first programming	• Test-driven development is a XP practice and is described in Chapter 4.
Incremental design	• Incremental design and development is central to all agile methods; see Chapter 1, 6, and 7 for more details.

Table I-8 XP Practices—secondary

Practice	Commentary
Real customer involvement	• Actual end users and customers with real and practical business knowledge should be the ones tapped to participate, and not necessarily users that are simply *available*.
Incremental deployment	• Product is deployed on a pace governed by the customer's ability to absorb change; parallel legacy operations may be required.
Team continuity	• Teams stay together so long as they are effective; turnover is anticipated to be minimal and thereby contributes directly to the stability of team metrics such as velocity.
Shrinking teams	• Team staffing is to be optimized to the circumstances, but generally smaller is more nimble, creative, and innovative—but only to a point. There is such a thing as too small to be effective; too small to have sufficient redundancy to withstand small staffing shortfalls.
Root cause analysis	• Always get to the bottom of problems; use Ohno's *five why's* process to drill down as described in the text of the book.
Shared code	• A tenant of XP, somewhat controversial in some quarters, is that everyone can work on any of the product code, and often code is a product of multiple collaborations.
Code and tests	• Code, test scripts, and test conditions are the permanent artifacts of the project. • Code and test scripts help bridge the gap among disparate developers on virtual teams.
Single code base	• Integrity of the design is maintained by keeping one gold copy; test and development copies are temporary expedients.
Daily deployment	• New design is integrated daily; add to production daily if the customer can absorb change rapidly.
Negotiated scope contract	• Work orders are contracted in short sequences where parameters can be stabilized. See details on this practice concept in Chapter 11 of this book.

value by building product incrementally according to the customer's priorities of importance and urgency. The first development cycle begins by designing the simplest object that is likely to be successfully coded. Thereafter, more complex objects are coded.

A project management tip	Architecture and XP
	• Experienced project managers and system engineers who apply XP to larger-scale development projects ordinarily create architecture and identify the critical success factors regarding feature, function, and performance.

Table I-9 summarizes the XP process. Note that it is very similar to SCRUM in terms of the process steps as shown in Figure I-1.

Table I-9 XP process

Process step	Commentary
0. A project is envisioned	• A project is chartered to meet a need, i.e. execute business strategy with the intended purpose of achieving a business goal • The goal encompasses a vision of the product, a community of users and stakeholders who will benefit, an investment plan, milestones, and a benefit plan
1. Requirements gathered and evaluated	• Requirements for the project outcomes, whether a product or a process, are gathered in the form of user stories and prioritized by the product master • There is an expectation that the unallocated backlog will change over the course of the project
2. Release planning meetings	• One or more release planning meetings map the backlog of customer and end-user requirements to fixed-duration releases
3. Development iterations	• The first allocation of the backlog to the first development iteration is most important • It is expected the backlog and user stories will be modified as the iterations deliver functionality and users become more aware of what they need and want
4. Spike and iteration	• Refactor for quality and correct serious defects
5. Close-out and lessons learned	• Feedback and a retrospective look at the iteration execution in near real time to the completion of the iteration is necessary to correct faults going into the next iteration
6. Releases to production	• The outcome of a iteration may or may not go to production. As the backlog allocation is made, release-to-production plans are developed

Crystal Methodology Is Human Powered

Computers must support the way in which people naturally and comfortably work.... I care about whether the team is thriving, and whether the software is being delivered. Keeping the people trained and the process light are keys to both.

Alistair Cockburn

The Crystal methodologies are called *people-powered*. The central theme is: *people drive methodologies and are responsible for outcomes*; people are not focused on management artifacts such as documents and metrics. So, Crystal advocates the minimization of documentation and other overhead, and a maximization of and dependency on human interaction. And, in a definite contrast with XP, Crystal assumes that people do not and will not adhere rigidly to a set of rules—the methodology is deliberately tolerant of variant behaviors. In fact, it is assumed that some people act irrationally, unpredictably, and fail to maintain a constant productivity. People, in other words, are not entirely linear. As such, planning must account for these behavior variations. Each team is empowered to set its own minimum behavior and accountability standards.

Crystal Beginnings

Cockburn began promoting his ideas even before his participation in the 2001 group-of-17 meeting in Utah. From the outset Cockburn advocated small, highly interactive teams but was quick to say that one size does not fit all. He conceived Crystal as a group of methodologies distinguishable by team size, project complexity, and practice details. To keep it all straight, Cockburn labeled each with a distinctive color, beginning with *clear*. The principal book on the topic was published in 2005, *Crystal Clear: A Human-powered Methodology*.[5]

Clear is the color given by Cockburn to the smallest team-size for the simplest projects—a team of between six and nine. The optimum situation is engaged people working face-to-face with generous interaction. Cockburn accepts that people are fallible, not good at repetitive tasks that require discipline, and usually unable to meet demands for uniformly the same quality time after time. Frankly, if Cockburn has an argument with XP, it is on this point: as a methodology, in his opinion, XP is too demanding about discipline and sticking with the rules, even though a beneficial side-effect of XP's disciplined behavior is less required documentation.

Dr. Cockburn posits that from one person to the next, performance expectations must allow for some variance, maybe even unpredictability. Cockburn calls this the non-linear attribute of human behavior.[6] He rejects the plan-driven project development lifecycle planning premise that people can be plugged into roles—like components into sockets—with an expectation that they will perform day-in and day-out according to the planning model just so long as they meet the requisites of the role specification. He argues that plans that forecast outcomes according to the performance of role models are bound to end up badly.

Nonlinear Behavior
Nonlinear behavior simply means that the output of a process or activity is not uniformly proportional to input, and the output may even reverse itself even if the input direction remains unchanged. Linear behavior is just opposite: linear systems obey the rule that states that "Output follows input proportionately and directionally; at zero input, the output may be zero or some other bias value."

Crystal Body of Knowledge

Like the other agile methods we will discuss, Crystal has its own body of knowledge. At the top level are seven principles. Although authored in a Crystal context, these principles are applicable to all agile methodologies, and if read in a value-added sense, they really apply to all project methodologies. Most have their roots in prior quality movements, but they provide a nice grouping that is easy to internalize. The main ideas are in Table I-10.[7]

Table I-10 Crystal principles

Principle	**Commentary**
Frequent delivery	• Put product into production as often as the customer can accept it • In this book, we advocate the concept of business preparation as a necessary work stream to complement project development • The mission of business preparation is to smooth the way for frequent deployment to production of the incremental deliverables
Osmotic communication	• Osmotic communication is a concept label unique to Crystal, but in practice the concept is shared by all agile methods • It means to benefit from informal communication by word, gesture, and by general association; listen to what is going on around you • Obviously, for the virtual team, osmotic communication is much harder to do effectively
Reflective improvement	• A principle similar to all agile methods that advocate pausing between iterations to consider the lessons learned, reinforce the things that work, and improve or discard weak practices

Table I-10 *(continued)*

Principle	Commentary
Personal safety	• Safety is a strong suit in Crystal, although a similar thought is part of the XP practice set • Essentially, it means direct energy and passion constructively—do not attack people; only attack problems • It also means tolerate challenge and don't kill the messenger. Make it easy to derail groupthink
Focus	• Do not multiplex between problems; teams should work one backlog at a time, and team members should work on one team at a time; and to the extent possible, members should not scatter themselves among multiple problems in the same interation
Easy access to subject-matter experts	• Make experts available quickly and easily • Unlike SCRUM, Crystal does not mandate continuous embedded participation, but does insist that functional experts from the business are readily available • Time should not be lost waiting for business members to show up when needed
Technical environment	• Make the technical environment effective for supporting project objectives—tools, training, support systems, space, and working conditions

Implementation strategies support the Crystal Family as given in Table I-11.[8]

Crystal embraces a number of day-to-day techniques, many of which are adapted from other methodologies. They are applied at the discretion of the team as situations arise. Cockburn makes the point that if somebody has a good idea, then put it to work. It's all part of methodology shaping, the first technique on Table I-12.

An important technique listed on Table I-12 not yet discussed in any detail is the burn-down and burn-up chart. Burn charts are a common tool recommended by all agile methods, not just by the Crystal family. Burn charts are used within the development team to show progress earned. In Crystal and in SCRUM, charts are shown as burn-down to zero remaining value to be earned; in XP, it is common to show burn-up charts to an accumulated goal. There is no standard chart template, but in Figure I-2, an example is shown that captures many of the planning elements. There are several features in this template.

A quick status is given by comparing the intended XP Red-Green-Refactor status at the end of each week with the actual status achieved. Effort can be in any standard unit of measure: hours, standard days, standard units, or dollars. Effort should relate directly to the team's benchmark for velocity. The chart in Figure I-2 is laid out in a flat format that facilitates filtering each column in a spreadsheet to create custom views.

Table I-11 Crystal strategies

Strategy	Commentary
Explore 360	• Look at the envisioned need from many perspectives and take into account supply chain, sales and marketing, customer support, customer use, and overall satisfaction of the balanced scorecard for the business
Early victory	• Do something simple to get into production and reinforce a *can-do* attitude • This is similar to other agile method practices that call for starting as quickly as possible after architecture is in place • Generally, as different from the Spiral method, an early victory means start with something simple for which feasibility is not in question
Walking skeleton	• Build an end-to-end functionality that works and can be used to build more functionality incrementally; gives the customer an early first look • In some quarters, this is means building a minimally functional framework that demonstrates how the overall application will be presented to the end user
Incremental rearchitecture	• Be prepared to reexamine the architecture after every release • See the planning chapters in this book that discuss the relationship of architecture to the rolling wave planning horizon
Information radiators	• Radiators are dashboards, whiteboards, newsletters, and other media distribution • The principle is be open with team communications; make it easy to find and use information, and easy to maintain

One charting problem all agile teams face is that the baseline is subject to change as requirements are shuffled, making the total count in the project backlog go up and down. In turn, the total project burn-down and burn-up progress is a moving target. So naturally, the question is whether the project will ever finish or whether burn-down and burn-up charts are useful for forecasting a finish. Of course, within one iteration or sprint, backlog is stable and the changing project target is not visible. However, at the next iteration, it will be obvious if the overall project burn-down and burn-up baseline has changed, as it is expected and encouraged to do.

The project manager should focus on the macro picture of requirements: how the baseline target is moving up or down. Project managers may want to plot the total requirements up-and-down iteration-by-iteration as shown in Figure I-3. Because the team's velocity is stable from one iteration to the next, the story points produced in each iteration remains relatively constant. What will change is the total number of iterations required to complete the project. See examples in Chapter 7.

Table I-12 Crystal techniques

Technique	Commentary
Methodology shaping	• Shape the project methodology for unique aspects of each project. In effect, Crystal is not rigidly wedded to a process with specific practices. • Crystal is the only agile methodology of the four discussed in this book that explicitly recognizes the need to modify practices to accommodate scale and the vagaries of the enterprise.
Reflection workshop	• Use a workshop to thoroughly examine lessons learned.
Blitz planning	• Rapid fire, just-in-time planning, using a planning game or other quick means to plan. • See planning poker detail in Chapter 7.
Delphi estimating	• Apply estimates from many independent experts. See Chapter 7 for discussion of Delphi and wideband Delphi, and the related game planning poker.
Daily stand-up	• Time-boxed meeting, as in SCRUM, to hear daily plans of team members.
Essential interaction design	• Share the design experience with users, customers, and sponsors.
Process miniature	• Run a benchmark of the team process with a scaled-down process for quick turnaround of benchmark numbers.
Burn charts	• See Figure I-2 for an example of a control chart for tracking objects planned, started, and completed.
Side-by-side programming	• See XP's pair programming.

Burn charts, whether burn-down or burn-up, show earned value progress against plan for developing objects for production

Effort to go is the difference between the operating plan and the effort burned for the object for the week
When R-G-RF [red – green – refactor] is in status RF, the object is considered complete

Object	Assigned to	Complexity	Baseline effort	Iteration week	Operating plan effort	Effort burned	Effort to go	Planned R-G-RF	Actual R-G-RF	Variance R-G-RF
1	AB	10	40	1	45	40	5	G	G	No
2	BC	25	100	1	100	100	0	R	R	No
3	RF	25	100	1	100	100	0	R	R	No
4	JG	5	20	1	25	25	0	RF	RF	No
5	RH	10	40	1	45	40	5	G	G	No
1	AB	10	40	2	40		40	RF		
2	BC	25	100	2	100		100	R		
3	RF	25	100	2	100		100	R		
6	JG	5	20	2	20		20	RF		
5	RH	10	40	2	40		40	G		
7	AB	10	40	3	40		40	G		
2	BC	25	100	3	100		100	R		
3	RF	25	100	3	100		100	R		
8	JG	5	20	3	20		20	RF		
9	RH	10	40	3	40		40	G		
7	AB	10	40	4	40		40	RF		
2	BC	25	100	4	100		100	RF		
3	RF	25	100	4	100		100	RF		
10	JG	5	20	4	20		20	RF		
9	RH	10	40	4	40		40	RF		
			1200		1215	305	910			

Figure I-2 Burn charts

Although outcomes are being steadily earned in each iteration, the NET backlog is influenced also by the changing project backlog

Metric	Iteration cycle			
	1	2	3	4
Project backlog, total*	1000	900	975	1100
Iteration backlog earned burn-down**	125	120	125	122
Project backlog earned, cumulative** [burned down]	125	245	370	492
Project NET backlog unearned to date	875	655	605	608

* Count subject to new additions and deletions by customer
**Based on nearly constant velocity

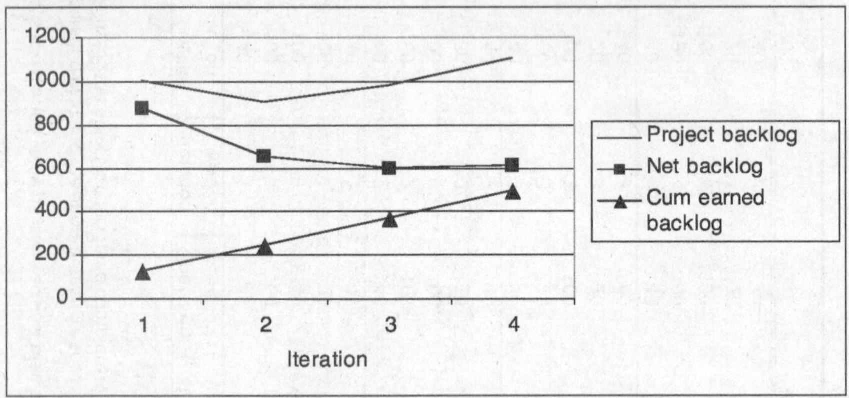

Figure I-3 Backlog variation

The strategies and techniques given in Tables I-11 and I-12 fit into a process. Table I-13 provides an overview of the Crystal clear process steps.

EVO Methodology Is PDCA-centric

We cannot know all the right requirements in advance, but we can discover them more quickly by attempts to deliver real value to real stakeholders.

Tom Gilb

EVO is built from system engineering principles and the quality ideas of W. Edwards Deming. Tom Gilb, renowned systems engineer, is the inventor and driver of EVO. EVO is a play on the word *evolutionary*, emphasizing that EVO is both incremental and evolutionary. Like all agile methods, it encourages customer in-

Table I-13 Crystal clear process

Process step	Commentary
Project	• The project has three major components: the charter, the deliveries (one or more), and the wrap-up and close-out
Delivery	• The delivery consists of one or more iterations, the actual go-live event (actually, a process with an event or milestone at the end), and then time for reflection
Iteration	• The iteration is led off by a planning activity; then there are day-to-day activities consisting of the daily stand-up, design episodes, code and unit test, integration into the code base, and then reflection and celebration
Episode	• The design episode is the actual design activity • Requirements from the backlog, as assigned by the plan to the iteration, are committed to design with tools like the UML Use Case and CRC cards • Actual design is allowed to be refactored, so objects are started quickly by coding an outline based upon the CRC data and the use case

volvement and feedback after every release. Feedback is the driver for evolving the design over the course of several releases.

EVO Principles

Similar to other methodologies, EVO has its value ideas and statements of principles. Many are shared with other agile methods, such as frequent delivery of product and close interaction with the end user, but because of the system engineering underpinning, some are unique and distinguish EVO among its peers. Table I-14 provides details of EVO's 10 principles.[9]

EVO Cycle

EVO is envisioned as a network of mini-waterfalls, each one a plan-do-check-act (PDCA) cycle. Each mini-waterfall, time boxed to a couple of weeks, is intended to be complete insofar as real product is delivered at the end of each cycle. Actual go-live-to-production scheduling is governed by the customer's ability to absorb change.

The EVO cycle—also called the EVO Step—is the building block of an EVO project. A project is a linkage of many cycles. Each cycle is planned carefully as the cycle's time in the box comes up for implementation. Planning details are dependent not only on legacy requirements, but also on the accomplishments of the prior cycles. In this sense, each cycle is individually plan-centric, and the cycle scope is drawn from a preplanned architecture. However, like all agile methods, EVO shares the idea that architecture should be elastic, allow for generous customer feedback, and adapt cycle-by-cycle.

Table I-14 EVO principles

Principle	Commentary
Deliver real results early	• Each delivery should be usable by the customer, and each delivery should be incrementally as soon as possible
Prioritize value	• Deliver the most stakeholder value possible at each delivery step
Evolve the solution	• Details of the solution come from an emerging understanding of the need
Discover requirements incrementally	• Discover requirements more quickly by delivering real value to real stakeholders frequently
Be all-inclusive with system engineering	• All necessary aspects of the system must be complete and correct
Value open architecture	• Change project ideas as often as necessary
Focus on the current step* or cycle	• Focus energy, as a team, towards success in the current step* or cycle
Learn from mistakes	• Learn from hard experiences as fast as possible
Meet milestones	• Achieve on-time product delivery to learn to get things right early
Adapt processes	• Prove new work processes, and get rid of bad ones early

**Step* is the word used in the EVO method for iteration. Step is used interchangeably with *cycle*. Typically a step is a couple of weeks in duration; the EVO recommendation is that any steps not consume more than 2 percent of project resources.

The planning principle for the EVO project and cycles is much like what is described in this book and in the literature as a rolling wave.[10] In the first wave of planning, near-term cycles are planned in detail, whereas subsequent cycles are beyond the planning horizon. Cycles over the horizon are essentially black boxes. The planning horizon is fixed during the planning activity, but then as time passes and the first horizon approaches present time, the next horizon is planned. Planning waves are repeated as often as necessary.

Just like in the agile sprints and iterations, the EVO cycles are planned to be short compared to the longer business cycles. One can imagine several cycle turns, to borrow an idea from inventory management, within one business turn. For many businesses, strategic planning is updated annually with road maps revised every three years or so. Within that timeframe, annual planning sets the goals for the year.

Planning the EVO Cycle

Like all other agile methodologies, the objective of the EVO cycle is working product. Project planning is directed toward putting product into production, not planning individual tasks and activity. Each cycle has a delivery date, and that date is fixed first. Then scope is allocated to the fixed cycle schedule. Each cycle is conservatively planned somewhat like a three-point estimate:

1. The minimum scope that will be delivered
2. The target scope
3. The maximum scope that might be delivered if everything goes optimally well

The planning principle is that a must-have minimum scope requirement must exist and it must be more conservative than the target scope requirement—certainly more conservative than the maximum scope requirement. Figure I-4 illustrates the points.

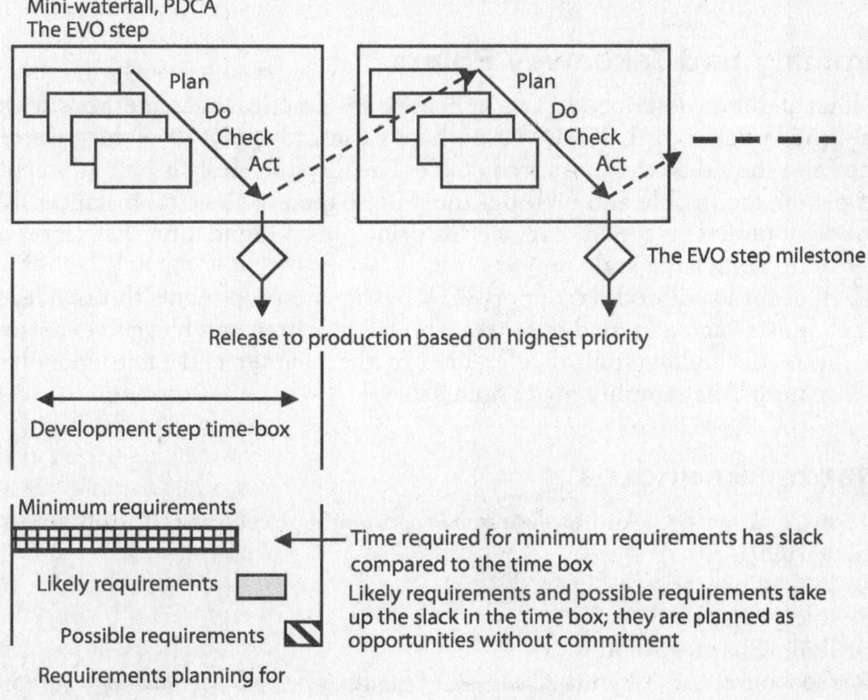

Figure I-4 EVO cycle plan

Staffing the EVO Project

There are three important points to grasp regarding staffing an EVO project:

1. Skilled people are assigned to fill roles. EVO shares an attitude about resources that is similar to plan-centric models, to wit: there are roles in the project that call for a variety of skills; skilled people are required to fill them, but the project should be able to function with anyone qualified, not just the best hand picked people.
2. Teams are allowed to handoff. Unlike other agile methods, there is no hard and fast concept that the same team is going to carry through from one cycle to the next without handoffs, so there is a commitment to documentation as a communication and control tool.
3. In contrast to Crystal but similar to XP, EVO participants are disciplined to closely follow the protocols of the methodology. In the case of EVO, there is a strong embrace of the plan-do-check-act doctrine.

Summary and Takeaway Points

All four methods described in this appendix are practical agile methods with an established track record. SCRUM is perhaps easiest to apply. XP is the most disciplined and should be the most predictable. The Crystal family is best at accepting that people are fallible and methods must be shaped to the circumstances. EVO is solidly founded on system engineering principles, a foundation that serves well when addressing large-scale projects.

Each of these methods is supported by passionate proponents through leaders in the industry and a myriad of others who have written and blogged extensively. See the many bibliographical references in the chapter and table endnotes of other material that amplify many points.

Chapter Endnotes

1. Beck, K. with C. Andres, *Extreme Programming Explained* (Boston: Addison-Wesley, 1999).
2. Ibid., Chapter 4
3. Ibid., Chapter 5
4. Ibid., Chapter 7 and 9
5. Cockburn, A., *Crystal Clear—A Human-powered Methodology for Small Teams* (Boston: Addison-Wesley, 2005).
6. For more on Cockburn's ideas, see his article presented at the Fourth International Multi-Conference on Systems, Cybernetics and Informatics, Orlando, Florida, June, 2000, "Characterizing People as First Order Non-linear Components" (1999).

7. Cockburn, A., *Crystal Clear—A Human-powered Methodology for Small Teams* (Boston: Addison-Wesley, 2005), 19–39.

8. Ibid., 46–55.

9. Paraphrased from paper prepared as "Overview of 10 EVO process principles originally intended for participants of the Tom and Kai Gilb February 2002 training sessions," April 2002, http://www.gilb.com.

10. See Goodpasture, J., "A Risk Perspective: Rolling Wave Planning is a Bet," *Projects and Profits Magazine: ICFAI University Press*, December 2007, 48–53.

This book has free material available for download from the Web Added Value™ resource center at *www.jrosspub.com*

Appendix II
Glossary

The following glossary defines the terms used in this book.

Item	Definition
adaptive	To be responsive to circumstances that then changes behavior or outcome; feedback enables adapting to circumstances. Adaptive situations are often emergent in character. See emergent.
agile methods and practices	Methodologies that are more situational-driven, less centrally managed and more self-managed, with an emphasis on near-continuous responsiveness to customer need. The focus is on the quality of the result, even if the result is not very predictable at the outset and not according to plan. Example: extreme programming (XP).
blitz planning	Rapid fire, just-in-time planning, using a planning game or other quick means to plan. A Crystal practice.
burn charts	Burn charts are a form of progress (i.e. earned-value) accounting wherein planned and expended effort per deliverable object is tracked versus progress toward accomplishing all the work. *Burn* refers to effort. Burn-up or burn-down refers to working up or down a chart of required objects until are all the objects are complete and delivered to production.
business	The organization or enterprise that hosts the project. The business may be a governmental unit, nonprofit, or a business unit within a larger enterprise. *Organization, enterprise*, and *business* are used interchangeably.

Item	Definition
calendar	A time display of absolute dates, days, and months, organized in date order.
chaos	A system concept that characterizes the sensitivity of system responses to system stimulus. Systems that have large, unpredictable, or unforecasted responses to relatively minor stimulus are chaotic or near-chaos.
chargeback rate	Chargeback rate is the rate per unit of time that the individual or entity is charged to the paying organization. The rate may be the base salary or the salary lifted by a factor for benefits, or it could be a rate that includes a lift for both benefits and overhead. In some organizations, and particularly if contracted, the chargeback rate may be a standard cost. See standard cost.
CMM (I)	CMM (I) is the *Capability Maturity Model*-Integration developed by Carnegie Mellon University. It integrates software and system engineering with product integration in a set of recommend practices loosely framed in a methodology. CMM (I) is a service mark of Carnegie Mellon University.
COCOMO	COCOMO is an acronym taken from the phrase *COnstructive COst MOdel*, emphasizing the model's focus on the construction phase of the project. COCOMO II is a follow-on model to the original COCOMO 81 developed by Dr. Barry Boehm and his associates in 1981.
complexity	Complexity is quality described by how many ways units can interact, a measure of how many unique states a system can be in, and how many responses one stimulus causes.
containment	A concept that seeks to prevent defect creep from one code base.
contractor	*Provider, supplier*, and *contractor* are used interchangeably to denote the entity that is doing the work governed by a contract. The project is the entity that does the contracting with the provider.
CRC cards	*Class-Responsibility-Collaborator* is the expansion of CRC. Typically written on index cards and posted on bulletin boards and whiteboards, CRC is a model of an object that specifies a class name, such as *order*, one or more responsibilities, such as *knows item*, and collaborators, such as *inventory item*.
critical path	The critical path is the longest connected path through the network.
customer	The people and organization that are the principal beneficiaries of the project. End users or users are customers with detailed functional knowledge. Customers may be external or internal to the organization.
defined process control	Defined process control is a concept from manufacturing, promoted strongly by the work of W. Edwards Deming and others in the post-World War II era. It presumes definable error limits that are acceptable in the finished product, a means to measure conformance to the error limits, and a means to correct processes that yield too many defects.

Item	Definition
Delphi	A process to arrive at a consensus opinion by many experts who examine the same problem independently.
DoD	*U.S. Department of Defense.*
EIA	*Electronics Industry Association.*
emergent	A characteristic of systems where the interaction of simple rules and parts creates very complex systems and responses. The narrative among rules, in effect the interconnectedness of the rules, is not fixed, but is situational and dynamic. Emergent systems have output based upon agents and agent processes interacting in seemingly unpredictable ways, adapting to circumstances, but bounded by rules set down by governance. Emergent systems are not linear.
entropy	A system concept that characterizes the number of stable states the system can be in; a system with large entropy has many stable states, some of which may not be known to developers.
epic	The top-level business story or theme from which all use cases and user stories are developed.
episode	The actual design activity within an iteration. Episode is a Crystal term.
finish-to-start	Finish-to-start is a scheduling precedence taken from the precedence diagramming method. It means that the finishing activity of a task must be completed before the starting activity of the successor task can begin.
Gantt chart	A bar chart with individual bars representing activities. The length of the bar is schedule duration for that activity. The overall timeline of the project can be computed by summing the nonoverlapping bar segments. Dependencies between bars are not usually shown. The chart is named after its inventor, Henry Gantt, mechanical engineer and industrialist, who introduced the chart in the 1910s. Gantt was a college roommate and professional associate of F. W. Taylor, the father of Taylorism, who we introduced in other chapters.
IEC	*International Electrotechnical Commission.*
IEEE	*Institute of Electrical and Electronics Engineers.*
information radiators	Dashboards, whiteboards, newsletters, and other media displays and distribution.
investment	Money put up by the business to fund a project. Investment is the money on the business side of the project balance sheet; funding demand is the project estimate that corresponds to investment. Investment and demand may not be equal.
ISO	*International Organization for Standardization.*

Item	Definition
JAD	*Joint Application Design*. A practice whereby users and developers sit together for a design session. JAD sessions can be part of an agile iteration.
knowledge area	A body of knowledge about how to do tasks or activities that has a common association. Example: risk management.
method or practice	A means of doing a specific activity within a knowledge area. Generally speaking, there are inputs which drive actionable steps, thereby producing outcomes. Example: Monte Carlo simulation of schedule outcome.
methodology	Activities linked to produce an outcome, with the specific methods or practices of each activity identified. In effect, a methodology is a lifecycle of the project, a PDLC as we have described elsewhere. Example: Crystal Clear.
N^2	The number of unique communication paths between N individuals is given by the formula $N \times (N - 1)$. When N is large, this formula is effectively N^2. For example, if there are five people on the team, named A, B, C, D, and E, then there are 20 independent paths that can be used to communicate among the five parties. A can talk to B, C, D, and E, and B, C, D, or E can talk back to A, just to identify eight paths. Add three people to the team, and the number of ways to communicate increases to 56.
operating model	A synonym for the organization chart of the project. Operating model also stands for the roles, responsibilities, and relationships of individuals in the project operation, even if not full-time or administratively assigned.
osmotic communication	Refers to communication by osmosis: absorbing information in your immediate vicinity, whether directly or indirectly intended for you.
pipeline	Pipelines and pipelining are terms that describe the use of a scorecard to capture data that flows by.
planning poker	A card game form of Delphi. See *Delphi*.
PMI	*Project Management Institute*. A professional association for project managers.
practice	See method.
practice standard	An agreed upon way of doing a practice, where the agreement is managed by a standards body (organization) with credentials in the standards community. Example: ISO/IEC 12207 practice standard for software engineering.
process	Similar to a methodology, activities linked to produce an outcome, although the methods may not be specified. Example: project initiating process.

Item	Definition
process miniature	A benchmark of the team process with a scaled-down process for quick turnaround of benchmark numbers. A Crystal practice.
product	The intended outcome or deliverables of a project that is useful to a customer and fits the customer's idea of quality in the large sense: feature, function, effective in application, efficient to use, environmentally compatible, and economically operable and supportable throughout a useful lifespan. Product may be tangible or intangible, and it may be a process, system, application, or product for internal or external customers.
product base	The current *gold copy* of the product that is in production. The gold copy is the standard to which all other copies are compared. Increments of new product are added to the product base at each release.
providers	See *contractor.*
PSP	*Personal Software Process*. PSP is a service mark of Carnegie Mellon University.
pull	A lean methods concept whereby external ideas from the customer community are pulled into the design rather than relying on developer whim to push new ideas out.
RAD	*Rapid Application Design*. A prototyping methodology for quick-reaction design and coding.
RAM	*Resource Assignment Matrix*. A matrix presentation of the operating model and the work breakdown.
RUP	*Rational Unified Process*. A set of practices—more so than a process—from IBM/Rational.
schedule	A timeline affixed to a calendar.
self-organizing	A team has successfully arrived at self-organization when it can operate autonomously, cross-fertilize itself with knowledge from its participants, and set its own goals that may in some cases transcend those of management.
Six Sigma	A quality management process in which a problem analysis protocol is followed by solutions that implement error control within approximately 3.4 defects allowable outside control limits in a million opportunities. Errors are sensed and corrective information is fed back to bring the process within the Six Sigma boundaries.
SOA	*Service Oriented Architecture.*
stakeholder	Primarily a business unit or individual who is in the supply chain, or who provides some resources to the project, but has no specific commitment to project success. In other words, involved but not committed.

Item	Definition
standard cost	*Standard cost* is a fixed rate by labor or job category, regardless of the person's paid-out compensation; in some cases, the standard cost is greater than the actual compensation. Other practices may use a rolling average of actual compensation as the chargeback rate. Standard cost is sometimes computed as a rolling average.
story	See *user story.*
story point	A quantity of effort to develop one unit of product with minimum relative complexity; in effect, *a story point results in a unit of outcome*.
supplier	See *contractor.*
team	A social structure wherein all members individually and mutually work collaboratively toward the achievement of a common goal that is attainable only through committed, collective contribution of all members.
throughput	The quantity of product produced by an agile performance team in one iteration. The metric is velocity. See *velocity.*
timeline	Duration measured in units of time, but has no reference to a calendar. When a timeline is affixed to a calendar, it becomes a schedule.
time box	A prescribed length of time for a set of multifunctional activities. Scope is modified to fit the time box, not the other way round. The daily stand-up meeting is done within a time box. Each development iteration and planning wave is time boxed.
TPM	*Technical performance measures*. Periodic measurements of technical achievement, comparison of achievements to benchmarks, and then actions to mitigate variances.
traditional methodologies	Methodologies that are planned-out at the outset and managed centrally according to the plan-to-produce outcomes. The emphasis is on predictable results according to the specifications of the plan, a PD-PDLC as we have described elsewhere. Example: waterfall.
TSP	*Team Software Process*. TSP is a service mark of Carnegie Mellon University.
UML	*Unified Modeling Language*. A text and diagrammatic language for specifying the interaction of actors and systems.
uncertainty	Risk without knowledge of an unfavorable event or neutralizing mitigation.
Unified Modeling Language	See *UML.*
untraditional methodologies	See *agile methods*.
use case	A text or diagrammatic specification within the UML that specifies a specific operational scenario involving actors and systems.

Item	Definition
user	See *customer*.
user story	A short vignette of a functional need, requirement, or capability.
velocity	An XP term applied generally to all agile methods that is a measure of throughput: objects actually put into production per iteration.
walking skeleton	Build an end-to-end functionality that works and can be used to build more functionality incrementally; gives the customer an early first look.
waterfall	The name given to a sequential project plan that roughly moves along from gather requirements, design the solution, develop and test the solution, and then deliver the outcomes. It gets its name from the appearance on charts of a series of cascading steps. To improve the waterfall sequencing, iteration back to prior steps was added in the 1970s.
WBS	*Work breakdown structure*. A means to depict how project deliverables are related and organized.
wicked	A problem description whereby the problem is described by the solution; typically, there are so many competing and circular dependencies that no up-front problem statement is possible.
wideband Delphi	A modification of the Delphi method to encourage communication and collaboration among experts working to estimate the same problem. See *Delphi*.

References

Ambler, S. Roles on Agile Teams: From Small to Large. *Ambysoft Best Software Practices*. http://www.ambysoft.com/essays/agileRoles.html.

Anderson, C. 2009. *Free, the Future of a Radical Price*. New York: Hyperion e-books, HarperCollins.

Anderson, D. 2004. *Agile Management for Software Engineering: Applying the Theory of Constraints for Business Model*. The Coad Series. Upper Saddle River, NJ: Prentice Hall Professional Technical Reference.

Astels, D. 2003. *Test-Driven Development: A Practical Guide*. Upper Saddle River, NJ: Prentice Hall.

Beck, K. 2003. *Test-Driven Development: By Example*. Boston: Addison-Wesley.

Beck, K. and M. Fowler. 2001. *Planning Extreme Programming*. Boston: Addison-Wesley.

Beck, K. with C. Andres. 2005. *Extreme Programming Explained: Embrace Change*. 2nd ed. Boston: Addison-Wesley Professional.

Berg, C., and K. Colenso. 2000. "Work Breakdown Structure Practice Standard Project—WBS vs Activities." *PM Network*, April.

Boehm, B. 1988. "A Spiral Model of Software Development and Enhancement." *Computer*, May, 61.

Boehm, B. and R. Turner. 2004. *Balancing Agility and Discipline: A Guide for the Perplexed*. Boston: Addison-Wesley.

Boehm, B. et al. 2000. *Software Cost Estimation with* COCOMO *II*. Upper Saddle River, NJ: Prentice Hall.

Boehm, B. 1981. *Software Engineering Economics*. Upper Saddle River, NJ: Prentice Hall.

Booch, Grady, Rumbaugh, and Jacobson. 1999. *The Unified Modeling Language User Guide*. Reading, MA: Addison-Wesley.

Brooks, F. 1995. *The Mythical Man-month Essays on Sofware Engineering Anniversary Edition*. New York: Addison-Wesley.

Cockburn, A. 1999. Characterizing People as Non-linear First Order Components in Software Development, HaT technical report.

Cockburn, A. 2005. *Crystal Clear—A Human-Powered Methodology for Small Teams*. Boston: Addison-Wesley.

Cockburn, A. 2001. *Writing Effective Use Cases*. Boston: Addison-Wesley.

Cohn, M. 2004. *User Stories Applied: For Agile Software Development*. Boston: Addison-Wesley.

Cohn, M. 2007. *Agile Estimating and Planning*. Upper Saddle River, NJ: Pearson Education.

Conklin, J. and W. Weil. 1998. Wicked Problems: Naming the Pain in the Organization. 3M meeting network white paper, Group Decision Support Systems. http://www.leanconstruction.org/pdf/wicked.pdf.

Cooper, R. 1993. *Winning at New Products*, 2nd ed. Reading, MA: Perseus Books.

Coutu, D. 2009. "Why Teams Don't Work," Interview with Dr. J. Richard Hackman. *Harvard Business Review* (May).

Covey, S. 1999. *7 Habits of Highly Effective People*. New York: Free Press Simon & Schuster.

Covey, S. 2004. *7 Habits of Highly Effective People*, 15th ed. New York: Simon & Schuster Free Press.

Covey, S. 1989. *7 Habits of Highly Effective People*, New York: Simon and Schuster. 95 Habit #2: Begin with the End in Mind.

Cox, J. and E. Goldratt. 1984. *The Goal: A Process of Ongoing Improvement*. Croton-on-Hudson, NY: North River Press.

D'Este, C. 1984. *Decision in Normandy*. Old Saybrook, CT: Konecky & Knoecky.

Downing, D. and J. Clark. 1997. *Statistics: The Easy Way*, 3rd ed. Hauppage, NY: Barron's Educational Series.

Dyer, W., et al. 2007. *Team Building: Proven Strategies for Improving Team Performance*. New York: John Wiley & Sons.

Editors. 2009. Requirements Engineering. From A Framework for Software Product Line Practice Version 5.0. Software Engineering Institute. http://www.sei.cmu.edu/productlines/frame_report/req_eng.htm.

Farquhar, J. 1970. *A Preliminary Inquiry into the Software Estimation Process*. RM-7271-PR, Santa Monica, CA: The Rand Corporation.

Fleming, Q. and J. Koppelman. 2000. *Earned Value Project Management*, 2nd ed. Newtown Square, PA: Project Management Institute.

Fowler, M. 2003. *Patterns of Enterprise Application Architecture*. Boston: Addison-Wesley.

Fowler, M. 2004. Mocks Aren't Stubs. MartinFowler.com, July 08. Page references are to the January 2007 revised edition.

Geller, E. 2001. *The Psychology of Safety Handbook*, 2nd ed. Boca Raton, FL: CRC Press.

Gladwell, M. 2009. "Highly Effective Underdogs." *The New Yorker*, May.

Goldratt, E. 1997. *Critical Chain*. Great Barrington, MA: The North River Press.

Goldratt, E. and R. Fox. 1986. *The Race*. Croton-on-Hudson, NY: North River Press.

Goodpasture, J. 2007. "A Risk Perspective: Rolling Wave Planning is a Bet." *Projects and Profits Magazine: ICFAI University Press* (Panjagutta, India), December.

Goodpasture, J. 2004. *Quantitative Methods in Project Management*. Ft. Lauderdale, FL: J. Ross Publishing.

Goodpasture, J. 2002. *Managing Projects for Value*. Vienna, McLean, VA: Management Concepts.

Grenning, J. 2002. *Planning Poker, or How to Avoid Analysis Paralysis while Release Planning*. Renaissance Software Consulting.

Hallowell, D. 2005. Software Development Convergence: Six Sigma-Lean-Agile. *iSixSigma.com,* March 2. http://www.isixsigma.com/library/content/c050302b.asp (Retrieved June 2009.)

Hammer, M. and J. Champy. 1993. *Re-engineering the Corporation: A Manifesto for Business Revolution*. New York: Harper Collins.

Haywood, M. *1998. Managing Virtual Teams: Practical Techniques for High-technology Project Managers*. Boston: Artech House Publishers.

Henderson, W. 1985. *Cohesion, the Human Element in Combat*. Washington DC: National Defense University Press.

Hersey, P., K. Blanchard, and D. Johnson. 2001. *Management of Organizational Behavior: Leading Human Resources*, 8th ed. Upper Saddle River, NJ: Prentice-Hall.

Highsmith, J. 2004. *Agile Project Management: Creating Innovative Products*. Boston: Addison-Wesley.

Hoare, C. 1969. An axiomatic basis for computer programming. Communications of the ACM.

Kaplan, R. and D. Norton. 1992. "The Balanced Scorecard: Measures that Drive Performance." *The Harvard Business Review*, (January–February).

Katzenbach, J. and D. Smith. 1994. *The Wisdom of Teams*. New York: HarperBusiness.

Katzenbach, J. and D. Smith. 1993. "The Discipline of Teams." *Harvard Business Review*, (March–April).

Kerzner, H. 2003. *Project Management: A Systems Approach to Planning, Scheduling, and Controlling*, 8th ed. Hoboken, NJ: John Wiley & Sons.

Kimble, C., F. Li, and A. Barlow, 2000. Effective Virtual Teams through Communities of Practice. Research Paper 2000/9, Strathclyde Business School, Glasgow, UK, September.

Kripalani, M. with Port O. 2005. "Watts Humphrey: He Wrote the Book on Debugging." *Business Week*, May 9. http://www.businessweek.com/magazine/content/05_19/b3932038_mz009.htm.

Kulak, D. and E. Guiney. 2000. *Use Cases: Requirements in Context*. Boston: Addison-Wesley.

Lencioni, P. 2002. *The Five Dysfunctions of a Team: A Leadership Fable*. San Francisco: Jossey-Bass.

Malotaux, N. 2006. Evolutionary Project Management Methods. Booklet focusing on EVO issues and first experience gained in 2001, Philips, Belgium. Version 1.4, www.malotaux.nl/ nrm/EVO. April.

Malotaux, N. 2008. Timeline: Getting and Keeping Control over Your Project. White paper prepared as for the October 2007 PNSQC conference, Portland, OR. www.malotaux.nl/nrm/Evo.

McConnell, S. 1993. *Code Complete*. Redmond, WA: Microsoft Press.

McConnell, S. 2007. *Software Estimating: Demystifying the Black Art*. Redmond, WA: Microsoft Press.

McCracken, D. and M. Jackson. 1982. Lifecycle Concept Considered Harmful. ACM Software Engineering Notes, April.

McQuaririe, E. 1993. *Customer Visits: Building a Better Market Focus*. Newbury Park, CA: Sage Publications.

Molokken-Ostvold, K., and N. Haugen. 2007. Combining Estimates with Planning Poker—An Empirical Study. 18th Australian Software Engineering Conference.

National Institute of Standards and Technology. 2002. Software Errors Cost U.S. Economy $59.5 Billion Annually. Press release. NIST 2002-10. (June 28). http://www.nist.gov/public_affairs/releases/n02-10.htm.

Paulish, D. 2002. *Architecture-Centric Software Project Management: A Practical Guide*. Boston: Addison-Wesley Professional.

Project Management Institute. 2008. *A Guide to the Project Management Body of Knowledge (The PMBOK® Guide)*, 4th ed. Newton Square, PA: Project Management Institute.

Robbins, H. and M. Finley. 2000. *The New Why Teams Don't Work: What Goes Wrong and How to Make it Right*. San Francisco: Berrett-Koehler,

Rogers, E. 2003. *Diffusion of Innovations*, 5th ed. New York: Free Press of Simon and Schuster.

Saaty, T. 1997. *Multi-criteria Decision Making: The Analytic Hierarchy Process*. R W S Publications.

Saaty, T. 2008. "Decision Making with the Analytic Hierarchy Process." *International Journal of Services Sciences*, 1:1.

Schawber, K. 2004. *Agile Project Management with SCRUM*. Redmond, WA: Microsoft Press.

Sherif, Muzafer and Sherif, W. Carolyn. 1956. *An Outline of Social Psychology*, rev. ed. New York: Harper & Brothers.

Sommerville, I. and P. Sawyer. 1997. *Requirements Engineering: A Good Practice Guide*. New York: John Wiley & Sons.

Stellman, A. and J. Greene. 2007. *Applied Software Project Management*. Sebastopol, CA: O'Reilly Media, Inc.

Takeuchi, Hirotaka; Nonaka, Ikujiro. 1986. The New New Product Development Game (PDF). *Harvard Business Review* (January-February).

Thiry, M. 1997. *Value Management Practice*. Newtown Square, PA: Project Management Institute.

Treacy, M. and F. Wiersema. 1993. "Customer Intimacy and Other Value Disciplines." *Harvard Business Review*. (January-February)

Treacy, M. and F. Wiersema. 1995. *The Discipline of Market Leaders*. New York: Perseus Books.

Tuckman, B. 1965. Developmental Sequences in Small Teams. *Psychological Bulletin, 63*:6.

Wall Street Journal, 1997. "Frederick Taylor, Early Century Management Consultant." *The Wall Street Journal Bookshelf*, June 13.

Walther, S. 2009. TDD Tests are not Unit Tests. StephenWalther.com, April 11.

Weaver, W. 1948. "Science and Complexity." *American Scientist*, 37:537.

Wiegers, K. 1999. *Software Requirements*. Redmond, WA: Microsoft Press.

Wikipedia, Forming-Storming-Norming-Performing. Wikipedia, www.wikipedia.com.

INDEX

N

O

P